Ubuntu®

Powerful Hacks and Customizations

Dr. Neal Krawetz

WILEY

Wiley Publishing, Inc.

Ubuntu® Powerful Hacks and Customizations

Published by
Wiley Publishing, Inc.
10475 Crosspoint Boulevard
Indianapolis, IN 46256
www.wiley.com

Copyright © 2010 by Wiley Publishing, Inc., Indianapolis, Indiana

Published by Wiley Publishing, Inc., Indianapolis, Indiana

Published simultaneously in Canada

ISBN: 978-0-470-58988-5

Manufactured in the United States of America

10 9 8 7 6 5 4 3 2 1

For general information on our other products and services please contact our Customer Care Department within the United States at (877) 762-2974, outside the United States at (317) 572-3993 or fax (317) 572-4002.

Wiley also publishes its books in a variety of electronic formats. Some content that appears in print may not be available in electronic books.

Library of Congress Control Number: 2010922555

To my parents, for systematically crushing my dreams of becoming a cartoonist while encouraging my interest in computers.

About The Author

Neal Krawetz earned his Ph.D. in Computer Science from Texas A&M University and Bachelors degree in Computer and Information Science from the University of California, Santa Cruz. In 2002, he founded Hacker Factor (www.hackerfactor.com), where he specializes in non-classical computer forensics, online profiling, and computer security. He is the author of three books (including this one) and numerous articles. He is a popular speaker at local and national conferences. Neal has been active in the security community for more than 20 years and has worked with the open source community for more than 25 years.

While most people have sane hobbies like bird watching or drinking beer at football games, Neal collects operating systems. He currently runs Fedora, Ubuntu, Mac OS X, OpenBSD, Solaris, HP-UX, and Microsoft Windows (with dozens of other operating systems ready to go). He has been a Linux user since 1993 and has enjoyed Ubuntu since 2005 (Hoary Hedgehog). Neal has configured Ubuntu on everything from personal workstations and netbooks to archival database systems and mission-critical servers.

Credits

Executive Editor
Carol Long

Project Editor
Kenyon Brown

Technical Editor
Timothy Boronczyk

Production Editor
Eric Charbonneau

Copy Editor
Foxxe Editorial Services

Editorial Director
Robyn B. Siesky

Editorial Manager
Mary Beth Wakefield

Production Manager
Tim Tate

Vice President and Executive Group Publisher
Richard Swadley

Vice President and Executive Publisher
Barry Pruett

Associate Publisher
Jim Minatel

Project Coordinator, Cover
Lynsey Stanford

Proofreader
Jen Larsen, Word One

Indexer
Johnna VanHoose Dinse

Cover Designer
Ryan Sneed

Acknowledgments

I have never thought of myself as a writer; I am a programmer. Yet, when Jenny Watson at Wiley contacted me and asked if I wanted to update the first edition of *Hacking Ubuntu*, I jumped at the opportunity. The first edition was a wild ride—a full book in less than five months with a focus on Ubuntu's Dapper Drake 6.06 (June 2006). But that was three years ago, and the operating system has evolved. I was eager to rewrite the book.

Writing a book takes time and commitment. I sincerely thank my friends and family for standing by me and giving me words of encouragement (between playful insults).

This book is intended for power users. However, I am only one type of power user: I usually turn off all the glitz and flash in lieu of speed and robustness. Fortunately, my friends are different types of power users: they love graphics, flash, bang, wow, and cutting edge. They provided a wealth of information that really helped cover all types of advanced Linux and Ubuntu needs. Many enlightening discussions were incorporated into parts of this text. To all of these people, I offer my sincerest thanks: Bill Tucker, Kyle Teague, Mark Litscher, Mark Rasch, Valdis Kletnieks, Paul Ferguson, Joe Battin, Erik Lillestolen, Paul Hummer, Jamie Leben, and the Northern Colorado Linux Users Group, as well as the people who helped with the first edition: Bill Hayes, Ragavan Srinivasan, LaMont Jones, Jer/ Eberhard, Paul Whyman, April Lorenzen, Marc Sachs and his band of Internet Storm Center handlers, the Department of Defense's Cyber Crime Center, and all of the folks who put together the Blackhat Briefings security conference. I must also thank my father, Howard, for all of the hardware he sent my way, including the various graphic cards and network interfaces. And my mother, Sharon, for her words of encouragement.

Although I have done my best to make this book as complete, accurate, and understandable as possible, I must offer my gratitude to the people who have reviewed, tested, and helped enhance this manuscript: Timothy Boronczyk for his thoroughness and ideas, and Michelle Mach for, well, *everything*. Their patience, feedback, and helpful comments have been an invaluable asset. Any errors in this book are strictly my own, but without them, there would be many more errors. I thank Carol Long, Kenyon Brown, Jenny Watson, Foxxe Editorial Services, and the staff at Wiley Publishing for this opportunity. And most importantly, I thank Neil Salkind and StudioB for the advice, assistance, and support.

Finally, nobody can use Linux without using software created by literally thousands of developers. I offer my deepest respect and gratitude to the entire open source community, and to Mark Shuttleworth and Canonical Ltd. for packaging up the best of the best into one distribution: Ubuntu.

Contents at a Glance

Contents

Introduction

I started seriously using Linux in 1995. Back then, Slackware 3.0 was the popular distribution, but RedHat 2.1 and Debian 1.0 were gaining a following. Ah, the good old days of the 1.2.13 kernel . . .

Over the last decade, I have used Linux on all types of systems and platforms—from personal computers to mission-critical servers, and from Intel's x86 to PowerPC, SGI, and Sun platforms. I view the operating system as a tool, and the right job needs the right tool. Ten years ago, the flexible Linux system filled a niche that Microsoft, Sun, and other proprietary operating systems could not fill. It had all the power and programming hooks that a developer could want but was seriously lacking in usability and support. Custom device drivers did not exist unless you built them, and compatibility with Microsoft Windows was limited to FTP and the web.

Today, the kernel is up to version 2.6 and Ubuntu is one of the fastest-growing Linux distributions available. Ubuntu combines all the desirable features—usability, security, and support—into one distribution.

Moving Targets

Writing for an open source operating system is like taking a picture of a moving target. While some parts remain focused and accurate for years, others lose focus and become outdated quickly.

The first edition, titled *Hacking Ubuntu*, really contained three types of hacks: enhancements, administration, and workarounds. While most of the enhancements and administration hacks continue to work today, the open source community has spent the last three years adding new features and addressing many of the workarounds. For example, wireless encryption (WPA) support under Dapper Drake (Ubuntu 6.06) required manual tweaking configuration files. But three years later Ubuntu's Jaunty Jackalope (9.04) included a working graphical interface. Now you only need hacks for working from the command line.

The first edition focused on the Dapper Drake 6.06 LTS version of Ubuntu. Although other versions of Ubuntu have an 18-month support life, Dapper was given five years of support from its corporate sponsor, Canonical Ltd. In this edition, I have tried to not write for a specific version of Ubuntu. These hacks are relevant for Hardy Heron (8.04 LTS) as well as Jaunty Jackalope (9.04) and Karmic Koala (9.10), and likely long past the next LTS (due in April 2010).

NOTE *LTS stands for Long-Term Support.*

Ubuntu is constantly changing. Knowing Hardy Heron (8.04 LTS) like the back of your hand does not mean that you know Karmic Koala (9.10). While much of the basic functionality remains the same, many of the actual implementation details have dramatically changed. Menus are altered, configuration files moved, and even core functionality, such as the default instant messaging software, is totally replaced. These details become much more noticeable when a cool hack suddenly stops working. Although I have tried not to write for specific Ubuntu versions, I do include notes and caveats about differences between versions that impact certain hacks.

Living Dangerously

There are usually many ways to implement the same hack. The hacks that I include in this book are the ones that I have found to be the easiest to implement (even if "easiest" is still a complicated hack), the simplest to maintain, and the most stable of the available options.

Having said that, however, any changes you make to your operating system could result in completely screwing up the system. Unless you enjoy reinstalling the operating system or spending hours trying to undo a mistake, I strongly recommend the following precautions:

- **Make a backup!** Before editing any files or making system changes, be sure to save everything that you cannot afford to lose. Although most hacks are easy to undo, others—like upgrading the operating system—have a point of no return.

TIP See Chapter 3 for a simple system backup script.

- **Save system files!** Before you edit any system file, make a local copy of it. For example, before editing `/etc/ssh/ssh_config`, save a copy of the original (`sudo cp /etc/ssh/ssh_config /etc/ssh/ssh_config.bak`). This way, you can put back the original file quickly in case you mess something up. I also recommend commenting out undesirable configuration options rather than deleting them. (It's easier to uncomment a line to restore functionality than it is to remember what it looked like before you deleted it.)

- **Don't play on mission-critical systems!** If you cannot afford to have downtime, then you should not be trying new tricks on the system. Instead, tinker on a test system, make sure it works, and then apply known-stable changes to your more serious systems.

Who This Book Is For

This book is written for the power user. Power users want the most out of their system: the most speed, the most glitz, the most sounds, or the most security. This book shows how to do just that.

Although you don't have to be a programmer to get the most out of this book, you should be familiar with Linux and know how to edit files. In particular, knowing how to download, install, and use the basic operating system is a must. You should be familiar enough with the Linux `bash` shell to create and traverse directories, search for applications, read man pages, and edit system files using whatever editor you are most familiar with. You should be familiar with commands like `grep`, `find`, and `sudo`.

Under Linux and Ubuntu, there are many ways to get the same results and many competing applications. There is rarely only one solution. Yet, some applications can trigger emotional responses. For example, debating the best editor (`vi` versus `emacs`) or the best desktop (e.g., Gnome, KDE, or Xfce) can quickly turn into a religious war. Although examples in this book may use one type of editor or desktop, the tasks can usually be accomplished just as easily with some other application.

WARNING This is *not* an introductory book on Ubuntu. Most bookstores have a shelf dedicated to introductory books on Linux. This book is for intermediate and advanced users. It contains hacks, tips, and techniques for power users.

This book does not completely encompass all the things you can do with Ubuntu. For most of the applications covered, there are dozens of alternate tools. And even the tools covered contain additional options and settings for doing more things than described here. The goal of this book is to show you some of the tricks, hacks, and tweaks that you can do with the system so that you can better customize it to your needs. I fully expect people to build on and extend these hacks.

How This Book Is Organized

Different power users have different needs. This book is divided into four parts, depending on the type of power user.

- **Part I: Optimizing Your System**—The first part of this book focuses on usability. Chapter 1 covers the different options for installing Ubuntu. The decisions made during the installation will dramatically impact how the system functions. Chapter 2 addresses the user interface and desktop. Although the default user interface is pleasant, it can be customized into an awesome interface. Chapter 3 focuses on devices and low-level drivers, including hard drives and printers. Chapter 4 targets common input devices: keyboards, mice, touch pads, and tablets.

- **Part II: Working with Compatibility**—In today's networked world, few people work in isolation. Part II focuses on compatibility with other systems. Chapter 5 discusses software management and how to install files for interoperability. Chapter 6 looks at networking tools such as e-mail, instant messaging, and the web. Chapter 7 covers collaboration with non-Linux systems.

- **Part III: Improving Performance**—Whereas Part I focuses on usability and Part II discusses compatibility, Part III looks at efficiency. Chapter 8 focuses on tuning the operating system's performance. Chapter 9 shows different ways to navigate the desktop, manage windows, and multitask between applications. Chapter 10 covers performance for video and graphics systems, including how to use multiple monitors to extend your desktop.

- **Part IV: Securing Your System**—It is all fun and games until someone's system gets compromised. This section shows tricks to check for vulnerabilities and prevent undesirable access. Chapter 11 provides different approaches to lock down the system and protect your files. Chapter 12 looks at advanced networking options such as proxies and wireless networking. Chapter 13 provides options for safely opening up the system with external network services.

What You Need to Use This Book

To use this book, you will need:

- A computer for running Ubuntu Linux. This book specifically supports versions 6.06 (Dapper Drake) through 9.10 (Karmic Koala), including the long-term support version 8.04 (Hardy Heron). This book primarily focuses on the PC (x86) platform but includes sections for the Macintosh (PowerPC). Although other platforms are not explicitly discussed, most of the hacks will work on these, too.
  - For the desktop installation, you will need at least 256 MB of RAM and 3 GB of disk space.
  - For the server installation, you will need at least 64 MB of RAM and 500 MB of disk space.
- Internet access for downloading ISO images and additional software packages from the online Ubuntu repositories. You will also need Internet access for the chapters that cover network services.
- For Chapter 1 ("Hacking the Installation"), you will need a CD-ROM burner and blank CD-R or CD-RW media. For playing with USB media, you should have one or more USB thumb drives or a USB hard drive.
- Chapter 3 ("Configuring Devices"), Chapter 4 ("Adapting Input Devices"), and Chapter 10 ("Getting Graphical with Video Bling") cover a variety of peripherals. You will need the peripherals in order to do the hacks. For example, you cannot do a printer hack without a printer and you cannot expand your desktop across monitors if you only have one monitor.
- Chapter 7 ("Collaborating") is best done with access to other operating systems. A computer running Apple's MacOS X or Microsoft Windows is a good option. However, other operating systems are also acceptable. These computers should be located on the same network and have network connectivity.

Conventions

I've used a few conventions throughout the book to help you get the most from the text and keep track of what's going on:

- Inline code and URLs within the text is presented with a monospaced font, like this: `System.capabilities`.

- Example blocks of source code are presented like this for code snippets:

```
statusTitle._text = "Look at the line below.";
```

or like this for code listings:

```
statusTitle._textColor = 0xFFFFFF;
```

In this book, you will find occasional notes, tips, and warnings. These are used to highlight subtle issues.

NOTE Notes point out minor items related to the topic.

TIP Tips provide small, helpful hints to make hacks work better.

WARNING Warnings alert you to possible hazards that can result from the hacks.

Source Code

It would be unfair for a book on modifying an open source operating system to include complex scripts and not make them easily available to the open source community. All of the source code written for this book is available for download at `http://www.wrox.com`. Once at the site, simply locate the book's title (either by using the Search box or by using one of the title lists) and click the Download Code link on the book's detail page to obtain all the source code for the book.

NOTE Because many books have similar titles, you may find it easiest to search by ISBN; this book's ISBN is 978-0-470-58988-5.

Once you download the code, just decompress it with your favorite compression tool. Alternately, you can go to the main Wrox code download page at `http://www.wrox.com/dynamic/books/download.aspx` to see the code available for this book and all other Wrox books.

Errata

We make every effort to ensure that there are no errors in the text or in the code. However, no one is perfect, and mistakes do occur. If you find an error in one of our books, such as a spelling mistake or faulty piece of code, we would be very grateful for your feedback. By sending in errata, you may save other readers hours of frustration and at the same time you will be helping us provide even higher-quality information.

To find the errata page for this book, go to `http://www.wrox.com` and locate the title using the Search box or one of the title lists. Then, on the book details page, click the Book Errata link. On this page you can view all errata that has been submitted for this book and posted by Wrox editors. A complete book list, including links to each book's errata, is also available at `http://www.wrox.com/misc-pages/booklist.shtml`.

If you don't spot "your" error on the Book Errata page, go to `http://www.wrox.com/contact/techsupport.shtml` and complete the form there to send us the error you have found. We'll check the information and, if appropriate, post a message to the book's errata page and fix the problem in subsequent editions of the book.

p2p.wrox.com

For author and peer discussion, join the P2P forums at `http://p2p.wrox.com`. The forums are a web-based system for you to post messages relating to Wrox books and related technologies and interact with other readers and technology users. The forums offer a subscription feature to e-mail you topics of interest of your choosing when new posts are made to the forums. Wrox authors, editors, other industry experts, and your fellow readers are present on these forums.

At `http://p2p.wrox.com` you will find a number of different forums that will help you not only as you read this book but also as you develop your own applications. To join the forums, just follow these steps:

1. Go to `http://p2p.wrox.com` and click the Register link.
2. Read the terms of use and click Agree.
3. Complete the required information to join as well as any optional information you wish to provide, and click Submit.
4. You will receive an e-mail with information describing how to verify your account and complete the joining process.

NOTE You can read messages in the forums without joining P2P, but in order to post your own messages, you must join.

Once you join, you can post new messages and respond to messages other users post. You can read messages at any time on the web. If you would like to have new messages from a particular forum e-mailed to you, click the "Subscribe to This Forum" icon by the forum name in the forum listing.

For more information about how to use the Wrox P2P, be sure to read the P2P FAQs for answers to questions about how the forum software works as well as many common questions specific to P2P and Wrox books. To read the FAQs, click the FAQ link on any P2P page.

Optimizing Your System

In This Part

Hacking the Installation

What's In This Chapter?

Which version of Ubuntu should you install?
Running Ubuntu from a USB drive, SD Card, and other kinds of removable
    media
Using Ubuntu on a netbook
Upgrading Ubuntu
Tips for modifying the GRUB boot loader

This chapter explores options for installing and configuring devices. Where you choose to install Ubuntu, which variation you install, and what options you select will impact the system's usability.

Before You Begin

Before you install the operating system, be sure to create a backup of anything you want to keep. Copy all data on the system. You can save it to a CD-ROM, copy it to a spare computer, or physically change hard drives—the method does not matter. Do not keep sensitive data on the same system, even if it is kept on a different hard drive or in a separate partition. If you accidentally format or repartition a working hard drive that contains data you wanted to keep, then the data will be gone.

WARNING This chapter deals with drive partitioning, formatting, and installing operating systems. If you play with a system that contains customized settings or personal files, there is a serious risk of accidentally deleting your working configuration and private data.

Drive device identifiers can be confusing—the label `/dev/sda1` looks a lot like `/dev/sda2` and `/dev/hda1`. Before every partition, format, and copy, be sure to *triple-check* the device identifier! When you make a mistake, there will be no going back.

Selecting a Distribution

Ubuntu is a Linux distribution based on Debian Linux. Different Linux distributions target different functional niches. The goal of Ubuntu is to bring Linux into the desktop workspace. To do this, it needs to provide a stable user interface, plenty of office tools, and drivers for a myriad of peripherals, while still being user-friendly. Although different groups manage nearly every open source project, Canonical Ltd. provides a central point for development and support. Canonical, along with the Ubuntu community, can answer most of your technical (and not so technical) questions.

WHICH DISTRIBUTION IS RIGHT FOR YOU?

Different Linux distributions fill specific needs. For example, although RedHat started life as a unifying distribution, it primarily supported English applications. SuSE was a popular internationalized distribution. Many distributions were maintained by modifying other distributions. For example, ASPLinux is a version of RedHat with multilingual support for Asian and Slavic languages, and the Beowulf clustered computing environment is based on RedHat.

Although RedHat has seeded many different distributions, it is not alone. Debian Linux is another distribution with a significant following. As with RedHat, Debian has been used to spawn many different niche distributions. Although Ubuntu is based on Debian, it is also seeding other distributions.

Different distributions of the Linux operating system are sometimes called *flavors*. There are hundreds different supported flavors of Linux, each with a different focus. You can see the listing of official distributions at www.linux.org.

Ubuntu is the basis for a variety of Linux distributions—most only differ in the user interface, although some do include specific software configurations. The basic Ubuntu distribution uses the Gnome desktop and is geared toward desktop or server systems. Other distributions based on Ubuntu include:

- **Kubuntu**—A variation of Ubuntu with the K Desktop Environment (KDE)
- **Xubuntu**—A variation of Ubuntu with the Xfce Desktop Environment
- **Edubuntu**—A modified version of Ubuntu that is loaded with educational applications

In each case, it is possible to switch from one installed version to another. For example, you can install Ubuntu, add in KDE, and remove Gnome, and you'll have an environment that looks like Kubuntu. To convert an Ubuntu installation to Kubuntu requires changing the desktop, office applications (OpenOffice to KOffice), and swapping other tools. Instead of modifying one distribution to look like another, you should just start with the right distribution.

NOTE Most people won't install KDE and remove Gnome in order to change their desktop. Instead, they will *add* KDE to the system and keep both Gnome and KDE installed.

To give you an example of the complexity, here's how to add KDE to an Ubuntu system that already uses the Gnome desktop:

1. Install KDE.

   ```
   sudo apt-get install kubuntu-desktop
   ```

   This requires about 700 MB of disk space. The installation will ask if you want Gnome (gdm) or KDE (kdm) as the default desktop.

2. Log out. This gets you out of the active Gnome desktop.
3. On the login page, select the user.
4. Select KDE from the Sessions menu (see Figure 1-1).
5. Log in using KDE.

Understanding Ubuntu Names

Each Ubuntu release is associated with a number and name. The release number is the year and month of the release in an internationalized format. So "6.06" is July 2006 and "9.04" is April 2009 (and not September 2004). Each release is also associated with a common name. Table 1-1 shows the current names and release numbers. Releases are commonly referred to by their names. For example, 9.04 is commonly called *Jaunty Jackalope* or simply *Jaunty*.

NOTE As a convention in this book, releases are referenced by their full names and version numbers. This way, you do not need to remember that Hardy came out in 2008.

Figure 1-1: The login menu on Karmic Koala (9.10) after adding KDE to Ubuntu

Table 1-1: Ubuntu Releases

NAME	VERSION	END OF SUPPORT
Warty Warthog	4.10	April 2006
Hoary Hedgehog	5.04	October 2006
Breezy Badger	5.10	April 2007
Dapper Drake	6.06 LTS	July 2009 (desktop), June 2011 (server)
Edge Eft	6.10	April 2008
Feisty Fawn	7.04	October 2008
Gutsy Gibbon	7.10	April 2009
Hardy Heron	8.04 LTS	April 2011 (desktop), April 2013 (server)
Intrepid Ibex	8.10	April 2010
Jaunty Jackalope	9.04	October 2010
Karmic Koala	9.10	April 2011
Lucid Lynx	10.04 LTS	April 2013 (desktop), April 2015 (server)

While most releases have 18 months of support, every other year a long-term support (LTS) version is released. The LTS releases provide three years of updates for the desktop, and five years for servers. The LTS is an excellent option for systems that cannot afford to be completely replaced every 18 months.

NOTE This book focuses on the actively supported versions: Hardy Heron (8.04 LTS), Jaunty Jackalope (9.04), and Karmic Koala (9.10). Dapper Drake (6.06 LTS) is also discussed but to a lesser degree.

Selecting the Ubuntu Version

Each Ubuntu release is designed to require only one CD-ROM for installing the system. This reduces the need for swapping disks during the installation. Unfortunately, one disk cannot hold everything needed for a complete environment. To resolve this issue, Ubuntu has many different types of initial install images that address different system needs.

- **Desktop**—This image provides a Live Desktop. This can be used to test-drive the operating system or install a desktop or workstation system. The installation includes the Gnome graphical environment and user-oriented tools, including office applications, multimedia players, and games.

- **Alternate**—Similar to the Desktop image, this image installs the desktop version of Ubuntu, but it does not use a graphical installer. This is a very desirable option when the graphics or mouse does not work correctly from the Desktop installer.

- **Server**—This minimal install image has no graphical desktop. It is ideal for servers and headless (without monitor) systems. The image includes server software such as a Secure Shell server, web server, and mail server, but none is installed by default (see Chapter 13).

- **Netbook**—Introduced with Jaunty Jackalope (9.04), the netbook edition (also called the Ubuntu Netbook Remix) is a version customized for portable netbook systems. (See "Using Ubuntu on a Netbook" in this chapter for the differences between the netbook and desktop releases.)

TIP From the Ubuntu web site (ubuntu.com), it can be difficult to find anything other than the Desktop and Server versions of the current and LTS releases for download. The web sites releases.ubuntu.com and cdimage.ubuntu.com provide easy access to all of the release images.

The names for the installation images do not exactly match the functionality. The names were chosen to avoid confusion with previous Ubuntu releases.

(If they called the Desktop CD-ROM *Install*, people might not realize it also contains a Live Desktop.) Better names might be Live CD with Desktop Install, OEM with Text Desktops, and Server with Minimal System Configuration. But then again, these are pretty long names, so we'll stick with Desktop, Alternate, Server, and Netbook.

There are more installation options than these four CD-ROM images. For example, there is an Ubuntu DVD image. The DVD contains everything found on all of the CD-ROM images, including the live operating system. There are also unofficial ports to other platforms. For example, installation disks for the PowerPC, Sun UltraSPARC, IA-64, and other architectures are available from `http://cdimage.ubuntu.com/ports/releases/`. While these platforms may not receive immediate updates and first-tier support, they are community supported.

Each installation disk has the option for a basic install as well as a few other common options. For example, you can verify the installation media using the check for CD defects, test your hardware with the Memory Test, and access an installed system using the Rescue option. There are also options specific to certain installation disks.

USING THE SMART BOOT MANAGER

One of my computers is so old that it does not support booting from the CD-ROM drive. However, all is not lost! On all the Ubuntu installation CD-ROMs is a small disk image: `install/sbm.bin`. This is the Smart Boot Manager, one of the best-kept secrets on the installation CD-ROMs. This is an image made for a floppy disk. To create the disk from a Linux system, use:

```
dd if=sbm.bin of=/dev/fd0
```

If you boot off of this floppy disk, you will see a menu that includes booting from the hard drive or CD-ROM. Using this disk, you should be able to boot off any of the installation CD-ROMs. Unfortunately, SBM does not support booting off USB or FireWire devices.

Configuring Dual Boot

Dual-boot systems were very popular during the late 1990s and early 2000s. Since different operating systems are incompatible, users would boot into the appropriate system to run native applications.

Today, dual-boot systems are less common. Computers are relatively inexpensive, so it is easier to have separate Windows and Linux computers, and many options exist for exchanging files and data between systems (see Chapter 7). In addition, virtual machines such as VMware and Qemu enable you to run native applications within a window, so there is rarely a need to dual-boot.

Some users still have a need for a dual-boot system. Many games, for example, are more responsive under the native operating system and outside of a virtual machine. If you need a dual-boot system, there are a few configuration steps:

1. Partition the disk for multiple operating systems. The easiest way is to just create one partition that does not use the entire disk. If you have multiple disks, then each disk can contain a different operating system.

2. If you will be using a Windows system, install it on the allocated partition. (You can use the Windows Partitioner to create the first partition.) Be sure to install Windows *first* since Windows has a bad habit of disabling boot loaders during its installation.

3. After you have installed the first operating system, use any of the Ubuntu install methods to install Ubuntu.

   ■ Do *not* select the entire disk for installation (unless you are installing on a separate drive).

   ■ Use the partitioner to create a new partition for Ubuntu—do not modify the existing partition.

The Ubuntu installer is smart enough to identify other operating systems and add them to the boot menu for dual-booting. This enables you to easily dual-boot Ubuntu with Windows, BSD, and other operating systems. On PowerPC systems, you can dual-boot between Ubuntu and Mac OS X without a problem.

TIP Configuring a dual-boot system is relatively easy. However, configuring a multi-boot computer with three or more operating systems can add complexity to the boot menu. I recommend installing Ubuntu last, since its boot manager installation will automatically detect other operating systems and label them properly.

Using the Desktop CD-ROM

The Desktop CD-ROM installation starts a graphical Live Desktop. This can be used for system recovery, debugging, or browsing the web.

NOTE The Desktop CD-ROM boot selection gives you 30 seconds to make a decision before it selects the English language and boots the graphical Live Desktop. If you want to select a different option, be sure to watch it boot (don't walk away) and make a menu selection. Pressing any key while on the menu will stop the 30-second timer.

When the CD-ROM boots, you will see a graphical desktop. On the desktop is an Install icon that can be used for installing the file system (see Figure 1-2). The same option exists on the menu under System ➪ Administration ➪ Install.

Figure 1-2: Hardy Heron's Live Desktop and install menu

If something goes wrong during the installation, you only have a few options for debugging the problem. After the graphical desktop appears, you can press Ctrl+Alt+F1 through Ctrl+Alt+F4 to provide command-line terminals. Ctrl+Alt+F7 returns to the graphical display. Otherwise, you may want to consider using the Alternate CD-ROM image for text-based installation.

NOTE Pressing Ctrl+Alt with F1 through F4 keys takes you out of the graphical desktop. Once out of the graphical mode, you don't need to use Ctrl. Simply pressing Alt+F1 through Alt+F8 will switch between terminals. This is because Alt+F1 through Alt+F12 are keyboard signals used by the desktop; Ctrl with Alt is used to distinguish between graphical desktop and console requests.

FAST RECOVERY

The Desktop installation CD-ROM provides a Live Desktop for exploring the operating system without performing an installation. It can also access an existing system in order to perform repairs or recovery. However, the Live Desktop is not the fastest of systems. On a fast computer (for example, 2 GHz with a 40x CD-ROM drive) it can still take three minutes to go from boot to Live Desktop. This can seem like an eternity if you just need to fix one text file on a critical server.

If you require a recovery system for repairs, or for using Linux without a hard drive, consider an alternative system. Knoppix, Gnoppix, and DSL (Damn

Small Linux) are designed for speed. Each is built for a fast start time when booting from a single CD-ROM or DVD.

Sometimes graphics are not even a concern. If you just need a command prompt to repair a system, consider the Ubuntu Server or Alternate CD-ROM images. Both contain a recovery option that will allow you to access the local system and make quick fixes. And if you really need a prompt fast, select any of the installation options on the Server or Alternate images and press Alt+F2. This will give you a prompt where you can mount the hard drive and perform repairs quickly.

Using the Alternate CD-ROM

The Alternate CD-ROM image enables you to install a desktop image with graphics disabled, or an OEM-configurable system (see Figure 1-3) by highlighting the Install option, pressing F4, and selecting a different install mode.

Figure 1-3: Hardy Heron's Alternate CD-ROM boot selection menu

Text Mode Installation

The text mode and OEM installations both create user workstations. However, they have very different configurations. The text mode system lacks the graphical installer, but everything else is present. This is ideal for computers with limited resources or low RAM. It is also a very fast method to perform the installation.

OEM Installation

The OEM mode installs the graphical desktop and creates the user account oem. This account can be used to customize the system. After the install, log in, and run the oem-config script if you need to change any of the original installation responses, or oem-config-prepare to remove the temporary oem account and enable configuration prompting during the next boot (for end-user configuration).

WARNING During the OEM installation, the Alternate CD-ROM prompts for a password but not a username. It is not until after the installation completes that you are told the account name for the password is oem. Both the account and password are removed when oem-config-prepare is used.

The OEM mode is an ideal choice for installers who want to customize the system (and remove the installation account) before the system is passed to someone else. Original equipment manufacturers (OEM) can use this option to install custom applications before shipping the computer to a customer. Similarly, corporate system administrators may configure the network, applications, and other subsystems before handing the computer to a new employee.

Networkless Upgrades and Repairs

The Alternate CD-ROM contains all of the necessary packages for upgrading a previous Ubuntu installation. This means that the CD-ROM can be used to perform upgrades when network access is unavailable.

Unlike the Desktop CD-ROM, the Alternate CD-ROM does not run a live graphical system. But, it does have a rescue mode for repairing a nonfunctioning operating system.

Installing an LTSP Server

Beginning with Hardy Heron (8.04 LTS), the Alternate CD-ROM includes the option to install an LTSP server. The Linux Terminal Server Project (LTSP) allows you to connect thin-client systems to the LTSP server.

NOTE A *thin client* is a minimal resource workstation. These systems generally contain very little disk space and are designed to boot off the network, load the operating system image from a remote server, and store files on a remote system.

The LTSP installation installs an Ubuntu server and configures it for use with LTSP clients. You can also configure a running Ubuntu system for use as an LTSP server:

1. Install the LTSP server packages. This will install the LTSP server, SSH server, DHCP server, and all other required packages.

```
sudo apt-get install ltsp-server-standalone openssh-server
```

2. Build the thin client environment by running `sudo ltsp-build-client` `—arch i386` (or—`arch powerpc`). This command takes a while as it identifies packages and prepares everything for the client image.

Eventually the client environment will be built. The client image files are located in `/opt/ltsp/i386/` and the compiled image is stored under `/opt/ltsp/images/`. To change the image, modify the files under `/opt/ltsp/i386/` and then run `sudo ltsp-update-image`. To update only the kernel, use `sudo ltsp-update-kernels`.

LTSP clients expect the server to be located at a specific network address and connect using Secure Shell (SSH). SSH associates cryptographic keys with network addresses. If the server changes network addresses, then the client image needs to be updated: `sudo ltsp-update-sshkeys`.

TIP To test your LTSP configuration, consider using a virtual machine as a LTSP client. See Chapter 7 for installing the Qemu emulator. A quick script for using Qemu as an LTSP client is installed on the LTSP server:

`/usr/share/doc/ltsp-server/examples/qemu-ltsp`

Using the Server CD-ROM

While the Alternate CD-ROM is focused on OEM customizations, the Server CD-ROM only installs a basic server and a minimal system image. Everything else needs to be installed as an add-on.

NOTE With Dapper Drake (6.06 LTS), the server image includes an option to install LAMP: Linux, Apache, MySQL, and PHP/Perl/Python. However, LAMP is not an option in later Ubuntu releases. To create a LAMP server, you will need to install and configure the components separately. See Chapters 5 and 13.

Debugging problems with the Server and Alternate installations is much easier than diagnosing problems with the Desktop CD-ROM. At any time during the installation, you can press Alt+F4 and see the current installation's progress. If the system hangs, you can tell which subsystem caused the problem. Pressing Alt+F2 provides a command prompt, and Alt+F1 returns you to the user-friendly installation screen.

The server installation sets up a system very quickly. Although the Desktop CD-ROM installs a graphical desktop, the installer is very slow. In contrast, the Server CD-ROM installs a text-only operating system, but it is very quick. After installing the text-based operating system, you can install additional packages using `apt-get` (see Chapter 5). For example, you may want to install the Gnome desktop using `sudo apt-get install ubuntu-desktop`. This creates the same system as the Desktop CD-ROM but is much faster than booting the Live Desktop and performing the graphical installation. All the necessary files are found on the Server CD-ROM.

TIP The Live Desktop is also relatively slow for installations. For a significantly faster installation time, consider using the Alternate or Server images. Both of these options use text-based installers.

Changing Options

The Desktop, Alternate, and Server ISO images are bootable and include a CD-ROM tester (for making sure that the CD-ROM was created correctly) and a memory tester. The System and Alternate CD-ROMs include recovery shells for debugging an installed system, while the Desktop CD-ROM includes a live system that can also be used for repairing the local host.

Depending on your computer, any of these disks may fail to run. The most common issues concern kernel parameters that conflict with the hardware. You can change the kernel parameters when booting the disks in order to address any issues. Some common parameters include:

- Configure a RAM disk. The default is 1 GB for the Desktop ISO and 16 MB for the Alternate and Server ISOs. For example, the Server ISO uses:

  `ramdisk_size=16384`

- Specify an alternate root disk. The default specifies the RAM disk (`/dev/ram`), but for debugging a system, you can specify a hard drive such as `/dev/hda`.

  `root=/dev/ram`

  or

  `root=/dev/hda`

- The Advanced Configuration and Power Interface (ACPI) support on some hardware can cause the installer to fail. ACPI support can be explicitly disabled using `acpi=off`.

- Similarly to ACPI, some PCMCIA chipsets (particularly on older motherboards and some Dell systems) can cause the installer's auto-detection to hang. The `start_pcmcia=off` boot option disables PCMCIA, allowing you to bypass this type of problem.

At the initial installation menu, you can press F6 to see the current options and make changes. Pressing F1 shows you other kernel options that are common remedies when the system fails to install.

Installing a Minimal System

Sometimes you want to start with a minimal configuration and add packages as needed. This is usually the case for hardware that has limited disk space, little

RAM, or a slow CPU. Minimal systems are also desirable for mission-critical and Internet-accessible servers, where unnecessary applications may consume critical resources or add security risks.

The Server CD-ROM provides the simplest minimal installation option. The basic configuration does not install any additional software packages and uses less than 300 MB of disk space. The Alternate CD-ROM does provide a basic install but does not enable many of the packages—these packages are placed on the system but not turned on.

In both cases, unnecessary packages can be removed. For example, the Alsa sound driver can be uninstalled, freeing 200 KB of disk space. The command to list all installed packages is:

```
dpkg -l | more
```

If you want to see what files are included in the package, use dpkg -L **packagename**. For example:

```
dpkg -L alsa-base | more
```

Many packages have dependent packages, so removals are not always simple. To identify conflicts before removing a package use:

```
sudo apt-get -s remove alsa-base
```

The -s option says to simulate the removal of the alsa-base package—it does all of the safety checks and lists all dependencies and conflicts without actually doing the removal. If there are no conflicts, then you can remove the -s and perform the actual removal. You can replace alsa-base with any of the packages installed on the system. You can also list multiple packages on the apt-get command line.

UNSAFE REMOVALS

The apt-get **program tries to not break dependencies, so removing one package may remove a dependent package.**

Be careful: if you select the wrong dependent package, you can end up removing critical parts of the operating system. For example, the package perl-base **cannot be removed without removing the** console-data **package. Removing** perl-base **and** console-data **will also automatically select and remove** cron, debconf, **LVM support,** python, wget, **and dozens of other system packages. Even if you have no plans to program in Perl, removing it will cripple your system. Use the** -s **option before doing the removal to check if there will be undesirable consequences.**

Installing over the Network

Although installing from a CD-ROM can be convenient, it does not scale well when you need to manage dozens or hundreds of systems. In addition, systems without CD-ROM drives need an option for installing the operating system. Ubuntu provides a bare-minimum boot image for installing Ubuntu over the network. There are different versions of the mini-image based on the desired architecture. For example, to install Hardy Heron (8.04 LTS) over the network, use the installer images found at `http://archive.ubuntu.com/ubuntu/dists/hardy/main/installer-i386/current/images/netboot/`.

This directory contains the Hardy Heron (8.04 LTS) mini-image for the i386. There are similar directories for the AMD64 (`install-amd64`) and any other supported platforms. Similarly, there are directories for Jaunty, Karmic, and other Ubuntu releases. Each of the directories contains similar preconfigured boot images.

- **boot.img.gz**—A compressed image of a bootable installer
- **mini.iso**—The `boot.img` file ready for burning to a CD-ROM
- **netboot.tar.gz**—The boot.img contents, ready for installing over the network
- **pxelinux.0**—The Preboot eXecution Environment (PXE) for network installation. This requires a DHCP and TFTP server
- **pxelinux.cfg**—A directory required for PXE installations
- **ubuntu-installer**—A directory required for PXE and TFTP installations

CHOOSING AN INSTALLATION METHOD

There are many different installation options. Which one to use really depends on your environment and how many times you plan to do an installation. For example, if you have a very slow or unreliable network connection, then you will want to install from one of the CD-ROM or DVD images. Don't bother with a network install if you don't have a good network connection.

If you want to install over the network and you only plan to install one or two systems, then the `boot.img` and `mini.iso` options provide the most convenience and require a minimum amount of effort.

However, if you plan to install many computers *and* each can boot from the network, then consider using the PXE option. While PXE takes a little effort to configure, you can quickly install hundreds of computers over the network.

With each of the network install options, you can either use one of the official Ubuntu servers or your own local server. Installing over the network gives you the flexibility to use your local network or servers located across the Internet.

To use the mini-images, simply copy the image onto a device. For example, to use an external hard drive for installing Ubuntu, use the Linux command:

```
zcat boot.img.gz | dd of=/dev/hdb
```

This command uncompresses the image and copies it to the external drive (/dev/hdb). This works for most external media.

To boot the network installer from the CD-ROM, just burn the mini.iso image to the CD-ROM. This can be done in two ways. From the Ubuntu desktop, you can right-click the ISO and select Write to Disc from the menu (see Figure 1-4), or you can burn it from the command line using the cdrecord command:

```
cdrecord dev=/dev/hdc blank=fast mini.iso
```

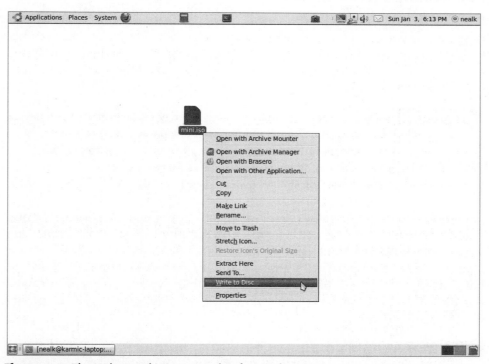

Figure 1-4: The Write to Disc menu option for ISO images

NOTE Other operating systems, such as Windows and Mac OS X, have their own options for writing an ISO file to a CD-ROM.

The result of all of these different boot options is a disk (or CD-ROM or PXE configuration) that can install Ubuntu over the network.

Using a USB Drive

The ubiquitous USB flash memory drives (also called *thumb drives*) have replaced floppy disks. They are smaller, less fragile, and store much more data. For convenience, they can also be used to kick off an installation, repair a damaged system, run a standalone operating system, or simply share files.

TIP These instructions work with *any kind* of removable media, including SD Cards, Compact Flash, and even your old MP3 player that looks like a thumb drive when you connect it to the computer. You are not strictly limited to USB thumb drives.

Formatting a USB Drive

USB drives support two basic formats: floppy drive and hard drive. A USB floppy drive consists of one large formatted drive. In contrast, USB hard drives contain partition tables and one or more formatted partitions. If you purchased a thumb drive and never formatted it, then it is most likely configured as a USB hard drive with one large partition.

WARNING Before formatting or partitioning any device, be sure that the device is unmounted! Use the mount command (without any parameters) to see if it is mounted, and then use umount to unmount any partitions. For example, to unmount /dev/sdc1 mounted at /media/usbdrive, you can use sudo umount /dev/sdc1 or sudo umount /media/usbdrive.

Thumb drives are usually partitioned just like regular hard drives. Commands such as fdisk and cfdisk can easily modify the drive partitions, and mkfs can be used to format a partition.

Besides capacity, speed is a significant difference between thumb drives and hard drives. When you change the partition table on a flash drive or format a partition, wait a few seconds before removing the drive; otherwise, some data may be buffered and not yet transferred.

TIP When writing to a thumb drive, I usually run the sync command (sudo sync). This flushes all cached data to the disk. When the command returns, it is safe to remove the drive.

When you use the fdisk or cfdisk command on a thumb drive, you configure it as a USB hard drive. However, you can also configure it as a USB floppy drive. The difference is that floppy drives do not use partitions. For example, to make an ext2-formatted USB floppy drive on my 1-GB USB thumb drive (/dev/sdb), I can use:

```
$ sudo mkfs /dev/sdb
mke2fs 1.41.9 (22-Aug-2009)
/dev/sdb is entire device, not just one partition!
Proceed anyway? (y,n) y
Filesystem label=
OS type: Linux
Block size=4096 (log=2)
Fragment size=4096 (log=2)
62976 inodes, 251648 blocks
12582 blocks (5.00%) reserved for the super user
First data block=0
Maximum filesystem blocks=260046848
8 block groups
32768 blocks per group, 32768 fragments per group
7872 inodes per group
Superblock backups stored on blocks:
        32768, 98304, 163840, 229376

Writing inode tables: done
Writing superblocks and filesystem accounting information: done

This filesystem will be automatically checked every 36 mounts or
180 days, whichever comes first.  Use tune2fs -c or -i to override.
$ sudo sync
```

WARNING When you first plug in a USB hard drive, all the partitions will appear and automatically mount. However, to create a USB floppy drive, be sure to unmount all partitions and then format the main device (for example, /dev/sda or /dev/sdc) and not a partition (for example, /dev/sda2 or /dev/sdc1).

You will need to disconnect and reconnect the device after you format it in order to remove any stale device partition identifiers:

```
sudo sync; sudo eject /dev/sdb
```

Sharing Files with a USB Drive

The simplest and most common use for a USB drive is to share files between systems. Ubuntu supports most USB drives. Simply plugging the drive into the USB port will automatically mount the drive. From there, you can access it as you would access any mounted partition.

TIP Many thumb drives have a light to indicate that the drive is being accessed. Even if the drive is not mounted, do not unplug the drive until the light indicates that all activity has stopped.

Linux, Windows, Mac, and most other systems support FAT file systems. In order to share files with other users, consider formatting the drive with mkdosfs. For example:

1. Install the dosfstools package if mkdosfs is not already installed:

   ```
   sudo apt-get install dosfstools
   ```

2. Unmount the drive (for example, /dev/sda1) if it is currently mounted:

   ```
   sudo umount /dev/sda1
   ```

3. Format the drive using either FAT16 or FAT32:

   ```
   mkdosfs -F 16 /dev/sda1  # format FAT16
   mkdosfs -F 32 /dev/sda1  # format FAT32
   ```

TIP If you want to create a FAT-formatted USB floppy drive, then use the -I option. For example: sudo mkdosfs -I -F 32 /dev/sda.

WARNING FAT16 supports a maximum of 2 GB per partition and no more than 512 entries per directory. If either is larger, then you must use FAT32.

If you do not mind restricting file sharing to Linux-only systems, then you can format the drive using an ext2, ext3, or ext4 file system, using any of the following commands:

```
mkfs /dev/sda1          # default format is ext2
mkfs -t ext2 /dev/sda1  # explicitly format type as ext2
mkfs -t ext3 /dev/sda1  # explicitly format type as ext3
mkfs -t ext4 /dev/sda1  # explicitly format type as ext4 (Jaunty
                                                and later)
mkfs.ext2 /dev/sda1     # directly call format ext2
mkfs.ext3 /dev/sda1     # directly call format ext3
mkfs.ext4 /dev/sda1     # directly call format ext4 (Jaunty and later)
```

NOTE The ext4 file system was introduced in Jaunty Jackalope (9.04). It is a backward-compatible extension to the ext3 journaling file systems. Ext4 includes performance enhancements as well as support for partitions up to 1 EiB. (One exibyte, or EiB, is 2^{60} bytes or 1,152,921,504,606,846,976). With Karmic Koala (9.10), ext4 is the default file system.

Booting from a USB Drive

Beyond file sharing, USB drives can be used as bootable devices. If your computer supports booting from a USB drive, then this is a great option for developing a portable operating system, creating an emergency recovery disk, or installing the OS on other computers.

Although most systems today support USB drives, the ability to boot from a USB thumb drive is inconsistent. Even if you create a bootable USB drive, your BIOS may still prevent you from booting from it. It seems like every computer has a different way to change BIOS settings. Generally, you power on the computer and press a key before the operating system boots. The key may be F1, F2, F10, Del, Esc, or some other key or combination of keys. It all depends on your computer's BIOS. When you get into the BIOS, there is usually a set of menus, including one for the boot order. If you can boot from a USB device, this is where you will set it. However, every computer is different, and you may need to have the USB drive plugged in when you power on before seeing any options for booting from it.

WARNING **Making changes to your BIOS can seriously mess up your computer. Be careful!**

Different USB Devices

Even if your computer supports booting from a USB device, it may not support all of the different USB configurations. In general, thumb drives can be configured one of three ways:

- **Small USB floppy drives**—Thumb drives configured as USB floppy devices (that is, no partitions) with a capacity of 256 MB or less are widely supported. If your computer cannot boot this configuration, then the chances of your computer booting any configuration is very slim.

- **Large USB floppy drives**—These are USB floppy devices with capacities greater than 256 MB. My own tests used two different 1-GB thumb drives, a 2-GB SD Card, and a 250-GB USB hard drive.

- **USB hard drives**—In my experience, this is the least-supported bootable configuration for older hardware. I only have one computer that was able to boot from a partitioned USB hard drive. However, every laptop I tested seems to support this configuration.

Changing between a USB hard drive and a USB floppy drive is as simple as formatting the base device or using `fdisk` and formatting a partition. However, converting a large USB floppy device into a small USB floppy device cannot be done directly.

1. Use dd to create a file that is as big as the drive you want to create. For example, to create a 32-MB USB drive, start with a 32-MB file:

```
dd if=/dev/zero of=usbfloppy.img bs=32M count=1
```

2. Treat this file as the base device. For example, you can format it and mount it.

```
mkfs usbfloppy.img
sudo mkdir /mnt/usb
sudo mount -o loop usbfloppy.img /mnt/usb
```

3. When you are all done configuring the USB floppy drive image, unmount it and copy it to the real USB device (for example, /dev/sda). This will make the real USB device appear to be a smaller USB floppy device.

```
sudo umount /mnt/usb
dd if=usbfloppy.img of=/dev/sda
```

The 10-Step Boot Configuration

Creating a bootable USB thumb drive requires 10 basic steps:

1. Unmount the drive. When you plug a USB drive into the computer, Ubuntu immediately mounts it. You need to unmount it before you can partition or format it.

   Use the mount command to list the current mount points and identify the USB thumb drive. Be aware that the device name will likely be different for you. In this example, the device is /dev/sda1 and the drive label is NEAL.

```
$ mount
/dev/hda1 on / type ext3 (rw,errors=remount-ro)
proc on /proc type proc (rw)
/sys on /sys type sysfs (rw)
varrun on /var/run type tmpfs (rw)
varlock on /var/lock type tmpfs (rw)
procbususb on /proc/bus/usb type usbfs (rw)
udev on /dev type tmpfs (rw)
devpts on /dev/pts type devpts (rw,gid=5,mode=620)
devshm on /dev/shm type tmpfs (rw)
lrm on /lib/modules/2.6.15-26-686/volatile type tmpfs (rw)
/dev/sda1 on /media/NEAL type vfat (rw,nodev,quiet,umask=077)
```

   Use the unmount command to free the device:

```
sudo umount /dev/sda1
```

2. Initialize the USB device. This is needed because previous configurations could leave residues that will interfere with future configurations. The simplest way to zero a device is to use dd. Keep in mind that large drives (even 1-GB thumb drives) may take a long time to zero. Fortunately, you usually only need to zero the first few sectors.

```
dd if=/dev/zero of=/dev/sda            # format all of /dev/sda
dd if=/dev/zero of=/dev/sda count=2048 # format the first 2048
                                         sectors
```

Use the sync command (sudo sync) to make sure that all data is written. After zeroing the device, unplug it and plug it back in. This will remove any stale device partitions. Ubuntu will not mount a blank device, but it will create a device handle for it.

3. If you are making a USB hard drive, then partition the device:

```
sudo fdisk /dev/sda
```

4. Format the partitions. If you are making a USB floppy drive, then format the base device (/dev/sda). For USB hard drives, format each of the partitions (/dev/sda1, /dev/sda2, etc.).

5. Mount the partition.

6. Copy files to the partition.

7. Place the kernel and boot files on the partition.

8. Configure the boot menus and options.

9. Use the sync command (sudo sync) to make sure that all data is written and then unmount the partition.

10. Install the boot manager.

Now the device should be bootable. The next few sections show different ways to do these 10 steps.

Starting the Network Install from a USB Drive

USB drives can be used to simplify system installations. For example, if the computer can boot from a USB drive, then you can use it to launch a network installation.

NOTE The preconfigured network boot image, boot.img, is very small—only 8 MB. It should work on all USB drives.

Configuring the thumb drive for use as a network installation system requires some simple steps:

1. Plug in the USB drive. If it mounts, unmount it.

2. Download the boot image. There is a different boot image for every platform. Be sure to retrieve the correct one for your Ubuntu release. For example, for Hardy Heron (8.04 LTS), use:

   ```
   wget http://archive.ubuntu.com/ubuntu/dists/\
   hardy/main/installer-i386/current/images/netboot/boot.img.gz
   ```

3. The boot image is preconfigured as a USB floppy drive. Copy the image onto the thumb drive. Be sure to specify the base device (for example, /dev/sda) and not any existing partitions (for example, /dev/sda1).

   ```
   zcat boot.img.gz > /dev/sda
   ```

4. Use sync to ensure that all writes complete, and then eject the thumb drive:

   ```
   sudo sync; sudo eject /dev/sda
   ```

Now you are ready to boot off the thumb drive, and the operating system will be installed over the network.

Every PC that I tested with Boot from USB support was able to run the default network installer: boot.img.gz. However, since USB support is not consistent, this may not necessarily work on your hardware. If you cannot get it to boot, then make sure your BIOS is configured to boot from the USB drive, that it boots from the USB before booting from other devices, and that the USB drive is connected to the system. If you have multiple USB devices connected, remove all but the bootable thumb drive.

Using the Boot Image

The boot.img.gz image is a self-contained file system and only uses 8 MB of disk space. If you have a bigger thumb drive (for example, 64 MB or 2 GB), then you can copy diagnostic tools or other stuff onto the drive.

In order to create a bootable USB drive, you will need a boot loader. The choices are GRUB or SYSLINUX. There are significant tradeoffs here. GRUB is the default boot loader used when Ubuntu is installed. However, using GRUB requires you to know the drive identifier, such as /dev/sda1.

TIP An alternative to the drive identifier is a universally unique identifier (UUID). Using UUIDs to identify drives is described in Chapter 3.

Since you may plug in and remove USB devices, the identifier may change, breaking the boot loader's configuration. SYSLINUX does not use a static drive identifier, but is limited to supporting FAT12 or FAT16 drives. Since USB devices are expected to be portable, use SYSLINUX:

```
sudo apt-get install syslinux mtools
```

The main steps require you to format the drive as FAT16 and use `syslinux` to make it bootable.

1. Start a shell with root privileges:

   ```
   sudo bash
   ```

2. Unmount the USB drive, if it is already mounted.

3. Format the drive as a FAT16 USB floppy drive (in this example, `/dev/sdc`) and mount it:

   ```
   mkdosfs -I -F 16 /dev/sdc
   sync
   mkdir /mnt/usb
   mount -o loop /dev/sdc /mnt/usb
   ```

4. Mount the `boot.img` file. You will use this to provide the boot files.

   ```
   zcat boot.img.gz > boot.img
   mkdir /mnt/img
   mount -o loop boot.img /mnt/img
   ```

5. Copy the files over to the USB drive. This can take a few minutes.

   ```
   sudo bash  # become root, run these commands as root
   (cd /mnt/img; tar -cf-*) | (cd /mnt/usb; tar -xvf -)
   sync
   ```

6. Set up the files for a bootable disk. This is done by copying over the SYSLINUX configuration files for an ISO image (`isolinux.cfg`) to a configuration file for a FAT16 system (`syslinux.cfg`):

   ```
   mv /mnt/usb/isolinux.cfg /mnt/usb/syslinux.cfg
   rm /mnt/usb/isolinux.bin
   sync
   ```

7. Unmount the drive and make it bootable by installing the boot loader:

   ```
   umount /mnt/usb
   syslinux /dev/sdc
   sync
   eject /dev/sdc
   exit  # leave the root shell
   ```

Now you can boot from the USB drive in order to install the operating system.

Installing a Full File System from USB

The Holy Grail for USB hacking is the ability to boot a standalone operating system from a thumb drive. In addition, given a large enough USB drive (and a computer that can boot from the USB port), you can configure a thumb drive as a standalone operating system.

WARNING There are many different methods discussed in online forums for configuring a USB drive as a bootable system. Unfortunately, most of the instructions are either incomplete or very complicated. Even if you follow these steps exactly, you may still be unable to boot from the USB device because of hardware limitations.

There are two configurations for making a bootable file system: a huge USB floppy drive or a large USB hard drive. In both of these examples, I will use the Hardy Heron (8.04 LTS) Live Desktop CD as the bootable device.

Using the Live CD from a USB Floppy Drive

Converting the Live CD to a bootable USB floppy drive requires at least a 1-GB thumb drive.

1. Start a shell with root privileges. This is done for convenience since nearly every command must be done as root.

   ```
   sudo bash
   ```

2. Unmount and blank the thumb drive. (See the section "The 10-Step Boot Configuration" for directions.)

3. Format the disk as one big FAT16 drive. The -I parameter to mkdosfs says to format the entire device. In this example, the USB drive is /dev/sdc.

   ```
   mkdosfs -I -F 16 /dev/sdc
   sync
   ```

TIP FAT16 only supports drives up to 2 GB. If you have a larger USB drive, then you will need to use the hack found in the "Different USB Devices" section to convert a large USB drive into a smaller one.

4. Mount the Live CD and the USB drive:

   ```
   mkdir /mnt/usb
   mkdir /mnt/iso
   mount -o loop ubuntu-8.04.3-desktop-i386.iso /mnt/iso/
   mount /dev/sdc /mnt/usb
   ```

5. Copy over the files. This can take 20 minutes or longer. Go watch TV or have lunch. Also, ignore the errors about symbolic links, since FAT16 does not support them.

   ```
   cp -rpx /mnt/iso/* /mnt/usb/
   sync
   ```

NOTE FAT16 does not support symbolic links. This copy command replaces links with the linked file contents.

6. Set up the files for a bootable disk. Since SYSLINUX does not support subdirectories for kernel files, you need to move these to the top directory on the USB drive.

```
# move the kernel files and memory tester
mv /mnt/usb/casper/vmlinuz /mnt/usb/vmlinuz
mv /mnt/usb/casper/initrd.gz /mnt/usb/initrd.gz
mv /mnt/usb/install/mt86plus /mnt/usb/mt86plus
# move boot files to top of the drive
mv /mnt/usb/isolinux/* /mnt/usb/
mv /mnt/usb/isolinux.cfg /mnt/usb/syslinux.cfg
rm /mnt/usb/isolinux.bin
# Optional: Delete Windows tools and ISO files to free space
rm -rf /mnt/usb/start.* /mnt/usb/autorun.inf
rm /mnt/usb/bin /mnt/usb/programs
rm -rf /mnt/usb/isolinux
# All done
sync
```

7. Edit the /mnt/usb/syslinux.cfg file and correct the kernel paths. Remove the paths /casper/ and /install/ wherever you see them. This is because Step 6 moved the files to the root of the USB drive. There should be eight occurrences of /casper/ and one of /install/. After you write your changes, run sync.

8. Unmount the drive and make it bootable:

```
umount /mnt/usb
syslinux /dev/sdc
sync
eject /dev/sdc
exit  # leave the root shell
```

The USB thumb drive should now be bootable! You can run the Ubuntu Live operating system or install the operating system from this USB thumb drive.

For customization, you can change the boot menu by editing the /mnt/usb/syslinux.cfg file and modifying the kernels.

Using the Live CD from a USB Hard Drive

Converting the Live CD to a USB hard drive is much more complicated. Many computers that support booting from USB devices do not support this configuration. Even if the basic configuration is supported, there may be BIOS restrictions on the disk's layout. In addition, the boot loader needs to support partitions. Finally, the USB drive's identifier cannot change after installation. This final issue is the main reason that I do not use GRUB or LILO as the boot loader on USB drives.

Hard drives are defined by a combination of heads, sectors, and cylinders. Although heads and cylinders used to match physical drive heads and platters, this is no longer the case. In general, each sector contains 512 bytes of data, each cylinder contains multiple sectors, and there are multiple cylinders per head. However, when booting from a USB hard drive, many BIOS manufacturers assume the drive has 64 heads and 32 sectors per cylinder. This is the configuration used by ZIP drives. If you use a different configuration, then it may not boot. In addition, the first partition must not be larger than 1023 cylinders.

Although the syslinux command only supports FAT12 and FAT16 file systems, the syslinux package includes extlinux, which supports the ext2 and ext3 file systems. For this example, we will use extlinux as the boot loader with an ext2 file system on the bootable partition.

There are 10 steps to configure a bootable operating system on the USB drive:

1. Open a shell with root privileges:

   sudo bash

2. Connect the USB drive and unmount it.

3. Use fdisk of cfdisk to partition the drive (for example, /dev/sdc). Be sure to specify 64 heads and 32 sectors. The last cylinder of the first partition must not be larger than 1023. If you have additional disk space after allocating the first partition, then you can allocate additional partitions.

```
# fdisk -H 64 -S 32 /dev/sdc
Command (m for help): d
No partition is defined yet!
Command (m for help): n
Command action
   e   extended
   p   primary partition (1-4)
p
Partition number (1-4): 1
First cylinder (1-983, default 1): 1
Last cylinder or +size or +sizeM or +sizeK (1-983, default 983): 983
Command (m for help): a
Partition number (1-4): 1
Command (m for help): p
Disk /dev/sdc: 1030 MB, 1030750208 bytes
64 heads, 32 sectors/track, 983 cylinders
Units = cylinders of 2048 * 512 = 1048576 bytes
   Device Boot      Start         End      Blocks   Id  System
/dev/sdc1   *           1         983     1006576   83  Linux
Command (m for help): w
The partition table has been altered!
```

WARNING The partition must be marked as "active"; otherwise, you will not be able to boot from it.

4. Format the partition as an ext2 file system:

```
mkfs.ext2 /dev/sdc1
```

5. Mount the Live CD and the USB drive:

```
mkdir /mnt/usb
mkdir /mnt/img
mount -o loop ubuntu-8.04.3-desktop-i386.iso /mnt/img/
mount /dev/sdc1 /mnt/usb
```

6. Copy over the files. As mentioned in the previous section, this can take 20 minutes or longer.

```
cp -rpx /mnt/iso/* /mnt/usb/
sync
```

7. Create the boot files. Unlike `syslinux`, the boot files for `extlinux` can be located in a directory. In this case, you will reuse the `casper` directory, since it already contains the kernel files.

```
cp /mnt/usb/isolinux/* /mnt/usb/casper/
rm /mnt/usb/casper/isolinux.bin
mv /mnt/usb/casper/isolinux.cfg /mnt/usb/casper/extlinux.conf
sync
```

NOTE The extension for the boot configuration file is `.conf`, not `.cfg`.

8. *Do not unmount* the drive yet! Making it bootable with `extlinux` requires the mounted directory containing the `extlinux.conf` file.

```
extlinux -z /mnt/usb/casper
sync
```

9. Copy over the boot loader. There is a file missing from the `syslinux` binary package, but it is available in the source package. This file is called `mbr.bin` and is a master boot record containing the boot loader. Download the source package:

```
apt-get source syslinux
```

This creates a directory, such as `syslinux-3.53/`. In this directory is the missing file. Install it on the drive using:

```
cat mbr.bin > /dev/sdc
sync
```

> **WARNING** If you are configuring a file image instead of the actual drive, then this `cat` command will truncate your file. Instead, use `dd if=mbr.bin of=usbdrive.img bs=1 notrunc` to install the master boot record to your USB drive image file (in this case, `usbdrive.img`).

10. Now, make sure all writes complete and then unmount the drive:

```
sync; umount /dev/sdc; eject /dev/sdc
```

If all goes well, you should have a working, bootable USB thumb drive. This drive can be used as a bare-bones recovery and repair system.

As an alternative configuration, you can format the drive with FAT16 and use `syslinux` to make the partition bootable. In this case, you will also need to copy the boot files to the top of the partition and edit the `syslinux.cfg` file as described in the previous section.

Booting Variations and Troubleshooting

I used a variety of computers for testing the USB boot process. Every computer acted differently to different boot configurations.

- Every computer with Boot from USB support was able to boot the original `boot.img` file. They were all able to install over the network.

- Most computers were able to boot the Ubuntu Live Desktop operating system when my 1-GB thumb drive was formatted as a USB floppy drive. However, one computer gave a generic boot error message.

- Only my newer computer systems could boot the USB hard drive with the ext2 file system. It didn't make any difference if I used a real USB hard drive or thumb drive. In addition, specifying the ZIP configuration was the only way to make the hard drive configuration work on one of the computers.

- My Asus netbook had no issues booting from any of these configurations, and it even worked from a 2-GB SD Card.

Depending on the configuration variation and hardware that you use, you may see some well-known errors.

- **Blank screen**—If all you see is a blank screen with a blinking cursor, then something definitely did not work. This happens when the boot loader fails. It could be the result of failing to install the boot loader properly, or it could be a BIOS problem. Try rebuilding the USB drive in case you missed a step. Also, try booting the USB drive on a different computer. If it works on one computer and not on another, then it is a BIOS problem. But if it fails everywhere, then it is probably the boot loader.

- **"PCI: Cannot allocate resource region. . ."**—This indicates a BIOS problem. You may be able to boot using additional kernel parameters to bypass the PCI errors, for example:

```
live noapic nolapic pci=noacpi acpi=off
```

   However, you may not be able to get past this. Check if there is a BIOS upgrade available for your computer.

- **Root not found**—There are a variety of errors to indicate that the root partition was not available during boot. This usually happens when the USB drive is still initializing or transferring data, and not ready for the root partition to be mounted. You can fix this by extracting the initrd file (see the next section, "Tweaking the BusyBox") and editing the conf/initramfs.conf file. Add in a mounting delay of 15 seconds (the new line should say: WAIT=15). This delay gives the USB time to initialize, configure, and transfer data.

Tweaking the BusyBox

During the text-based installation, you have the option to access a command prompt by pressing Alt+F2. Unlike a full operating system, this prompt contains a very minimal environment with few commands.

The minimal operating system is part of an application called BusyBox. BusyBox is a very small executable that provides the installation environment. The BusyBox system files are stored in the initrd archive. Depending on your Ubuntu version, the file is named either initrd.gz or initrd.lz.

By hacking the initrd file, you can add commands to the basic installation environment. For example, you can add an editor or diagnostic tools to the /bin directory. Be sure to copy over any shared libraries used by commands. For example, file /bin/nano shows a dynamically linked executable, and ldd /bin/nano lists all of the libraries. You will be unable to use a linked executable unless you also include all of the libraries.

```
$ file /bin/nano
/bin/nano: ELF 32-bit LSB executable, Intel 80386, version 1 (SYSV), for
GNU/Linux 2.6.8, dynamically linked (uses shared libs), stripped
$ ldd /bin/nano
        linux-gate.so.1 =>  (0xb7fa1000)
        libncursesw.so.5 => /lib/libncursesw.so.5 (0xb7f4e000)
        libc.so.6 => /lib/tls/i686/cmov/libc.so.6 (0xb7dff000)
        libdl.so.2 => /lib/tls/i686/cmov/libdl.so.2 (0xb7dfa000)
        /lib/ld-linux.so.2 (0xb7fa2000)
```

NOTE Don't worry about the linux-gate.so.1 library. It does not really exist. You only need to copy over libraries that include paths, such as /lib/libncursesw.so.5.

In contrast, any executable identified as statically linked (not dynamically linked) is good to go! There are no additional libraries required.

```
$ file /usr/bin/rar
/usr/bin/rar: ELF 32-bit LSB executable, Intel 80386, version 1 (SYSV),
for GNU/Linux 2.6.0, statically linked, stripped
$ ldd /usr/bin/rar
        not a dynamic executable
```

TIP If you are compiling programs, then you can use `gcc -static` to generate statically linked executables. You can also download package source code using `apt-get source`. (See Chapter 5 for information on installing the compilation environment and downloading the source for packages.)

To modify `initrd`:

1. Extract the archive. The `initrd` file is actually a compressed archive containing all of the executables, libraries, and configuration files needed during boot. Depending on your Ubuntu version, the file is named either `initrd.gz` or `initrd.lz`. For example, the Hardy Heron (8.04 LTS) Live Desktop CD uses `casper/initrd.gz`, while the Live CD for Karmic Koala (9.10) uses `casper/initrd.lz`.

   ```
   mkdir extract
   cd extract
   zcat /mnt/usb/casper/initrd.gz | cpio -imvd  # for initrd.gz
   lzma -dc -S .lz /mnt/usb/casper/initrd.lz | cpio -imvd
                                   # for initrd.lz
   ```

2. The extracted contents look like a file system. Add or edit files in this directory. For example, to add a binary, place the binary in `./bin/` and any libraries in `./lib/`.

3. Repackage and replace the `initrd` file:

   ```
   find . | cpio -o -L--format='newc' |
           gzip -9 > /mnt/usb/casper/initrd.gz
   find . | cpio -o -L--format='newc' |
           lzma -7 > /mnt/usb/casper/initrd.lz
   ```

Using Ubuntu on a Netbook

Beginning with Jaunty Jackalope (9.04), specialized version of Ubuntu has been created for netbook systems. Netbook computers are a class of low-end laptops. They are generally smaller, less powerful computers. Physically, they usually have smaller keyboards, smaller screens, and no CD or DVD drive.

While you would not want to run a multi-user or high-volume web server on a netbook, they are ideal for simple tasks when you are out of the office. For example, you can check e-mail, surf the web, do some basic word processing, and even occasionally develop software (like patching while on the road). Netbooks are also great for watching movies on airplanes.

Installing on a Netbook

Most netbooks include multiple USB connectors and usually have a slot for an SD Card or similar memory device. Since netbooks lack CD and DVD drives, all include the ability to boot from USB, SD Card, or other types of removable memory. Many also include the ability to boot from the network.

NOTE Even though the netbook release is relatively new and still undergoing major revision changes (the Jaunty desktop looks very different from the Karmic desktop), the installation is one of the most painless processes I have ever experienced.

While there is a wide range of netbooks on the market, not all are supported by Ubuntu. While some work right straight out of the box, others may need you to manually install drivers or patches, and a few have completely unsupported hardware. Usually the issues concern sound, video camera, or network support.

TIP Before trying to use Ubuntu on a netbook, consult the list of supported hardware at `https://wiki.ubuntu.com/HardwareSupport/Machines/Netbooks`.

Creating the Netbook Installation Media

To create the netbook installation media, you will need to download the netbook ISO (for example, `ubuntu-9.10-netbook-remix-i386.iso`). If your netbook has a CD-ROM drive, then simply burn the ISO to a disk and boot from it.

However, most netbooks lack a CD-ROM drive. In this case, you will need a 1-G USB thumb drive, SD Card, or other form of media that is supported by your netbook. You will also need a computer to create the CD-ROM.

The easiest way to make a bootable netbook installation image on a USB thumb drive or SD Card is to use `usb-creator`. This tool automates the processes of putting a CD-ROM image onto other types of removable media.

- **Intrepid Ibex (8.10) and later**—Install `usb-creator` using `sudo apt-get install usb-creator`. The executable is called `usb-creator-gtk`.

- **Hardy Heron (9.04 LTS)**—There is an ugly hack for installing `usb-creator` on Hardy. Hardy and Intrepid are very similar and can run much of the same code.

1. Download Intrepid's `usb-creator` package from

   `https://launchpad.net/ubuntu/intrepid/i386/usb-creator`

   The file will have a file name like `usb-creator_0.1.10_all.deb`.

2. Install the dependent packages:

   `sudo apt-get install syslinux mtools`

3. Install Intrepid's `usb-creator` package on Hardy:

   `sudo dpkg -i usb-creator_0.1.10_all_deb`

4. The executable is called `usb-creator`.

The `usb-creator` program allows you to select the ISO image and destination device. (See Figure 1-5.) When it finishes the installation, you can connect the USB device (or SD Card) to your netbook and boot from it.

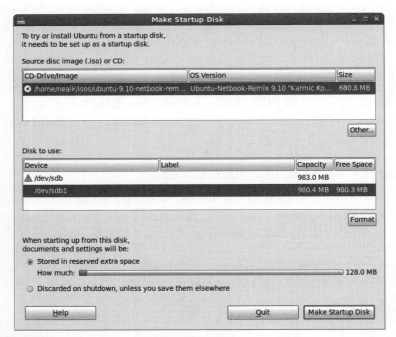

Figure 1-5: The `usb-creator` under Karmic Koala

If `usb-creator` is not an option (for example, if you are running Dapper Drake 6.06 LTS), then follow the steps in the section "Installing a Full File System from USB" to copy the netbook installation image to an SD Card or USB device. Use the USB hard drive configuration.

Installing with Only a Netbook

There are two other options that work really well for installing Ubuntu on a netbook, or any other kind of Windows system. The approach is a little roundabout, but you can install Ubuntu using only a netbook and a USB drive and not burn anything to CD-ROM.

Most netbooks ship with Microsoft Windows XP or Windows 7 installed. Using Windows, download the netbook installation disk onto the netbook. At this point, you have two options: create a bootable USB device from Windows or use the Windows Ubuntu Installer.

To create a bootable USB drive, download `unetbootin` for Windows from `unetbootin.sourceforge.net`. This program works like the `usb-creator`, allowing you to select an ISO and install it on a USB device.

With Windows, you can also open up the ISO image. Sitting at the root of the disk image is a program called `wubi.exe`. This is the Windows Ubuntu Installer. Using Wubi, you can install Ubuntu as an application under Windows that runs a separate operating system. Wubi works by adding itself to the Windows boot menu. This effectively turns the Windows system into a dual-boot computer.

After installing Wubi, reboot the system. You will see Ubuntu listed in the boot menu. If you boot Ubuntu, it will use the Windows boot manager to run an Ubuntu environment. From Ubuntu, you can access the host Windows system through `/host` and `/media`. More importantly, you can download the `usb-creator` for Ubuntu and create a bootable USB device.

Regardless of the approach you take, you should now have a bootable USB drive (or SD Card or other type of removable memory). Tell your netbook to boot off the new media. For example, with an Asus 1005HA netbook, you can press Esc after pressing the power-on button and select the SD Card or USB drive as the boot device. At this point, you can install Ubuntu for the netbook.

HIDDEN DISK PARTITIONS

Many netbooks and laptops have a boot option to restore the operating system. This works by accessing a separate partition on the hard drive that contains a bootable operating system and will restore the system to factory defaults.

During the install process, use the advanced disk partitioning option. This will show you the name of the emergency recovery partition. (It is usually named something like "XP recovery.") There may also be a small Extensible Firmware Interface (EFI) partition used to improve boot times.

If you don't want to accidentally press a button and overwrite your Ubuntu netbook with Windows, then be sure to reformat the drive (or remove the XP recovery partition) during the installation. If you remove the emergency recovery partition, then the operating system will ignore requests for recovery.

(continued)

HIDDEN DISK PARTITIONS *(continued)*

While removing the EFI partition (fdisk partition type 0xEF) will not harm anything, keeping the small (usually 8 MB) partition can dramatically improve boot times.

Upgrading Ubuntu

People who already use Ubuntu have the option to upgrade rather than reinstall. Ubuntu follows a strict upgrade path between major revisions; you should not just upgrade straight from Dapper to Karmic. The upgrade path is only supported for one-off and LTS releases. For example, you can upgrade from Dapper Drake (6.06 LTS) to the next release (Edgy Eft 6.10) or to the next LTS release (Hardy Heron 8.04 LTS). However, skipping a release, such as upgrading from Hardy Heron to Karmic Koala (9.10) and skipping Jaunty Jackalope (9.04), is not supported.

NOTE Although you could upgrade directly from Dapper or Hardy to Karmic, this is likely to cause problems. Each upgrade assumes that you are upgrading from the previous version. Skipping a version may break this assumption and cause upgrade problems.

UPGRADE VERSUS FRESH INSTALL

Even though Dapper, Hardy, and Karmic are all versions of Ubuntu, they are all major releases. Treat them as different operating systems. Just as the upgrade path from Windows 2000 to Windows XP is not recommended, I don't recommend the upgrade path between Ubuntu revisions. Instead, back up your files, inventory the software you need, and perform a clean install. After the install, restore your personal files and add your software. This is faster and less painful than debugging Ubuntu after an upgrade.

WARNING The success of an upgrade depends on your system and customizations. Upgrades do not always work.

The safest upgrade approach is to save your files off the system and perform a clean install. However, if you still want to go through with the upgrade, then you will need to determine your Ubuntu version and run a few upgrade commands.

TIP Consider putting the /home directory on its own partition. This way, you can upgrade or reinstall without losing all of your personal files.

Determining the Version

Upgrading gets complicated when Ubuntu users refer to the operating system by name, while the operating system reports numeric versions. The question becomes: How can you tell which version of Ubuntu is in use?

One approach is to use the graphical desktop. On the menu bar, System ⇨ About Ubuntu displays the version number and common name. Unfortunately, this is not an option for text-only systems such as the Ubuntu Server. This is also not practical for automated systems.

Another approach is to look at the current /etc/apt/source.list file. Assuming that nobody has drastically modified the file, the common name for the operating system should be listed on the deb installation lines.

A better option is the lsb_release command. This command displays distribution-specific information from the Linux Standard Base.

```
$ lsb_release -a
No LSB modules are available.
Distributor ID: Ubuntu
Description:    Ubuntu 8.04.3 LTS
Release:        8.04
Codename:       hardy
```

Performing the Upgrade

When you start the upgrade, there is no going back. Attempting to stop the upgrade will likely screw up the system, and a power outage during the upgrade can be disastrous. Be sure to make a backup before beginning the upgrade.

The automated upgrade command is:

```
sudo apt-get install update-manager-core
sudo do-release-upgrade
```

Depending on your system's state, these commands may direct you to run additional commands. Eventually, you will be directed to reboot the system. If all goes well, the system will come up. During the first login, the system may be a little slow as it performs some post-upgrade configurations. After that, you should be good to go.

Upgrading Issues with Ubuntu

Ubuntu upgrades are not always painless. (I have not yet had a simple upgrade.) Although upgrading from a new Dapper install (with no additions) to Edgy to Hardy works well, you are unlikely to be running a new installation of Dapper or Edgy. Customizations lead to upgrade complications. For example:

- **Custom system files**—Customizing files, such as /etc/gdm/gdb.conf (see Chapter 10), will prompt you to resolve installation conflicts. You can either overwrite or keep the old file, but you cannot merge changes.

- **Proprietary drivers**—Binary and custom drivers, ranging from the Macromedia Flash player to wireless network support, may break. You will need to uninstall and reinstall the software.

- **Shared Libraries**—Different versions of Ubuntu use different linked libraries. For example, Jaunty uses newer libraries than Hardy. Code that is compiled for one set of libraries may break under the new system; be prepared to recompile as needed.

- **Moving files**—Required system files may move between upgrades. For example, the w32codec files (for playing multimedia files, see Chapter 6) may be located in /usr/lib/win32/, /usr/lib/codec/, or some other directory, depending on when and how you installed it. You may even have different versions of the same files in different directories, leading to run-time compatibility issues.

The time required to do an upgrade is another significant issue. An upgrade usually takes at least three times longer than a clean install. This is because the upgrade checks files before modifying the system. While a 2-GHz computer may install in 15 minutes and upgrade in under an hour, a slower computer can take many hours. My 2-GHz PC upgraded over the network from Dapper to Hardy in roughly 5 hours. The same computer completed a network install of Hardy in less than 30 minutes.

Finally, your graphical desktop may not look like a new installation. Menus and applications change between Ubuntu versions, but upgrades do not receive the changes, For example, if you migrated from Hardy Heron to Jaunty Jackalope to Karmic Koala, then you will still have the System ⇨ Preferences ⇨ Removable Drives and Media menu, even though the popup window no longer describes any settings for removable drives or media. Under a clean install of Karmic, this menu option does not exist.

WARNING Be prepared to devote time to upgrading. Because you may be prompted occasionally to resolve conflicts, you cannot walk away and expect the upgrade to finish without your intervention. If the upgrade takes two hours, you should be near the computer for two hours. After the upgrade has been completed, you may need to spend additional time fixing broken drivers and recompiling software. (Be sure to stock up on coffee and order in for lunch.)

Configuring GRUB

When you first boot your Ubuntu system, there is a small text screen that says GRUB Loading, and you have three seconds to press Esc before it boots the default operating system. GRUB is the GRand Unified Bootloader and determines which operating system you want to run. If you press Esc during the boot loader screen, you can select alternate operating systems, kernels, and kernel parameters.

If you don't press Esc in three seconds, then GRUB will boot the default operating system. You can change the GRUB configuration by editing /boot/grub/menu.1st. For example, if you change the timeout value to 15 (from timeout 3 to timeout 15), then GRUB will wait 15 seconds before booting the default operating system. This is very useful if your monitor takes a few seconds to wake up from power-save mode or if you are just slow to press Esc.

Similarly, menu.1st file includes the list of known kernels and operating systems at the end of the file. The first one listed is item 0, the second is item 1, and so on. At the beginning of menu.list is a line that says Default 0. This identifies the default operating system configuration as the first one in the list. If you change it to Default 3, then the fourth system listed will become the default.

Altering Boot Parameters

The /boot/grub/menu.1st file contains three main sections. The first section, found at the top of the file, contains basic parameters such as timeout and default.

The second section is denoted by a line that says BEGIN AUTOMAGIC KERNELS LIST. This section contains parameters used for automatic kernel configuration. Each of these lines begins with one or two hash signs (# or ##). Usually a hash sign denotes a commented line. However, the automated script actively removes the first hash in order to obtain customized kernel parameters. Real comments have two hash signs; configuration parameters have one.

For example, one of my computers requires the kernel parameter pci=nobios in order to boot properly. Rather than pressing Esc and manually entering it each time I reboot, I can add it to the boot options line. It needs to have one hash character so that it becomes a configuration parameter.

```
## additional options to use with the default boot option, but not with
## the alternatives
## e.g. defoptions=vga=791 resume=/dev/hda5
# defoptions=pci=nobios
```

The final section of the file comes after the line that says `End Default Options`. Do not modify anything below this line. Whenever you update the system and install a new kernel or make changes to GRUB, this section is regenerated. Anything manually changed after this line will be lost the next time you install a kernel upgrade.

Updating GRUB

The boot loader does not actually reside in the Linux partition. Instead, it is hooked into the sector containing the partition table on the hard drive. After you make any changes to the GRUB configuration files, you need to update the installed boot loader:

```
sudo update-grub
```

This command regenerates the `/boot/grub/menu.lst` file and updates the boot loader on the hard drive.

CONFIGURING GRUB UNDER KARMIC KOALA

GRUB's configuration was very consistent though all versions of Ubuntu . . . until Karmic Koala (9.10) showed up. While GRUB essentially works the same way, all of the configuration files moved.

For example, earlier Ubuntu versions use `/boot/grub/menu.lst` for setting the timeout, default operating system, and associated parameters. With Karmic, the configuration has been split. The file `/etc/default/grub` contains generic settings, including the timeout (`GRUB_TIMEOUT`) and default parameters (`GRUB_DEFAULT` and `GRUB_CMDLINE_LINUX_DEFAULT`).

Additional configuration scripts have been moved under `/etc/grub.d/`. For example, the actual Linux boot command is stored in `/etc/grub.d/10_linux`, and the memory tester is in `20_memtest86+`.

The final significant change comes from the list of kernels and operating systems. With earlier versions of GRUB, the kernel list was automatically detected from the `/boot/` directory and then added to the final automated section of the `menu.lst` file. The new version of GRUB still automatically discovers all installed kernels, but the list is now stored in `/boot/grub/grub.cfg`. This configuration file is completely auto-generated. Do not edit this file. Instead, make any configuration changes to the `/etc/default/grub` and `/etc/grub.d/` files.

When you finish customizing GRUB, be sure to run `sudo update-grub` to refresh the automatically generated files and update the boot loader.

Summary

The initial Ubuntu configuration determines the ease and flexibility available when modifying the operating system. A right decision at the beginning can make everything else easier. The questions addressed in this chapter include:

- Do you upgrade or reinstall?
- Do you want a desktop, server, or custom installation?
- Should you install from a floppy disk, CD-ROM, USB, or across the network?
- If you upgrade, what are some problems you may run into?

Chapter 2 covers the post-installation environment and discusses options that you might want to change after you first log in. In Chapter 3, you'll learn how to configure the different types of devices and peripherals that you may want to use with your system, and Chapter 4 helps you get the most out of your keyboard, mouse, and other manual interfaces.

## CHAPTER 7

Customizing the User Environment

What's In This Chapter?

What should you do after you first log in?
Adjusting the desktop's look and feel
Adding easy access buttons
Configuring the Nautilus file browser
Tips for changing the login screen

The basic install of Ubuntu provides a usable system. But *usable* is not the same as *optimal*. When you first log into the system, there are some things that you will definitely want to change, like the colors (nobody likes brown—seriously, what can brown do for you?). This chapter discusses options for making the desktop and workspace environment more usable.

Logging in for the First Time

When you first log in to Ubuntu, a few things will get your attention, like the login music. With Dapper Drake (6.06 LTS), it is an increasing tone with twinkles that sound like an orchestra tuning up; later Ubuntu versions sounds like bongo drums. And the desktop color scheme: brown. Before you can call the system usable, you will need to change these and other things.

Changing the Startup Music

Prior to Karmic Koala (9.10), the startup music is one of the easiest items to change. From the menu at the top, select System ➾ Preferences ➾ Sound. This brings up the Sound Preferences applet (see Figure 2-1). From here, you can assign sounds to system events. For example, I have a blood-curdling scream for error messages, and a telephone ringing for question dialog boxes.

WARNING New sound selections are not always used immediately. If you find that your new sounds are not immediately used, log out and log back in. This seems to be a bug in the Gnome Sound Preferences applet.

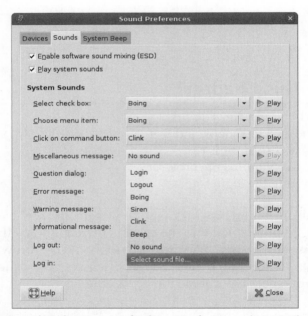

Figure 2-1: The Sound Preferences applet from Hardy Heron (8.04 LTS)

Converting Audio Files

You may select any WAV audio file for any of the audio events. If you want to use a different audio format, such as MP3 or OGG, you will need to convert it to a WAV file. The easiest way to convert audio files is with sox—the universal sound exchanger.

1. The `sox` package comes from the universe repository, but this repository is not enabled by default. As root, you will need to edit `/etc/apt/sources.list` and uncomment the two universe lines. These should be near the top of the file and look similar to:

   ```
   deb http://us.archive.ubuntu.com/ubuntu/ hardy universe
   deb-src http://us.archive.ubuntu.com/ubuntu/ hardy universe
   ```

   You will also need to update the repository cache:

   ```
   sudo apt-get update
   ```

   NOTE The `/etc/apt/sources.list` file and the `apt-get` process are detailed in Chapter 5.

2. Install `sox` if it is not already installed.

   ```
   sudo apt-get install sox
   ```

3. Use `sox` to convert the audio file. By default, `sox` determines file types by the file extension.

   ```
   sox fileIN.mp3 fileOUT.wav
   ```

4. Test the sound file using the `play` command:

   ```
   play fileOUT.wav
   ```

5. From the Sound Preferences applet, select the pull-down menu for the desired system sound, for example, "Login" and click "Select Sound File".

6. Select the WAV file you just created.

SOX AIN'T LAME

The `sox` application is a great tool for converting and modifying sound files, but it does not support all formats for all functions. In particular, even though it can read MP3 files, it cannot be used to create MP3 files without additional libraries. To resolve this constraint, you can use the `lame` package to encode MP3 files from WAV files.

Just as GNU is a recursive acronym, GNU is Not Unix, LAME uses a recursive name: LAME Ain't an MP3 Encoder. Ignoring the name, `lame` is a powerful tool for creating MP3 files. First, make sure that the package is installed: `sudo apt-get install lame`. Then, convert your WAV file to an MP3 file: `lame fileIN.wav fileOUT.mp3`.

The MP3 file from LAME cannot be used for system sounds (because system sounds do not support MP3 files) but can be used by other audio applications and portable music devices.

Modifying Audio Files

Most WAV files are longer than a few seconds, and you probably do not want a three-minute song playing every time you click a button. The `sox` program can be used to trim audio files, but you will need to know the starting time for the sound you want and the length. For example, to start 3 seconds into the file and keep a 2.31 second duration, use:

```
sox fileIN.mp3 fileOUT.wav trim 3 2.31
```

Trim times can be written in a variety of formats. You can specify seconds (and fractions of a second) or actual time values. The value 125.6 can be written as 2:05.6 or 0:2:5.6. The notations indicate seconds (with fractions), minutes, and hours. Also, if you do not specify the duration, then it goes to the end of the file.

The `sox` command can also add effects such as echos, high-pass and low-pass filtering, stretching, and reversing. For a full list of functions, refer to the `sox` man page (`man sox`).

Changing Sounds under Karmic Koala

With Karmic Koala (9.10), modifying the system sounds is a little more complicated. The System ⇨ Preferences ⇨ Sound menu options permit you to change the entire sound theme, but you cannot alter specific sounds. (See Figure 2-2.) Moreover, the desktop login sound is not even listed.

The startup sound is actually found under System ⇨ Preferences ⇨ Startup Applications. To disable the desktop login sound, uncheck the GNOME Login Sound item.

Creating your own audio theme is more complicated in Karmic because there is no GUI interface.

1. Open a terminal window and go to the `/usr/share/sounds/` directory.

   ```
   cd /usr/share/sounds
   ```

2. Copy the Ubuntu default audio theme to your own theme:

   ```
   sudo cp -r ubuntu newtheme
   ```

3. In your *newtheme* directory is a file called `index.theme`. Change the theme's name from `name=Ubuntu` to your own theme name (for example, `name=My Cool Audio Theme`).

4. Under *newtheme*/`stereo/` are a bunch of OGG sound files. The file name tells you when each is used. For example, `desktop-login.ogg` is played

when the GNOME Login Sound plays. Replace these OGG files with your own OGG files. You can use `sox` to convert other audio formats to OGG.

5. When you are finished, go to System ➪ Preferences ➪ Sound and select your new sound theme from the list.

Figure 2-2: The Sound Preferences applet from Karmic Koala (9.10)

Changing the Background

The default background for the Ubuntu desktop is a brown screen with a bright highlight. As my fashionable coworker tells me, "Nobody likes brown." So the background must be changed. Right-click on the background, and select Change Desktop Background from the popup menu. The System ➪ Preferences ➪ Desktop Background menu item brings up the Desktop Background Preferences applet.

TIP You can also bring up the Desktop Background Preferences applet from the menus. With most Ubuntu versions, you can use System ➪ Preferences ➪ Appearance and click on the Background tab. With Dapper Drake (6.06 LTS), the menu is System ➪ Preferences ➪ Desktop Background.

Although Ubuntu does include some very colorful backgrounds, you can always add your own. Unlike the Sound Preferences, where you are limited to one type of audio file format, the desktop supports many graphic formats. GIF, JPEG, BMP, PCX, TIF, and PNG are all acceptable formats. Besides selecting an alternate image, you can also select whether the image should be tiled, stretched, or centered, or have a border color. In Figure 2-3, I selected my Safe-Computing logo, centered, with a vertical gradient background. Since my image is a GIF with a transparent background, the desktop's color scheme blends well with the picture.

NOTE Even though the desktop supports many different graphical formats, there are some graphics that it does not support. In particular, the desktop background displays static pictures. Animated GIFs are not animated, MPEG videos do not work as backgrounds, nor do Adobe Flash movies. In Chapter 10, you'll see how to create animated backgrounds.

TIP In case you need to crop or modify your picture, the Desktop installation automatically includes Gimp, a powerful graphics editor.

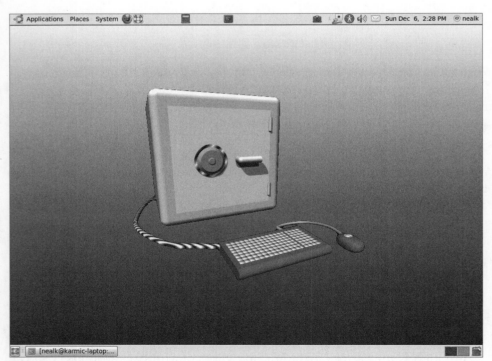

Figure 2-3: The Hacker Factor Safe-Computing logo as a background with a gradient color

Changing the Background As Needed

The picture and color on the desktop does not need to be static. You can use a simple program to change the picture (or color) as needed. The commands are:

```
gconftool-2 -t str-set /desktop/gnome/background/picture_filename \
    /path/picture.gif
gconftool-2 -t str-set /desktop/gnome/background/primary_color \
    "#AABBCC"
gconftool-2 -t str-set /desktop/gnome/background/secondary_color \
    "#112233"
```

The Gnome desktop keeps a set of configuration parameters, similarly to the Microsoft Windows registry. The `gconf-editor` command enables you to interactively view and edit the values (reminiscent of the Windows `regedit` command), and the `gconftool-2` command enables you to edit values from the command line. Within the registry, the `picture_filename` field stores the name of the background image (in this example, `/path/picture.gif`). Be sure to specify the *full path* to the image. As soon as you change the image in the registry, the image on the background changes.

As with `picture_filename`, the `primary_color` and `secondary_color` fields are used to control the background color. If you only have a solid background, then the color is defined by `primary_color`. The `secondary_color` is only used with a color gradient. Colors are represented by three hex bytes that denote red, green, and blue. Black is #000000, white is #FFFFFF, and a nice light blue is #2255FF. As with the background image, as soon as you change the color in the registry, the color on the background changes.

Using Informative Colors

The background color does not need to be a static color. With a simple script, you can change the color based on system events. For example, you can monitor a log file and change the background to red when something serious happens. As an example, Listing 2-1 is a Perl script that changes the background color to represent the system load.

NOTE The results from the script in Listing 2-1 will only be visible if you have some portion of the desktop background displaying the primary background color. If you have a graphic that covers the whole desktop, then you will not see anything.

Listing 2-1: Script to Change Background Color with Load

```perl
#!/usr/bin/perl
# Color the background based on system load
my $key = "/desktop/gnome/background/primary_color";
my $load; # system load
my $R, $G, $B; # Red, Green, Blue colors
while ( 1 )
  {
  $load=`uptime`; # get the current load
  # format is "duration, users, load average: 0.00, 0.00, 0.00"
  # remove everything except the first load value
  $load =~ s/.*: //;
  # load values: 1 minute, 5 minute, 15 minute averages
  # these are colored: 1=Red, 5=Green, 15=Blue
  ($R,$G,$B) = split(', ',$load);

  # scale up to the range 0-255, but cap it at 255
  $R = $R * 255; if ($R > 255) { $R = 255; }
  $G = $G * 255; if ($G > 255) { $G = 255; }
  $B = $B * 255; if ($B > 255) { $B = 255; }
  # convert to hex
  $load = sprintf "%02X%02X%02X",$R,$G,$B;

  # set the color
  system("gconftool-2 -t str—set $key '#$load'");
  sleep 15; # Update 4 times per minute
  }
Done
```

This script changes the background color every 15 seconds based on the system load. A reddish color indicates a very active system. Yellow indicates an active process that has been running at least 5 minutes; white means at least 15 minutes. If no processes are raising the system load, then the colors will cycle from green to blue to black. If you want to know when the system becomes busy, a sudden change in the background color should get your attention.

Changing the Fonts

By default, the Ubuntu desktop uses a 10 pt Sans font. You can change the font used by the desktop through the System ➪ Preferences ➪ Font applet. Changing the fonts immediately changes the desktop.

MAKING A POINT

There are three metrics for determining font size. First, there are pixels (px). These are the active elements on the screen. Screen coordinates such as 1024x768 usually describe absolute pixel values.

The dots-per-inch (dpi) describes the density of the pixels. A monitor that is 14 inches across at 1024x768 has approximately 73 horizontal pixels per inch (73 dpi), while a 20-inch wide screen at the same resolution has 51 pixels per inch (51 dpi).

Finally, a point (pt) is used to describe a portable density. There are 72 pt per inch. When rendering, a 12-pt font should have letters that are 0.17 inches wide (12 pt ÷ 72 pt per inch). If the screen is 96 dpi, then the letters should be 16 pixels wide (12 pt ÷ 72 pt per inch × 96 dpi = 16 px).

When rendering the font, the system maps the font pt to the known dpi. If the screen is not configured with the correct dpi value, then the font on a printed document may appear at a different size than in the same document on the screen. Usually people don't change the screen dpi setting, but that doesn't mean that you can't.

Changing the DPI

Different output devices render the fonts at different resolutions. Increasing the font size will make it appear larger on all devices, including the screen and printer. On the other hand, if you change the rendering resolution for a single device, then the same font size will be larger or smaller.

The default desktop fonts are rendered at 96 dpi. You can change the dpi value by opening the System ⇨ Preferences ⇨ Appearance applet, selecting the Fonts tab, and clicking the Details button.

NOTE With Dapper Drake (6.06 LTS), use System ⇨ Preferences ⇨ Font. Later versions of Ubuntu use the Appearance applet.

Although the Font applet is good for one-time changes, it cannot be easily automated. The dpi value can also be set through the `gconf-edit` registry under `/desktop/gnome/font_rendering/dpi`. This value can be adjusted to match your screen. For example, if you change the screen resolution or use a different size monitor, then fonts may appear larger or smaller.

To change the dpi value, use:

```
gconftool-2 -t float—set /desktop/gnome/font_rendering/dpi 96
```

Values larger than 96 will make the fonts appear larger (but not change the actual font size), whereas a smaller number decreases the rendered size. In general, changing the dpi setting only changes how fonts are rendered on the screen. It does not change the size of the application windows nor impact how documents will print.

NOTE Changing the rendering resolution only alters fonts rendered by the desktop. For example, the Gnome terminal (Applications ⇨ Accessories ⇨ Terminal) and Gnome Text Editor (`gedit`) both will change sizes, but an `xterm` window will not; xterm uses px, not pt. Also, some applications, such as xchat, use hard-coded window heights, so the tops or bottoms of large fonts may be brutally cropped.

Helping with Big Fonts

I have a couple of coworkers who wear reading glasses when sitting at the computer. More than once, they have come over to my work area and had to run back to get their glasses. To help them (and tease them), I created a *Grandpa Mode* macro that increases the screen font size—just for them. Permanently setting up the ability to use Grandpa Mode requires four commands. The first two define custom commands that change the dpi value. The second two bind the commands to key sequences.

```
gconftool-2 -t str-set /apps/metacity/keybinding_commands/command_7 \
  'gconftool-2 -t float-set /desktop/gnome/font_rendering/dpi 200'
gconftool-2 -t str-set /apps/metacity/keybinding_commands/command_8 \
  'gconftool-2 -t float-set /desktop/gnome/font_rendering/dpi 96'
gconftool-2 -t str-set /apps/metacity/global_keybindings/run_command_7 \
  '<Control>F7'
gconftool-2 -t str-set /apps/metacity/global_keybindings/run_command_8 \
  '<Control>F8'
```

Now pressing Ctrl+F7 changes the resolution to 200 dpi and makes the fonts appear large (and coworkers can read it without glasses). Ctrl+F8 returns the screen to the system default of 96 dpi (see Figure 2-4).

If you want to remove Grandpa Mode, you can use the gconftool-2-unset option:

```
# reset default dpi
gconftool-2 -t float-set /desktop/gnome/font_rendering/dpi 96
# unset key mappings
gconftool-2-unset /apps/metacity/keybinding_commands/command_7
gconftool-2-unset /apps/metacity/keybinding_commands/command_8
gconftool-2-unset /apps/metacity/global_keybindings/run_command_7
gconftool-2-unset /apps/metacity/global_keybindings/run_command_8
```

Tuning the Shell

Most of these Ubuntu hacks require you to use the command line and that means using the GNU Bourne-Again Shell (bash). bash has replaced shells such as sh, csh, and tcsh on most Linux distributions. When you open up a command prompt or terminal window, the default shell is bash. Bash uses the same syntax as the original Bourne shell (sh) but has many more features for usability. For example, the up and down arrows can be used to scroll through the shell history.

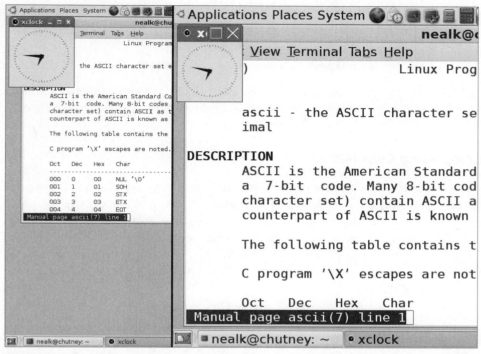

Figure 2-4: The desktop and Gnome terminal as seen at 96 dpi (left) and 200 dpi (right). Both screen shots are taken on the same 1280x1024 monitor.

TIP Beginning with Edgy Eft, the default shell is `/bin/dash` and not `/bin/bash`. However, `bash` is available on the system. If your user shell is not `bash` (`grep $USER /etc/passwd`) and you want extended features like command-line editing and a shell history, then you can change it with `chsh -s /bin/bash`. Chapter 5 covers additional differences between `bash` and `dash`.

Besides accessing the history of previous commands, `bash` enables you to edit command lines in either `vi` or `emacs` mode.

```
set -o vi    # enable vi-mode
set -o emacs # enable emacs-mode
```

The default edit mode under Ubuntu is `emacs`. If you want to specify the mode (rather than inherit default settings), then add the appropriate `set` command to the end of your `$HOME/.bashrc` file. This way, it will be set whenever you log in or open a new terminal window.

You can tell if `bash` is using `vi` or `emacs` mode by running `set -o` (with no other options) or with `echo $SHELLOPTS`.

You may also want to change the default editor for applications by adding one of these lines to your `$HOME/.bashrc` file:

```
export EDITOR=vi    # enable vi-mode
export EDITOR=emacs # enable emacs-mode
```

After modifying `$HOME/.bashrc`, you can reload it using: `. $HOME/.bashrc`. This is called *dotting in* because the command you are running is a single dot.

Completing Completion

`bash` includes file completion, so you don't need to type in very long file names. Pressing the Tab key fills out a partial file name with the available files. Pressing Tab twice lists the available files. For example, `ls a<TAB>` will complete the file name if there is only one file beginning with the letter `a`. And `ls a<TAB><TAB>` lists all files beginning with `a`. In these examples, if you use both `<TAB>` and `<TAB><TAB>` and see no file completion, then you have no file names that start with `a`.

SHELL GAMES

There are a few topics in the computer field that can start passionate arguments on the scale of religious wars. The first topic is "Windows or Unix?" Both sides have zealots who are willing to argue this topic to the death. (And anyone who is thinking "What about Macs?" knows the depth of this debate.) Even among Unix users, "Linux versus BSD" can spark heated debates. One of the most violent topics comes from the choice of editors. "`emacs` vs. `vi`" can lead to real bloody battles.

When you need to help someone else at his terminal, it is a common courtesy to ask before switching modes. A `vi` user who finds himself in `emacs` mode can become very miffed. Instead, consider creating a subshell while you work. Running `bash -o vi` or `bash -o emacs` will open a shell in your favorite mode. Now you can change directories, set aliases, or edit the command line without interfering with the system's owner. When you're done, just `exit` and the shell closes. This leaves the owner's terminal unchanged.

Under Ubuntu, the default `.bashrc` loads a set of predefined command-line completion options. For example, there is a special completion sequence for the command `apt-get`. Typing `apt-get up<TAB><TAB>` displays `update` and `upgrade`, since those are the available command-line parameters. The default completion files (`/etc/bash_completion` and `/etc/bash_completion.d/`) contain options for many widely used commands.

Awesome Aliases

Aliases are simple shortcuts for commonly typed commands. Usually people add aliases for the `ls` command to their `.bashrc` file. For example:

```
alias l.='ls -d .[a-zA-Z]*'    # list all system files
alias ll='ls -l—color=tty'     # detailed listing (-l) with color coded
                                       file types
alias llf='ls -l—full-time'    # list using the full timestamp
alias ls='ls -F'                      # make ls denote the file type after
                                     each filename
```

TIP If you don't want to use the aliased command, then preface the command with a backslash. For example `ls` uses the `ls -F` alias, but `\ls` will just run the regular command.

There are a couple of other aliases that I find very useful. The first two are `webhist` and `webbook`. Both of these aliases use the `sqlite3` command (`sudo apt-get install sqlite3`) to access Firefox database files.

NOTE The `webhist` and `webbook` aliases are designed for Firefox 3, which is found on Hardy Heron (8.04 LTS) and later versions of Ubuntu. These aliases access only the default Firefox profile. Chapter 6 covers alternate Firefox profiles.

The `webhist` alias accesses the Firefox `places.sqlite` file and displays your current history of visited web sites:

```
# The Firefox places.sqlite file will be locked if Firefox
                                    is running.
# The alias copies it to a new file in order to bypass
                                    file locking.

# webhist: List the current web history
alias webhist='(cd $HOME/.mozilla/firefox/*.default;
 cp -f places.sqlite places.bak;
 echo "select url from moz_places inner join moz_historyvisits
       on place_id=moz_places.id order by visit_date;"
       | sqlite3 places.bak)'
```

The `webbook` alias displays your Firefox bookmarks:

```
# webbook: List the current bookmarks
alias webbook='(cd $HOME/.mozilla/firefox/*.default;
  cp -f places.sqlite places.bak;
  echo "select url from moz_places inner join moz_bookmarks
        on fk=moz_places.id;" | sqlite3 places.bak)'
```

Using `webhist` and `webbook`, I can very quickly and easily automate tasks based on my URLs, or look up specific web sites that I previously visited.

> **TIP** The Firefox `places.sqlite` database contains much more information than just URLs. For example, if you change the `select url` to `select url,title`, then you can also see the URL and title of each web page. For database gurus, the schema is available at `http://www.firefoxforensics.com/research/firefox_places_schema.shtml`.

Another alias that I use often is `pinger`. This alias simply displays a number every five seconds. Many firewalls assume that no traffic after a while indicates a closed connection. If I know that I will be walking away from a live connection, I run the `pinger` alias just to generate traffic and keep the connection alive.

```
alias pinger='(i=0; while [ 1 ]; do sleep 5; echo $i;
              ((i=$i+1)); done)'
```

Fun Functions

Besides storing aliases, the `.bashrc` file can store shell functions that can be used in place of commands. For example, `pinger` can also be written in the `.bashrc` file as:

```
function pinger() { i=0; while [ 1 ]; do sleep 5; echo $i;
              ((i=$i+1)); done }
```

Another function that I use is `ccd`:

```
function ccd()
{
  if [ "$1" == "" ]; then
    echo "Usage: ccd location"
  elif [ -d "$1" ]; then
    # if it is a directory, go there
    cd "$1"
  else # must not be a directory
    # Cut off filename and cd to containing directory
    cd "${1%/*}"
  fi
}
```

The `ccd` function works similar to the `cd` command, except that it does not mind when you paste a line containing a file name. For example, `cd ~/public_html/logo.gif` will fail because the target must be a directory. But `ccd ~/public_html/logo.gif` will see that `logo.gif` is a file and place you in the same directory as the file.

My technical editor, Tim, suggested another great shell function for programmers. This alias searches `Makefile` results for errors and highlights them in red.

```
function make()
  {
  # Be careful with quotation marks: " on outside, ' on inside
  # echo -e '\033' prints an escape character
  Red="$(echo -e '\033')[41;37m"
  Reset="$(echo -e '\033')[0m"
  /usr/bin/make $@ 2>&1 |
  sed -e "s@\(.*\(error\|fail\|undef\).*\)@${Red}\1${Reset}@gi"
  }
```

Cool Commands

There are two other, lesser-known bash features. Ctrl+T transposes the last two characters at the cursor. This way, the common typing error sl can be quickly corrected to ls.

The other is the CDPATH environment variable. The PATH environment variable specifies where to look for commands. This usually looks something like:

```
export set PATH=/usr/local/bin:/usr/bin:/bin:/usr/bin/X11:/usr/games
```

When you run a command, the shell first checks if the program exists in /usr/local/bin, then in /usr/sbin, then in /usr/bin, and so on until it is found. The CDPATH variable tells cd where to look when the directory is not in your current directory. For example:

```
export set CDPATH=.:~:/usr:/etc
```

If you type cd bin, then the shell will first check for ./bin. If that does not exist, then it will try ~/bin followed by /usr/bin and /etc/bin. This can come in really handy if you find yourself frequently trying to type cd public_html (or some other directory) when you're in the wrong location.

TIP For other lesser-known bash commands, see the Bash man page (man bash).

Tweaking the Desktop

After you configure the color scheme, fonts, and sound, you'll want to modify the Gnome Desktop. This means adding buttons and menus for frequently used functions. You may also want to change the overall widget theme and application skins.

Adding a Prompt Button

The toolbars at the top and bottom of the screen are convenient locations for buttons. Buttons give you a quick way to run commands. I usually add buttons for X-terminals since I regularly use the command line. I also add a button for my favorite games and other applications that I regularly run.

Adding a new button is pretty straightforward: just right-click an empty part of either the top or bottom toolbar and select Add to Panel. The default options shows you common applications, like Weather Report and Workspace Switcher, that you can drag and drop onto the toolbar. But when the application you want does not exist, you'll need to select the Custom Application Launcher (see Figure 2-5).

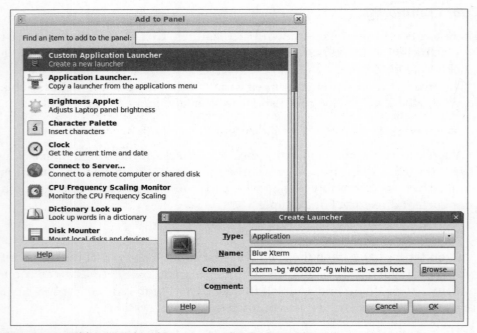

Figure 2-5: Add to Panel and Custom Application Launcher

The Custom Application Launcher prompts you for the button's name. This is the text that will appear when you hover the mouse over the button. The command is the active element—this is any line that you can enter on a command line. In Figure 2-5, I created an xterm with a dark blue (#000020) background, white text, and a scrollbar (-sb). Rather than opening a terminal on the local system, I use Secure Shell to connect to a remote host (-e ssh host). This way, I can color-code my terminal windows to specific hosts. You should also choose an icon for your button. Clicking the empty icon button shows you a large system of ready-to-go icons. Alternately, you can create your own; PNG is the best format for this.

NOTE The command can be any valid command line. If you want to use pipes or redirection, consider using the `bash` command. For example: `bash -c 'ls | more'`. Be sure to select the Run in Terminal option. This way, the command will run and you can see the output. Otherwise, it will never open a window (which could be desirable if you don't want to see any text results).

TIP If you want to run a command as root, preface it with `gksudo`. `gksudo` works like `sudo`, but with a graphical prompt. You can learn more about `sudo` in Chapter 11.

After you create your button, it will appear on the toolbar. You can always right-click the button to change its properties (name, command, icon, and so on). This menu also enables you to move the button along the toolbar, to another toolbar (for example, from the top to the bottom), or to lock the icon so that it won't move.

TIP Laptop computers can either use their own screen or an external monitor. The two screens are usually at different resolutions. If you find yourself switching resolutions often, you might want to enable the Lock to Panel property for each toolbar icon. Otherwise, they can move around and get bunched up in the middle of the toolbar.

Buttons are not restricted to the toolbars. They can also be created on the desktop.

1. On the desktop, right-click to bring up the desktop menu.
2. Select Create Launcher. The creation window looks just like the window from the panels.
3. Enter a name and command line for the button. You can also select an icon.
4. When you finish, click OK.

The new button appears on your desktop. Double-clicking the button starts the application.

Adding Panels

The default Ubuntu user interface has two panels (toolbars): one at the top and one at the bottom. Each panel has a limited amount of screen real estate for placing menus and buttons; you might run out of room. To resolve this, you can add more panels.

1. Right-click any empty space on any panel. This brings up the panel menu.
2. Select New Panel from the menu. A new panel will appear.

The first new panel will appear on the right side of the screen. To move the panel, grab it with the mouse (left button) and move it. It can reside along any screen edge or along another panel. For example, you can easily stack multiple panels along the top edge for adding lots of buttons.

Panels can also have subpanels, called drawers. A drawer is a pop-out panel where you can store more buttons. To create a drawer:

1. Right-click any empty portion of the panel to bring up the panel menu.

2. Select the Add to Panel option. This brings up the list of available applets.

3. Drag the drawer icon from the Add to Panel window to the panel.

4. Left-click the drawer icon in order to open the drawer.

Clicking the drawer icon once opens it. Clicking it a second time closes it. The open drawer acts as another panel, and you can add panel icons to it. The opened drawer is normally three icons tall. However, if you add more icons, then it will automatically widen.

Adding Menus

The default desktop contains one text-based top-level menu with three items in it: Applications, Places, and System. In Gnome2, the developers removed the ability to add custom menus. The implementation was reportedly unstable, so it was disabled. Hopefully, this will be added to a later version of Ubuntu. In the meantime, you can add custom menus under the existing top-level menu items (Applications and System) by right-clicking the menu and selecting Edit Menus.

The Gnome Menu contains two different types of items. First, they can contain additional menus. For example, Applications contains Games (Applications ⇨ Games). There is no limit to the depth of the menus; you can have a menu in a menu in a menu.

Second, the Gnome Menu contains entries. An entry is just like a panel button but uses text (with an optional graphic) to denote the functionality. Like buttons, entries can run any command on the system.

WARNING Only menu items that contain items are displayed, and only empty menus can be deleted.

Although adding menu items is easy, deleting them can be a little confusing (the Gnome interface is not exactly production quality in this regard).

1. Open the menu editor by right-clicking the main menu and selecting Edit Menu.

2. Delete all menu entries by right-clicking each item and selecting Delete. You can delete menus that started off empty, but you cannot delete a menu that you just emptied. The next steps (Steps 3–5) are for deleting an empty menu.

3. Close the menu editor. (That's right! Close it so that you can open it again to delete!) The menu editor is not updated until you close it and restart the process.

4. Reopen the menu editor.

5. Now delete the empty menu by right-clicking and selecting Delete.

Selecting Themes and Skins

The default widgets—window borders, scrollbars, and buttons—that ship with Ubuntu are nice, but they can be made nicer. You can change the desktop theme by selecting System ➪ Preferences ➪ Appearance. (With Dapper Drake the menu is called Theme.) From this menu you can select from a wide range of themes, color schemes, and control widgets (see Figure 2-6). Besides the existing theme selections, you can customize the control widgets, window borders, and icons. Your choices here will impact every application you run.

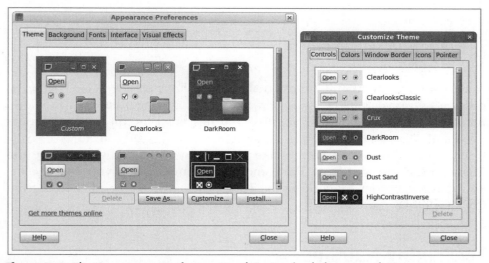

Figure 2-6: The Appearance Preferences and Customized Theme applets

Unfortunately, the theme selection applet does not give you as many options as in other operating systems. (Yes, Windows and even OS/2 both have more configurable options than Gnome.) But there are ways to tweak aspects that are not available from the graphical customization.

1. Become root. Open a terminal and type:

```
sudo bash
```

WARNING This starts a command prompt as root. You have the ability to delete and destroy the entire operating system. Be careful.

2. Go to the directory /usr/share/themes.

```
cd /usr/share/themes
```

3. Copy your favorite theme to a new directory. This uses the existing theme as a template. For example, if you like the AgingGorilla theme, then use:

```
cp -R AgingGorilla MyTheme
```

4. In the MyTheme/metacity-1 directory is a file called metacity-theme-1. xml (/usr/share/themes/MyTheme/metacity-1/metacity-theme-1.xml). Edit this file.

The theme file contains XML that describes the theme's name and attributes. By editing this file, you can change colors, border sizes, icons, and more. And this gives you much more editing power for creating a custom theme than other operating systems. As an example, I can set the title bar to have a couple of bars that grow by editing the title_tile section and specifying:

```
<draw_ops name="title_tile">
  <line color="#0000ff" x1="0" y1="0" x2="width" y2="0"/>
  <line color="#3030f0" x1="0" y1="1" x2="width" y2="1"/>
</draw_ops>
```

This sets two alternating horizontal stripes. One is blue (#0000ff) and the other is a grayish blue (#3030f0). If you want to change the icons for close, maximize, minimize, and so on, then you just need to edit the appropriate PNG file in the /usr/share/themes/MyTheme/metacity-1/ directory.

Changes to the active theme take effect immediately. If you change the theme using the System ➪ Preferences ➪ Theme applet, you can reselect your customizations by clicking the Theme Details button and choosing the MyTheme selection.

Navigating Nautilus

Nautilus is the graphical file browser that is incorporated into Gnome. It enables you to graphically view files, navigate directories, and start applications when you double-click icons. Besides appearing as a window with files in it, Nautilus also manages the desktop—the desktop is just another file folder that is open all the way.

You can create a button to quickly start Nautilus.

1. On the top panel, right-click to bring up the menu.

2. Select Add to Panel. This brings up the applet.

3. Click the Custom Application Launcher button.

4. Type **Nautilus** for the Name field of the button and **nautilus** (lowercase) as the Command field.

5. Choose an appropriate icon. I like `/usr/share/icons/gnome/24x24/apps /file-manager.png`.

6. Click OK to create the button.

Nautilus has many configurable items that are similar to other operating systems'. For example, you can set the background in the Nautilus window to be a color or an image. There is also a side pane (View ➪ Side Pane) that can list information about the directory or show the directory tree.

Beyond these common features, Nautilus offers a few uncommon features, such as emblems, scalable icons, and customized context-sensitive menus.

CONFIGURING NAUTILUS

Even though Gnome uses Nautilus for directory navigation, Nautilus is not the same as Gnome. This distinction becomes very apparent when customizing the system. Gnome uses `gconf-edit` to manage all configuration options. Any changes to this registry take effect immediately.

In contrast to Gnome, Nautilus uses a variety of configuration methods, and few take place immediately. To tell Nautilus about changes, your best option is to restart it. The command `nautilus -q` tells Nautilus to quit. If Gnome does not immediately restart Nautilus, then run `nautilus` to reactivate it. New configuration changes will be loaded when it restarts.

Embracing Emblems

Emblems are small accents that you can add to a file or directory icon. For example, critical files can all be tagged with an urgent emblem, and finance files can have a dollar sign on them. Emblems appear at the corner of the icons, so you can easily enable four emblems per file. There are many different ways to enable emblems:

- **Properties**—You can right-click an icon and select the properties option. In the properties menu, select the Emblem tab. This enables you to put a check box next to the desired emblem. If you select multiple files, then you can view the preferences and enable all of their emblems at once.

- **Backgrounds and Emblems**—Under the Nautilus menu you can select Edit ➪ Background and Emblems. A dialog box appears that enables you to drag over a different background (patterns or colors) for the Nautilus window. There are also icon emblems. Just drag the emblem onto the file icon, and it will be set (or if it is already set, then it will be removed).

- **Side Pane**—The Nautilus side pane has a pull-down menu that displays the emblems. As with backgrounds, you can drag the emblem onto an icon in order to enable or disable it.

Emblems provide visual cues about a file's purpose, but they have little use beyond human interpretation right now. You cannot automatically select files or sort them by emblem, enable emblems on subdirectories, or programmatically change them (without some serious programming efforts).

PRACTICAL USES FOR EMBLEMS

Although emblems have no functionality beyond human interpretation, they can be very useful. For example, I have a friend who is a freelance writer. She uses emblems to denote the status of different articles. One emblem denotes a submission, a different emblem marks a sale, and a third indicates work in progress.

Technical Details

Emblems are stored in a set of XML files found in `$HOME/.nautilus/meta files/`. There is one XML file per directory, and only customized directories are present. You can edit these XML files to make system changes, but you'll need to restart Nautilus for the change to take effect.

Listing 2-2 shows a simple script for changing emblems. In this case, every icon with the `important` emblem is changed to have an `urgent` emblem. More complicated scripts can be created to add emblems to specific files, manipulate files according to their emblems, or to set an emblem based on an event. For example, if an `important` icon is more than 48 hours old, then it can be set to `urgent` or an e-mail notification can be generated.

Available for download on Wrox.com

Listing 2-2: Script to Change "Important" Emblems to "Urgent"

```sh
#!/bin/sh
# for each of the meta files..
for i in ~/.nautilus/metafiles/*; do
    # convert any "important" emblems to "urgent"
```

```
  # save the result to a temporary file
  cat $i | sed -e 's/name="important"/name="urgent"/g' > $i.new
  # move the temporary file into place
  mv $i.new $i
done
# restart Nautilus so the changes take effect
nautilus -q
```

Stretching Icons

One of the coolest features in Nautilus is the ability to stretch icons. You can take any icon on the desktop and scale it—making it very tiny or extremely large. If the icon denotes a text document, then it can be scaled large enough to read the text. To scale an image:

1. For desktop icons, right-click the icon to bring up the icon's menu and select the Stretch Icon menu option. For icons within a Nautilus directory window, select the icon and choose Edit ➪ Stretch Icon from the Nautilus menu bar.

2. When you select Stretch Icon, four blue dots appear on the corners of the icon.

3. Grab one of the blue dots (left mouse button) and drag it. This will stretch or shrink the icon.

One great use for stretching icons is to unclutter desktops. When I'm working on a project, I may end up having dozens of files on my desktop. Before going to lunch, I can stretch the current file to a larger size—this way, I can find it quickly when I get back. Figure 2-7 shows a couple of stretched icons.

To unstretch the icon, bring up the icon's menu and select Restore Icon's Original Size.

> **NOTE** Under the previous section on emblems, I mentioned that you can have up to four emblems per icon. That isn't exactly true. Emblems are placed along the sides of the icon. If the icon is stretched to a very large size, then you can have lots of emblems without any overlap.

STRETCHING EXERCISES

Stretching icons is still a work in progress for Nautilus. As a result, not all options are available all the time. For example, when an icon is on the desktop, there is a menu option to stretch the icon's size. But the stretch

(continued)

STRETCHING EXERCISES *(continued)*

option is not on the icon menu when an icon is selected from inside a Nautilus window. Instead, you need to use Edit ⇨ Stretch Icon.

Nautilus enables you to drag and drop a stretched icon into a folder—and it will retain the stretched dimensions. Unfortunately, dragging an icon will remove the Restore Icon's Original Size menu entry. In order to restore the icon's size, you will need to first stretch the icon. This reactivates the Restore menu option.

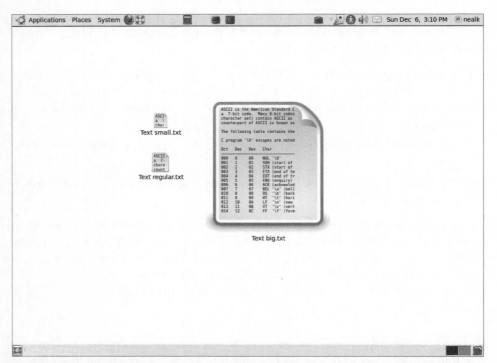

Figure 2-7: A regular icon, a shrunk icon, and a stretched icon that is very large. Icons for text files show the file contents.

Technical Details

As with emblems, the stretched value is saved in the `$HOME/.nautilus/meta files/` XML files. Scripts can be created to manipulate the size of the icons. This way, important files can be suddenly made larger. A great use, for example, would be to increase an icon in size right before an online meeting. This way, you can quickly find the files you need. As with emblems, making any automated changes to the stretched value requires you to restart Nautilus before they take effect.

Adjusting Fonts

The System ➪ Preferences ➪ Appearance ➪ Fonts window enables you to set font types but not font colors. The default font uses white lettering with a dark shadow. Although this font is nice when you have a dark (or brown) background, it can appear hard to read with a light background. Changing the font color under Nautilus requires a $HOME/.gtkrc-2.0 file. In your favorite editor, create (or edit) this file. Add or modify a section for desktop icons:

```
style "desktop-icon"
{
NautilusIconContainer::frame_text = 1
NautilusIconContainer::normal_alpha = 0
text[NORMAL] = "#000000"
}
class "GtkWidget" style "desktop-icon"
```

In this example, the font color is set to black (#000000). The frame_text value indicates that you are specifying the text format, and the normal_alpha field controls the transparency of the font (0 is not transparent). After editing the file, you can save your changes and restart Nautilus (nautilus -q). The text color matches your setting and (hopefully) offers a higher contrast than the default colors.

Tuning Templates

On the Nautilus menu (including the desktop menu) is an option called Create Document. The Create Document option enables you to make a new file that is based on a template file. By default, there is only one template file—empty file. This creates a zero-sized file just as if you ran the touch command. You can create your own templates by placing files in a Templates directory.

1. Create a directory called Templates in your home directory:

   ```
   mkdir $HOME/Templates
   ```

2. Place any template file in this directory. The template file name (without extension) appears in the Create Document menu.

For example, you can start up Open Office (Applications ➪ Office ➪ Open Office.org Word Processor) and save an empty file called WordProcessor.doc in the Templates directory. As soon as you save it, you will have the WordProcessor option listed in the Create Document menu. Selecting this menu option creates a file called WordProcessor.doc, with the name WordProcessor highlighted for renaming.

Scripting Menus

The single most powerful feature of Nautilus is the ability to create context-sensitive menu items. For example, you can create a special menu item that only appears when you select an MP3 file. You can control the types of files, directories, or both where the menu item appears, and whether it appears for one selected item or multiple selections.

To do this, you will first need to install Nautilus Actions:

```
sudo apt-get install nautilus-actions
```

Now you can create custom menus. For example, Figure 2-8 shows a menu for securely deleting files.

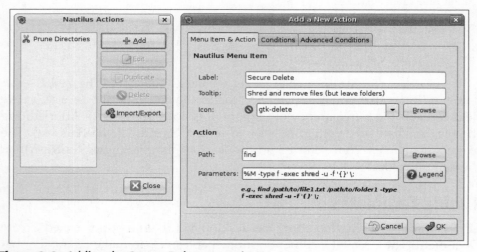

Figure 2-8: Adding the Secure Delete menu item

1. Run `nautilus-actions-config`. This brings up the configuration menu.

TIP You can also find this tool on the top menu under System ➪ Preferences ➪ **Nautilus Actions Configuration.**

2. Click Add to create a new menu script. A new window opens.

3. For the label, enter `Secure Delete`. This is the text that will appear on the menu.

4. You can add a tooltip, such as "Safely delete files." This appears when the mouse hovers over the menu item.

5. Optionally select an icon for this menu item. The icon appears in the menu.

6. Path is the command to run. Any command that can be used on the command line can be entered here. For this command, use `find` (or `/usr/bin/find`) as the path.

7. The parameters will be passed to the `Path` command. An example of the command line is displayed below the Parameter field as you type. The `%M` parameter becomes the list of selected files. If you click the Legend button, you will see other variables that can be used. For this action, use `%M -type f -exec shred -u -f '{}' \;`. This parameter tells `find` to identify all files and run the command `shred`, forcefully unlinking (deleting) each file.

NOTE The `shred` command does not securely delete directories. The result is a bunch of empty directories. See the Shred Everything entry in Table 2-1 for a solution to this problem.

8. Under the Conditions tab, you can select when the menu item appears. You can make the selections based on any combination of file name, Meta type, file or directory, and single or multiple selections. In this case, you should select both files and directories (even through directories are not deleted), and allow multiple file selections.

9. Click OK to add the action to the menu.

10. Click Close to end the Nautilus action application.

11. Restart Nautilus so that it loads the new menu item.

    ```
    nautilus -q
    ```

You can test the new menu item by bringing up Nautilus and deleting something. Right-clicking an icon should show the Secure Delete menu item. Selecting the delete item should remove all of the files selected.

WARNING Shred overwrites files with garbage before deleting them. There is no prompt to check if this is what you really want to do, and anything deleted will be gone forever.

Action scripts can be used to convert files (for example, for any GIF, make it a PNG), e-mail a file (such as a Mail To command), or view a file under the web browser. Actions are limited to one command line, but you can specify a shell script for performing multiple-step commands. Some useful custom menu items are included in Table 2-1.

Table 2-1: Examples of Useful Custom Menu Commands

NAME	PATH	PARAMETERS	CONDITION	NOTES
Command Prompt	gnome-terminal	g—working -directory ='%M'	Folders only, no multiple selection.	Opens a terminal window.
Open in Firefox	firefox	'%M'	Both files and folders, no multiple selection.	Firefox must be opened first; otherwise, nothing may happen.
Shred Everything	bash	-c 'find %M -type f -exec shred -u -f "{}" \;; rm -rf %M'	Files or folders with multiple selections.	Although you can only run one command, this only runs the bash command. The bash argument translates as two commands.
Convert WAV to MP3	bash	-c "lame %M %d/ `base name %M .wav` .mp3 "	Only for files ending in .wav, no multiple selections.	This converts file.wav to file.mp3 in the same directory. Instead of running lame directly, bash is used to create the subshell basename (used to rename the file). Without the basename program, you would end up with a file named file.wav.mp3.

NOTE Only one command can be specified. You cannot use &, |, or; to join multiple commands.

WARNING Some commands, such as shred and lame, may take minutes (or longer) to process very large files. During this time, result files (for example, Convert WAV to MP3 files) may be created even though they are incomplete.

Requesting the same task multiple times may result in many running processes that all interfere with each other. The net result may not be what you want. Instead, wait for the task to finish. See Chapter 8 for different ways to monitor processes.

TIP While the previous examples use `shred` to erase files, `shred` is not compliant with government regulations. An alternative is diskscrub (`http://code.google.com/p/diskscrub/`). This program is compliant with specifications from the United States Department of Defense (DoD) and other government agencies. Invoke it using `scrub -rSLp dod` *filename*.

Replacing Nautilus

While the Gnome desktop is pretty solid and easy to use, Nautilus seems to regress to less stable versions with each release of Ubuntu. With Dapper Drake (6.06 LTS), Nautilus was stable but feature-limited. Three years later, Nautilus under Karmic Koala (9.10) has become seriously buggy and offers no new features. Nautilus has too many quirks and limitations to be considered "ready for prime time."

Alternatives to Nautilus include the graphical Rox (`sudo apt-get install rox-filer`) and the text-oriented Gnome Commander (`sudo apt-get install gnome-commander`). The Gnome Commander looks like a modern version of the 1986 DOS program Norton Commander.

However, my personal preference is to leave Nautilus for managing the desktop and use the very professional-looking X File Explorer (`sudo apt-get install xfe`) for folder navigation. The `xfe` command has a very configurable layout and only one major limitation: The default helper applications are not included in the installation. To fix this, set the application preferences before you get too frustrated (Edit ⇨ Preferences ⇨ Programs). I suggest setting the default text editor and viewer to `gedit`, image viewer to Eye of Gnome (`eog`), and terminal to `gnome-terminal`.

Altering the Login Screen

Now that you have your desktop configured, it is time to do something about that login screen. Every Ubuntu version has a different default login screen. How you change it depends on the version of Ubuntu.

With every Ubuntu version up through Jaunty Jackalope, including Dapper Drake (6.06 LTS) and Hardy Heron (8.04 LTS), you can open up the Login Window Preferences applet (System ⇨ Administration ⇨ Login Window). This lets you select different styles, themes, backgrounds, colors, and even security options such as an automatic login and the list of users who are permitted to log in.

Beginning with Karmic Koala (9.10), the login screen settings have become significantly feature limited. The only thing you can do is enable or disable the automatic login. Under Karmic, you will need to change the login configuration manually. You can change the background, colors, widget set, and fonts by running the `gnome-appearance-properties` applet as the Gnome Display Manager (user `gdm`).

```
sudo -u gdm dbus-launch gnome-appearance-properties
```

Alternately, you can change specific properties using `gconftool-2`. For example, you can get and set the login screen's background image using:

```
# Get the current background image filename
sudo -u gdm gconftool-2 -g /desktop/gnome/background/picture_filename
# Set the background image to a new file
sudo -u gdm gconftool-2 -s /desktop/gnome/background/picture_filename \
 -t string /path/to/background.png
```

The other aspect of the login screen that I usually change is the user list. By default, it lists every user on the system. However, if you want your privacy (and to not show every name on your system) or have dozens of users on the system and don't want a long scroll window, then you will need to disable the user list.

```
# Get the current user list setting
sudo -u gdm gconftool-2 -g /apps/gdm/simple-greeter/disable_user_list
# Set the value to true for disabling the list
sudo -u gdm gconftool-2 -s /apps/gdm/simple-greeter/disable_user_list \
 -t bool true
```

You can alter other options using the graphical `gconf-editor`. I suggest looking under the configuration path `/apps/gdm/simple-greeter`. This is where you can find options to set the greeter text message, change language settings, and even disable the login screen's restart button.

```
sudo -u gdm dbus-launch gconf-editor
```

After you make these changes, log out and view your handiwork.

Modifying Login Scripts

Usually there are common tasks that you want to run when you first log in to the system, and some tasks to run when you finally log out. While you can set the program to run using System ➪ Preferences ➪ Sessions, I have found the options to be too limiting; I don't want to run single commands, I want to run complicated scripts.

The GDM runs a set of scripts each time a user logs in and out of the graphical desktop. The `/etc/gdm/PostLogin/Default` script is started every time any user is logged in. This script runs as root.

In contrast, the `/etc/gdm/PreSession/Default` and `/etc/gdm/PostSession/Default` scripts are executed with the user's privileges during the graphical desktop login and logout. For user-specific scripts, I added the following line to the end of my `PreSession/Default` script:

```
if [ -x $HOME/ .gui_login]; then (cd $HOME; ./.gui_login); fi
```

This checks to see if the user has an executable file called `.gui_login` and runs it. I have a similar check for `.gui_logout` in `/etc/gdm/PostSession/Default`. These scripts allow me to run specific applications during the graphical login, and clean up temporary files during the graphical logout.

WARNING Make sure that your login and logout scripts do not prompt for users' input or hang indefinitely. Otherwise, your login and logout will hang.

Summary

Just as a home isn't a home until you add furniture, the default installation of Ubuntu is fine for short-term use, but to really be usable over the longer term, it needs to be customized. Changing the background, sounds, fonts, buttons, and themes enables you to configure the desktop for whatever is best for you. For some users, static environments are best, but the user interface supports scripts that can dynamically change the desktop based on the current environment. Informative backgrounds, changing icons, smart menus, and adjustable fonts can really add to the system's usability and your own productivity.

Configuring Devices

What's In This Chapter?

How to install loadable kernel modules
Methods for configuring startup services
Adding and configuring printers, hard drives, TV cards, and other peripherals
Creating a RAID with backups, and surviving a hard drive failure

Linux is a powerful operating system, and much of that power comes from its ability to support different hardware configurations and peripheral devices. Everything from multiple CPUs and video cards to printers and scanners requires device drivers and kernel modifications. In this chapter, we'll look at getting some common devices configured properly.

Working with Device Drivers

Under Linux, there are a couple of required elements for working with devices. First, you need a kernel driver that can recognize the device. This is usually a low-level driver, such as a parallel port driver for use with parallel printers or USB support (regardless of the USB device).

The second element depends on the type of hardware—some devices need software support for managing the device. The kernel driver only knows how to address the device; the software driver actually speaks the right language. This means that different versions of the same device may speak different languages but communicate over the same kernel driver. Printers are one such example. A printer may use PostScript, HP PCL, oki182, or some other format to communicate data. The kernel driver knows how to send data to the printer, but the software driver knows what data to send. The same is true for most scanners, cameras, pointer devices, and even keyboards.

The final element is the user-level application that accesses the device. This is the program that says "print" or the audio system that says "play."

There are four steps needed before using any device:

1. Install a device driver, if one is not already installed.

2. Create a device handle if one is not created automatically.

3. Load any required software drivers and configuration parameters.

4. Configure applications as necessary for using the device.

In some cases, some or all of these steps are automated. In other cases, devices will need manual configuration.

USEFUL PROGRAMS

Many computer peripherals and add-ons are either pointer or video devices. There are two programs that are very useful when trying to test these devices. The first is the GNU Image Manipulation Program or gimp **(**www.gimp.org**), a very powerful drawing tool that supports most types of pointer devices and can also capture input from video devices such as cameras, scanners, and TV cards.**

The second useful program is called Scanner Access Now Easy or sane **(**www.sane-project.org**). This is strictly used for capturing images from a video device such as a scanner, digital still camera, digital video camera, or TV card. The** xsane **program provides an X-Windows front end for** sane**. As with** gimp**,** xsane **can capture images from a variety of input devices.**

The sane**,** xsane**, and** gimp **programs are installed by the default Ubuntu desktop configuration.**

Loading Modules

Very early versions of Linux had all the necessary kernel drivers compiled into the kernel. This meant that the kernel knew exactly what was supported. If you needed to add a new device, you would need to compile a new kernel.

Unfortunately, including every driver in the kernel led to a big problem: the kernel became too large. Back in the days of floppy disks, it would take two

1.44-MB disks to boot Linux—one for the kernel and the other for the rest of the operating system. The kernel developers introduced compressed kernels, but even those became too large for floppy disks.

Fortunately, the barbaric days of compiling all desired modules into the kernel are long gone. Today, Linux uses loadable kernel modules (LKMs). Each LKM can be placed in the kernel as needed. This keeps the kernel small and fast. Some LKMs can even perform a check to see if they are required. If you don't have a SCSI card on your computer, then the SCSI LKM driver won't load and won't consume kernel resources. Usually, hardware is found through device identifiers, but sometimes you need to tell the operating system to enable the device.

Ubuntu includes a healthy selection of common and uncommon kernel modules. If the device has any type of stable Linux support, then it is very likely that Ubuntu has the LKM on the system.

Viewing Modules

The basic command to see what modules are currently loaded is `lsmod`. Running `lsmod` displays the LKM's common name, size of the LKM, and any other LKMs that depend on it. For example:

```
$ lsmod | head
Module               Size  Used by
floppy              64676  0
rfcomm              43604  0
l2cap               28192  5 rfcomm
bluetooth           54084  4 rfcomm,l2cap
ppdev                9668  0
speedstep_lib        4580  0
cpufreq_userspace    6496  0
cpufreq_stats        6688  0
freq_table           4928  1 cpufreq_stats
```

This shows that the bluetooth module is loaded and is in use by the rfcomm and l2cap modules. A second command, `modprobe`, can be used to show the actual LKM files.

```
$ modprobe -l bluetooth
/lib/modules/2.6.24-26-generic/kernel/net/bluetooth/bluetooth.ko
```

The `modprobe` command can also list available modules—not just ones that are loaded. For example, to see all the asynchronous transfer mode (ATM) network drivers, you can use:

```
$ modprobe -l -t atm
/lib/modules/2.6.24-26-generic/kernel/drivers/usb/atm/cxacru.ko
/lib/modules/2.6.24-26-generic/kernel/drivers/usb/atm/usbatm.ko
```

```
/lib/modules/2.6.24-26-generic/kernel/drivers/usb/atm/speedtch.ko
/lib/modules/2.6.24-26-generic/kernel/drivers/usb/atm/ueagle-atm.ko
/lib/modules/2.6.24-26-generic/kernel/drivers/usb/atm/xusbatm.ko
/lib/modules/2.6.24-26-generic/kernel/drivers/atm/idt77252.ko
/lib/modules/2.6.24-26-generic/kernel/drivers/atm/iphase.ko
/lib/modules/2.6.24-26-generic/kernel/drivers/atm/he.ko
/lib/modules/2.6.24-26-generic/kernel/drivers/atm/atmtcp.ko
/lib/modules/2.6.24-26-generic/kernel/drivers/atm/fore_200e.ko
/lib/modules/2.6.24-26-generic/kernel/drivers/atm/nicstar.ko
/lib/modules/2.6.24-26-generic/kernel/drivers/atm/lanai.ko
/lib/modules/2.6.24-26-generic/kernel/drivers/atm/suni.ko
...
```

The -t atm parameter shows all modules with the ATM tag. LKMs are stored in an organized directory, so the tag indicates the directory name. This is different from using modprobe -l '*atm*', since that will only show modules containing "atm" in the LKM file name.

Along with modprobe, you can use modinfo to learn more about a particular LKM. The modinfo command lists information about a module, or it can be used to retrieve specific information. For example:

```
$ modinfo lp  # list information about the lp module
filename:       /lib/modules/2.6.31-15-generic/kernel/drivers/char/lp.ko
license:        GPL
alias:          char-major-6-*
srcversion:     84EA21D13BD2C67171AC994
depends:        parport
vermagic:       2.6.31-15-generic SMP mod_unload modversions 586
parm:           parport:array of charp
parm:           reset:bool
```

If you only need to see a particular field from the modinfo output, then you can use the -F parameter with any of the listed fields. For example, -F filename only displays the file name for the module.

```
$ modinfo -F filename lp  # only list the filename field
/lib/modules/2.6.31-15-generic/kernel/drivers/char/lp.ko
```

Installing and Removing Modules

Modules are relatively easy to install. The insmod command loads modules, and rmmod removes modules. The modprobe command actually uses insmod and rmmod but adds a little more intelligence. The modprobe command can resolve dependencies and search for modules.

As an example, let's look at the suni.ko ATM driver (you probably do not have it installed, and you probably don't need it). Listing 3-1 shows different queries for the driver, installing the driver, and removing it.

NOTE Asynchronous transfer mode (ATM) network cards are uncommon on home PCs, so this is a good type of device driver to play with when learning how to load and unload LKMs. If we used a common driver for this example, then you could end up disabling your hard drive, printer, or other device. If you do happen to have a Saturn User Network Interface (SUNI) ATM card, then consider using a different driver for this example, such as `pppoatm`.

Listing 3-1: Sample LKM Queries and Management

```
$ modinfo suni          # information about the module
filename: /lib/modules/2.6.24-26-generic/kernel/drivers/atm/suni.ko
license:    GPL
srcversion: 4F4DC0C890932441A81CC12
depends:
vermagic:   2.6.24-26-generic SMP mod_unload 586
$ lsmod | grep suni   # see if it is installed
[none found]
$ modprobe -l -t atm  # show all ATM modules
/lib/modules/2.6.24-26-generic/kernel/drivers/usb/atm/cxacru.ko
/lib/modules/2.6.24-26-generic/kernel/drivers/usb/atm/usbatm.ko
/lib/modules/2.6.24-26-generic/kernel/drivers/usb/atm/speedtch.ko
/lib/modules/2.6.24-26-generic/kernel/drivers/usb/atm/ueagle-atm.ko
/lib/modules/2.6.24-26-generic/kernel/drivers/usb/atm/xusbatm.ko
/lib/modules/2.6.24-26-generic/kernel/drivers/atm/idt77252.ko
/lib/modules/2.6.24-26-generic/kernel/drivers/atm/iphase.ko
/lib/modules/2.6.24-26-generic/kernel/drivers/atm/he.ko
/lib/modules/2.6.24-26-generic/kernel/drivers/atm/atmtcp.ko
/lib/modules/2.6.24-26-generic/kernel/drivers/atm/fore_200e.ko
/lib/modules/2.6.24-26-generic/kernel/drivers/atm/nicstar.ko
/lib/modules/2.6.24-26-generic/kernel/drivers/atm/lanai.ko
/lib/modules/2.6.24-26-generic/kernel/drivers/atm/suni.ko
...
$ modprobe -l '*suni*'   # Show only the suni.ko module
/lib/modules/2.6.24-26-generic/kernel/drivers/atm/suni.ko
$ modprobe -l -a 'suni'  # Show all suni modules
/lib/modules/2.6.24-26-generic/kernel/drivers/atm/suni.ko
$ sudo modprobe -a suni  # install all suni modules
$ lsmod | grep suni      # show it is installed
suni                  7504  0
$ sudo modprobe -r suni  # remove it
$ lsmod | grep suni      # show it is removed
[none found]
```

TIP Using `modprobe -l` without any other parameters will list every module on the system.

The installation step could also be accomplished using

```
sudo insmod /lib/modules/2.6.24-26-generic/kernel/drivers/atm/suni.ko
```

Similarly, removal could also use any of the following commands:

```
sudo rmmod /lib/modules/2.6.24-26-generic/kernel/drivers/atm/suni.ko
sudo rmmod suni.ko
sudo rmmod suni
```

To make the installation permanent, you can add the module name to either `/etc/modules` or `/etc/modprobe.d/`. (See the man pages for `modules` and `modprobe.conf`.) In general, `/etc/modules` is simpler for adding a new module, since it just lists one module per line. However, the `/etc/modprobe.d/` configuration files permit more configuration options.

Optimizing Modules

If you're trying to streamline your system, you may not want to have all of the various modules installed or accessible. Although unused modules take virtually no resources (even if they are loaded into memory), systems with limited capacity or that are hardened for security may not want unnecessary LKMs. Between the `lsmod` and `modprobe -l` commands, you can identify which modules are unnecessary and either remove them from the system or just not load them.

For example, if you do not have a printer on your parallel port, then you probably do not need the `lp` module loaded. Similarly, if you want to disable the floppy disk, you can remove that driver, too.

```
sudo modprobe -r lp
sudo modprobe -r floppy
```

You can make these changes permanent by removing `lp` from `/etc/modules` and adding both `lp` and `floppy` to `/etc/modprobe.d/blacklist` (or `blacklist.conf`). Alternately, if you need the disk space, then you can just delete the drivers from the system (use `modinfo -F filename lp` and `modinfo -F filename floppy` to find the files).

Starting Services

After the device driver is loaded into the kernel, it usually needs to be configured. Each device driver has its own set of tools for doing the configuration. For example, the network uses `ifconfig` to configure addresses, and PCMCIA support uses `cardmgr` to notify the operating system when a new card is added or removed. Each driver is different. Some software drivers are only needed once to configure the system (for example, network, audio, and system clock); others are needed continually, while the device is in use (for example, high-resolution graphics and the mouse). A few KLM drivers require no additional assistance—keyboard, hard drives, and USB fall into this category.

In addition to configuring and managing kernel drivers, some software drivers are software-only (no KLM needed). These services include virtual file systems, displays, and schedulers. Finally, application and network services, such as Secure Shell (SSH) and the web, can be configured.

While kernel modules are managed by the LKM subsystem, the Init and Upstart systems manage the configuration and management of application and network services.

Using Init.d

As the system boots, kernel drivers are loaded into memory and the `init` process begins setting the runlevel. At each runlevel, different software drivers and services are started. Which ones are started and the order in which they are started is determined by `/etc/init.d/` and the `rc` script. There are eight `rc` directories: `/etc/rc0.d`, `/etc/rc1.d`, ... `/etc/rc6.d`, and `/etc/rcS.d`. These correspond with the different runlevels: 0 through 6, and S for system startup.

In each of these directories are symbolic links to files in `/etc/init.d/`. The name of the symbolic link determines whether the script is called when starting (S) or leaving (K for kill) the runlevel (see Listing 3-2). Each name also has a number, used to order when the service is started. This way, dependent processes can be started in the right order. For example, `S13gdm` is started before `S99rmnologin` since the Gnome Display Manager (`gdm`) should be started before the user login prompt.

The directory `/etc/init.d/` contains the actual control scripts (without the S/K and number). Each script has a start, stop, and restart option. So, for example, if you want to restart the network and stop the `cron` server, you can run:

```
sudo /etc/init.d/networking restart
sudo /etc/init.d/cron stop
```

To make system changes happen after the next reboot, add the appropriate S or K script to the appropriate runlevel directory.

Listing 3-2: Directory Contents of /etc/rc6.d

```
$ ls /etc/rc6.d
K01gdm              K20zvbi
K01usplash          K21postgresql-8.3
K01xdm              K25hwclock.sh
```

(continued)

Listing 3-2: Directory Contents of /etc/rc6.d (*continued*)

```
K09apache2              K25mdadm
K16dhcdbd               K50alsa-utils
K19aumix                K59mountoverflowtmp
K20apport               K80nfs-kernel-server
K20avahi-daemon         K99laptop-mode
K20cpufreqd             README
K20dkim-filter          S01linux-restricted-modules-common
K20dkms_autoinstaller   S15wpa-ifupdown
K20libvirt-bin          S20sendsigs
K20nas                  S30urandom
K20nfs-common           S31umountnfs.sh
K20nvtv                 S32portmap
K20postfix              S40umountfs
K20privoxy              S51dmraid
K20snort                S60umountroot
K20sysstat              S90reboot
K20xinetd
```

RUNNING RAGGED

Ubuntu includes seven different runlevels: 0–6 and S. Many of the runlevels provide very specific services. For example, level 0 is a system halt, 1 provides for single-user mode, 6 reboots the system, and S provides services that are needed to start the system regardless of runlevel.

The remaining runlevels provide different types of multi-user support. Usually the system uses level 2. This provides a graphical user interface (when available) and network support. The default level 3 provides support for accessibility devices, such as a Braille TTY display. Finally, levels 4 and 5 usually look like level 2, but you can modify them if you need customized run-time environments.

Understanding Upstart

Starting with Edgy Eft (Ubuntu 6.10), the System V init was replaced with an event-driven process manager called Upstart. The location of the Upstart configuration files varies with the Ubuntu version. (It's new, so you can expect it to move around until it becomes more standard.) Under Jaunty Jackalope (9.04), the configurations files are in /etc/event.d/. With Karmic Koala (9.10), they are under /etc/init/.

Each Upstart control file lists the runlevels where it should start and stop, which commands to execute, and the set of dependencies. Besides the required command to run, Upstart supports optional pre- and post-command scripts. For example, a `pre-script` may prepare the environment, the command (`script` or `exec`) starts the service, and `post-script` can clean up any unnecessary files after running the command.

> **TIP** If the service is started with a single command, then use **exec**. More complex services can be started using a **script** block that contains the script to run.

Karmic's `dbus.conf` file is a good example of a simple Upstart script. This file uses a `pre-start script` block to create the required directories and initialize the system. It runs a single command to start the service (`exec dbus-daemon --system --fork`), and then it runs a single command after starting the service.

```
# dbus - D-Bus system message bus
#
# The D-Bus system message bus allows system daemons and user
# applications
# to communicate.

description     "D-Bus system message bus"

start on local-filesystems
stop on runlevel [06]

expect fork
respawn

pre-start script
    mkdir -p /var/run/dbus
    chown messagebus:messagebus /var/run/dbus

    exec dbus-uuidgen --ensure
end script

exec dbus-daemon --system --fork

post-start exec kill -USR1 1
```

To control Upstart scripts, you can use the start, stop, and restart commands. In addition, the status command lets you know if a service is running. For example, the following commands exercise the `cron` daemon.

```
$ sudo stop cron      # same as: sudo /etc/init.d/cron stop
cron stop/waiting
$ sudo status cron
cron stop/waiting
$ sudo start cron      # same as: sudo /etc/init.d/cron start
cron start/running, process 30166
$ sudo status cron
cron start/running, process 30166
```

```
$ sudo restart cron   # same as: sudo /etc/init.d/cron restart
cron start/running, process 30182
$ sudo status cron
cron start/running, process 30182
```

For backward compatibility, Upstart includes scripts that will run any init scripts located under the /etc/rc*.d/ directories. You do not need to port scripts from init to Upstart, and you don't need to worry about installing software that is not configured for using Upstart.

Configuring Services with the GUI

Managing services by hand can be time-consuming. Ubuntu includes an easy applet for enabling and disabling some system services: System ⇨ Administration ⇨ Services (see Figure 3-1). Enabling or disabling services only requires changing a check box.

> **NOTE** The Services applet was removed from Karmic Koala (9.10). To configure startup services, either use the command line or install bum.

Figure 3-1: Hardy Heron's Services Settings applet

Checking or unchecking a service will immediately change the service's current running status. It will also alter the service's boot status. This way, if you uncheck a service, you don't need to manually stop any running processes and it will not start at the next boot. Checking a service starts it immediately and schedules it to start with the each reboot.

Although this tool does identify some of the better-known services, it does not list custom services and does not identify different runlevels. Since Ubuntu normally runs at runlevel 2, you are only modifying services that start during runlevel 2. In order to control more of the boot options, you either need to modify the files in the `/etc/init.d` and `/etc/rc*.d` directories, or you need a better tool, like `bum` or `sysv-rc-conf`.

Configuring Boot-Up Services with bum

The Boot-Up Manager (`bum`) is a powerful GUI for managing startup services. Unlike the default Services applet, `bum` lists all startup services, including ones that you created. `bum` also includes an advanced menu for changing the startup priorities and viewing the startup sequence by runlevel. And best yet: `bum` is available for all Ubuntu platforms and is even Upstart-aware.

To use `bum`, you first need to install it: `sudo apt-get install bum`. To run it, use `sudo bum`. `bum` might take a minute to start up; it looks for package descriptions related to each startup service. The basic window shows the service name with a one-line description. An icon indicates whether the service is currently running, and a check box allows you to enable or disable it (see Figure 3-2).

TIP With the default Services applet, changes take effect as soon as you click on a check box. With `bum`, alterations are not performed until you press the Apply button.

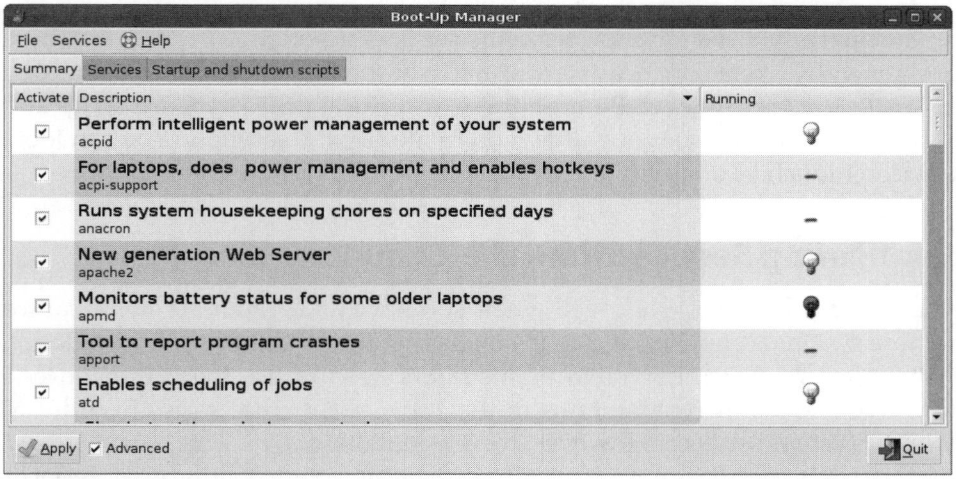

Figure 3-2: The Boot-Up Manager basic window

The most power part of `bum` comes from the tiny check box labeled Advanced at the bottom of the screen. This check box creates three tabs: Summary, Services, and Startup, and shutdown scripts. The Summary tab contains the basic window. However, the Services tab is just plain awesome (see Figure 3-3). It lists every service and the startup order for each runlevel. The table permits sorting by service name, runlevel startup order, or even current status. But the best part happens when you highlight any service: the text box provides a description of the service, so you can tell exactly what it does.

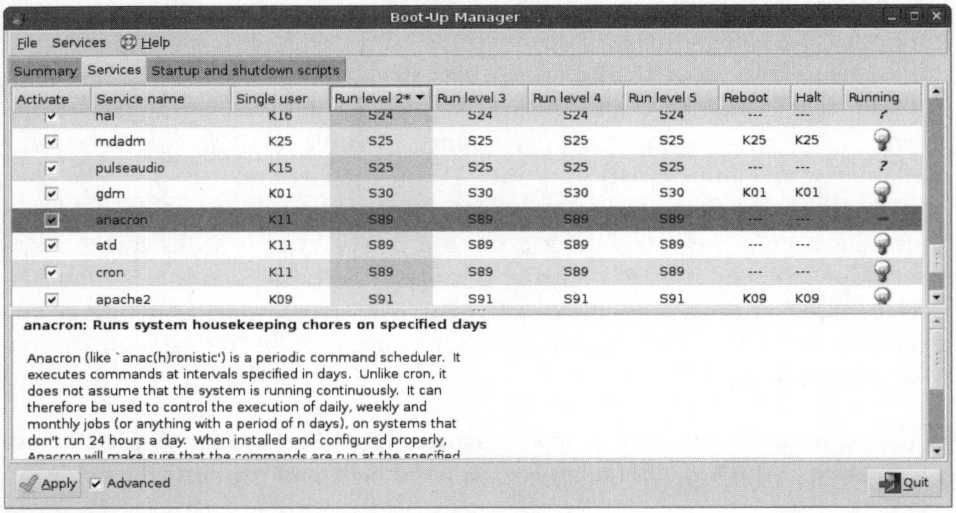

Activate	Service name	Single user	Run level 2* ▼	Run level 3	Run level 4	Run level 5	Reboot	Halt	Running
✔	hal	K16	S24	S24	S24	S24	---	---	?
✔	mdadm	K25	S25	S25	S25	S25	K25	K25	💡
✔	pulseaudio	K15	S25	S25	S25	S25	---	---	?
✔	gdm	K01	S30	S30	S30	S30	K01	K01	💡
✔	anacron	K11	S89	S89	S89	S89	---	---	—
✔	atd	K11	S89	S89	S89	S89	---	---	💡
✔	cron	K11	S89	S89	S89	S89	---	---	💡
✔	apache2	K09	S91	S91	S91	S91	K09	K09	💡

anacron: Runs system housekeeping chores on specified days

Anacron (like `anac(h)ronistic`) is a periodic command scheduler. It executes commands at intervals specified in days. Unlike cron, it does not assume that the system is running continuously. It can therefore be used to control the execution of daily, weekly and monthly jobs (or anything with a period of n days), on systems that don't run 24 hours a day. When installed and configured properly, Anacron will make sure that the commands are run at the specified

Figure 3-3: The Boot-Up Manager Services window

The final advanced tab shows you the services found in /etc/rcS.d/. These are generally system critical startup and shutdown scripts that are needed regardless of the runlevel. Because these are critical (like keyboard setup and console drives), bum does not allow you to modify the settings. (You can look, but don't touch.) To modify these, you will need to use the command line.

Configuring Services from the Command Line

The GUI applications work well when you have a GUI, but are not ideal for remote system administrating or for managing the Ubuntu Server installation (which lacks a GUI). Usually administrators need to use the command line to create, delete, or rename links in the /etc/rc*.d/ directories in order to modify system services. However, there is an alternative. The sysv-rc-conf tool offers a middle ground by allowing easy access to the boot services without requiring manual modification of the different startup files found in /etc/init.d/ and /etc/rc*.d/.

```
sudo apt-get install sysv-rc-conf
```

Running this tool (sudo sysv-rc-conf) brings up a text list of all services and runlevels (see Figure 3-4). Using this tool, you can immediately start or stop services by pressing + or -, and spacebar enables or disables the service in specific runlevels. The tool also supports the mouse; clicking a check box enables or disables the service.

```
┌─────────────────────────────── Terminal ───────────────────── _ □ x ┐
│ File  Edit  View  Terminal  Tabs  Help                               │
│  ┌─SysV Runlevel Config  -: stop service =/+: start service h: help q: quit─┐ │
│  │                                                                    │ │
│  │  service      1     2     3     4     5     0     6     S          │ │
│  │  -------------------------------------------------------------     │ │
│  │  acpi-supp$  [ ]   [X]   [X]   [X]   [X]   [ ]   [ ]   [ ]          │ │
│  │  acpid       [ ]   [X]   [X]   [X]   [X]   [ ]   [ ]   [ ]          │ │
│  │  alsa-utils  [ ]   [ ]   [ ]   [ ]   [ ]   [ ]   [ ]   [ ]          │ │
│  │  anacron     [ ]   [X]   [X]   [X]   [X]   [ ]   [ ]   [ ]          │ │
│  │  apache2     [ ]   [X]   [X]   [X]   [X]   [ ]   [ ]   [ ]          │ │
│  │  apmd        [ ]   [X]   [X]   [X]   [X]   [ ]   [ ]   [ ]          │ │
│  │  apparmor    [ ]   [ ]   [ ]   [ ]   [ ]   [ ]   [ ]   [X]          │ │
│  │  apport      [ ]   [X]   [X]   [X]   [X]   [ ]   [ ]   [ ]          │ │
│  │  atd         [ ]   [X]   [X]   [X]   [X]   [ ]   [ ]   [ ]          │ │
│  │  aumix       [ ]   [X]   [X]   [X]   [X]   [ ]   [ ]   [ ]          │ │
│  │  avahi-dae$  [ ]   [X]   [X]   [X]   [X]   [ ]   [ ]   [ ]          │ │
│  │  bluetooth   [X]   [ ]   [ ]   [ ]   [ ]   [ ]   [ ]   [ ]          │ │
│  │  bootclean   [ ]   [ ]   [ ]   [ ]   [ ]   [ ]   [ ]   [ ]          │ │
│  │                                                                    │ │
│  └────────────────────────────────────────────────────────────────┘ │
│  Use the arrow keys or mouse to move around.       ^n: next pg   ^p: prev pg │
│                       space: toggle service on / off                 │
└──────────────────────────────────────────────────────────────────────┘
```

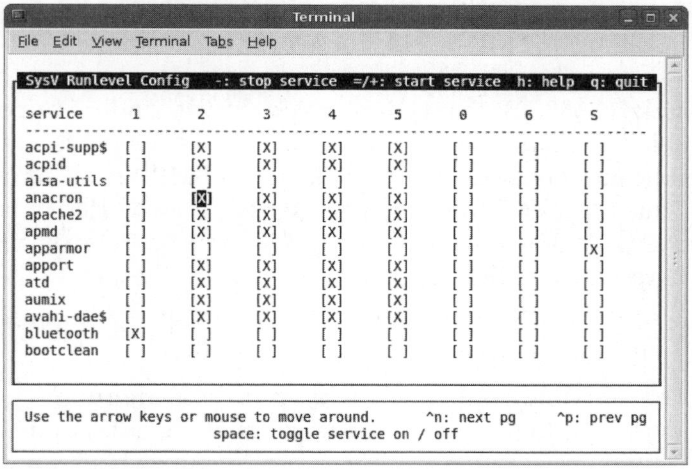

Figure 3-4: The sysv-rc-conf tool

WARNING The `sysv-rc-conf` tool only recognizes services in the `/etc/rc*.d/` and `/etc/init.d/` directories. It is not Upstart aware. Upstart scripts for `cron`, `hal`, `bootclean` and other services do contain scripts in `/etc/init.d/`, but they are listed by `sysv-rc-conf` as not being used in any runlevel.

As with the default Services applet, selecting or clearing a service will immediately change the service's running status and alter the service's boot-up configuration.

Enabling Multiple CPUs (SMP)

Many of today's computers have multiple CPUs. Some are physically distinct and others are virtual, such as hyperthreading and dual-core CPUs. In any case, these processors support symmetric multiprocessing (SMP) and can dramatically speed up Linux.

NOTE The kernel supports multiple CPUs and hyperthreading. If your computer has two CPUs that both support hyperthreading, the system will appear to have a total of four CPUs.

Older versions of Ubuntu, such as Hoary and Breezy, had different kernels available for SMP. To take advantage of multiple processors, you would need to install the appropriate kernel.

```
sudo apt-get install kernel-image-2.4.27-2-686-smp
```

Without installing an SMP kernel, you would only use one CPU on an SMP system.

Dapper Drake (6.06 LTS) changed this requirement. Under Dapper, all of the default kernels have SMP support enabled. The developers found that there was no significant speed impact from using an SMP kernel on a non-SMP system, and this simplified the number of kernels they needed to maintain.

There are a couple of ways to tell if your SMP processors are enabled in both the system hardware and kernel:

- `/proc/cpuinfo`—This file contains a list of all CPUs on the system. Alternately, you can use `sudo lshw -class cpu`.

- `top`—The `top` command shows what processes are running. If you run `top` and press 1, the header provides a list of all CPUs individually and their individual CPU loads. (This is really fun when running it on a system with 32 CPUs. Make sure the terminal window is tall enough to prevent scrolling!)

- **System Monitor**—The System Monitor applet can be added to the Gnome panels. When you click it, it shows the different CPU loads (see Figure 3-5).

In each of these cases, if only one CPU is listed, then you are not running SMP. Multiple CPUs in the listings indicate SMP mode.

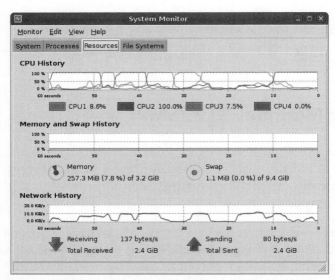

Figure 3-5: Hardy Heron's System Monitor applet showing multiple CPUs

Disabling SMP

In some situations, such as application benchmarking or hardware debugging, you may want to disable SMP support. This can be done with the kernel parameters `nosmp` or `maxcpus=1`. If this is a temporary need, then you can boot the system, catch GRUB at the menu by pressing Esc, and enter `boot nosmp maxcpus=1` at the prompt. If you have multiple boot options, then you may need to edit the kernel line and add `nosmp maxcpus=1` to the kernel boot line.

WARNING Some kernels may not work with `nosmp`, but in my experience `maxcpus=1` always works.

NOTE The default boot loader gives you three seconds to press the escape key before it boots the operating system.

For a longer-term solution, consider adding these parameters to boot configuration. See Chapter 1 for configuring GRUB.

Missing SMP?

If you find that you only have one active CPU on a multiple CPU system, then there are few generic debugging options. The problem is unlikely to be related to Ubuntu—it is probably a general Linux kernel problem.

- Check with the motherboard's manufacturer to see if Linux supports the chipset. For example, I have an old dual-CPU motherboard that is not supported by Linux.

- Check the Linux Hardware FAQ for the motherboard or chipset. This will tell you if other people managed to get it to work. Web sites such as `https://wiki.ubuntu.com/HardwareSupport` and `www.faqs.org/docs/Linux-HOWTO/SMP-HOWTO.html` are good places to start.

- If all else fails, post a query to any of the Linux or Ubuntu hardware forums. Maybe someone else knows a workaround. Some good forums include `ubuntuforums.org`, `www.linuxhardware.org`, and `www.linuxforums.org`. Be sure to include details such as the make and model of the motherboard, Ubuntu version, and other peripherals. It is generally better to provide too much information when asking for help, rather than too little.

Unfortunately, if SMP is not enabled after the basic installation, then it probably will not work. But you might get lucky—if someone has a patch, then you will probably need to recompile the kernel.

WARNING Compiling the kernel is not for the weak-of-heart. Many aspects of Linux are now automated or have easy-to-use graphical interfaces, but compiling the kernel is not one of them. There are plenty of help pages and FAQs for people daring enough to compile their own kernel.

Adding Printers

Printers are one of the most common types of external device. Today, many computer manufacturers bundle printers with new computers—it's hard *not* to have a printer. Printers used to come with one of two types of connectors: serial or parallel. Today, USB printers are very common. In corporate and small-office/home-office (SOHO) environments, networked printers are the norm. Ubuntu supports an amazing number of printers; making Ubuntu work with most printers is relatively easy.

Changing Paper Size

Before you install your first printer, be sure to set the system's default paper size. This is found in the file `/etc/papersize`. The default paper size probably says `A4` or `letter`—this depends on the geographical location you selected during the installation. If the default paper size is not set right, then every printer you add to the system will be configured with the wrong default paper size. Changing `/etc/papersize` *after* you create a printer will not alter any already existing printers.

To change the default paper size, edit `/etc/papersize` and change the value. Common values are `A4`, `letter`, and `legal`. A4 is the standard paper in Europe. Letter and legal refer to the 8.5 inch × 11 inch and 8.5 inch × 14 inch paper sizes common in the United States. Less common paper sizes that I have come across include `A5`, `B2`, `C2`, `ledger`, and `10x14`.

TIP If you have multiple printers that take different paper sizes, change the value in `/etc/papersize` before adding each printer.

PAPERS PLEASE

Paper sizes, such as A0, A1, A2, B3, C4, and D4, refer to ratios from a larger piece of paper. For example, A0 has a total area of one square meter. The A0 dimensions are 841 x 1189 mm. A1 is half of A0's longest direction: 594 x 841 mm. A2 is half of A1 (420 x 594), and so on. As a result, 16 sheets of A4 cover

a surface area of 1 m². Other paper types follow the same ratios—four sheets of B2 can fit in one B0 sheet. B0 is 1000 x 1414 mm and C0 is 917 x 1297 mm.
  Specific fields use different paper sizes. For example, A is common in publishing, while C is used in construction for building plans. If you have a large printer or plotter, be sure to set up /etc/papersize with the right default before adding the printer.

Adding a Printer

Adding a printer under Ubuntu is straightforward. Go to System ➪ Administration ➪ Printing to open the printer applet. From there, you can double-click New Printer to configure the device.

The first step in adding a printer requires specifying which kernel device communicates with the printer (see Figure 3-6). The system will search for local and network printers. You also have the option to configure a local printer using a USB or parallel port, or a network printer. Although the local printer configuration is easy (select the detected USB printer or parallel port), networked printers require additional information.

- **CUPS Printer (IPP)**—The Common Unix Printing System allows the sharing of printers between different Unix computers. You will need to provide a URL for the printer, such as ipp://server/printer_name.

- **Windows Printer (SMB)**—Windows printers are very common. In small offices, a user with a printer directly connected to a Windows host can share the printer with the network. You will need to provide the Windows hostname, printer name, and any username and password needed to access the device.

- **Unix Printer (LPD)**—The Line Printer Daemon protocol is one of the oldest and most reliable network printing options. Most standalone network printers support LPD. For this option, you will need to provide the hostname and the name of the LPD print queue.

- **HP JetDirect**—This is another common protocol for standalone printers. You only need to provide the hostname (and port number if it's not the default 9100).

NOTE The printer configuration applet's layout changes with each Ubuntu version. However, the core functionality remains the same.

TIP Use sudo apt-get install cups-pdf to add a printer for generating PDF files.

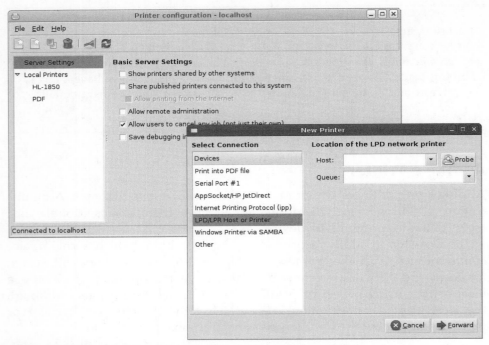

Figure 3-6: The applet for adding a new printer under Hardy Heron

The second step for adding a printer requires you to specify the type of printer. If your exact printer model is not listed, chances are good that there is a model that is close enough. In the worst case, you can always select one of the generic printer options.

Finally, you should name the printer. Give it a descriptive name so that you can recognize it later.

Sharing Your Printer

After you have added your printer, you can share it with other people on the network. Sharing the printer requires knowing who will use it: other system using CUPS, other devices using LPD, or other computers running Windows.

Sharing a Printer with CUPS

To share the printer with CUPS, you will need to configure both the printer server and the client.

On the print server:

1. Edit `/etc/cups/cupsd.conf` and change the line that reads `Listen localhost:631` to `Port 631`. This tells CUPS to allow printing from any remote system, and not just `localhost`.

2. (Optional) Edit `/etc/cups/cupsd.conf` and change `Browsing off` to `Browsing on`. This allows the server to announce the printer's availability to other hosts on the network.

TIP The default is an announcement every 30 seconds. You can change this by specifying a `BrowseInterval`. For example, `BrowseInterval 15` will announce every 15 seconds, and a value of `300` will announce every five minutes.

3. Restart the CUPS subsystem on the print server:

```
sudo /etc/init.d/cupsys restart # Hardy Heron (8.04 LTS) and older
sudo /etc/init.d/cups restart   # Jaunty Jackalope and newer
```

On the print client:

1. Go to System ➪ Administration ➪ Printing to open the printer applet.
2. Add a New Printer.
3. Select a Network Printer and the CUPS Printer (IPP) protocol.
4. Enter the printer hostname and printer name as a URL. For example, if the server is named *printer.home.com* and the printer is called *Okidata*, then you would use `ipp://printer.home.com/printers/Okidata`.
5. Click the Forward button and select the printer model.
6. Create a description for the printer
7. Click on the Apply button to create the printer.

TIP If you enabled browsing in Step 2 of the server configuration, then Ubuntu clients will try to automatically discover and configure the remote printer.

CUPS RUNNETH OVER

CUPS provides many configuration options, but it has a long history of being a security risk. The CUPS installation includes a web-based administration interface. By default, it is not accessible remotely. (But if you followed the steps under Sharing With CUPS, then it *is* remotely accessible.) The URL for this interface is `http://localhost:631/`.

Although you can use the CUPS web interface to view and manage the print queue, the default administration interface does not permit adding new printers or changing configurations. This functionality is disabled in Ubuntu, primarily because of security risks. Enabling this interface is not recommended. Instead, if you need to modify printer configurations, use the System ➪ Preferences ➪ Printing application.

Sharing a Printer with LPD

Enabling LPD support is a little more complex, since Ubuntu does not normally include servers.

On the print server:

1. Install `xinetd` on the print server. This is the extended Internet daemon for running processes.

   ```
   sudo apt-get install xinetd
   ```

2. Create a configuration file for the printer service. This requires creating a file called `/etc/xinetd.d/printer`. The contents should look like this:

   ```
   service printer
   {
     socket_type = stream
     protocol = tcp
     wait = no
     user = lp
     group = sys
     server = /usr/lib/cups/daemon/cups-lpd
     server_args = -o document-format=application/octet/stream
   }
   ```

3. Restart the `xinetd` server:

   ```
   sudo /etc/init.d/xinetd restart
   ```

On the printer client:

1. Go to System ➪ Administration ➪ Printing, to open the printer applet.

2. Double-click New Printer to configure the device.

3. Select a Network Printer and the Unix Printer (lpd) protocol.

4. Enter the print server hostname (or IP address) in the Host field and the CUPS printer name under the Queue field.

5. Continue through the remaining screens to select the printer type and configure it.

Sharing a Printer with Windows

It is usually best to use a native printing protocol. For Ubuntu, LPD and CUPS are native. Most versions of Windows support network printing to LPD servers, so sharing with LPD should be enough, but it requires users to configure their printers.

Native Windows environments can share printers using the Server Message Block (SMB) protocol. This allows Windows users to browse the Network Neighborhood and add any shared printers—very little manual configuration is required. For Ubuntu to share a printer with Windows users requires installing SAMBA, an open source SMB server.

On the print server:

1. Install SAMBA on the print server. This provides Windows SMB support:

   ```
   sudo apt-get install samba
   ```

2. Create a directory for the print spool:

   ```
   sudo mkdir /var/spool/samba/
   ```

3. Edit the SAMBA configuration file: /etc/samba/smb.conf.

4. Under the [global] section, change workgroup = to match your Windows Workgroup. For example, my office workgroup is SLUGGO:

   ```
   [global]
      workgroup = SLUGGO
   ```

5. Under the [global] section is an area for printer configuration. Uncomment (remove the leading ;) the load printers = yes and CUPS printing lines.

   ```
   ########## Printing ##########

   # If you want to automatically load your printer list rather
   # than setting them up individually then you'll need this
   load printers = yes

   # lpr(ng) printing. You may wish to override the location of the
   # printcap file
   ;    printing = bsd
   ;    printcap name = /etc/printcap

   # CUPS printing.  See also the cupsaddsmb(8) manpage in the
   # cupsys-client package.
   printing = cups
   printcap name = cups
   ```

6. Set the [printers] section to look like this:

   ```
   [printers]
      comment = All Printers
      browseable = no
      security = share
      use client driver = yes
      guest ok = yes
      path = /var/spool/samba/
      printable = yes
      public = yes
      writable = yes
      create mode = 0700
   ```

This setting allows any Windows client to access the printers without a password.

7. (Optional) Under the `[printers]` section, set `browseable = yes`. This allows Windows systems to see the printers through the Network Neighborhood.

8. Restart the SAMBA server:

```
sudo /etc/init.d/samba restart
```

On the Windows client, you can add the printer as if it were a Windows printer. For example, if the server's name is *printer.home.com* and the printer is *Okidata*, then the shared printer resource would be `\\printer.home.com\Okidata`. Windows clients will need to install their own print drivers.

Adding Drives

Back in the good old days, people would buy computer components separately. After gathering the necessary components, such as a motherboard, case, memory, video card, and monitor, they would slap together a working computer. Today, it is usually cheaper to get a pre-built system. Few people (except power users like yourself) upgrade the video card or memory after buying the computer; most people will just replace the entire system. Even though most of the hardware stays the same, there is one thing that is usually upgraded: the hard drive. This could be because you need more disk space, or maybe you want a second drive for backups or additional storage.

Upgrading Drives

When you upgrade your hard drive, you'll want to make sure that you transfer over all of your personal files. This could be as simple as transferring the contents of /home from one system to another. But if you have installed any custom applications (very likely) or tuned any configurations, then you will probably need to transfer system files, too. Here's an easy way of doing it:

1. Shut down the system, remove the old drive, and install the new drive. Do not leave the old drive in the system, since you do not want to accidentally reformat the wrong drive.

2. Install Ubuntu on the system (see Chapter 1). Be sure to use the same base install. Don't bother customizing this new install—it is only needed for making the drive bootable.

3. Shut down the system and install the old hard drive as the second drive. Do not boot from the old hard drive.

4. Start up the computer and boot from the new drive.

5. Log in when the computer has rebooted and open a terminal.

6. Now for the hard part—finding the drive's device handle for the old drive. This is a two-step process. First, use `mount` to identify the current drive. It will be the one that is mounted. Second, use `sudo lshw -class disk` to find the unused drive that needs to be mounted. In this example, the current drive is `/dev/sdb` and the new drive is `/dev/sdc`.

```
$ mount | grep -e /dev/sd -e /dev/hd
/dev/sdb1 on / type ext3 (rw,relatime,errors=remount-ro)
$ sudo lshw -class disk
*-disk:0
        description: ATA Disk
        product: ST3500320AS
        vendor: Seagate
        physical id: 0
        bus info: scsi@4:0.0.0
        logical name: /dev/sdb
        version: SD15
        serial: 9QM52R9R
        size: 465GiB (500GB)
        capabilities: partitioned partitioned:dos
        configuration: ansiversion=5 signature=00070904
*-disk:1
        description: ATA Disk
        product: ST31500341AS
        vendor: Seagate
        physical id: 1
        bus info: scsi@5:0.0.0
        logical name: /dev/sdc
        version: CC1H
        serial: 9VS2N2QN
        size: 1397GiB (1500GB)
        capabilities: partitioned partitioned:dos
        configuration: ansiversion=5 signature=00052eee
```

7. Mount the old drive partition(s). The partitions will be enumerated. Since drive `/dev/sdc` is a working drive, there should be `/dev/sdc1`, `/dev/sdc2`, etc. If you know the data partition, then you can mount it. Otherwise, you can blindly mount each of the partitions.

```
cd /dev
for i in sdc[0-9]* ; do
  sudo mkdir /media/$i
  sudo mount /dev/$i /media/$i
done
```

NOTE Don't worry if some partitions fail to mount. Swap and other specialized partitions are not data partitions. We only care about the data partitions, since we want to copy over data.

8. As root, copy over all of the old files to the new system. For example, if /dev/sdc1 was the old / partition, then copy the data from /media/sdc1/ to the new /.

```
$ cd /media/sdc1
$ ls
bin    dev    initrd          lib          mnt    root   sys  var
boot   etc    initrd.img      lost+found   opt    sbin   tmp  vmlinuz
cdrom  home   initrd.img.old  media        proc   srv    usr  vmlinuz.old
$ sudo tar -cf - * | ( cd / ; tar -xvf - )
```

NOTE You may want to remove temporary and device directories first, such as /mnt/disk/mnt, cdrom, tmp, dev, and proc. Alternately, you could only list the directories to keep in the tar -cf command.

9. Repeat Step 8 with each of the data partitions. Be sure to copy data to the correct directory. For example, if /dev/sdc2 was /home, then copy the contents to /home, not /.

10. Since the copy may have brought over a newer kernel, you will want to reset the boot loader:

```
sudo update-grub
```

11. Now that everything is copied, you can reboot the system immediately. You don't want to use shutdown, since that can save desktop settings over your new settings. To force an immediate reboot, use the -f parameter:

```
sudo reboot -f
```

When the system comes back up, you should have all of your old files right where you left them, and a minimal amount of residue (undesirable files) that you did not originally want. This method is great for switching partition layouts, since it only copies files, but it should not be used to upgrade operating systems.

Mounting Systems

In Chapter 1, we covered how to partition and format a drive. Now, since you have a second drive in the system, you can make it mount each time you boot the system.

1. Unmount the drive, partition, and format it. For this example, we will assume that you have configured it with one partition as /dev/sdb1.

2. Identify the drive's universally unique identifier (UUID) and optional label:

```
$ sudo blkid | sort
/dev/sda1: UUID="357948d2-281e-444e-bcec-2fa67b498330" TYPE="ext3"
/dev/sda3: UUID="b14b1292-0165-4e61-8f70-f23b319d62ad" TYPE="ext4"
/dev/sda5: UUID="99ab3ba2-63bb-4c90-82fa-c1f7391fd732" TYPE="swap"
/dev/sda6: UUID="d24160cb-d2bc-44dd-aa0a-d4d67837bad0"
           SEC_TYPE="ext2" TYPE="ext3"
/dev/sdb1: UUID="93736c75-920c-4533-b4c1-ea1346c16958"
           SEC_TYPE="ext2" TYPE="ext3" LABEL="Backup"
```

TIP With ext2, ext3, and ext4 file systems, you can assign a label to the drive using `e2label` or `tune2fs`. For example, `sudo e2label /dev/hdb1 Backup` or `sudo tune2fs -L Backup /dev/sdb1`.

3. Create a place to mount the drive. For example: `sudo mkdir /mnt/backup`.

4. Add the drive to the `/etc/fstab` file so that it is mounted automatically. You can refer to the drive by its device name (`/dev/hdb1`), its UUID, or an optional label.

Listing 3-3: Mounting a New Drive

```
# /etc/fstab: static file system information.
#
# <file system> <mount point>   <type>  <options>        <dump>  <pass>
# / was on /dev/sda3 during installation
UUID=b14b1292-0165-4e61-8f70-f23b319d62ad /   ext4 errors=remount-ro 0   1
# swap was on /dev/sda5 during installation
UUID=99ab3ba2-63bb-4c90-82fa-c1f7391fd732 none swap sw 0        0
/dev/scd0  /media/cdrom0  udf,iso9660 user,noauto,exec,utf8 0       0
# Add the new drive by device handle
# /dev/hdb1         /mnt/backup      ext3      defaults       0       0
# Add the new drive by label
# LABEL=Backup     /mnt/backup      ext3      defaults       0       0
# Add the new drive by UUID
UUID=93736c75-920c-4533-b4c1-ea1346c16958 /mnt/backup ext3 defaults 0 0
```

Using device names is only useful if the device handles never change. Don't use this option unless you never change hardware.

Labels are great for multiple removable drives that all need to mount in the same place. Swappable external drives for backups are a great example.

However, UUIDs are best for partitions that are always mounted in unique locations. Even if the drive's device handle changes, the UUID will remain the same.

5. Mount the new file system using either `sudo mount -a` or `sudo mount /mnt/backup`.

With these changes in place, the new drive will be mounted every time you boot.

ALMOST UNIQUE

UUIDs are not always unique. For example, if you mirror a drive, then the mirror will have the same UUID. Use `uuidgen` **to generate a new UUID, and** `tune2fs` **to set the UUID.**

```
sudo tune2fs -U $(uuidgen) /dev/sdb1
```

This approach can also be used to force a specific UUID onto a drive, simplifying recovery from a hard drive failure. You just need to restore your system backup onto a new drive and use `tune2fs -U` **to assign the UUIDs onto the partitions. This way, you don't need to edit** `/etc/fstab`**, GRUB, or other system files in order to make the drive bootable.**

Labels and UUIDs are just the start of the configurable options. For example, you can use `sudo tune2fs -c 20 /dev/sda1` **to perform a file system check (**`e2fsck`**) after every 20 mounts. Use** `sudo tune2fs -l /dev/`*partition* **to list all of the configurable parameters.**

Using Simple Backups

Back in the old days, I would make backups using floppy disks. As drives increased in size, I switched over to magnetic tapes. Today, home systems can be cheaply backed up using a second hard drive. Listing 3-3 is a simple script that I use to back up my Ubuntu system onto a second hard drive.

Listing 3-4: Very Simple Backup Script: /usr/local/bin/backup2disk-full

```
#!/bin/sh
# backup files to disk
for i in bin boot etc home lib opt root sbin sys usr var ; do
   tar -clzf /mnt/backup/backup-$i-full.tgz "/$i" 2>/dev/null
done
```

This simple script creates a bunch of compressed TAR files containing all of my data. For example, `/mnt/backup/backup-home-full.tgz` contains the contents of my `/home` partition. You can also create a version that does incremental backups by replacing the `tar` command in Listing 3-3 with:

```
tar --newer "$(date -r /mnt/backup/backup-$i-full.tgz)" \
   -clzf /mnt/backup/backup-$i-inc.tgz "$i" 2>/dev/null
```

For my system, I added the full backup script to my root `crontab` and configured it to run once a week. The incremental runs nightly.

1. Edit the root `crontab`. This allows files to run at specific times.

   ```
   sudo crontab -e
   ```

2. Add a line to make the full backup run weekly and the incrementals run daily. (See Chapter 8 for details on `cron`.)

   ```
   # minute hour day-of-month month day-of-week    command
   5 0 * * 0 /usr/local/bin/backup2disk-full
   5 0 * * 1-6 /usr/local/bin/backup2disk-inc
   ```

Using this script, I can restore any file or directory using `tar`. For example, to restore the `/home/nealk/book3` directory, I would use:

```
cd /
sudo tar -xzvf /mnt/backup/backup-home-full.tgz home/nealk/book3
sudo tar -xzvf /mnt/backup/backup-home-inc.tgz home/nealk/book3
```

WARNING This backup script is very simple and can still lead to data loss. It does not keep historical backups, and you can lose everything if a crash happens during the backup. Although this script is a hack, it is better than having no backups. However, it should not be depended on for critical backup needs. For long-term or critical data recovery, consider using a professional backup system.

ALTERNATE BACKUP METHODS

Not everyone likes compressed `.tar` files. While these archives usually reduce disk space requirements for long-term storage, they are not always convenient when searching for specific files to recover.

For a simple directory mirror, consider using `sudo cp -axruf /home /mnt/backup/home`. The `cp` parameters will archive (`-a`) all files on one file system (`-x`) and recursively process directories (`-r`). All newer or missing files will be updated (`-uf`). This command preserves owners, permissions, timestamps, and links.

Another alternative is to use `rsync`. This acts just like the `cp` command (`rsync -av /home /mnt/backup/home`) but can also store files over the network. For example, `rsync -av /home rsync://user@host/backup` will copy the local `/home` directory into the `/backup` directory on `host`. It will connect using SSH as the specified user. To recover, swap the source and destination parameters: `rsync -av rsync://user@host/backup /home`.

Configuring a RAID

A redundant array of inexpensive disks (RAID) is a simple solution to surviving a disk crash. Ubuntu supports hardware RAIDs as well as software RAIDs. A hardware RAID needs no extra configuration for use with Ubuntu. The entire RAID just appears as a single disk. On the other hand, software RAIDs require some configuration.

RAID LEVELS

The RAID level identifies the number of drives that can be lost before a data failure. Common RAID levels include:

- **RAID0—This concatenates all of the RAID drives into a single hard drive. There is no data redundancy; if you lose a drive then your entire partition will be corrupted. However, data can be striped across drives, so you can potentially increase your data access rate. Use this level if you have many small drives and want to store temporary (non-critical) data.**

- **RAID1—This level mirrors the disks. Since every disk contains all of the data, your data will remain intact as long as at least one drive is good. If your RAID only contains two drives, then this is your safest option.**

- **RAID5—This level splits and mirrors the data across multiple drives. If you have three or more drives, then this option gives you the best storage capacity with redundancy. The actual amount of redundancy depends on the partition size and number of drives. (A partition may be larger than one drive.)**

- **RAID10—For the truly paranoid, this option combines mirroring with data striping. While it may be an expensive option (and does not scale well), it is very fast and highly fault tolerant.**

Other RAID levels do exist, but have mostly become obsolete. For example, RAID2 includes error-correcting code (ECC). However, most drives already include ECC so this feature is redundant. Similarly, RAID3 and RAID4 use different methods to split data across drives. Both RAID3 and RAID4 have been replaced by the more efficient RAID5.

A software RAID requires multiple hard drives. The simplest option, RAID1, uses two identical hard drives. I recommend buying the same make and model at the same time because they are certain to be identical. Other people recommend buying similar—but not identical—drives in case the drives have an unknown common problem. The choice really depends on your level of paranoia. I have had identical drives die within months of each other but never both at the same time.

After installing the drives (for example, sda and sdb), partition them, using fdisk or gparted, with the same size partitions (sda1 and sdb1). Now comes the fun part, turning them into a RAID.

NOTE This example assumes that you have added two additional hard drives to your systems and they are already partitioned. The software RAID works by combining multiple real partitions into one virtual partition. Usually the partitions are on different hard drives, since having a RAID hosted on a single hard drive does not protect against hardware failure.

WARNING Creating a RAID requires modifying disk partitions and format. If you accidentally specify the wrong partition, you may end up destroying some or all of your system.

1. Use the mdadm tool to create the RAID. The man page for mdadm contains many additional options for striping, setting the RAID level, and so on. In this example, we will create a simple RAID1, or mirrored disks, configuration using the two partitions. The result is one RAID drive called /dev/md0.

   ```
   sudo mdadm --create /dev/md0 --level=1 \
           --raid-devices=2 /dev/sda1 /dev/sdb1
   ```

2. Creating the RAID happens in the background and can take hours to complete. Do not continue until it finishes. To watch the progress, use:

   ```
   nice watch cat /proc/mdstat
   ```

3. Now you can create the file system for the RAID. You can use any file system on the RAID. For example, to create an ext2 file system, you can use:

   ```
   sudo mkfs.ext2 /dev/md0
   ```

When the process finishes, you can view the RAID's details by using sudo mdadm -Q --detail /dev/md0. You can also mount the partition (sudo mount /dev/md0 /mnt/disk) and add it to your /etc/fstab.

BETWEEN A ROCK AND A HARD DISK

In 2004 I had a hard disk crash that hurt. Years worth of research was on that drive, and it had a head crash. Although I did have simple backups, that's not the same thing as having the entire working system. Although 98 percent of the data was recovered (thanks to Reynolds Data Recovery in Longmont, Colorado!) and the lost 2 percent was easily recreated, I quickly learned my lesson: don't store critical data on one hard drive.

(continued)

BETWEEN A ROCK AND A HARD DISK *(continued)*

Today, my main research computer has four hard drives. One is the main operating system, one is configured as a removable backup, and two are identical drives used in a software RAID for storing research and critical files. When I had a second disk failure, I ended up not losing any data.

I also use daily backups and off-site, out-of-state storage. A massive file system corruption might take a day or two to recover and result in a few hours of lost work, but the majority of my data is safe.

Although this type of configuration may sound like overkill for most home and SOHO environments, you need to ask yourself: Which costs less, configuring a software RAID and a simple backup script, or rebuilding everything after a total loss? Even the hourly costs for recovery time are less when you maintain a minimal backup system.

For home users, consider using a simple RAID and backup system for storing irreplaceable files. This includes tax documents, personal emails, and digital photos of little Billy's first birthday. If you cannot afford to lose the data, then mitigate potential loss with data redundancy.

Detecting a RAID Failure

It is one thing to configure a RAID but another thing to actually see a RAID fail and recover from it. As luck would have it, one of my RAID drives died while writing this chapter! So my description of what I saw and how I recovered from it is not theoretical—this is what worked well for me.

Before you can address a RAID problem, you have to know that your RAID is failing. In my case, two things happened. First, I noticed that writes would temporarily hang. This is because one RAID drive was working but the other was timing out. Second, my administrative account received an e-mail from the RAID subsystem informing me that a drive died. The e-mail looked like this:

```
To: root
Subject: DegradedArray event on /dev/md0:slushy
Date: Sun,  6 Dec 2009 10:57:59 -0700 (MST)

This is an automatically generated mail message from mdadm
running on slushy

A DegradedArray event had been detected on md device /dev/md0.

Faithfully yours, etc.

P.S. The /proc/mdstat file currently contains the following:
```

```
Personalities : [linear] [multipath] [raid0] [raid1] [raid6]
[raid5] [raid4] [raid10]
md0 : active raid1 sdb1[1]
      976759936 blocks [2/1] [_U]

unused devices: <none>
```

My RAID normally consists of two drives: sda1 and sdb1. In this case, sda died, since only sdb1 is listed. The notation [_U] indicates that the first drive is dead and the second is up (U). A working RAID will look like [UU] (with one U per drive).

Not knowing any better, I did a quick backup (good idea) and rebooted my system (bad idea). As it turns out, mdadm will not reconstruct the RAID (needed for mounting) if a disk has failed. What I should have done before rebooting: sudo mdadm /dev/md0 -f /dev/sda1. This marks the drive as being faulty and allows the RAID to come up after a reboot.

However, if you are like me and didn't mark the drive as faulty, then all is not lost. You can always force the RAID to reassemble using fewer disks.

```
# trying to assemble will fail
$ sudo mdadm --assemble /dev/md0 /dev/sdb1
mdadm: /dev/md0 assembled from 1 drive - need all 2 to start it
(use --run to insist).
# force it to assemble
$ sudo mdadm --assemble --force /dev/md0 /dev/sdb1
mdadm: /dev/md0 has been started with 1 drive (out of 2).
$ mdadm -Q --detail /dev/md0  # check the RAID
/dev/md0:
          Version : 00.90.03
    Creation Time : Sat Sep 20 14:27:40 2008
       Raid Level : raid1
       Array Size : 976759936 (931.51 GiB 1000.20 GB)
    Used Dev Size : 976759936 (931.51 GiB 1000.20 GB)
     Raid Devices : 2
    Total Devices : 1
  Preferred Minor : 0
      Persistence : Superblock is persistent

      Update Time : Sun Dec  6 10:58:37 2009
            State : clean, degraded
   Active Devices : 1
  Working Devices : 1
   Failed Devices : 0
    Spare Devices : 0

             UUID : 4f11630b:69c64ebc:b066c2d5:6a53b630 (local to host
                    slushy)
           Events : 0.101020
```

```
      Number    Major    Minor    RaidDevice  State
        0          0        0         0        removed
        1          8       17         1        active sync   /dev/sdb1
$ sudo mount -a   # It works!
```

Granted, running a two-drive RAID with only one drive is not robust. However, it did let me continue to work while I waited for the new hard drives I ordered to arrive.

Adding to a RAID

Replacing a dead drive and adding a new drive to a RAID is a very painless procedure:

1. Install the new hard drive(s). Assuming that your system is not hot pluggable, you will need to power down the computer first.

2. If you are using SATA or other internal hard drives, make sure that the computer's BIOS recognizes the new disks. This ensures that the hardware is installed properly. With USB drives, you just need connect them to the computer.

3. Boot the computer. It should come up and the drives should be assigned device handles. In my case, the new drives are /dev/sda and /dev/sdc; /dev/sdb is my original RAID drive. (Having had one drive fail, I decided to replace it with two additional drives.)

4. Partition the new drives using fdisk as root. When using RAID level 1 (mirror), the partitions need to be as large or larger than the existing RAID. This is not a requirement for RAID levels 5 or 6, since data is stripped across partitions.

> **WARNING** There are other ways to partition disks. For example, Karmic Koala (9.10) includes Palimpsest (sudo palimpsest). Older Ubuntu versions use the graphical gparted. However, gparted failed to partition my 1.5-terabyte (TB) hard drives. It works fine with 1-TB and smaller drives. Although fdisk may be text-based and cryptic, it works well with large drives.

5. Add the new partition(s) to the RAID. To add sda1 and sdc1, use:

   ```
   sudo mdadm --manage /dev/md0 --add /dev/sda1 /dev/sdc1
   ```

6. Watch /proc/mdstat as it copies over the data: nice watch cat /proc/mdstat. Depending on the size of your RAID, this process could take hours.

In my case, I had three disks in a two-disk RAID. The extra partition was marked as a spare drive in /proc/mdstat (denoted by the s after the partition name).

```
md0 : active raid1 sda1[2](S) sdb1[3] sdc1[1]
      976759936 blocks [2/1] [_U]
      [>...................]  recovery =   2.6%
         (25578432/976759936) finish=185.
```

To alter the RAID to use all three drives, wait for it to finish the recovery, and then use:

```
sudo mdadm --grow /dev/md0 --raid-devices=3
```

As with the other commands, this one will take hours to complete. When it finishes, /proc/mdstat will identify three active drives.

```
md0 : active raid1 sda1[2] sdb1[3] sdc1[1]
      976759936 blocks [3/3] [UUU]
```

TIP You can add drives, remove drives, and alter a RAID's configuration while it is mounted and in use.

NOTE The mdadm command allows you to alter most RAID attributes but not all of them. For example, you cannot change the RAID level. If mdadm --version reports 3.1 or later (not yet included in any Ubuntu release), then you can change the RAID level. For example, mdadm --grow /dev/md0 --level 5 alters it to RAID level 5.

SPEEDING UP RAID REBUILDS

Rebuilding the RAID can take hours. You can try to speed it up using:

```
echo 50000 | sudo tee /proc/sys/dev/raid/speed_limit_min
echo 200000 | sudo tee /proc/sys/dev/raid/speed_limit_max
```

This says to increase to minimum rebuild speed to 50 Kps, and max to 200,000 Kps. The defaults are 1,000 and 100,000.

Changing the speed limits may improve recovery time but also makes the system sluggish as more bandwidth is devoted to the RAID. For some systems, the hardware bus is already a bottleneck, so increasing the limits will have no impact.

Adjusting Default Devices

With Ubuntu, different peripherals will cause different events. For example, a USB storage device will generate a drive letter and be mounted. A new DVD drive will become another /dev/dvd device (dvd1, dvd2, etc.), and a new network card will create a new network interface (eth1, eth2, wlan1, etc.). While the default action is usually desirable, you may want to alter it.

Disabling USB Drive Auto-Mount

With USB storage devices, such as thumb drives and external hard drives, the default action is to assign a drive letter and immediately mount the drive. There are two ways to cause the auto-mount. First, you can have the disk listed in /etc/fstab with an auto-mount parameter. For example:

```
/dev/sdb1 /mnt/backup ext3 defaults,auto 0 0
```

To disable the auto-mount, you can either remove the offending /etc/fstab line or change the entry so that it has the option noauto. The noauto option allows you to use sudo mount /dev/sdb1 or sudo mount /mnt/backup and have the system do the right thing based on the existing /etc/fstab entries.

The second situation in which automatic drive mounting occurs is when you are logged in to the graphical desktop and attach a new storage device, such as a USB drive. Plugging in the USB drive before you log in will not mount the drive.

Disabling the desktop's auto-mount means changing the Gnome configuration. Use gconf-editor and change the value of /apps/nautilus/preferences/media_automount to false, or you can use gconftool-2 to alter it from the command line.

```
gconftool-2 -t bool -s /apps/nautilus/preferences/media_automount false
```

Altering Network Interface Preferences

Adding in a second network interface card (NIC) can become troublesome. For example, if you are using the built-in wired network interface and then turn on the wireless network interface, all of your traffic may try to route over the wireless network. It does not matter that the wired network may be faster or more reliable; the default settings give all NICs the same priority, and the newest one becomes the default.

The problem is, the newest NIC may not be properly configured when you first enable it. Attaching it to the system can cause you to lose all network connectivity. The solution is to change the network interface priority.

Before you connect the new network interface, install ifmetric (sudo apt-get install ifmetric). The NIC priority is based on a stored ranking (the interface metric). Lower values have higher priorities and are accessed first. The default value is zero. To change the network priority, specify the interface and priority value, such as `sudo ifmetric eth1 10`. To make the change permanent, edit `/etc/network/interfaces` and set the metric for each network interface. For example:

```
auto lo
iface lo inet loopback

# My manually configured network interface
iface eth0 inet static
  address 192.168.107.6
  netmask 255.255.255.0
  gateway 192.168.107.1
  metric 0

# My second network which uses DHCP
iface eth1 inet dhcp
  metric 10

auto eth0
```

NOTE Wireless network configuration is covered in Chapter 12.

Adding Other Devices

Printers, network cards, and hard drives are just the start of the list of devices that people use with their computers. Scanners, modems, and video capture devices are also common. Unfortunately, hardware support within the open source community is hit or miss. Some devices have plenty of support, some have drivers that almost work, and some have no support at all. Adding to this problem, Ubuntu natively supports a smaller set of hardware options than Linux in general. As a result, some drivers may need to be downloaded and compiled from scratch.

There is a basic rule of thumb when looking for Linux and Ubuntu support. If the device is standard and has been around for a while, then it is likely to have support. Proprietary devices and closed technologies are unlikely to have drivers. Most peripherals that are new and cool either lack support, or are supported by standard drivers.

ALMOST COMPATIBLE

Some vendors provide drivers for Linux in binary format only. Although these will work for specific platforms, they may not work with all platforms.

(continued)

ALMOST COMPATIBLE *(continued)*

When choosing new hardware that requires Linux drivers, make sure that they support *your* version of Linux. A kernel driver for RedHat Enterprise Linux 5.4 may not work with Ubuntu's Hardy Heron, and a device driver for Edgy Eft may not work with Karmic Koala.

In general, the best hardware vendors use standard protocols and do not require specialized kernel drivers. This means that drivers have been around for a long time. Your second choice should be vendors that provide source code. This enables you to recompile the code for use with other kernels and operating system versions. In the worst case, you may need to tweak the driver to work, but at least you will have the source code for tweaking. Finally, if you have no other option, choose a vendor that has a long track record of Linux support. Hardware that does not support Linux today should not be expected to support Linux tomorrow.

For example, Timex offers a set of watches with USB ports. This enables you to synchronize the alarms with your computer's calendar program. (This is a huge cool factor in geek terms.) Unfortunately, the watches use a nonstandard USB protocol. Moreover, drivers are only available for Windows. Even though a few open source groups have tried to create drivers for other operating systems, Mac OSX and Linux users are currently out of luck.

NVIDIA is another example of a vendor with proprietary protocols. But instead of USB watches, NVIDIA manufacturers video cards. In contrast to the Timex nonexistent drivers, NVIDIA supports Linux by providing proprietary video drivers, including versions that work with Ubuntu (see Chapters 5 and 10). Although source code is not available, NVIDIA has a long history of providing drivers for Linux.

Under Linux, it is generally easier to find drivers for legacy hardware. Few devices have ever been completely dropped. (The notable exceptions are the original 80386 and older CPU architectures because of their lack of a math coprocessor.) Although Windows XP may not have drivers for the Colorado Memory Systems' QIC-80 tape backup system, the Linux `ftape` driver's source code should be available for decades (although you may need to download, compile, and install it manually).

Tuning TV Cards

TV capture cards are a must-have for any power user. These add-on cards allow you to watch TV through your computer and configure a video recorder such as MythTV (an open source video recorder system). The driver for video devices is called video4linux (v4l and v4l2 for version 2). The video4linux driver supports bt848, bt878, saa7130/34, and conexant 2388x TV cards.

NOTE Most TV cards use the bt848 or bt878. If you look at the card, you should see a 1-inch chip with "848" or "878" printed on it.

Although Karmic Koala (9.10) includes video4linux by default, you have to add it to older Ubuntu versions. Configuring TV cards is relatively easy.

1. Install the video card and hook up the TV cable to it. Most TV cards support both broadcast and cable TV signals.

2. Install the v4l driver:

   ```
   sudo apt-get install xserver-xorg-driver-v4l
   ```

3. Edit `/etc/X11/xorg.conf` and add v4l to the "Modules" section so that X-Windows knows about the video driver:

   ```
   Section "Module"
           Load    "i2c"
           Load    "bitmap"
           Load    "ddc"
           Load    "dri"
           Load    "extmod"
           Load    "freetype"
           Load    "glx"
           Load    "int10"
           Load    "type1"
           Load    "vbe"
           Load    "v4l"
   EndSection
   ```

4. Restart the X-server using Ctrl+Alt+Backspace.

5. Test the video configuration. The `xsane` program has a scan option and menu for selecting the TV as input (see Figure 3-7). If you see a picture (or static), then the v4l driver is working properly.

Now that the video4linux driver is working, you can install capture, recording, and viewing programs that can configure and use the video card. My favorite is `xawtv`. This is a simple program for tuning the TV, watching channels, capturing images, and recording shows.

```
sudo apt-get install xawtv xawtv-plugin-qt tv-fonts xawtv-tools
```

When you first start `xawtv`, it will display the TV screen but may need a little configuration. Right-clicking the TV window will bring up the configuration menu. Be sure to set the norm (PAL, NTSC, and so on), type of signal (for example, us-cable), and input source (Television). Use the up and down arrows to change channels. When you find a configuration that works for you, save it using E. This option is actually used to set channel names, but saves the entire configuration in $HOME/.xawtv. At this point, xawtv should be working for you, and the TV card should be fully configured (see Figure 3-8).

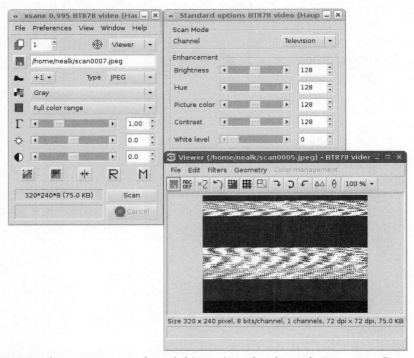

Figure 3-7: Using xsane to test the v4l driver. Since the channels are not configured, only static is captured.

Figure 3-8: The xawtv program showing the TV in a window

With a working TV card, you can also configure your screen saver to grab pictures from the TV.

TIP If you change the screen saver from the default `gnome-screensaver` to `xscreensaver` (see Chapter 10), then you can configure some of the screen savers to use the TV card. You will find this option in the `xscreensaver`'s preferences as Grab Video Frames under the Advanced tab settings. Screen savers such as Distort and Flipscreen3D manipulate TV captures.

Using Digital Cameras, Scanners, and Web Cameras

Although TV cards are cool, they are not as common as digital cameras, scanners, and webcams. Unfortunately, this is where hardware support really becomes hit or miss. My eight-year-old SCSI scanner is supported, whereas my USB scanner is not. And although both of my digital cameras can work as webcams under Windows, neither can work as a webcam under Linux.

NOTE Not every camera provides the same compatibility. If your camera does not support a capture mode, then you cannot use the computer to take pictures with it, and you cannot use it as a high-resolution webcam.

A tool that you may want to consider installing is `gphoto2`. This program provides support for over 700 different camera models. It enables you to scan for compatibility with the camera and query for supported functionality.

1. Install `gphoto2` as well as the graphical front end (`gtkam`) and the GIMP plug-in to allow captures from cameras:

   ```
   sudo apt-get install gphoto2 gtkam gtkam-gimp
   ```

2. Plug your camera into the USB port. There is no need to restart the X-server in order to load the drivers. If any windows, such as the camera import applet, pop up with prompts to import images or show the camera's contents, just close them.

3. Determine if the camera is supported. If the `gphoto2` command does not auto-detect your camera, then the camera is not supported. You may need to use a different driver if one is available. If the camera is mounted as a disk, then it will not be listed as a camera device.

   ```
   $ gphoto2 --auto-detect
   Model                            Port
   ─────────────────────────────
   HP PhotoSmart 618                usb:
   ```

NOTE Depending on your camera model and capabilities, you may see multiple lines of output from the `gphoto2 --auto-detect` command.

4. List the camera's capabilities. Most digital cameras have two PC-connect modes. The first mode is usually called something like *digital device*

and makes the camera appear as an actual USB camera. The second mode makes the camera appear as a USB drive. The different camera modes provide different attributes. For example, here are the attributes for the HP PhotoSmart 618 in digital device mode:

NOTE The ability to switch PC-connect modes depends on the camera. You will need to hunt through the camera's configuration menu to see if mode selection is supported and to change modes.

```
$ gphoto2 --abilities
Abilities for camera            : HP PhotoSmart 618
Serial port support             : yes
USB support                     : yes
Transfer speeds supported       :
                                : 9600
                                : 19200
                                : 38400
                                : 57600
                                : 115200
Capture choices                 :
                                : Capture not supported by the
                                  driver
Configuration support           : no
Delete files on camera support  : yes
File preview (thumbnail) support : yes
File upload support             : no
```

For a comparison, here are the attributes for the same camera in USB disk drive mode:

```
$ gphoto2 --abilities
Abilities for camera            : USB PTP Class Camera
Serial port support             : no
USB support                     : yes
Capture choices                 :
                                : Capture not supported by
                                  the driver
Configuration support           : yes
Delete files on camera support  : yes
File preview (thumbnail) support : yes
File upload support             : yes
```

Depending on your supported capture modes, you may be able to use the camera with scanner software such as GIMP and xsane, or with VoIP and teleconference software like Skype (see Chapter 6). Even if the camera does not support captures or webcam mode, you can still access the device as a USB drive and copy (or move) images. In USB disk drive mode, the camera appears no different than a USB thumb drive. You can transfer files by opening the drive via Nautilus and copying the files. In digital device mode, use `gtkam` to view the photos and copy them to the desktop.

Summary

Hardware support for Linux, and Ubuntu in particular, varies greatly. Although printers, hard drives, and TV cards have excellent support, other devices have more spotty support options. In many cases, installing the driver is not the last step; you will also need to configure the driver and dependent applications. Fortunately, once Linux supports a device, it is effectively supported for life. You can still find drivers for ancient MFM hard drives and 10-year-old scanners.

The best resources for hardware support are the Linux and Ubuntu forums and sites that specialize in specific hardware types, such as the following:

- `https://wiki.ubuntu.com/HardwareSupport` lists hardware that is supported by Ubuntu, as well as any particular quirks and issues.
- `www.linux.org/hardware` provides a very complete list of hardware that has known support for the Linux kernel.
- `www.gphoto.org` lists more than 1,100 supported digital camera models.

Loading the device and making it work is one thing, but making it work well can be something entirely different. In Chapter 4, you'll learn how to configure various input devices, including mice with extra buttons, special keyboard keys, and drawing tablets. Chapter 5 shows how to get the most out of video and audio devices by installing different codecs. Chapter 7 covers hardware emulation. In Chapter 10 you will start playing with screen resolutions and multiple monitors, and in Chapter 13 you will dive into advanced networking.

Adapting Input Devices

What's In This Chapter?

Modifying keyboard layouts and key functions
Supporting Ubuntu on Macs
Enabling multi-button mice and drawing tablets

Ordinary users might be content to use the keyboard "as is," but power users want custom shortcuts, multifunction keyboards, and complex tasks to start with the touch of a button. Mice, tablets, and other input devices can also be tweaked to maximize, optimize, and customize performance.

Empowering Keyboards

The default Ubuntu installation is optimized for a PC system, so there is not much modification required to make the keyboard or mouse function. Most peripherals that need tuning are physical devices, which are covered in Chapter 3. The only real PC-only functionality that may need tweaking is the use of special keyboard keys and the Ctrl+Alt+Delete sequence.

Changing Keyboard Layouts

While the Ubuntu installation has become virtually painless (see Chapter 1), people usually breeze through the crucial part: the keyboard configuration. Fortunately, the keyboard layout usually does not become an issue until after you change keyboards. For example, when the spacebar on my old keyboard wore out after years of use, I upgraded from a 101-key keyboard to a 105-key layout. During the interim period (between when the keyboard broke and when I could replace it), I plugged in a spare Apple USB keyboard. Each of these keyboards uses a different layout. The result would have been a painful experience had I not altered the active layout configuration; with each keyboard, important keys moved and new buttons were added.

There are two independent places that manage the keyboard configuration. The first is the graphical desktop and the second is the text console.

NOTE Changing the text console's keyboard does not alter the keyboard configuration for the graphical desktop, or vice versa. To fully reconfigure your keyboard, you will need to modify both the console and the graphical desktop—and neither configuration impacts remote login access.

From the Gnome desktop, use System ⇨ Preferences ⇨ Keyboard to select an alternate layout. Changing the layout takes effect immediately, but it only impacts the graphical desktop.

TIP While you can only have one default keyboard, you can load multiple layouts. Under Layout Options, select the key combination to switch between keyboard layouts. For example, you can choose to press both Alt keys at the same time to switch the keyboard mode (the *mode switch*).

Changing the console's configuration is nearly as painless. With Hardy Heron (8.04 LTS) and later Ubuntu versions, reselect the console's keyboard using `sudo dpkg-reconfigure console-setup`. This command will allow you to select the appropriate keyboard model, nationality, and additional key sets for your keyboard.

For older Ubuntu systems, such as Dapper Drake (6.06 LTS), install `console-tools` (`sudo apt-get install console-tools`). Then, use `sudo kbd-config` to reconfigure the console's keyboard.

Understanding Keyboards

Keyboards are one of the most complex subsystems in the entire operating system. Each button on the keyboard generates a raw value called the *scancode*. There are two scancodes per key, one for key down and the other for key up.

The operating system maps the scancodes to keycodes. *Keycodes* are the actual letters that appears on the screen. So the "a" key generates a scancode that the keyboard driver maps to the keycode that represents the letter "a". When you set the keyboard layout, you assign a default scancode-to-keycode mapping table.

Viewing the actual scancodes and keycodes requires a terminal window. Press Ctrl+Alt+F2 to get to a console window and log in.

- `showkey -s`: This command displays the scancode of every key you press. Most keys generate 1-byte scancodes. However, some keys, such as the Menu, Scroll Lock, and arrow keys generate multibyte scancodes. Every key on the keyboard generates different scancodes. Even the left shift is differentiated from the right shift. The only exceptions are special function keys, like those found on laptops. These do not generate scancodes but do alter the scancodes returned from other keys.

TIP The `showkey` program exits after 10 seconds of inactivity. When you finish, stop pressing keys for 10 seconds. Pressing Ctrl+C and other break sequences will not stop the program.

- `showkey -k`: This command shows the mapped keycodes from the scancodes. If you do not have the proper keyboard layout, then some keys will not generate keycodes.

Enabling Unused Keys

You won't be able to use a keyboard key if there is no keycode associated with the scancode. Moreover, every application that uses a custom keyboard driver tracks its own keyboard mapping. This means that you will need to map keycodes for both the console and graphical desktop.

Mapping Console Keys

The kernel includes a set of built-in mappings that are standard among keyboard manufacturers. Additional mappings can be created in the boot-time keymap, which is used by the console. The location of the boot-time keymap varies by operating system. For example:

- Dapper Drake (6.06 LTS) and Hardy Heron (8.04 LTS) use `/etc/console/boottime.kmap.gz`.

- Jaunty Jackalope (9.04) uses `/etc/console-setup/boottime.kmap.gz`.

- Karmic Koala (9.10) uses `/etc/console-setup/cached.kmap.gz`.

The compressed keymap (kmap) file contains lines that follow a basic format:

```
[modifier] keycode number = keysym keysym keysym...
```

The keycode's number is effectively the scancode value. It may be in decimal or hex. The key symbols (keysym) define the keycodes that are generated. Usually there is one or two keysym values listed. The first is the basic, unmodified key, and the second is a combination with the shift key.

The keysym value can be a character, like "a" or a common name. The keyboard driver recognizes names like grave and asciitilde, so the actual character is not required in the file.

For example, Hardy Heron's default keymap file maps scancode 6 to the "5" key, and shift with the scancode is a percent (%). Other key combinations include holding down the modifiers Control, Alt, and Alt+Shift.

```
keycode   6 = five          percent
        control keycode   6 = Control_bracketright
        alt     keycode   6 = Meta_five
        shift   alt   keycode   6 = Meta_percent
```

KEYMAP STRINGS AND COMPOSITION

The keymap file contains other types of mappings. For example, strings can be assigned to a scancode. If a single scancode is seen, it can generate a series of letters. Defining string F9 = "Hello" **will generate** Hello **every time you press F9. The default configuration assigns ASCII terminal escape sequences to function keys.**

The keymap also includes composition mappings. Using the compose key (found on non-English keyboards), you can select two keys and generate a character. For example, the default setting includes compose 'a' 'e' to '<E6>'. **Pressing the compose key followed by "a" and "e" will create the ae ligature, æ (character 0xE6).**

Of course, using this composition requires a Compose key on your keyboard. Since the Compose key is usually not found on U.S. keyboards, you will need to define one. For example, on my keyboard keycode 100 **is the right Alt key (also called Alt Graph or AltGr). Using** keycode 100 = Compose **allows me to redefine the key to be the Compose key. Then, I can press** Compose " y (pressing one key at a time) to generate a ÿ character.**

To create your own keyboard mapping, start with the current mapping.

1. Press Ctrl+Alt+F2 and log in to the text console.

2. Uncompress the current boot-time keymap or generate a new one by using dumpkeys.

```
cd $HOME
zcat /etc/console/boottime.kmap.gz > boottime.kmap # Hardy or Dapper
dumpkeys > boottime.kmap # all versions of Ubuntu
```

3. Edit the uncompressed keymap file, and insert your own mappings.

4. Recompress the file using gzip, and replace the old file.

5. Load the new keymap.

```
sudo loadkeys /etc/console/boottime.kmap.gz # Hardy or Dapper
```

Your new keymap will be activated when you load it, and it will be loaded with each reboot.

Mapping Desktop Keys

The X-server manages the desktop key mappings. The command xmodmap -pke displays the list of keycode and keysym mappings. The keysym mappings are: keycode *num* = *1 2 3 4*... where the positions are:

1. The unmodified key.
2. Shift+key.
3. Mode_switch+key. The mode switch key sequence alternates the keyboard layout mode.
4. Shift+Mode_switch+key.

NOTE Don't be surprised if xmodmap -pke shows keycodes without keysym values. The keycode comes from your keyboard, and there are some codes that your keyboard cannot generate.

For example, the default U.S. keyboard layout maps keycode 29 to the letter Y:

```
keycode  29 = y Y
```

I can assign an alternate mode using:

```
xmodmap -e "keycode 29 = y Y yen cent"
```

This maps the keyboard character ''y'' to the letter ''y'' and shift+y generates a capital ''Y''. Pressing the mode-switch key (such as Alt+Alt) enables the alternate mode, where the keyboard character ''y'' generates a Japanese Yen symbol (¥) and shift+y creates a cent symbol (¢). Pressing the mode switch again returns to the letter mode.

Altering Keycode Assignments

To find a particular keycode, open a command prompt and use the X Event Tester (xev) program. This pops up a small window and displays every X-server event, including mouse movements and key presses, in the terminal window. For example, pressing the ''h'' key displays the key-down event, key-up event, keycode value, and any active keysym values (see Figure 4-1).

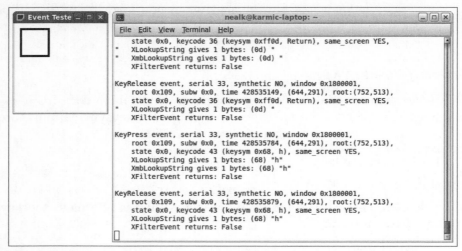

Figure 4-1: The xev application, showing keycodes

To modify the active keyboard map, use xmodmap -e *expression*. The *expression* assigns a keycode to a set of keysym values. However, this assignment will only remain until you log out.

For a permanent configuration, create $HOME/.xmodmap and list your keyboard changes. The changes will only take effect when you log in (not other users), and Gnome will prompt you about using a new .xmodmap.

TIP After creating .xmodmap, test it using the command xmodmap .xmodmap. Be sure to correct any errors; otherwise, the configuration will not load.

For a systemwide configuration change, consider adding the xmodmap commands to /etc/X11/xinit/xinirrc or /etc/X11/Xsession.

SHAS'T NOS FUNNY!

There's an old practical joke where people pry the keys off a keyboard and replace them out of order. A user who is not a touch typist can get really confused when looking for the right letters. The xmodmap command can be used as an excellent alternative to this prank. For example, you can add the following commands to the victim's .bashrc file:

```
xmodmap -e 'keycode 91 = t T'
xmodmap -e 'keycode 92 = s S'
```

This prank swaps the s and t keys on the keyboard without requiring any physical keyboard modifications. Alternately, if you can pry up and replace the keys on the keyboard, follow it up by remapping the keyboard so that the keycodes match the keysym values! Be sure to wear tennis shoes if you do this, since your coworker will either get a big laugh out of it, or you will need to run.

Running Commands with the Push of a Button

Now that you can identify unused keys and map them to characters, it is time to put them to use. The X-server includes some special-function keysym values. For example, XF86WWW and XF86HomePage are the buttons that should start your web browser. My keyboard includes a special key that looks like a globe; xev identifies it as keycode 180. This button is supposed to start my web browser. To make it fully functional, I need to make the following changes:

1. Use xmodmap to assign the key to the XF86HomePage keysym:

   ```
   xmodmap -e 'keycode 180 = XF86HomePage'
   ```

2. Open System ➪ Preferences ➪ Keyboard Shortcuts.

3. Scroll down to the "Launch web browser" setting.

4. Click on the shortcut. It will prompt for you to select a new shortcut key.

5. Press the globe key, and the shortcut should say XF86HomePage. Now, every time you press the globe button, it will start up a new web browser.

TIP If you like this hack, then be sure to either add `keycode 180 = XF86HomePage` to $HOME/.xmodmap, or add the entire xmodmap line to /etc/X11/xinit/xinitrc. Otherwise, this change will be lost the next time you log in.

Besides the default events listed in the Keyboard Shortcuts applet, you can define your own. Use the graphical gconf-editor or command-line gconftool-2 to alter your Gnome configuration. There are 12 run_command options under /apps/metacity/global_keybindings. These allow you to bind key combinations to commands. The commands to run when the binding is found are listed under /apps/metacity/keybinding_commands. For example, to map Alt+Shift+T so that it opens a new terminal window, use:

```
gconftool-2 -t str -s /apps/metacity/global_keybindings/run_command_9 \
  '<Alt><Shift>t'
gconftool-2 -t str -s /apps/metacity/keybinding_commands/command_9 \
  'gnome-terminal --geometry 80x40'
```

Of course, the predefined events in the Keyboard Shortcuts and 12 user-defined sequences may not be enough for some people. In that case, use xbindkeys to associate any arbitrary key sequence with a shell command.

1. Install xbindkeys.

```
sudo apt-get install xbindkeys
```

2. Create a configuration file. The program looks for $HOME/.xbindkeysrc. You can create a default configuration using:

```
xbindkeys --defaults > $HOME/.xbindkeysrc
```

3. Each mapping consists of two lines. The first is a quoted string containing the command to run. The second is indented and lists the key combinations. For example:

```
"gnome-terminal --geometry 80x40"
  alt + shift + t
```

TIP xbindkeys **is not limited by the type of key combination. For example,** control + b:1 + alt **will run the command when the combination control key, alt key, and mouse button #1 (left mouse button) are pressed at the same time.**

4. Run the xbindkeys daemon. For a permanent configuration, be sure to add xbindkeys & to /etc/X11/Xsession.

OUT OF KEY

With Jaunty Jackalope and Karmic Koala, the audio volume control on my Toshiba laptop causes the popup notification box to go bonkers and freezes the desktop. This happens because the dial generates an infinite stream of key volume events. Adding to this problem, the little dial is far too easy to bump.

If you experience this problem, then consider disabling the volume dial. One way do this is to open the Keyboard Shortcuts and remove the Volume Up and Volume Down shortcuts by pressing the backspace key. Alternately, you can use xmodmap to remove the key assignments.

```
$ xmodmap -pke | grep -e XF86AudioRaise -e XF86AudioLower
keycode 122 = XF86AudioLowerVolume NoSymbol XF86AudioLowerVolume
        NoSymbol XF86AudioLowerVolume
keycode 123 = XF86AudioRaiseVolume NoSymbol XF86AudioRaiseVolume
        NoSymbol XF86AudioRaiseVolume
$ xmodmap -e 'keycode 122 = NoSymbol'
$ xmodmap -e 'keycode 123 = NoSymbol'
```

If you need volume control, you can always map it to a different key setting. For example, I installed a command-line audio mixer (sudo apt-get install `aumix`). **The following code for** `xbindkeys` **maps two key sequences that alter the volume level by 10%.**

```
"aumix -v+10"
  Control+Shift+F7
"aumix -v-10"
  Control+Shift+F6
```

Examples of Keyboard Shortcuts

There are many great shortcuts that can be mapped to key combinations. For example, my system contains the following mappings:

- The left Super key (usually has a Microsoft logo on PC keyboards or a flower symbol on Macs) is mapped to Audio Mute. When the phone rings, I may not be able to quickly stop every music player, web page with background sounds, and other audio applications. Instead, I press Super_L and immediately mute the entire computer. Pressing it again unmutes the system.

- While Macintosh keyboards have a button to eject the CD, most PC keyboards lack this button. My Menu key (found on the bottom right, next to the Control key) ejects the CD-ROM drive.

- The key combination Alt+Shift+B immediately starts a systemwide backup. I also installed the `notify-send` command (`sudo apt-get install libnotify-bin`). This way, completed backups show a notification popup on the desktop, and the message remains up for 60 seconds.

  ```
  notify-send -t 60000 "Backup completed"
  ```

- Control+Alt+b:2 (using `xbindkeys`, the middle mouse button) runs `"sleep 1; xkill"`. This allows me to click on any window and immediately kill it. (The `sleep` statement provides time to release the key sequence. Otherwise, `xkill` cannot grab the cursor.)

- The combination Alt+Shift+G runs my favorite game (`bzflag`).

Many of the Gnome applications use Ctrl+*key* and Alt+*key* combinations. I generally stay away from using these in customized key sequences because of potential conflicts. However, three-key combinations, including Ctrl+Alt+*key* and Alt+Shift+*key*, rarely conflict with other applications. Similarly, the Super_L and Super_R keys are usually not used by other applications.

Trapping Ctrl+Alt+Delete

The Ctrl+Alt+Delete (CAD) key sequence has a special historical function. In the good old days, it was used to immediately reboot the computer. Later Linux versions modified it to perform a clean reboot (with a proper shutdown), while Microsoft Windows uses it to bring up the list of running processes.

Today, different versions of Linux either have the CAD key sequence enabled or disabled. With Ubuntu, this key sequence is enabled but does different things depending on the system's state.

For example, if you log in to the graphical desktop, then the Gnome desktop intercepts the CAD sequence. Pressing CAD brings up the Shutdown menu, allowing you to choose to Shutdown, Logoff, or Restart, or perform other operations. However, what if you really want CAD to reboot and not see a menu selection? The easiest option is to modify what happens when CAD is intercepted by the desktop.

```
gconftool-2 -t str --set \
 /apps/metacity/global_keybindings/run_command_10 '<Control><Alt>Delete'
gconftool-2 -t str --set /apps/metacity/keybinding_commands/command_10 \
  'gksudo reboot'
```

These two commands bind CAD to command #10, and command #10 will run `gksudo reboot`. Pressing CAD will graphically prompt you for your password (because `reboot` must run as root) and then reboot the computer.

An alternative to rebooting is to show a process list, similar to pressing CAD under Microsoft Windows. To do this, map CAD to the `gnome-system-monitor`. The monitor allows you to see running processes and terminate programs as needed.

```
gconftool-2 -t str --set \
 /apps/metacity/global_keybindings/run_command_10 '<Control><Alt>Delete'
gconftool-2 -t str --set /apps/metacity/keybinding_commands/command_10 \
  'gnome-system-monitor'
```

SYSTEM REQUESTS

The desktop intercepts the Ctrl+Alt+Delete key sequence, so it does not immediately reboot the system. However, Linux adds in a few other key sequences that use the System Request key—the SysRq key is the same as the Print Scrn key.

To immediately reboot the computer, press Alt+SysRq+b. (The b stands for boot.) This is faster than doing a `shutdown` or running the `reboot` command; it is just like pulling the power on the computer. Similarly, Alt+SysRq+o immediately turns the computer off.

> The problem is, Alt+SysRq+b and Alt+SysRq+o do not sync the disks or cleanly terminate processes the way that `shutdown` or `reboot` does. At minimum, consider pressing Alt+SysRq+s to sync the disks before rebooting with Alt+SysRq+b.
>
> You can disable SysRq by editing `/etc/sysctl.conf` and adding in `kernel.sysrq=0`. Then, run `sudo sysctl -p` to reload the configuration.
>
> But what if you just want to reboot? To properly reboot the system, leave the graphical desktop by pressing Ctrl+Alt+F2. This brings up a text terminal (you don't need to log in). At the terminal, press Ctrl+Alt+Delete. This will perform a proper shutdown and reboot the computer.

Disabling Ctrl+Alt+Delete

Depending on your requirements, you may want to prevent CAD from rebooting the system. For example, disable CAD on a critical server to prevent someone from playing with the keyboard and cycling the system. How you disable it depends on your Ubuntu version.

Disabling Ctrl+Alt+Delete with Init

With pre–Hardy Heron systems, such as Dapper Drake (6.06 LTS), CAD is handed by `init`.

1. Edit the `/etc/inittab` file:

   ```
   sudo vi /etc/inittab
   ```

2. Find the line that says:

   ```
   ca:12345:ctrlaltdel:/sbin/shutdown -t1 -a -r now
   ```

   This line says, for all init levels (1, 2, . . . 5), run the shutdown command and reboot now.

3. To disable CAD, comment out the line by inserting # at the beginning of the line:

   ```
   #ca:12345:ctrlaltdel:/sbin/shutdown -t1 -a -r now
   ```

4. To alter the CAD action, change the `/sbin/shutdown` command to run your own program. For example, you may want to send an alert to an administrator or play some disco music to let the user know that CAD is outdated.

   ```
   ca:12345:ctrlaltdel:/usr/bin/play /home/nealk/disco.mp3 > /dev/null
   ```

Only one application can use the audio driver at a time, so this will only play music if nothing else is playing.

5. After changing the `inittab` file, reload it using: `sudo telinit q`.

> **WARNING** Unmapped keyboard signals can be lost. If you disable CAD, then you may find that you cannot reenable it without rebooting the system. But if you change the functionality (without disabling the command) then you do not need to reboot.

TELL INIT

The `init` process is the parent of all processes. It kicks off processes to start and stop at different run levels. For example, runlevel 1 is a single-user mode. It contains a minimal number of running processes and is usually used to fix a broken system. Usually Ubuntu operates at runlevel 2, supporting multiple users and graphics. To view the current and previous runlevel, use the `runlevel` command. (If there was no previous runlevel, then N is displayed.)

If you want to tell `init` to change run levels, use the `telinit` command. For example, to switch from the current runlevel to single-user mode, change to a text window (Ctrl+Alt+F1) and use `sudo telinit 1`.

Running the shutdown command is similar to running `sudo telinit 0`. Runlevel 0 is the shutdown mode.

The file `/etc/inittab` tells `init` what to do at each run level, what processes to spawn, and how to handle hardware signals, such as Ctrl+Alt+Delete, and power modes, such as low battery. After modifying the `inittab`, you will need to tell `init` to reexamine (query) the file. This is done by using `sudo telinit q`.

Disabling Ctrl+Alt+Delete with Upstart

Beginning with Hardy Heron (8.04 LTS), Upstart is used to intercept the CAD sequence. Although the file that handles the intercept configuration is different from `init`, the basic hack remains the same.

1. Edit the `/etc/event.d/control-alt-delete.conf` file (or `/etc/init/control-alt-delete.conf` with Karmic Koala 9.10).

2. Find the line that says:

```
exec shutdown -r now "Control-Alt-Delete pressed"
```

3. To disable CAD, comment out the line by inserting # at the beginning of the line:

```
# exec shutdown -r now "Control-Alt-Delete pressed"
```

4. To alter the CAD action, change the `shutdown` command to run your own program.

5. After changing the file, reload it using: `sudo telinit q`. The `telinit` command informs Upstart to reload the configuration.

Blinking Keyboard Lights

Besides being an input device, keyboards have the ability to provide a limited amount of feedback to the user. The typical keyboard has three lights that identify when CapsLock, NumLock, and ScrollLock are engaged. However, the lights can be used to represent other kinds of information. For example:

- **Alternate keyboards:** Under System ➪ Preferences ➪ Keyboards are configurable Layout Options. One of the options is to use the keyboard LEDs to identify when an alternate keyboard layout is in use.

- **Network monitor:** The `tleds` program monitors network traffic. By default, the NumLock light blinks whenever a packet is received, and ScrollLock flashes with packet transmits.

```
sudo apt-get install tleds
sudo /etc/init.d/tleds start
```

NOTE The blinking from `tleds` can get annoying very quickly. Consider using it for debugging network connectivity or monitoring traffic from relatively isolated systems (where there should be very little network traffic). You can also use it in server rooms, for that boss who associates blinking lights with productivity.

- **E-mail notification:** The `ixbiff` program (`sudo apt-get install ixbiff`) is great for single-user systems. The program monitors up to three directories for incoming e-mail. When new e-mail is received, the associated keyboard light blinks to let you know that you have new mail. After you check your e-mail, the lights stop blinking. For example, my `/etc/ixbuff.conf` monitors `/var/mail/` and `/home/nealk/mail/` for new e-mail.

```
led2 = "/home/nealk/mail"
led3 = "/var/mail"
```

TIP `ixbiff` monitors all e-mail folders in the specified directory. To monitor a single file, make a directory and create a symbolic link to the specific e-mail folder:

```
mkdir $HOME/mail; ln -s /var/mail/nealk $HOME/mail/nealk
```

BURNT OUT LIGHTS

There are other programs to toggle the keyboard LEDs, but many do not always work correctly. For example, the `xset` command claims to support toggling keyboard lights (`xset led 1` or `xset -led 2`). However, it does not work on all keyboards. (Some forums report problems dating back to 1999.) The `xset` command may do nothing depending on your configuration.

The `setleds` command (`sudo apt-get console-tools`) works great from a terminal console but not from the graphical desktop. Other programs, such as `mailleds` and `ledcontrol`, do not work properly on my systems.

In general, the keyboard lights can only be managed by one application. If one program is already managing the LEDs, then another program will either be unable to set the lights or both programs will compete by overwriting the LED settings. In other words, don't use `ixbiff` and `tleds` at the same time.

Changing Xorg.conf

The X-server provides the base graphics used by Gnome, KDE, and other desktops. It also manages common input devices, such as keyboards, mice, and tablets. Configuration changes to these devices require editing `/etc/X11/xorg.conf` and restarting the X-server.

For configuring the system, it is best to run the server manually.

1. Press Ctrl+Alt+F2 to get to a text console and log in.

2. Stop the running desktop.

   ```
   sudo /etc/init.d/gdm stop
   ```

3. If you are running Karmic Koala (9.10), then you won't have an `xorg.conf`. The system relies of default settings. To generate `xorg.conf`, use:

   ```
   Xorg -configure  # create xorg.conf.new in the current directory
   sudo cp xorg.conf.new /etc/X11/xorg.conf # copy and install
   ```

4. Make a backup of the working `/etc/X11/xorg.conf`.

5. Make whatever changes are necessary to `xorg.conf`.

6. Start the server manually by running `startx`.

TIP There are other options for restarting the X-server. For example, Ctrl+Alt+Backspace immediately restarts the server. However, beginning with Jaunty (9.04) this key sequence is disabled. See Chapter 10 for information on reenabling it.

One of two things will happen when you start the X-server. Either it will start up your desktop or it will spew a ton of text and abort, leaving you back at the text terminal. All of the logs are recorded in `/var/log/Xorg.0.log`. Use the logs to diagnose the problem. Most likely, the `xorg.conf` contains one or more invalid entries.

When you are done tuning the X-server configuration, exit the graphical desktop and restart the system using `sudo /etc/init.d/gdm start`.

TIP If you feel that you have totally corrupted your `xorg.conf` settings, copy back the backup file. In the worst case, you can always reset to the default installation using:

```
sudo dpkg-reconfigure xserver-xorg
```

Supporting Serial Mice

One of the first problems I encountered when installing Ubuntu was the mouse. By default, Ubuntu only supports a USB mouse, but my mouse uses the serial port. This problem is resolved by editing the `/etc/X11/xorg.conf` file, which describes the screens and input devices that should be used with the graphical desktop.

1. As root, make a backup of `/etc/X11/xorg.conf`.

   ```
   sudo cp /etc/X11/xorg.conf /etc/X11/xorg.conf.original
   ```

2. Edit the file. You may want to make the window wide enough so that lines do not wrap.

   ```
   sudo gedit /etc/X11/xorg.conf
   ```

3. Search for the sections titled `"InputDevice"`. One will refer to the keyboard with an identifier like `"Generic Keyboard"` or `"Keyboard0"` and the other will refer to the mouse (`"Configured Mouse"` or `"Mouse0"`).

4. Add a new section after the mouse for the serial mouse. In this example, the mouse is on `/dev/ttyS0` (first serial port). Other port options include `/dev/psaux` (for a PS/2 mouse) and `/dev/ttyS1` for the second serial port. This example configuration also supports three-button emulation, whereby pressing the left and right mouse buttons acts the same as pressing the middle mouse button. If you have a three-button mouse, then you can choose to leave this line out of the configuration. Other options include specifying the mouse protocol, such as "Microsoft" or "Logitech" for most serial mice, and "PS/2" for a PS/2 mouse.

   ```
   Section "InputDevice"
           Identifier      "Serial Mouse"
           Driver          "mouse"
           Option          "CorePointer"
   ```

```
        Option          "Device"            "/dev/ttyS0"
        Option          "Emulate3Buttons"   "true"
#       Option          "Protocol"          "Microsoft"
#       Option          "Protocol"          "Logitech"
#       Option          "Protocol"          "PS/2"
EndSection
```

5. Go to the ServerLayout section. Add a line for the serial mouse.

```
Section "ServerLayout"
        Identifier      "Default Layout"
        Screen          "Default Screen"
        InputDevice     "Generic Keyboard"
        InputDevice     "Configured Mouse"
        InputDevice     "Serial Mouse" "SendCoreEvents"
        InputDevice     "stylus" "SendCoreEvents"
        InputDevice     "cursor" "SendCoreEvents"
        InputDevice     "eraser" "SendCoreEvents"
EndSection
```

TIP If you leave in the original mouse configuration (such as "Configured Mouse" for the USB mouse), then you can connect a USB mouse at any time and have it immediately work. There is no configuration conflict from having multiple mouse definitions.

6. Save your changes and restart the X-server.

When the system comes up, moving the serial mouse should work.

Debugging Xorg.conf

There are a few things that could go wrong here. First, you could have entered the wrong information for your mouse (for example, specifying /dev/ttyS0 instead of /dev/ttyS1) or the wrong protocol (such as Microsoft instead of Logitech). This appears as a mouse pointer that does not move. You can press Ctrl+Alt+F2 to get to a command prompt where you can stop the X-server and re-edit your /etc/X11/xorg.conf file.

The other common problem is a black screen (maybe with a cursor blinking). This means that you did something wrong and the server failed to start. Use Alt+F3 (or Ctrl+Alt+F3—both key combinations work) to get to a command prompt where you can edit the /etc/X11/xorg.conf file. Look in the /var/log/Xorg.0.log file for error messages. Common things that can go wrong include:

- **Typographical error**—A mistake when entering the configuration file can stop the server from booting.

- **Driver conflict**—If you have another device using the same driver (such as two mice definitions that both specify /dev/ttyS0), then there is a driver conflict with the serial mouse. That will block the server.

Unfortunately, if the server crashes, you will be unable to restart it with Ctrl+Alt+Backspace. Instead, use `startx` to bring up the X-server. If the server fails, it will display a lot of debugging information that you can use to resolve the problem. In the worst case, restore from the backup file (`sudo cp /etc/X11/xorg.conf.backup /etc/X11/xorg.conf`) and try again. When you finally have a working X-server, you can run `sudo /etc/init.d/gdm restart` to restart the graphical login.

Enabling Extra Mouse Buttons

The built-in functionality found in computer mice keeps changing. First there was one button, then two, then three. Then someone added in a scroll wheel. Today, newer mice have a scroll wheel that toggles left and right—the toggles are two more mouse buttons. If your mouse has all of these buttons, then how can you put them to use?

The `xmodmap` command maps buttons for both keyboards and mice. While `-pke` prints keyboard expressions, `-pp` prints pointer mappings. The `xmodmap -pp` command lists physical buttons and button codes; it usually lists many more buttons than found on your mouse. The default button codes are:

- Buttons 1, 2, and 3 are the left, middle, and right buttons. With left-handed mice, the buttons are reversed.
- Buttons 4 and 5 are the vertical scroll wheel.
- Buttons 6 and 7 are for the horizontal scroll wheel.

Use `xev` to identify any extra mouse buttons. With the mouse over the `xev` window, press each mouse button and spin every scroll wheel. Each should generate a press and release event.

```
ButtonPress event, serial 26, synthetic NO, window 0x4200001,
    root 0x93, subw 0x0, time 3342078709, (102,103), root:(112,176),
    state 0x0, button 6, same_screen YES

ButtonRelease event, serial 26, synthetic NO, window 0x4200001,
    root 0x93, subw 0x0, time 3342078709, (102,103), root:(112,176),
    state 0x0, button 6, same_screen YES

ButtonPress event, serial 26, synthetic NO, window 0x4200001,
    root 0x93, subw 0x0, time 3342081421, (102,103), root:(112,176),
    state 0x0, button 7, same_screen YES

ButtonRelease event, serial 26, synthetic NO, window 0x4200001,
    root 0x93, subw 0x0, time 3342081421, (102,103), root:(112,176),
    state 0x0, button 7, same_screen YES
```

Reassigning buttons requires listing the physical buttons in the order that matches the button code's position. For example, to swap the left and right mouse buttons, use `xmodmap -e "pointer = 3 2 1"`. This maps physical button 3 to button code 1 (position 1), and button 1 to code 3. Similarly, if the vertical scrolling is reversed, you can swap it using `"pointer = 1 2 3 5 4"`.

For a permanent change, add the pointer configuration to `$HOME/.xmodmap` or include it in the mouse section of `/etc/X11/xorg.conf`. For example, my Hardy Heron `xorg.conf` includes button modifications (in bold):

```
Section "InputDevice"
        Identifier      "Configured Mouse"
        Driver          "mouse"
        Option          "CorePointer"
        Option          "Protocol" "evdev"
        Option "Buttons" "8"
        Option "ButtonMapping" "1 2 3 6 7 8 4 5"
        Option "XAxisMapping" "4 5"
        Option "YAxisMapping" "6 7"
        Option "HWHEELRelativeAxisButtons" "7 6"
        Option "VWHEELRelativeAxisButtons" "4 5"
        Option "Emulate3Buttons" "no"
EndSection
```

All of the `xorg.conf` mouse options are optional. The options include defining the number of buttons (`Buttons`), mapping physical buttons to button codes (`ButtonMapping`), specifying the horizontal and vertical scroll buttons, and indicating whether the middle mouse button (#2) can be emulated by pressing the left and right buttons at the same time.

Supporting a Touch Pad

Another type of pointing device that you will likely come across is a touch pad. Touch pads are very common with laptops. Normally, these are identified by the mouse driver and used without any additional configuration.

On pre–Hardy Heron systems (before 2008), the default mouse driver did not support special features such as double-tapping the pad in place of double-clicking, or hot corners in place of shortcuts. These features can be added through the Synaptics mouse driver.

```
sudo apt-get install xserver-xorg-input-synaptics
```

TIP Beginning with Hardy Heron (8.04), the Synaptics TouchPad driver is installed by default.

As with other devices, you will need to install the device driver, configure `/etc/X11/xorg.conf`, and restart the X-server. The basic `"InputDevice"` section will look something like this:

```
Section "InputDevice"
  Identifier "Synaptics Touchpad"
  Driver "synaptics"
  Option "SendCoreEvents" "true"
  Option "Device" "/dev/psaux"
  Option "Protocol" "auto-dev"
  Option "HorizScrollDelta" "0"
  Option "SHMConfig" "on"
EndSection
```

You will also need to add `InputDevice "Synaptics Touchpad"` to the `"ServerLayout"` section of `xorg.conf` and restart the X-server.

Tuning Ubuntu on a Macintosh

Many versions of Linux have been ported to the Macintosh. Unfortunately, Dapper Drake (6.06 LTS) was the last Ubuntu version to include an official port with support for Macintosh hardware. However, ports for other platforms, including the Mac, are available from `http://cdimage.ubuntu.com/ports/`. (These ports are not official and lack the same level of community support.)

For anyone trying to use Ubuntu on a Mac, there are some very notable differences. Some PC features do not exist on the Mac, and some Mac features lack support under Ubuntu.

Using a One-Button Mouse in a Three-Button World

The biggest issue with using Ubuntu on a Mac is the lack of a three-button mouse. Under Ubuntu, the left mouse button performs actions, such as selecting icons and moving windows. The right button brings up menus, and the middle button is used for pasting from the clipboard.

TIP There are many different types of PC mice. Some have only two buttons. The middle button can be emulated by clicking both the right and left buttons at the same time. Others have a scroll wheel that can be pushed in for the third button.

Most Macs include a one-button mouse. If you swap the one-button mouse for a three-button model, it will work fine with Ubuntu. However, if you do not want to swap hardware then how do you use the other buttons?

By default, Ubuntu on the Mac (PowerPC platform) maps the F11 and F12 keys to the middle and right mouse buttons. This is configured in the `/etc/sysctl.conf` file. On the PowerPC installation, this file contains the following additional lines:

```
# Emulate the middle mouse button with F11 and the right with F12.
dev/mac_hid/mouse_button_emulation = 1
dev/mac_hid/mouse_button2_keycode = 87
dev/mac_hid/mouse_button3_keycode = 88
```

On a Mac, keycode 87 is F11 and keycode 88 is F12.

Missing Keys and Functionality

PC keyboards usually do not look like Mac keyboards. The standard 104-key PC keyboard contains many extra keys that are not found on a Mac. Some of the missing keys include:

- **Two Alt keys**—Every Mac keyboard has a left Alt key (Alt_L), but the right Alt key (Alt_R) is not always present.

- **Two Ctrl keys**—While Control_L always exists, Control_R may be missing on some Mac keyboards.

- **System keys**—The Print Screen, System Request, Scroll Lock, Pause, and Break keys are missing. With Ubuntu on a PC, the Print Screen button is mapped to the screen capture application. Without this button, you will need to remap the functionality to another key combination.

- **Edit keys**—Most PC keyboards have a set of keys for Insert, Delete, Home, End, Page Up, and Page Down. Although Mac keyboards do have Page Up and Page Down, they are not in the same location as a PC keyboard. Different Mac keyboards can have very different keys. For example, the Mac iBook G4 has Home/End, while the older iMac G3 keyboard has Home and Help (where Help generates the same keycode as Insert).

- **Windows keys**—The Windows keys do not exist on the Mac keyboard (for obvious reasons). Similarly, the Menu key does not exist.

- **Numeric keyboard**—Although they are usually not labeled on the Mac, the numeric keyboard does have the same arrows (KP_Up, KP_Down, KP_Left, and KP_Right) and navigation keys as a standard PC keyboard.

WARNING Many Mac keyboards do not have an indicator light to show when NumLock is enabled, so switching between keypad navigation and numeric entry may be confusing.

There are also some keys that exist on the Mac but not on the PC. By default, these are not mapped to anything but they can be mapped to other keys.

- **Command keys**—On a Macintosh keyboard, there is at least one and possibly two Command keys. These are located on either side of the spacebar and are labeled with a flower pattern. Mac users call this the Apple or Command key. Under Linux, it is called the Super key. The left one (Super_L) is mapped to keycode 115 and the right key (Super_R) is keycode 116.

■ **Keypad Equal (=)**—On a standard PC keyboard, there is no equal sign on the numeric keypad, but there is one on the Mac. This key is mapped to keycode 157 but is not mapped to any keyboard value.

NOTE Specialized keyboards may have additional keys, such as volume up/down, power, and even buttons labeled for e-mail or the web. Each generates a distinct keycode. Use xev to see the codes. This way, you can map the keys to functions.

Remapping the Command and Alt Keys

One of the biggest distinctions for Mac users is the use of the Command key. Under Mac OS, this key modifier is used for most shortcuts. For example, Command+W closes the window and Command+Q quits an application. Under Ubuntu and on most PC operating systems, the Ctrl key has the same usage (for example, Ctrl+W instead of Command+W). Adding to the confusion, a PC keyboard has Alt next to the spacebar, whereas a Mac has the Command keys in that location. What this means is that a Mac user running Ubuntu will need to learn how to use the Alt key instead of the Command key, or just remap the keys.

To remap the Command keys, use xmodmap. The easiest way to remap the Command keys is to simply change the modifiers. First, remove the Control and Command keys, then add the Ctrl keys again.

```
xmodmap -e "remove control = Control_L Control_R" # unmap control
xmodmap -e "remove mod4 = Super_L Super_R"         # unmap old Super keys
xmodmap -e "add control = Super_L Super_R"         # map Super to Ctrl
```

Alternately, you could actually remap the Command and Ctrl keys.

```
xmodmap -e "remove control = Control_L Control_R" # unmap Ctrl
xmodmap -e "remove mod4 = Super_L Super_R"         # unmap super
xmodmap -e "keycode 115 = Control_L Control_L"     # map Command to Alt
xmodmap -e "keycode 116 = Control_R Control_R"     # map Command to Alt
xmodmap -e "keycode 64 = Super_L Super_L"          # map Alt to Command
xmodmap -e "keycode 113 = Super_R Super_R"         # map Alt to Command
xmodmap -e "add control = Control_L Control_R"     # map new Ctrl to Ctrl
```

Mapping the keyboard using xmodmap only creates a temporary change. If you reboot the computer or restart the X-server, the changes will be lost. To make the changes permanent, add the xmodmap commands to

/etc/X11/xinit/xinitrc for systemwide changes. Alternately, you can add the specific mappings to $HOME/.xmodmap for an individual user's configuration.

```
remove control = Control_L Control_R
keycode 115 = Super_L Super_L
keycode 116 = Super_R Super_R
remove mod4 = Super_L
add control = Super_L Super_R
```

Supporting USB Devices

Ubuntu supports many types of USB devices. Some devices are recognized instantly and are very usable, but others need additional drivers and some configuration. The first step for configuring a USB device is simple enough: plug it in. The core USB kernel driver should immediately recognize that a USB device has been connected. You can check this with the lsusb command.

```
$ lsusb
Bus 004 Device 001: ID 1d6b:0001 Linux Foundation 1.1 root hub
Bus 003 Device 002: ID 056a:0014 Wacom Co., Ltd
Bus 003 Device 001: ID 1d6b:0001 Linux Foundation 1.1 root hub
Bus 001 Device 002: ID 04f2:b008 Chicony Electronics Co.,
              Ltd USB 2.0 Camera
Bus 001 Device 001: ID 1d6b:0002 Linux Foundation 2.0 root hub
Bus 005 Device 001: ID 1d6b:0001 Linux Foundation 1.1 root hub
Bus 002 Device 001: ID 1d6b:0001 Linux Foundation 1.1 root hub
```

You should also see the device listed at the end of /var/log/messages.

```
$ dmesg | grep usb
[  113.596064] usb 3-1: new low speed USB device using uhci_hcd and
                           address 2
[  113.770293] usb 3-1: configuration #1 chosen from 1 choice
[  113.773363] input: Wacom Graphire3 6x8 as
/devices/pci0000:00/0000:00:1d.1/usb3/3-1/3-1:1.0/input/input10
```

USB supports hot-plug devices. This means that USB devices can be disconnected and reconnected without advance notice to the operating system. The operating system will not crash or become unstable just because a USB device is suddenly unplugged.

WARNING Although the core USB subsystem permits disconnections at any time, other subsystems can have problems. Disconnecting a USB thumb drive while it is being written to can corrupt the thumb drive's partition, and disconnecting an X-Windows input device can crash the computer or hang the desktop.

Creating Static USB Devices

Every device on the system needs a device handle in the /dev directory. This can lead to problems with hot-plug devices: each time a device is connected, it may be assigned a different device handle. One time the tablet may be on /dev/input/event0, and the next time it could be /dev/input/event3.

The maintenance of these devices is handled by udev, the dynamic device management system. You can configure the udev daemon (udevd) to assign static names to specific devices. For example, if you have a Wacom USB drawing tablet, you can have it automatically assigned to /dev/wacom or /dev/input/wacom rather than using the dynamic device driver handle.

TIP The same approach for assigning the tablet to /dev/wacom can be used for assigning a mouse, scanner, or other USB character input device.

NOTE The Wacom graphic tablet is used throughout this example because it requires each of the configuration steps. Other USB character input devices may need some or all of these steps.

1. Connect the device. Look in /dev/ or /dev/input/ for symbolic links pointing to the event driver and that match the timestamp for when you connected the table. For example:

```
$ ls -ld /dev/* /dev/input/* | grep ^l | grep event
lrwxrwxrwx  1 root root         6 2009-12-26 17:16
/dev/input/tablet-graphire3-6x8 -> event9
lrwxrwxrwx  1 root root         6 2009-12-26 17:16
/dev/input/wacom -> event9
```

If you see symbolic links, then stop here: the system already recognizes the device and has created a static device handle.

If you do not see a link for the input device, then continue on to create one.

2. Determine the event driver(s) assigned to the device by looking in /proc/bus/input/devices. In this example, the device is a Wacom Graphire3 6x8 tablet and it uses the device handlers /dev/input/mouse0, /dev/input/event2, and /dev/input/ts0 for the mouse, stylus, and touch screen, respectively.

```
$ more /proc/bus/input/devices
...
I: Bus=0003 Vendor=056a Product=0014 Version=0314
N: Name="Wacom Graphire3 6x8"
P: Phys=
S: Sysfs=/class/input/input3
H: Handlers=mouse0 event2 ts0
B: EV=f
```

```
B: KEY=1c43 0 70000 0 0 0 0 0 0 0 0
B: REL=100
B: ABS=3000003
...
```

3. Determine the driver attributes using the event driver (`event2` in this example) identified in `/proc/bus/input/devices`. The `udevadm` command (or `udevinfo` on older systems) traverses the chain of USB device drivers, printing information about each element. (There will be similar entries for `/dev/input/mouse0` and `/dev/input/ts0`.)

NOTE Hardy Heron (8.04 LTS) denotes the transition from older `udevinfo` to the newer `udevadm` systems. Hardy supports both commands, while Dapper Drake (6.06 LTS) supports only `udevinfo`, and later systems only include `udevadm`.

```
$ sudo udevinfo -a -p $(udevinfo -q path -n /dev/input/event2) #
older
$ udevadm info --attribute-walk -n /dev/input/event2 # newer
...
looking at parent device '/devices/pci0000:00/0000:00:1d.1/usb3/3-
1/3-1:1.0':
    KERNELS=="3-1:1.0"
    SUBSYSTEMS=="usb"
    DRIVERS=="wacom"
    ATTRS{bInterfaceNumber}=="00"
    ATTRS{bAlternateSetting}==" 0"
    ATTRS{bNumEndpoints}=="01"
    ATTRS{bInterfaceClass}=="03"
    ATTRS{bInterfaceSubClass}=="01"
    ATTRS{bInterfaceProtocol}=="02"
    ATTRS{modalias}=="usb:v056Ap0014d0314dc00dsc00dp00ic03isc01ip02"
    ATTRS{supports_autosuspend}=="1"
...
```

4. Udev uses a directory that stores device configurations. For older systems, the directory is `/etc/udev/rules.d/`. Newer systems use `/lib/udev/rules.d/`. Regardless of the directory, the file format remains the same.

NOTE If you do not see dozens of files in `/etc/udev/rules.d/`, then you are probably using a newer system. Look in `/lib/udev/rules.d/` instead.

Create (or edit) the `10-local.rules` file. Rules can consist of comparisons (such as `==` or `!=`) and assignments. Rules can use any of the fields displayed by `udevadm` or `udevinfo`. There are other rules files in the same directory if you need additional examples. The manual for udev (`man udev`) is also very informative.

5. Add the following line to the `10-local.rules` file. Be sure to use the name found in `/proc/bus/input/devices` and the driver name and fields found from the `udevadm` or `udevinfo` command.

```
BUS=="usb", DRIVER=="wacom", KERNEL=="event[0-9]*", SYMLINK="wacom"
```

This says to match any device where the bus is `usb`, the driver is `wacom`, and the kernel is the string `event` followed by some digits. Any match will be assigned to the device link `/dev/wacom`.

> **NOTE** Try to make the rule as specific as possible, but be aware that fields like **ID** and **SYSFS{dev}** can change each time the device is plugged in. For example, if you don't specify the **KERNEL**, pattern, then the **mouse0** and **ts0** devices will also match the rule. But, if you add in **SYSFS{dev}=="13:66"**, then it may not match if you plug the device into a different USB port.

6. Restart the udev system:

```
sudo /etc/init.d/udev restart
```

If your tablet is already plugged in, you may also need to unplug the tablet from the USB socket and then plug it in again; otherwise, its device driver may not be recognized.

7. Check to see if the device appears:

```
$ ls -l /dev/wacom
lrwxrwxrwx 1 root root 12 2009-12-22 14:19 /dev/wacom -> input/event2
```

With these changes, every time the tablet is plugged in, it may still be assigned a dynamic device handle, but the well-known symbolic link will always point to the correct place. When the tablet is disconnected the symbolic link will be removed.

Associating Applications with USB

By default, all new device handles created by udev are only accessible by root. You can change the default ownership and permissions by including an OWNER, GROUP, or MODE assignment in your udev rule. For example:

```
SYSFS{idVendor}=="e2e3", SYSFS{idProduct}=="0222", MODE="664", \
  GROUP="floppy"
```

The udev rules can also run commands. For example, Hardy Heron's `/etc/udev/rules.d/85-ifupdown.rules` contains commands to auto-configure network devices.

```
ACTION=="add",    RUN+="/sbin/start-stop-daemon --start --background \
  --pidfile /var/run/network/bogus --startas /sbin/ifup -- --allow \
  auto $env{INTERFACE}"
```

```
ACTION=="remove", RUN+="/sbin/start-stop-daemon --start --background \
   --pidfile /var/run/network/bogus --startas /sbin/ifdown -- --allow \
   auto $env{INTERFACE}"
```

A similar rule could be added to start a program when a specific USB device is connected. For example, when you connect a scanner, you may want the drawing program gimp to start automatically. This way, you can immediately use Gimp to scan in images.

All commands executed by udev are run as root. This can be a security risk for multi-user systems and a problem for interactive applications. For example, if you start the gimp drawing program whenever a scanner is connected, it will try to run as root; it will also try to connect to the X display and fail. To resolve both of these problems, create a /usr/bin/run_gimp command to always run the program as the user who owns the display (see Listing 4-1). You can then add this script to the scanner's run line in /etc/udev/rules.d/45-libsane.rules. For example, to run Gimp when an HP ScanJet 4100C scanner (USB vendor 03f0, product 0101) is plugged in, you can use:

```
SYSFS{idVendor}=="03f0", SYSFS{idProduct}=="0101", MODE="664", \
   GROUP="scanner", RUN="/usr/bin/run_gimp"
```

NOTE Don't forget to make the script executable by using chmod a+x /usr/bin/run_gimp.

Now, every time the scanner with the USB identifier 03f0:0101 (as seen by lsusb) is connected, the driver will be added to group "scanner" and gimp will be started with the right permissions.

Listing 4-1: /usr/bin/run_gimp

```
#!/bin/sh
# Get the username of the person running the X-window on tty :0
name=$(/usr/bin/who |
 /bin/grep "(:0[.)]" |
 /usr/bin/head -1 |
 /usr/bin/awk '{print $1}')
# Udev runs as root but this needs to run as the user
# Run as the user and set the display
/bin/su - "$name" "/usr/bin/gimp --display :0"
```

WHEN PROGRAMS RUN . . .

There are many different places where a program can be told to run automatically. Some are easy to find, but others are more difficult to hunt down. More importantly, there is no single right place to install a program.

For example, if you want to start a program when a scanner is plugged in, you can either modify /etc/udev/rules.d/45-libsane.rules, or you can run gnome-volume-properties (System ⇨ Preferences ⇨ Removable Drives and Media, or on Karmic run nautilus and select Edit ⇨ Preferences ⇨ Media) and change the program that the desktop runs when a scanner is detected.

The main difference between these options is flexibility. Although Gnome knows about scanners and cameras, only udev knows about other types of devices. In contrast, Gnome is generally easier to configure, since udev has no graphical interface. Chapter 8 covers other ways to have programs to start automatically.

Enabling Drawing Tablets

Ubuntu supports the many types of drawing pads, but the Wacom drawing pad has drivers installed by default. Even though the drivers are installed, they are not completely configured. Although udev might recognize the device, the X-server still needs to be told about it. To complete the configuration, you will need to follow a few steps.

NOTE Karmic Koala (9.10) automatically recognizes most Wacom tables without any additional configuration. If your tablet is not recognized correctly, then you will need to follow these steps.

1. Follow the steps mentioned in the "Creating Static USB Devices" section to create the /dev/wacom driver handle, if one does not already exist.

2. The /etc/X11/xorg.conf should contain three "InputDevice" sections for the Wacom driver. It also needs these input devices listed in the "ServerLayout" section. Listing 4-2 shows the relevant Wacom configurations for xorg.conf.

3. Plug the Wacom drawing pad into the USB port and restart the X-server.

   The mouse cursor on the screen should now be controllable by the mouse or drawing pad.

NOTE Tablets and drawing pads may not be common, but installing them requires all of the device configuration steps. This is a fairly long example, but if you have trouble with any new device, then you can use this example to help debug the problem.

Listing 4-2: Part of /etc/X11/xorg.conf for Wacom Tablet Configuration

```
Section "InputDevice"
  Driver        "wacom"
  Identifier    "stylus"
  Option        "Device" "/dev/wacom"
  Option        "Type" "stylus"
#  Option         "ForceDevice"    "ISDV4" # Tablet PC ONLY
EndSection

Section "InputDevice"
  Driver        "wacom"
  Identifier    "eraser"
  Option        "Device" "/dev/wacom"
  Option        "Type" "eraser"
#  Option         "ForceDevice"    "ISDV4" # Tablet PC ONLY
EndSection

Section "InputDevice"
  Driver        "wacom"
  Identifier    "cursor"
  Option        "Device" "/dev/wacom"
  Option        "Type"           "cursor"
#  Option         "ForceDevice"    "ISDV4" # Tablet PC ONLY
EndSection

Section "ServerLayout"
        Identifier      "Default Layout"
        Screen          "Default Screen"
        InputDevice     "Generic Keyboard"
        InputDevice     "Configured Mouse"
        # Include the Wacom devices:
        InputDevice     "stylus" "SendCoreEvents"
        InputDevice     "cursor" "SendCoreEvents"
        InputDevice     "eraser" "SendCoreEvents"
EndSection
```

Debugging the Wacom Tablet

If the tablet does not work, start with the xorg.conf debugging instructions. This should help you resolve any problems with the graphical display not starting.

NOTE There is a set of Wacom diagnostic programs that may assist you with debugging issues (sudo apt-get install wacom-tools). However, the tools do not work on every Ubuntu version. For example, sudo wacdump /dev/input/

`wacom` **generates a segmentation fault under Karmic Koala (9.10) but works correctly under Hardy Heron (8.04 LTS) and earlier Ubuntu versions.**

Not all removable devices can be removed safely. Removing a USB device that is in use by the X-server may create problems. In the best case, the device can be removed and reinserted without any issue. In the worst case, the X-server can hang the desktop or crash the entire computer. Even with Karmic Koala (9.10)—which supports removable input devices—quickly unplugging and replugging a tablet can hang the desktop.

To be safe, if you want to disconnect the Wacom graphics tablet, first log out and then disconnect it. If you are running Dapper Drake, then *immediately* restart the X-server by pressing Ctrl+Alt+Backspace, since the server does not support hot-plug input devices. With newer Ubuntu versions, wait a few seconds before trying to plug it back in.

WARNING **Disconnecting a USB device that is used by the X-server can crash the computer or hang the desktop.**

Tuning the Tablet

Depending on the tablet model, the coordinates on the tablet may not match your screen resolution. You can resolve this by adding the following options to each of the Wacom `"InputDevice"` sections in the `xorg.conf` file.

To automatically set the coordinates on your tablet to match your screen resolution, you can use:

```
Option "KeepShape" "on"
```

The `KeepShape` option scales the active area of the tablet so that it matches the screen. For example, the tablet likely has a 4:3 aspect ratio. If your screen is 16:9, then the active area on your tablet will start at the top-left corner and scale to match a 16:9 region. The bottom of the active area on the tablet will not be usable, since it is outside of the 16:9 ratio.

DRAWING WITH GIMP

Drawing tablets are great for artists. The stylus acts like a pen, and it even has an eraser. If you are going to be drawing with Linux, then you are almost certainly going to use Gimp. The problem is that Gimp's use of the stylus is

(continued)

DRAWING WITH GIMP *(continued)*

unintuitive. One would think that the pen should draw and the eraser should erase, but one would be wrong.

The Gimp toolbox displays many different functions. There are different tools for area selection, drawing, scaling, and more. Gimp remembers which tool each end of the stylus last used. If you use the eraser end to select the eraser tool, then it will act like an eraser. If you use the eraser end with the area select tool, then it will work as an area select. The same applies to the drawing end; if you last used it with the gradient fill, then the drawing end will continue to do a gradient fill until you change the tool.

If this seems confusing, then think of it this way: with Gimp, the stylus is not a pen and an eraser. Instead, the stylus is a device for selecting two different toolbox items at the same time. Each tool is assigned to a different end of the stylus.

You can also enable the tablet's pressure sensitivity. Under Gimp, choose Edit ⇨ Preferences ⇨ Input Devices ⇨ Configure Extended Input Devices. Select the tablet and set the mode from Disabled to Screen. This turns the pen into a pressure sensitive device; more pressure creates a darker line.

Using Other Tablets

Although support for the Wacom tablet is included by default, other tablets require additional drivers. Use `apt-cache search tablet` to display the list of available drivers. In addition, some tablets may be compatible with other drivers or have drivers available for downloading from other sources. Your best bet is to research the tablet first and select one that has Linux, and preferably Ubuntu, support.

Each different tablet model will likely have different configuration requirements. Some of the requirements may be automated, while others may require manual modifications. Regardless of the specific requirements, they will all have the same basic steps:

1. Install a device driver, if one is not already installed.

2. Create the device handle if one is not created automatically.

3. Load any required software drivers and configuration parameters.

4. Configure `/etc/X11/xorg.conf`.

5. Restart the X-server using Ctrl+Alt+Backspace.

Summary

Keyboards, mice, and tablets often have plug-and-play functionality. However, you can greatly improve your productivity by knowing how to map additional buttons to specific tasks. This includes customizing your system to fit your needs, as well as adapting the input devices to your comfort level. Whether you use a PC or Mac, you will not have to train yourself to switch between different hardware configurations.

Working with Compatibility

In This Part

Managing Software

What's In This Chapter?

Adding software repositories
Installing software with and without a GUI
Enabling multimedia support
Configuring a software development environment
Compiling packages from source code

Operating systems evolve. There is a constant flow of patches and updates that needs to be reviewed and installed. And then there is custom software—packages that are not included in a standard distribution but which can be very valuable anyway. How do you even begin to browse for these packages? If you want compatibility with others, then you need a system that is up to date and contains the software *you* require.

As part of the Linux open source family, Ubuntu can use most open source packages. Large repositories such as SourceForge (`sourceforge.net`) and FreshMeat (`freshmeat.net`) store hundreds of thousands of projects. Unfortunately for some projects, downloading, compiling, resolving dependencies, and installing can be overwhelming. In addition, dead projects, unchanged in years with no active maintainers, are available for download.

Fortunately, the Ubuntu community maintains many different repositories of precompiled packages that are ready to install and use. All you need to do is specify the ones you want and they are installed—no manual compilation required. Programs such as the Advanced Package Tool (APT) and its graphical front end, Synaptic, simplify the search and install process.

Each package contains several items:

- Precompiled applications
- Dependency information for other packages needed by this package
- Install scripts
- Package information and description
- License information

You can obtain packages from the Ubuntu CD-ROM or DVD, or over the network from an Ubuntu package repository.

Not every package works immediately after a successful installation. Some packages require additional configurations before working properly. In the worst cases, you will need to download source code and compile it. For these situations, you will need to install a programming environment.

Understanding Package Repositories

Packages (precompiled executables) come from a variety of locations. Ubuntu maintains four main repository types (called *components*) where most software can be retrieved.

- **main**—This component contains all officially supported open source projects without restrictive licensing. Gnome, GDM, and the Linux kernel are all found in main.
- **restricted**—These packages are officially supported but have restrictive licenses. This component primarily contains third-party video and network drivers.
- **universe**—These packages are not officially supported by Ubuntu but are provided and maintained by the Ubuntu community. As with main, the universe component only contains open source projects without restrictive licensing. Games, compilers, and a wide variety of tools are found here.
- **multiverse**—This is the catchall component that contains community-supported packages with restrictive licensing. Example packages include Adobe's Acrobat PDF reader, some fonts, and MP3-related tools.

Packages from the main and restricted components are included on the Ubuntu installation CD-ROMs (see the /pool directory). Although Ubuntu officially supports these two components, the community provides the other two: universe and multiverse. This means that their contents may not be as thoroughly tested, updated, or patched as often as the official repositories.

By dividing software on the basis of licensing and support, software developers and corporations can make intelligent decisions according to their own needs. For example, a company that develops custom software may want to stay away from the restricted and multiverse repositories in order to reduce the risk of licensing contamination. A small office looking for reliable support may stick to fully supported packages from the main and restricted repositories.

UNRESTRICTED SOFTWARE

The Ubuntu Free Software Philosophy contains three core concepts:

1. **Every computer user should have the freedom to download, run, copy, distribute, study, share, change, and improve their software for any purpose, without paying licensing fees.**

2. **Every computer user should be able to use their software in the language of their choice.**

3. **Every computer user should be given every opportunity to use software, even if they work under a disability.**

The first core concept determines which repository contains the software. For example, some wireless drivers are proprietary and do not include source code. Without code, they cannot be easily studied. Even if you have the source code, you may not have the right to modify or redistribute the code due to licensing or patent issues. In these cases, the software is considered "restricted," and will either appear in the *restricted* or *multiverse* repositories. (*Multiverse* is for community-supported software, while *restricted* is for Ubuntu-supported packages.)

If the software is open source and unburdened by restrictive licensing or patents, then it is placed in the *main* or *universe* repositories. As with the restricted and multiverse repositories, *main* contains Ubuntu-supported software and *universe* contains community-provided packages.

Differentiating Distributions

Along with the four components (main, restricted, universe, and multiverse) are a variety of Ubuntu repositories. For Ubuntu, each repository contains the name of the Ubuntu version. For Dapper Drake (6.06 LTS), all distributions contain "dapper". Hardy Heron (8.04 LTS) uses "hardy", and Karmic Koala (9.10) uses "karmic".

- **hardy**—This indicates the primary distribution for the operating system.

- **hardy-updates**—This repository holds updates to the primary distribution. Updates are kept separate from the main distribution so an installation baseline is maintained.

- **hardy-security**—This is a special repository specifically used for security updates.

- **hardy-backports**—This repository contains software that has been back-ported—compiled from a newer version of Ubuntu to work with this version. For example, Karmic Koala uses use a newer version of Gnome than Hardy. Karmic's Gnome version may be backported to work with Hardy. Because these versions are not thoroughly tested under Hardy, the back-ported distributions are disabled by default.

- **hardy-proposed**—Before becoming an update, packages must first be tested. This repository holds packages that are currently being evaluated. Enable this repository if you want to play with potentially unstable, bleeding edge updates. However, only people interested in testing updates and providing feedback should use this repository. Do not enable this repository on mission critical systems or computers used in day-to-day activities.

DEBS, RPMs, AND REPOSITORIES

Most large Linux distributions provide some form of precompiled code. Red-Hat and SUSE Linux, for example, use the RedHat Package Manager (RPM) format. Although the `rpm` package tool exists for Ubuntu, it is not commonly used. Each RPM contains licensing information. A single RPM repository may contain packages with both restricted and unrestricted licenses.

Debian Linux uses the Debian Package Manager (`dpkg`) to install `deb` packages. Since Ubuntu is based on Debian, it too uses `dpkg` and `deb` packages. Other package management tools, such as APT and Synaptic, are actually wrappers around `dpkg`. As with Ubuntu, Debian divides packages according to licensing, but Debian uses slightly different divisions.

- **Debian main**—This is similar to the Ubuntu main component. All code is supported, open source, and provided with unrestrictive licensing.

- **Contrib**—This component contains open source with unrestrictive licensing but may be dependent on code that has restrictive licensing.

- **Non-Free**—As with the Ubuntu restricted component, these packages contain licenses that restrict use or distribution.

- **Non-US/Main**—These packages do not have restrictive licensing but may not be exported outside of the United States. This usually means that the packages contain cryptography.

- **Non-US/Non-Free**—This component is the counterpart to Non-US/Main. Most of these packages use proprietary cryptography or are restricted by patents.

Although you can install Debian deb packages under Ubuntu, most of these packages have been ported to the Ubuntu repositories.

Compatibility leads to big problems when using binaries from other platforms. Depending on the software and how it was compiled, some packages may not work under your version of Ubuntu. Different kernels and shared library versions can break executables.

If you can, consider sticking with Ubuntu binaries. If you can't find Ubuntu binaries, then be careful. Don't try binary kernel modules without knowing how to remove them first; incompatible modules can crash your system. For regular user applications, incompatible binaries may not run or may complain about missing libraries. Sometimes you can fix dependencies by installing older libraries, but you are probably better off looking for source code. If the binaries are proprietary, then you are out of luck unless you can use them in a virtual machine (see Chapter 7).

Each distribution contains main, restricted, universe, multiverse, and proposed repositories. Different servers may host some or all of the different distributions and repositories.

NOTE Not all Ubuntu servers provide the same software. Even though the official repositories are supposed to be mirrors, sometimes they contain different packages. Similarly, a mirror may only carry the main component for Hardy, whereas the original server may provide all components for Hardy and other Ubuntu versions.

Running Synaptic

Synaptic is the graphical interface for selecting packages for installation. To open it, choose the System ➪ Administration ➪ Synaptic Package Manager menu (see Figure 5-1). The Synaptic Package Manager displays the available sections on the left and the available packages on the right. At any time, you can select a package for installation or deselect an already installed package. If you select a package that has dependencies, then all dependencies are automatically selected (or deselected). The bottom status line of the window displays a summary of the selections.

When you are ready to make the system changes, select the Apply button. Although there are a few confirmation and status screens, the installations usually require no manual effort.

Searching with Synaptic

The most powerful part of Synaptic is its search capabilities. You can search for packages by name, description, version, dependencies, and more. Searches are listed as a category on the left side, with search results showing the packages on the right.

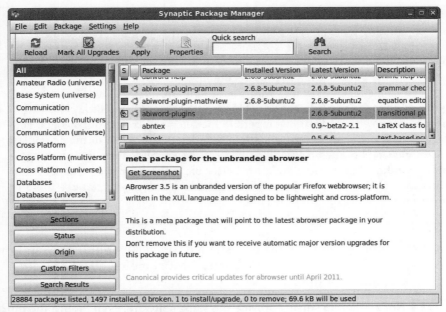

Figure 5-1: The Synaptic Package Manager

To switch back to the repository list, click the Sections button. You can always return to your search history by clicking the lower Search button.

SYNAPTIC GAPS

As powerful as Synaptic is, it has a couple of usability issues. First, there isn't a Stop button available when you do a search. If you have a slow computer (or slow network connection) and you search for a common term, such as the word *the*, you should be prepared to wait until the search completes.

Second, the search history is limited to the current session. When you close Synaptic, you will lose your search history.

The third limitation concerns the ever-changing search button. With Dapper Drake (6.06 LTS), there are two search buttons. One was the search itself, and the other shows the history of previous searches. With Hardy, the search button is labeled Search and the history is found by using the Search Results button.

However, the search button keeps changing. For example, Karmic Koala (9.10) does not have a search button. You need to use Edit ⇨ Search or press Ctrl+F. Karmic also introduced a Quick Search bar where you can refine searches without storing the results under the Search Results listing.

Changing Repositories

Different Ubuntu distributions include different default repositories. The default Dapper Drake (6.06 LTS) and Hardy Heron (98.04 LTS) installations only enable the officially supported (main and restricted) repositories. You may want to also enable the universe and multiverse repositories. In contrast, Karmic Koala (9.10) enables all four repositories. If you only want the fully supported repositories, then you will need to disable universe and multiverse.

You can modify the repository list with Synaptic through the Settings ⇨ Repositories menu. A list of standard distributions is provided—you can simply check the appropriate entries to enable them.

NOTE The experimental (proposed) component is not included in the listing. If you want to install software from this repository, you will need to manually add it to /etc/apt/sources.list. Also, items that are commented out of the sources.list file will appear here without a checked box (disabled).

Besides enabling distributions, you can select specific repositories from the distributions using the Add button (see Figure 5-2). After modifying the repositories, you will need to click Reload to rescan the list of packages.

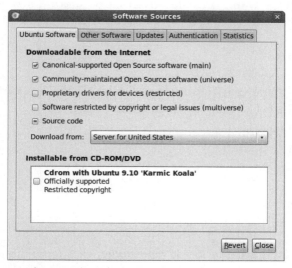

Figure 5-2: Adding to the repository list

WARNING Synaptic does little to prevent you from adding invalid repository-component combinations, or from adding the same distribution twice. Bad choices may result in error messages later, but you will get no warning when you make the selection.

Installing from a CD-ROM or Directory

Besides installing over the network, Synaptic supports installations from a CD-ROM drive or fixed directory. This can come in really handy when working without a network connection or in a closed network environment such as a mission-critical server room.

Installing from a CD-ROM is very easy—simply put the CD-ROM in the drive. Ubuntu will recognize the disc as being a repository and will prompt you to add it to the repository list. At this point, the CD-ROM will act like any other repository.

NOTE If the CD-ROM is not automatically recognized, you can use Settings ⇨ Repositories to get to the Add Cdrom button.

In closed environments, it is usually more convenient to install from a shared or local directory. You can configure this using Settings ⇨ Repositories. Rather than selecting a preset value, click on the Add button and then select Custom to add your own repository. For example, the following enables package installation from a downloaded ISO file:

1. Know your system. Dapper wants to install from a subdirectory named dapper. Hardy wants to install from hardy, and Jaunty wants a jaunty. Use lsb_release -c to identify the subdirectory that your system wants to use:

   ```
   $ lsb_release -c
   Codename:      hardy
   ```

2. Download one of the Ubuntu installation CD-ROMs that matches your system. Let's call it ubuntu-hardy.iso.

3. Mount the disk image:

   ```
   sudo mkdir -p /mnt/iso
   sudo mount -o loop ubuntu-hardy.iso /mnt/iso
   ```

4. Using the custom add button under Synaptic (Settings ⇨ Repositories ⇨ Add ⇨ Custom), add the following repository:

   ```
   deb file:/mnt/iso hardy main restricted
   ```

NOTE When using Synaptic to add repositories, each repository will appear at the end of the /etc/apt/source.list file. However, when searching for a package, the repositories are scanned from the top of the file to the bottom. If you want your new repository to be used first, you will need to edit /etc/apt/sources.list and change the order of the repositories.

Synaptic will look for the hardy distribution's main repository in the /mnt/iso/dists/hardy/main and /mnt/iso/pool/hardy/main directories. The dists directory contains the indexes for packages, whereas the pool directory contains the actual packages.

TURNING OFF REPOSITORIES

Using a repository from a CD-ROM or local directory can improve installation speeds, since you are not dependent on the network. Local repositories also give you the ability to customize the software your system can access.

However, as useful as it is to use a CD-ROM or local directory as a repository, you may want to disable it after you do an installation. If you do not turn it off, Synaptic will complain that the repository is no longer accessible after you remove the CD-ROM or disable the directory.

To turn off repositories, edit /etc/apt/sources.list and comment out the appropriate lines to disable, or delete lines to remove. Alternately, you can use Synaptic and select System ⇨ Repositories. You can clear the CD-ROMs and custom directories to turn them off. If you do not think you will need them again, you can click on the Remove button.

Managing Updates

The default Synaptic installation periodically checks for upgrades. If there are updates or patches for packages that you already have installed, then Synaptic can flag these or automatically install them.

When new updates are available, the system will alert you. With Hardy Heron and older systems, you will see an alert icon on the top panel. Hovering the mouse over this icon will show you the number of pending updates (see Figure 5-3), and clicking on the icon will allow you to apply updates. However, Karmic Koala (obnoxiously) opens a huge popup window that lists every package with pending updates.

Figure 5-3: The indicator on Hardy Heron (8.04 LTS) showing that updates are available

You can change the update settings by using Software Preferences applet. Either select it from the System ⇨ Administration ⇨ Software Sources menu, or by right-clicking the update indicator. The Updates tab shows the settings. You can tell Ubuntu to periodically check for updates (or never check), download updates (but not install), or automatically install security updates.

Some updates require a special confirmation before installation. These include kernel updates and critical libraries. Upgrading these usually requires a reboot and could break some applications. As a result, these packages require additional confirmation and are not automatically installed.

By default, Ubuntu checks for updates daily and notifies you about pending updates. (With Dapper Drake, it automatically installs critical security patches.)

For critical systems and controlled environments, you may want to completely disable automatic updates. This allows you to apply updates during a scheduled period rather than when updates they are available. In contrast, regular home users should keep the daily check for updates and consider enabling the automatic installation of security updates. If you are on a slow network connection, you may want to change the update frequency, but it should be at least every two weeks.

WARNING Completely disabling updates is usually a bad decision. While many updates apply security patches, others address stability issues. The only time you may want to disable auto-updates is when you have some other procedure for maintaining the system.

Shopping at the Ubuntu Software Center

While Synaptic provides a straightforward means for searching across all packages and installing selected items, it isn't ideal for just browsing the list of available software. Sure, Synaptic lists packages and even rough categories, but it does not distinguish dependent packages from whole applications. Beginning with Karmic Koala (9.10), the desktop includes an application called the Ubuntu Software Center.

Under the Ubuntu Software Center, all packages are grouped by applications and divided into categories such as Accessories, Games, and Programming (see Figure 5-4). The goal is to simplify installation. If you just want to browse and see what is available, then the Ubuntu Software Center is ideal.

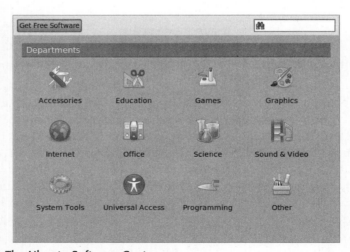

Figure 5-4: The Ubuntu Software Center

For example, let's say you want to install a planetarium application under Synaptic. You could search for "planetarium" and find `kstars`, `kstars-data`, and a half-dozen similar Celestia packages (`celestia`, `celestia-common`, `celestia-kde`, etc.). You could also search for "stars" and find everything from `kstars` and `stellarium` to `gcstars` (for movie manager collections) and arcade games like `defendguin` and `wing`. However, you won't find OpenUniverse unless you know what to search for.

With the Ubuntu Software Center, you would go into the Science category and easily find a dozen celestial programs. If you select the "OpenUniverse Space Simulator" then you will see a nice description, install button, and even a link to the web. All of the fine details, like cryptic package names and required dependencies, are kept behind the scenes.

The Ubuntu Software Center adds usability to application installation. Since it is relatively new, the user interface is likely to undergo changes with future Ubuntu releases. (The current software is a great improvement over the old system, but it could use some more refinement.) Eventually it may even replace Synaptic.

Using the Computer Janitor

Many Ubuntu packages have dependencies. If you install a package and later decide to remove it, the dependencies may just sit around on the system. Along with the Ubuntu Software Center, Karmic Koala has introduced the Computer Janitor (System ➪ Administration ➪ Computer Janitor). This application searches for applications that are no longer needed and makes it easy to select and delete.

As with the Ubuntu Software Center, the Computer Janitor needs some work but is a step in the right direction. It is certainly an improvement over using `sudo apt-get autoremove` under Hardy Heron (8.04 LTS) or `deborphan` (`sudo apt-get install deborphan`) to find unused packages.

```
# Removing one unused dependency may make another become unused.
# Repeat until all dependencies are removed
while [ "$(deborphan)" != "" ]; do
  sudo apt-get remove—purge $(deborphan)
done
```

Living without Synaptic

Synaptic and the Ubuntu Software Center are very useful utilities for keeping up to date on patches and installing new software. Unfortunately, both programs require human interaction and a graphical interface. If you have installed the Ubuntu server or are remotely logged into the system, then you probably do not have the graphical interface. And when managing dozens (or hundreds) of systems, depending on a graphical interface becomes an impediment.

Fortunately, Synaptic is a graphical front end to the Advanced Package Tool environment; every basic Synaptic function comes from APT. Using the APT commands, you can search for software, install packages, and perform upgrades from the command line.

Modifying Sources

APT uses a configuration file to tell it where repositories are located. The file `/etc/apt/sources.list` contains a list of servers, distributions, and repositories. Listing 5-1 shows some sample repositories. If you want to add or change repositories, simply edit the file (as root) and make your additions or modifications. There is no need to restart any services or processes.

> **NOTE** The `/etc/apt/sources.list` file is used by dpkg, APT, Synaptic, and the Ubuntu Software Center. Technically, APT is a wrapper around dpkg, and both Synaptic and the Ubuntu Software Center are graphical front ends to APT. Changes to this file affect all of these tools.

Each line within this file contains four key elements:

- **Type of data**—The available data is either precompiled binaries (deb) or source code for compiling binaries (deb-src).
- **Location**—A URL says how to get the data. This is usually an HTTP, HTTPS, or FTP server, but it can also be a local CD-ROM or a directory.
- **Distribution**—The name of the distribution is provided. Example names include hardy, hardy-updates, and hardy-security.
- **Component**—One or more components are specified, such as main, restricted, universe, or multiverse.

> **WHEN ALL ELSE FAILS . . .**
>
> Knowing how Synaptic works under the hood, and how to use APT from the command-line can be critical for system recovery. On August 21, 2006, the maintainers of Ubuntu accidentally released a bad update. This update disabled X-Windows, leaving users at a command line prompt. Graphical tools, such as Synaptic, suddenly became unavailable. The only mitigation option was to use apt-get to reinstall the X-server from the command line after Ubuntu fixed the error in the X-Windows packages.

Not all failures are due to bad updates. On Saturday, July 22, 2006, many of the servers hosting Ubuntu repositories went offline—and some stayed offline the entire weekend. Refreshing the Synaptic repository list generated a cryptic error message (and sometimes crashed Synaptic). Knowing how to manually change the servers from one region to another was the only way to apply patches and install essential software. And changing the servers is a task easier done without using Synaptic. (The downtime was later attributed to a series of server upgrades.)

Accidents happen, but without knowing how to identify errors or recover from them, you can end up with an unusable system. The command line `apt-get` **and** `apt-cache` **tools generate informative errors that can be used to diagnose these problems. In the case of a bad server or network connection, editing the** `/etc/apt/sources.list` **file so that it pointed to other servers provided a quick fix.**

Listing 5-1: Sample Entries from an /etc/apt/source.list

```
## The server "us.archive.ubuntu.com" contains packages.
## This server contains main and restricted components for karmic.
deb http://us.archive.ubuntu.com/ubuntu/ karmic main restricted
deb-src http://us.archive.ubuntu.com/ubuntu/ karmic main restricted

## Major bug fix updates produced after the final release of the
## distribution.
deb http://us.archive.ubuntu.com/ubuntu/ karmic-updates main restricted
deb-src http://us.archive.ubuntu.com/ubuntu/ karmic-updates main restricted

## The packages from the universe component are unsupported by
## Ubuntu, may not be updated or patched, and have not been
## checked by Ubuntu's security team.  If you use software from
## these repositories, then you are on your own.
#deb http://us.archive.ubuntu.com/ubuntu/ karmic universe
#deb-src http://us.archive.ubuntu.com/ubuntu/ karmic universe
#deb http://us.archive.ubuntu.com/ubuntu/ karmic-updates universe
#deb-src http://us.archive.ubuntu.com/ubuntu/ karmic-updates universe

## The packages from the multiverse component are unsupported by
## Ubuntu, make not be provided under a free license, may not
## include software, may not be updated or patched, and have not
## been checked by Ubuntu's security team.  If you use software
## from these repositories, then you are on your own.
#deb http://us.archive.ubuntu.com/ubuntu/ karmic multiverse
#deb-src http://us.archive.ubuntu.com/ubuntu/ karmic multiverse
#deb http://us.archive.ubuntu.com/ubuntu/ karmic-updates multiverse
#deb-src http://us.archive.ubuntu.com/ubuntu/ karmic-updates multiverse
```

> **TIP** If you want to exclude a specific repository, then make sure that the `/etc/apt/sources.list` file does not include it on any of the repository lines. For example, to exclude multiverse, make sure that all multiverse lines are commented out (with a # character) or removed from the uncommented lines.

After you make any changes to `/etc/apt/sources.list`, you will need to refresh the APT cache of available packages: `sudo apt-get update`. This updates the cache of available software. Without this command, you won't search the list of available software. When you enable the automatic check for patches, the system actually runs the `apt-get update` command.

> **NOTE** If you make changes to `/etc/apt/sources.list` and you use Synaptic, then you can click the Reload button to refresh the cache. Otherwise you need to run `sudo apt-get update`.

The list of servers should match your region. For example, `us.archive.ubuntu.com` is intended for users in the United States. The `uk.archive.ubuntu.com` server is for the United Kingdom, and `ca.archive.ubuntu.com` supports Canada. A few two-character country codes (for example, `uk` and `us`) are currently defined; undefined country codes are redirected to the United Kingdom because that is where Canonical is located. If you find that a particular region is temporarily unavailable, then try changing regions by modifying each of the server's names in `/etc/apt/source.list`. It is rare for all of the servers to be unavailable at the same time.

> **TIP** Official Ubuntu mirrors are associated with a country code, such as `us.archive.ubuntu.com` for the United States and `de` for Germany. But these hostnames are just aliases for actual sites. Some official mirrors perform better than others. The list of official registered mirrors is maintained at `https://launchpad.net/ubuntu/+archivemirrors`. The list includes the country, service provider, network protocol (http, ftp, or rsync), network capacity, and the last time it updated with the primary Ubuntu servers. If you find that a particular country code server is not working well for you, then consider checking this web site and explicitly using a different mirror.

Adding CD-ROM Repositories

Besides using Synaptic, there are two ways to add a CD-ROM to `/etc/apt/source.list`. The first way requires you to manually identify the CD-ROM label and then add it. The `apt-cdrom` command can list the disk's label. Let's assume that the Ubuntu installation CD-ROM is mounted at `/mnt/iso`:

```
$ apt-cdrom -m -d /mnt/iso ident
Using CD-ROM mount point /mnt/iso/
```

```
Mounting CD-ROM
Identifying. [246d1f9a6e6a7e92d0139dd36c36e257-2]
Stored label: Ubuntu 9.10 _Karmic Koala_—Release i386 (20091028.5)
```

TIP The **-m** parameter for `apt-cdrom` says to not mount and unmount the mount point. The **-d** parameter specifies the mount point for acquiring the label and `ident` directs the command to identify the CD-ROM label. If you don't use **-m** and **-d**, then the CD-ROM in the drive will be used.

After finding the CD-ROM name, you can add it to the `/etc/apt/sources.list` file with a `cdrom:` resource. For example, to install the main component, I would use:

```
deb cdrom:[Ubuntu 9.10 _Karmic Koala_—Release i386
    (20091028.5)]/ karmic main
```

Although you can add a disk manually, the easiest way to add a CD-ROM is to let `apt-cdrom` do it.

1. Insert the CD-ROM into the drive.

2. Run the following command:

   ```
   sudo apt-cdrom add
   ```

The CD-ROM is automatically added to the `/etc/apt/source.list` file.

NOTE After adding a CD-ROM to the `/etc/apt/sources.list` file, be sure to run `apt-get update`. This adds the packages on the CD-ROM to the cache of known packages.

Browsing the APT Cache

The `apt-cache` command enables you to search the repositories for a particular subject or file name. The search word will match any package's name or description. For example, if you are searching for a calculator, you could use:

```
$ apt-cache search calculator
bc—The GNU bc arbitrary precision calculator language
gcalctool—A GTK2 desktop calculator
dc—The GNU dc arbitrary precision reverse-polish calculator
bison—A parser generator that is compatible with YACC
```

TIP Searches are case-insensitive and look for substrings. You can search for multiple words in sequence using quotes like `apt-cache search "gnu bc"`. You can also list multiple terms (without quotation marks) that will be matched in any order. For example: `apt-cache search calculator calctool`.

It may seem odd that Bison (Yet Another Compiler-Compiler) is listed as a calculator, but another `apt-cache` command shows the entire package's description and lets us understand why it was listed. (Bison's description contains the word *calculator*.)

```
$ apt-cache show bison
Package: bison
Priority: optional
Section: devel
Installed-Size: 1580
Maintainer: Ubuntu Core Developers
          <ubuntu-devel-discuss@lists.ubuntu.com>
Original-Maintainer: Chuan-kai Lin <cklin@debian.org>
Architecture: i386
Version: 1:2.4.1.dfsg-1
Depends: m4, libc6 (>= 2.4)
Suggests: bison-doc
Filename: pool/main/b/bison/bison_2.4.1.dfsg-1_i386.deb
Size: 259028
MD5sum: b9f073b6ead38a0b448e3cb1fd9b1033
SHA1: e1eaf5fde901c727251ec1c624ce887d1dcbef88
SHA256: a4f633faa9a12caf642b29c646e91b66e14a2f5b5fd2cea9feca975f7151d84e
Description: A parser generator that is compatible with YACC
 Bison is a general-purpose parser generator that converts a
 grammar description for an LALR(1) context-free grammar into a C
 program to parse that grammar.  Once you are proficient with Bison, you
 may use it to develop a wide range of language parsers, from those used
 in simple desk calculators to complex programming languages.
 ..
```

Other options for `apt-cache` can show dependencies, requirements, and contents. The man page for `apt-cache` details other options (`man apt-cache`).

Organizing Search Results

The results from `apt-get search` are not sorted by package name. Instead, they are sorted by server repository. In the case of the calculator search, `bison` is listed after `dc` because it came from a different repository. If you want the results sorted by package name, then you will need to sort them yourself:

```
apt-cache search calculator | sort
```

Similarly, if you are searching for a specific package name or description, then you will need to apply a filter:

```
apt-cache search calculator | grep gcalctool
```

TIP You can use `grep` to restrict results to the displayed text. This is different from using multiple terms with `apt-cache search` since the matched results may not be in the displayed text.

Installing with APT

After you know what to install, you can use the `apt-get install` command to perform the installation. You can list one or more packages after the `install` instruction. If you want to see what will happen without actually doing the install, use the `-s` option to simulate the installation. You will see every warning and message without actually doing the install.

```
sudo apt-get -s install gcalctool  # check the install
sudo apt-get install gcalctool     # perform the install
```

Although the `gcalctool` application is installed by default, when you install the Ubuntu desktop, its source code is not installed. Source code is available for all packages in main and universe components. However, source may not be available for packages found in restricted or multiverse.

TIP While Synaptic gives cryptic error messages (or crashes) when `/etc/apt/sources.list` contains bad entries or is misconfigured, the `apt-cache` and `apt-get` commands will display plenty of errors and warnings.

Removing Packages with APT

Package removal is nearly as painless as installation.

1. First, find the name of the package you want to remove. You can use `apt-cache search` or `apt-cache pkgnames` to list all packages, but the easiest way is to use `dpkg`.

   ```
   dpkg -l | more
   ```

   Alternately, if you know a file that is in the package, then you can use `dpkg -S` to list all packages containing that file. For example, to remove whatever package provides the program `bc`, you can use:

   ```
   dpkg -S $(which bc)
   ```

2. Use `apt-get -s` to check what will be removed. Some package dependencies will force the removal of other packages. For example, to check the removal of the `bc` package, use:

   ```
   sudo apt-get -s remove bc
   ```

3. If the removal looks safe, then use `apt-get` to remove the package. For example, to remove the `bc` package, use:

```
sudo apt-get remove bc
```

WARNING The `bc` package is installed as part of the default desktop. Removing `bc` removes a dependency from a trivial package called `ubuntu-desktop`. This isn't the actual desktop, but it is used as a flag to indicate that the full desktop is installed. To see everything in the `ubuntu-desktop` package, use `dpkg -L` `ubuntu-desktop`. (The `ubuntu-desktop` only delivers two files: `copyright` and `changelog.gz`.)

Removing Residues

Most software removals are clean—everything that went in is taken out. Unfortunately, some removals leave residues, such as configuration and data files. Removing or reinstalling a package because it is misconfigured may not replace critical configuration files. This can result in the package remaining misconfigured after being reinstalled. A few examples:

- Removing and reinstalling a Web browser will not clear user caches or replace user settings. This is not a solution for fixing privacy issues from cached Web pages.
- Removing and reinstalling Gnome will not remove `$HOME/.gnome`, `$HOME/.gnome2`, and other Gnome-related files in user directories.
- Many packages check for modified configuration files. If you modify a configuration file, such as `/etc/X11/xorg.conf` or `/etc/gdm/gdm.conf`, then it may not be removed when these packages are removed.

NOTE If you are reinstalling software because of a configuration problem, be aware that this may not fix the problem.

Leftover files and other residues may need to be manually cleaned up (or deleted) before you decide to reinstall the package. In the case of a misconfiguration, reinstalling the package usually will not resolve problems—especially if the configuration problem is due to files stored in a user's directory or created after the installation.

Tracking Removals

As mentioned earlier, one of the biggest problems with removals comes from dependent packages. Removing one package may automatically select other packages and remove them too. Although using `apt-get remove -s` can be useful, always remember to use the `-s` to check first. If you forget the `-s` then you will need some way to see everything that was removed (so you can put back critical packages).

Fortunately, you have two options (besides restoring from a system backup). First, the /var/log/dpkg.log file contains a list of every addition and removal (see Listing 5-2). This log file is updated every time Synaptic, ATP, or dpkg installs or removes packages. Using this list, you can see what was removed and undo an accidental removal.

TIP The dpkg.log file is a great place to reference after an auto-update. This is particularly true if the update made the system unstable.

Listing 5-2: Sample Contents from /var/log/dpkg.log

```
2009-11-28 18:42:07 install openuniverse <none> 1.0beta3.1-6
2009-11-28 18:42:07 status half-installed openuniverse 1.0beta3.1-6
2009-11-28 18:42:07 status unpacked openuniverse 1.0beta3.1-6
2009-11-28 18:42:07 status unpacked openuniverse 1.0beta3.1-6
2009-11-28 18:42:08 startup packages configure
2009-11-28 18:42:08 configure openuniverse-common 1.0beta3.1-6 1.0beta3.1-6
2009-11-28 18:42:08 status unpacked openuniverse-common 1.0beta3.1-6
2009-11-28 18:42:08 status half-configured openuniverse-common 1.0beta3.1-6
2009-11-28 18:42:08 status installed openuniverse-common 1.0beta3.1-6
2009-11-28 18:42:08 configure openuniverse 1.0beta3.1-6 1.0beta3.1-6
2009-11-28 18:42:08 status unpacked openuniverse 1.0beta3.1-6
2009-11-28 18:42:08 status unpacked openuniverse 1.0beta3.1-6
2009-11-28 18:42:08 status half-configured openuniverse 1.0beta3.1-6
2009-11-28 18:42:09 status installed openuniverse 1.0beta3.1-6
2009-11-28 18:42:26 startup packages remove
2009-11-28 18:42:26 status installed openuniverse 1.0beta3.1-6
2009-11-28 18:42:26 remove openuniverse 1.0beta3.1-6 1.0beta3.1-6
```

The second option is to use the script command. This command logs all command-line output to a file:

```
$ script -c "sudo apt-get remove openuniverse-common" apt-get.log
Reading package lists.. Done
Building dependency tree
Reading state information.. Done
The following packages will be REMOVED:
  openuniverse openuniverse-common
0 upgraded, 0 newly installed, 2 to remove and 8 not upgraded.
After this operation, 5448kB disk space will be freed.
Do you want to continue [Y/n]? y
(Reading database .. 217775 files and directories currently installed.)
Removing openuniverse ..
Removing openuniverse-common ..
Script done, file is apt-get.log
```

From the `script` command, you will get a file called `apt-get.log` containing the entire removal session. This command can even be turned into a simple script that you can use instead of using the actual `apt-get` command (see Listing 5-3).

Listing 5-3: Replacement /usr/local/bin/apt-get for Logging Results

```
#!/bin/sh
# Run the apt-get command and append (-a) results to ./apt-get.log
script -a -c "sudo /usr/bin/apt-get $*" apt-get.log
```

Upgrading with APT

Applying upgrades is a two-step process. First, use `apt-get update` to retrieve the list of available software packages and upgrades based on your `/etc/apt/sources.list`. If there are any updates, then the update indicator will appear on the top panel. After getting the list of updates, use `apt-get upgrade` to perform the upgrade.

```
$ sudo apt-get update
Get:1 http://archive.ubuntu.com hardy Release.gpg [189B]
Get:2 http://archive.ubuntu.com hardy Release [34.8kB]
Get:3 http://archive.ubuntu.com hardy/universe Packages [2458kB]
Hit http://us.archive.ubuntu.com hardy Release
Hit http://us.archive.ubuntu.com hardy-updates Release
Hit http://us.archive.ubuntu.com hardy/main Sources
..
Fetched 3117kB in 7s (416kB/s)
Reading package lists.. Done
$ sudo apt-get upgrade
```

Installing Common Functions

When setting up an Ubuntu desktop system, there are some packages that most people want to install. Many of these center around multimedia functionality: playing MP3 files, DVD movie media, and multimedia streams with RealNetwork RealPlayer. Although downloading with `apt-get` is relatively easy, some packages still require configuration before they can be used.

Unfortunately, a few of these essential multimedia packages are unsupported by Ubuntu because of licensing issues (and in some cases, the software has been deemed illegal by the local authorities). So for these packages, installation is pretty much manual.

AIN'T SO EASY

For early versions of Ubuntu, like Dapper Drake (6.06 LTS) and Edge Eft (6.10), there were applications for automating the installation of license-restricted media libraries and players. Unfortunately, tools like EasyUbuntu and Automatix are no longer supported. You won't find these programs for Ubuntu versions newer than Edge Eft.

Installing Multimedia Support

Different multimedia formats need different libraries to encode and decode the formats. A variety of coder-decoder (codec) libraries are available for Ubuntu. Each of these packages is installed using `apt-get install package_name`. Some of these packages are located in the universe or multiverse repositories. With most of these packages, no additional configuration steps are required.

MOVING TARGETS

The location of the package depends on your version of Ubuntu. For example, the `ffmpeg` package for MP3 support is located in the Dapper universe, Hardy universe, and Karmic main repositories. Similarly, the `faad` package (for MPEG4 support) is located in Dapper's multiverse, but Hardy and Karmic's universe repositories.

To find out where the package comes from, use `apt-cache show` and look for the `Section` field. For example, `apt-cache show ffmpeg | grep "^Section:"`. You will either see something like `Section: universe/graphics` to indicate the universe repository, or you will see `Section: graphics` to indicate the main repository.

- **MP3**—MP3 is one of the most common and popular audio formats. As mentioned in Chapter 2, the `sox` and `lame` packages provide MP3 encoding and decoding support. While these tools do provide command-line support, they do not provide audio libraries. For libraries that will work with most audio players, you will need to install the `ffmpeg` package.

- **Ogg**—Ogg Vorbis is an alternate audio format that is free from MP3's licensing restrictions. To support Ogg Vorbis files, you will need to install the `vorbis-tools` package from the restricted repository.

- **MPEG and Video**—For MPEG and other video file formats, you will want to install the `mjpegtools` package. This multiverse package provides codecs for MPEG, AVI, QuickTime, and other video formats.

■ **MPEG4**—The `libxvidcore4` and `faad` packages provide video and audio support for this file format.

After you load the codecs onto the system, you will need to add plug-ins to your multimedia players so that they know the codecs exist.

■ **Gstreamer**—The Gstreamer interface provides multimedia support for most Gnome applications. Although there are generic plug-ins, their package-naming convention is less than descriptive.

■ `gstreamer0.10-ffmpeg`: This package provides support for the `ffmpeg` package.

■ `gstreamer0.10-pitfdll`: This package adds support for the controversial `w32codecs` package.

■ `gstreamer0.10-plugins-bad`: This package provides support for codecs, such as WAV audio codecs, that are not as refined as other codecs. The naming convention `bad` denotes codecs that are still under development. They are close to production quality, but are not there yet.

■ `gstreamer0.10-plugins-bad-multiverse`: This package provides support for multiverse codecs that are not as refined as other codecs. This includes `faad` and `libxvidcore4`.

■ `gstreamer0.10-plugins-ugly`: This package provides support for MPEG formats. While the `bad` codecs are just not refined, the `ugly` codecs may have distribution issues because of licensing restrictions or patents.

■ `gstreamer0.10-plugins-ugly-multiverse`: Similar to `gstreamer0.10-plugins-ugly`, this supports packages from the multiverse repository.

■ **Xine**—Xine is an audio and video player that provides an alternative to Gnome's totem player. As with the Gstreamer interface, Xine supports plug-ins. The `gxine` package installs the `gxine` base player. The `libxine-main1` and `libxine-extracodecs` packages provide codecs.

Adding Proprietary Media Support

Because of restrictive licensing, codecs for WMA, WMV, and other Microsoft proprietary formats are not supported by Ubuntu and may not exist in the Ubuntu repositories. Similarly, playing DVD movies requires decoding the Content-Scrambling System (CSS). The open source decoder (DeCSS) has been deemed illegal in some countries.

WARNING Packages such as libdvdcss2, libdvdread4, and w32codecs could cause legal headaches—particularly in corporate and government environments. If you have any questions here, you might want to consult legal counsel before installing these packages.

Although the Ubuntu distribution may not carry the needed packages, the Medibuntu distribution does. The Multimedia, Entertainment & Distractions In Ubuntu (Medibuntu) repository contains packages that are not included in the Ubuntu repositories because of legal restrictions.

WARNING The Medibuntu repository does not support every Ubuntu version. For example, at the time of this writing Dapper still has long-term support from Ubuntu. However, Medibuntu dropped Dapper from their repository. Medibuntu only supports the last few Ubuntu releases.

1. Add the Medibuntu repository to your list of APT sources. Rather than appending it to the /etc/apt/sources.list file, you should store it in a separate source file to keep a clear distinction between the Ubuntu repositories and non-Ubuntu repositories.

   ```
   sudo wget -O /etc/apt/sources.list.d/medibuntu.list \
       http://www.medibuntu.org/sources.list.d/$(lsb_release -cs).list
   ```

2. Install the Medibuntu key ring. This is used to authenticate the remote Medibuntu repository.

   ```
   sudo apt-get—yes -q—allow-unauthenticated install medibuntu-keyring
   ```

3. Update the repository content cache.

   ```
   sudo apt-get update
   ```

4. Install the Windows codecs. If you are running on a 32-bit system, then install w32codecs. Sixty-four-bit systems should use w64codecs.

   ```
   sudo apt-get install w32codecs # for 32-bit systems
   sudo apt-get install w64codecs # for 64-bit systems
   ```

5. Install RealPlayer for accessing RealNetworks' proprietary streaming media. This will automatically add RealNetworks RealMedia support to your web browser. (Just be sure to restart any open web browsers after installing the player.)

   ```
   sudo apt-get install realplayer
   ```

6. Install libdvdcss2 for playing encoded DVD videos.

   ```
   sudo apt-get install libdvdcss2
   ```

OTHER DVD OPTIONS

There are other options for adding DVD support to Ubuntu without adding in the Medibuntu repository. For example, the `libdvdread3` (or `libdvdread4` under Karmic) package prepares the system for DVD support. However, after installing the package, you will need to run a script to complete the configuration:

```
sudo apt-get install libdvdread3
sudo /usr/share/doc/libdvdread3/install-css.sh
```

The script will download and install the `libdvdcss2` package. When it is done, you will probably want to delete `/tmp/libdvdcss.deb` or `/tmp/dvdcss-*` since the temporary data is no longer needed. (The `libdvdread3` and `libdvdread4` packages are cute, but they leave installation residues sitting around the system.)

Getting Flashy

Macromedia provides a Flash player for Ubuntu. Installing the `flashplugin-nonfree` package from the multiverse repository will actually download and install the Linux Flash player from the Adobe web site.

```
sudo apt-get install flashplugin-nonfree
```

Unfortunately, the `flashplugin-nonfree` package is only available for PCs. For unsupported platforms, like the PowerPC, there are alternatives. The open source `libflash-swfplayer`, `swfdec-gnome`, and `swfdec-mozilla` packages provide basic SWF (Flash file) support for all Ubuntu platforms.

Although the open source SWF player is supported on both PCs and other platforms, it is not supported on every version of Ubuntu. For example, Dapper (6.06 LTS) has `libflash-swfplayer`, but not `swfdec-gnome`. Karmic (9.10) has `swfdec-gnome` but not `libflash-swfplayer`. And Hardy (8.04 LTS) has both.

The open source SWF packages also do not support all SWF versions. Newer versions of Flash animations may not play using `swfplayer` (from the `libflash-swfplayer` package) or `swfdec-player` (from `swfdec-gnome`).

Installing Font Packages

There are a few desktop packages that you will probably want to install. The first set of packages provides different desktop fonts. These are used by everything from text menus to PDF and PostScript viewers. If an application cannot find a particular font, then it will attempt to substitute it with a different font, and the results can be ugly.

Ubuntu supports three main types of fonts: xfonts, gsfonts, and ttf. Xfonts are used by X-Windows. These bitmapped fonts are designed for specific resolutions (dots per inch, dpi) and can appear blocky when scaled. For example, the `xfonts-100dpi` package provides fonts that render best at 100dpi.

Ghostscript fonts (gsfonts) are vector-based rather than bitmapped. These may take longer to render than bitmapped fonts, but they will look smoother and scale well. These are usually used for displaying documents, word processing, and printing but not for regular screen fonts.

The final group consists of TrueType fonts (ttf). These are also vector-based and are commonly used on Windows systems. If you receive a document in PDF or Word that has ugly or missing fonts, then you probably need to install a ttf font package.

Font definitions are relatively small and consume no system resources if they are not used. For best results, consider installing all of the available fonts for languages that you expect to encounter. This way, you won't end up rendering with poor substitutions.

WARNING Installing *all* fonts can negatively impact performance with some applications. For example, OpenOffice may spend a long time populating the font-list if you have hundreds of fonts and a slow computer with limited resources. Use your best judgment when deciding whether to install any particular font.

NOTE The default font in most cases is called *misc-fixed* and is a monospaced San Serif font. When converting between graphic formats, like PostScript and PDF, missing system fonts may be replaced with bitmapped fonts, resulting in very rough text that is readable but not pretty. The technical term for drawing text with bitmapped fonts is *ugly* rendering.

- **Ghostscript fonts**—Ghostscript is the open source PostScript rendering and viewing system. The fonts used by Ghostscript can be used by any available X-Windows application. The `gv` package provides the Ghostscript Ghostview program for viewing PostScript files. The `gsfonts` package provides Ghostscript fonts, and `gsfonts-x11` makes the fonts available for X11.

  ```
  sudo apt-get install gv gsfonts gsfonts-x11
  ```

- **International fonts**—There are many different packages for providing international language support. All of the most common languages are supported, as well as some lesser-known languages. Examples of font packages include:

  - `xfonts-intl-european` provides support for most European and Latin-based languages. This includes Spanish, German, and French.

- gsfonts-wadalab-common, gsfonts-wadalab-gothic, gsfonts-wadalab-mincho, konfont, and ttf-sazanami-mincho each provide support for Japanese.

- gsfonts-other provides Ghostscript fonts for Cyrillic, Kana (Japanese), and other typesets.

- There are a variety of Chinese font packages. They can be easy found by using apt-cache:

  ```
  apt-cache search font chinese | egrep 'ttf|xfont'
  ```

- ttf-farsiweb and ttf-paktype supplies Farsi and Urdu fonts.

- ttf-khmeros supplies fonts for the Khmer language of Cambodia.

- There are dozens of xfont packages (apt-cache search xfonts) for supporting most European, Asian, and Middle-Eastern languages.

- **Windows fonts**—The msttcorefonts (ttf-mscorefonts-installer under Karmic) package provides the core TrueType fonts found on Microsoft systems. While this does provide true compatibility with Windows systems, there may be licensing issues.

- **Free Windows-Compatible fonts**—The ttf-liberation package (for Hardy Heron 8.04 LTS and later) provides free fonts with the same metrics as the Windows fonts. If you can't use the true Windows fonts, then this is the next best thing.

After installing the fonts, you will need to inform applications that they exist. Fortunately, all standard applications look at the same cache directories. The command sudo fc-cache -f -v will scan and list the font directories, and update the shared font information.

> **NOTE** If the fonts do not appear after you install them, you may have forgotten to run fc-cache.

Compiling and Developing Software

The packages found in the Ubuntu repositories do not include all open source software (far from it!). The main and restricted repositories only include software explicitly supported by Ubuntu and its managing company, Canonical. The universe and multiverse repositories only include Ubuntu packages that are (or were) supported by someone in the community. There are also sites like GetDeb (www.getdeb.net) that offer some of the latest software releases in their own unofficial Ubuntu repositories.

Software can come from anywhere. There are hundreds of thousands of open source projects that are not in Ubuntu repositories, and many only require you to download and compile the source.

There are many reasons why you might want to download source code. Some of the common reasons include:

- **Cutting edge**—Software found in the Ubuntu repositories may be outdated. If you want the most recent version, you will probably need to visit the project's home page and download source code.

- **Tweaking**—If you don't like how some piece of software functions, you can download the source code and change it.

- **Fixing**—Some packages do not work. This may be the result of broken dependencies or outdated software components. In any case, you can retrieve the code, patch it as necessary, and install it on your system. You are not limited to precompiled software.

- **Educating**—If you want to understand how something works, you can download the source and look at the code. Code from open source projects can be used as excellent examples and templates.

- **Extending**—Many projects are extendible. By downloading the source code, you can see how to interface new software into a project.

- **Leveraging**—Why reinvent the wheel? If some source code does a function that you need, you can download the code and adapt it to your needs. Be sure to pay attention to the original author's licensing requirements; some source code cannot be freely used without restrictions.

- **Sharing**—Every package in the universe and multiverse repositories was compiled and tested by someone. Perhaps you would like to add your favorite project so the community can benefit?

- **Uniqueness**—Many open source projects not found in the Ubuntu repositories provide very unique and useful functions. If you cannot download the functionality in binary form, then you will need to acquire the source.

Regardless of the reason, you will need some way to retrieve the source code and compile it. Some open source code is built for specific platforms and operating systems. For example, the mail reader elm and the graphic program xv were both designed for very old versions of Linux and have not been maintained. Downloading the source to these projects is not enough. You will likely need to edit the files before you can build these executables. To compile any incompatible projects, you may need a full development environment.

Installing Package Source Code

Many packages are available as precompiled executables and as source code. If you plan to install any source code then you'll need to install the dpkg-dev package. This brings in one required executable: /usr/bin/dpkg-source. This is used to unpack source code packages.

Many packages include developer installs. For example, the linux-source package places source code on the system for people doing kernel development. Most major subsystems, including audio, USB, and X-Windows, provide developer packages.

The other way to retrieve source code from the Ubuntu repositories is to actually download the source, not an installation package. Source code is downloaded using apt-get source *package_name*. Every package in the main and universe repositories should include source code, but source code may be missing from the restricted and multiverse repositories.

NOTE Not every package includes source code, and some packages include source code, general patches, and Ubuntu-specific patches.

The installation of binary files requires you to run apt-get as root. This is because files are placed in privileged directories and the catalog of installed packages must be updated. In contrast, source files are deposited in the current directory, so root permission is not required. This also means that there is no automatic removal. For example, to download the source code to gcalctool and unpack it, use:

```
mkdir src
cd src
apt-get source gcalctool
```

If you also want to automatically compile it, add the --compile flag to the apt-get line:

```
apt-get --compile source gcalctool
```

WARNING While apt-get install downloads dependencies, the apt-get source command does not. You may be required to download and install different developer packages and additional source code. Do not expect automatic compilation to work perfectly every time.

If you are done with the source code, you can remove it without using apt-get:

```
rm -rf gcalctool*
```

Programming with C

Most open source projects are written in C, C++, Java, Perl, Python, or Shell Script. Perl, Python, and bash (for Shell Scripts) are installed by default. Although basic C and C++ compilers are installed, these are not the full development environments. You should consider installing full environments.

There are many components to the full C and C++ environment. The key ones to install are:

- The Gnu C Compiler (gcc) and Gnu C++ (g++). These packages also install the manuals and documentation in case you need to look up any standard library calls.

```
sudo apt-get install gcc g++
sudo apt-get install gcc-doc manpages-dev
```

- The `make` command is commonly used for building executables. Other build-environment tools include `autoconf`, `automake`, and `libtool`.

```
sudo apt-get install make autoconf automake libtool
```

- If the code uses any complicated state machines or lexical analyzers, then you will probably need `flex` and `bison`.

```
sudo apt-get install flex bison bison-doc
```

- The `zlib` library is very common. Most tools that perform compression use it. Some well-known examples include `gzip`, `bz2`, and `unzip`, but other tools such as PNG rendering systems and MP3 players also use `zlib`.

```
sudo apt-get install zlib1g zlib1g-dev
```

- Most graphic systems use the X11 graphic library. You will probably need the development environment since it provides the application programming interface (API) to X-Windows.

```
sudo apt-get install libx11-dev
```

- If you plan to do any hard-core development, you might want an integrated development environment (IDE). Under Ubuntu, you have a couple of options.

  - Anjuta is a fully functional IDE with a graphical interface. To install it, use `sudo apt-get install anjuta`.

  - Eclipse is a very popular IDE for Java, but it does have an extension for C programming. Use `sudo apt-get install eclipse eclipse-cdt` to install Eclipse and the C Developer Tools.

NOTE Anjuta is designed for C and C++ software development. In contrast, Eclipse is an extension of a Java IDE. As a result, Eclipse requires include a lot of additional packages that Anjuta does not need. The list of Eclipse requirements includes Ant (a Java build system that is comparable to `make`), Java (the full environment), and libswt (the standard widget toolkit).

Enabling Java

Java is a programming language that is used by some developers as an alternative to C and C++. Its strength is in portability: a program created in Java does not need to be recompiled on every platform.

> **NOTE** Despite the naming similarity, Java and JavaScript are very different languages. The JavaScript name was more of a marketing blitz than a functional expression. At the time the language was created, Java was popular and *scripts* implied *simple*. Unfortunately, many nonprogrammers still think that JavaScript uses Java.

In previous versions of Ubuntu, there were many options for installing Java, and all required multiple steps. The problem was the licensing: Sun Microsystems used a restrictive license that was not appropriate for the restrictive or multiverse repositories. When Ubuntu Dapper Drake (6.06 LTS) was released, Sun changed the licensing, allowing the package to be placed in the multiverse repository.

Today, there are many different variations of Java. This includes Sun Microsystem's Java, OpenJDK, and GCJ. For most practical purposes, you only need to install one of these.

- The Gnu Compiler for Java (GCJ) is part of the default Ubuntu installation, but it lacks a development environment. This Java version comes from the main repository.

    ```
    sudo apt-get install java-gcj-compat-dev
    ```

- Sun Java is the official version of Java maintained by Sun Microsystems. It exists in the multiverse repository.

    ```
    sudo apt-get install sun-java6-bin sun-java6-jre
    ```

- OpenJDK is an open source Java Development Kit that includes the java compiler and standard libraries. It is available for Hardy Heron (8.04 LTS) and later versions from the universe repository.

    ```
    sudo apt-get install openjdk-6-jre # run-time environment
    sudo apt-get install openjdk-6-jdk # optional java development kit
    ```

In addition to the Java development environment, you may also want to install some optional components:

- If you would like to use Java with the Mozilla Firefox web browser, you will need to install the Java plug-in and configure it as the default JRE. You will also need to run `update-alternatives` to update various links found throughout the operating system.

    ```
    sudo apt-get install sun-java6-plugin    # for Sun Java..
    sudo apt-get install icedtea6-plugin     # for OpenJDK..
    ```

```
sudo apt-get install icedtea-gcjwebplugin # for GCJ..
sudo update-alternatives—config java    # .. to update the system
```

- For build environments, Ant is the tool of choice (few Java environments use make):

```
sudo apt-get install ant ant-doc
```

- If you need a full IDE for Java, consider using Eclipse:

```
sudo apt-get install eclipse
```

Fixing Scripts

Shell scripts are found everywhere on the system. The startup commands under /etc/init.d/ are scripts. The Gnome Display Manager configuration in /etc/gdm/ and network configuration in /etc/network/ are scripts. Even the command-line prompt is actually an interactive script that you create as you go.

There is only one real problem with shell scripts, and that's the shell. Most shell scripts begin with the line #!/bin/sh. The first two characters are special: they tell the running shell that the file is a script and not a data file or compiled executable. Right after that comes the name of the shell to use for processing the commands in the script. In this example, everything will be processed using /bin/sh. Perl scripts usually use #!/usr/bin/perl and you can create an awk script using #!/bin/awk.

The issue is that /bin/sh isn't actually a program. It is a symbolic link to the actual shell. With Dapper Drake (6.06 LTS) and earlier versions of Ubuntu, /bin/sh links to /bin/bash. The Bourne Again Shell (bash) is a feature-rich shell that extends the original Bourne shell (sh) from the early days of Unix.

Beginning with Edgy Eft (6.10), /bin/sh was changed to link to /bin/dash. The Debian Almquist Shell (dash) is a slimmed down shell that loads faster, consumes less memory, and is ideal for most shell scripts. While dash is (mostly) POSIX-compliant and compatible with the Bourne shell, it lacks many of the additional features found in bash. Some of the missing features include:

- **No command-line editor**—With bash, you can use bash -o vi or bash -o emacs to specify command-line editing using vi or Emacs controls. Dash lacks an editor.

- **No in-variable expressions**—With bash, in-variable substitutions like ${!MODE_*} and ${MODEVAR//_/\/} are quick shortcuts for modifying a variable's content. Dash does not support this.

- **Missing POSIX features**—A few POSIX features, such as $LINENO to represent the shell script line number, are missing from dash. This means dash cannot store a history of previous commands, and commands like !! to rerun the last command and !-2 to rerun the penultimate command won't work.

Usually the difference between /bin/bash and /bin/dash isn't a problem. But it can bite you when code is ported over from other operating systems where /bin/sh is actually bash. Usually the shell differences crop up with complex shell scripts, but it can also appear in Perl or C code that runs system commands. (The system() and popen() calls run /bin/sh, which may be bash, dash, or some other shell.)

If you come across this problem, there are two ways to fix it. The best option is to replace the shell in the isolated instance where it does not work. If the script expects bash, then make it run bash: change the first line in the script from #!/bin/sh to #!/bin/bash.

The less desirable option is to replace the default system shell with bash:

```
sudo ln -sf /bin/bash /bin/sh
```

This second option isn't as desirable since it will slow down boot and run times; every boot and maintenance script uses /bin/sh; since dash runs faster and consumes less resources that bash, the change is a performance hit. However, this change won't break anything since bash can do everything dash does, plus a lot more.

NOTE For more information about the change from bash to dash, see `https://wiki.ubuntu.com/DashAsBinSh`.

Summary

Ubuntu provides many different ways to search for software, installation packages, and manage updates. Some of the methods require a graphic display—these are very easy to use but may limit remote administration. If the graphic display is unavailable (or inconvenient), you can always fall back to the command-line software management system. Although most of the common software that you might want is available from one of the four standard repositories, you should be prepared to download source code and compile software by hand since some cool projects are not readily available for Ubuntu.

Communicating Online

What's In This Chapter?

Enhancing Web access by improving browser features
Securing web access from remote locations
How to unify e-mail accounts
Chatting with IM and VoIP

The default Ubuntu desktop installation includes a web browser, e-mail reader, instant messaging and chat-room client, and even a VoIP system. Although anyone can use them as is, you can get much more out of them by performing a few tweaks and tuning a couple of parameters. Whether you want speed, security, or fancier graphics and cooler features, you are going to want to modify the default applications. In this chapter, you will see how to adjust the web browser settings, secure your web traffic using Secure Shell, access your mail on a variety of systems, and chat online.

Hacking the Firefox Web Brower

The default web browser for Ubuntu is Mozilla Firefox. This browser is fast and supports HTTP 1.0 and 1.1 protocols, as well as HTML, CSS, and JavaScript. Although you can immediately use the browser for accessing web sites, some of the default settings could use a little modification.

TIP Hardy Heron (8.04 LTS) and later versions of Ubuntu use Firefox 3.x. Older versions of Firefox have the same configuration options, but they are located under different preference tabs.

Tuning Preferences

Firefox has a set of common preferences that can be adjusted to fit your needs. Open the main preferences menu by starting the browser and choosing Edit ⇨ Preferences from the Firefox menu. The preferences menu is divided into categories, denoted by icons on the top of the window (see Figure 6-1). I change my preferences for security, speed, and convenience. Whenever I use a new browser, I immediately change the home page, Java and JavaScript settings, and cache options. If I plan to repeatedly use the browser (instead of a one-time install on a temporary system), then I also adjust the connection and privacy settings.

Figure 6-1: The Firefox Preferences window

Tuning the Main Preferences

The Main category provides basic settings for the browser. I usually make a few minor changes.

- **Change the default location.** I usually use a search engine or a blank page. If there is a particular site you usually go to first, put the URL here.

However, specifying a blank page gives you a faster startup time since the browser isn't busy accessing the network.

▪ **Set the download location.** The default location is `$HOME/Downloads/`. You can change this if you like; some people prefer downloading to the Desktop or to an alternate disk partition. I prefer downloading to a folder, but I make a link to the folder from my desktop for easy access:

```
ln -s $HOME/Downloads $HOME/Desktop/Downloads
```

Tuning the Tabs Preferences

Tabs enable you to open new pages in the same window rather than opening a new browser. I find this to be the most useful feature of Firefox. I always have tabs shown. This way, if I want to open a new tab, I can either press Ctrl+T or double-click on an empty part of the tab bar. Also, always having tabs displayed means the screen will not resize when I open a new tab bar.

TIP Pressing Ctrl+Shift+T will re-open the last closed tab. The list of closed tabs is stored under History ➪ Recently Closed Tabs.

Tuning the Content Preferences

The Content category provides settings for handling HTML content.

▪ **Enable popup blocking.** If a specific site wants to create a popup, Firefox will create a notice at the top of the page. Then I can choose to explicitly permit popups for that page.

NOTE Blocking popups does not stop all popups. JavaScript can also be used to spawn popup windows without being caught by this setting. However, enabling popup blocking does stop many of the annoyances.

▪ **Disable Java.** There are very few web sites that require Java and there are too many security risks.

▪ **Adjust JavaScript.** I used to recommend that people disable JavaScript, but today there are too many web sites using it for active web pages. If you do leave it enabled, be sure to look at the Advanced settings for JavaScript. Turn off anything you do not require. (And if you don't know, turn it off until you do know—usually you will not notice a difference.) I usually permit JavaScript to move or resize existing windows, but not anything else.

Adjusting Preferred Applications

The Applications category allows you to specify what applications will handle specific download formats. For example, if you download a video, then you can have it automatically play using VLC, Totem, or some other application; always save; or always ask you what to do. If you have a preferred application (or do not like the default settings), then you can change the settings here.

Tuning the Privacy Preferences

The Privacy category provides settings for managing cached information.

- **Alter history.** I usually reduce the history of accessed sites. With Hardy Heron (8.04 LTS), the default is 9 days; Karmic Koala (9.10) defaults to 90 days. I usually reduce it down to one day. If I need to visit a site often, then I bookmark the URL. Keeping nine days (or three months) of history just clutters the list of sites I have visited. But there are some reasons to keep a large history. For example, if you use the browser for researching a project, then a large history can allow you to quickly find places you visited days or weeks ago. Consider changing this value to match your needs.

- **Adjust saved passwords.** I usually disable saved forms and saved passwords. This is mainly for privacy; an unauthorized user cannot access my online accounts through the auto-login feature. However, enabling these options can really speed up access to some web sites. If you don't have privacy concerns and frequently visit the same sites that require forms or passwords, then you can enable these options.

- **Change download history.** Firefox keeps a history of downloaded files. The default setting enables you to manually clean up the list of files. I usually enable automatic removal of entries after downloads. This way, my list only shows failed downloads and ones in progress.

- **Handling cookies.** As much as privacy advocates complain about tracking people, cookies have become a way of life on the web. Yet, there are some safer ways to handle cookies. I suggest enabling cookies for only the originating site and blocking cookies for third-party sites (see Figure 6-2). Unless you have a need for maintaining cookies long after you close the browser, I suggest the "Keeping cookies: Until I close Firefox" setting. When you close the browser, all cookies are removed.

NOTE Firefox uses shared memory. You must close *all* Firefox browsers and windows to clear out the cookies when using the "Until I close Firefox" setting. Closing one browser does not do it since the shared memory is not released.

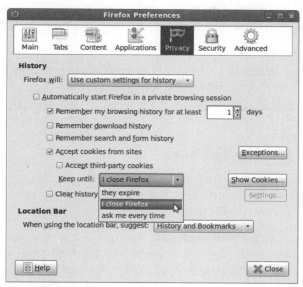

Figure 6-2: Changing the Firefox cookie preferences

PRIVATE BROWSING

Many people have privacy concerns when browsing. Whether you are borrowing from someone else's computer, letting someone use your computer, or worried about having your laptop stolen, there are some things you don't want cached. (Does your friend really need to have a cache of your Gmail account?)

Anyone using your browser can see the sites you have visited. If you have privacy concerns, consider lowering the history or disabling it completely by setting the number of days to zero and then clearing the history once. You can also clear your cached information using Tools ➪ Clear Private Data or by pressing Ctrl+Shift+Del.

Beginning with Firefox 3.5, you can use Tools ➪ Start Private Browsing (or press Ctrl+Shift+P) to switch the browser into a mode where it will not save any history, usernames, or cache files. Unfortunately, Hardy Heron and older Ubuntu versions do not have Firefox 3.5 available in the repositories. Karmic Koala (9.10) is the first Ubuntu release that includes Firefox 3.5 as the default.

Some Firefox plug-ins maintain their own cookies and are not impacted by browser settings. For example, the Macromedia Flash plug-in (see Chapter 5)

(continued)

PRIVATE BROWSING *(continued)*

stores cookies under `$HOME/.macromedia/Flash_Player/#Shared`
`Objects/`. **Clearing the browser's cookies and cache does not automatically**
clear these files. I added the following line to my `$HOME/.profile` **in order**
to clear my Flash cookies each time I login:

```
rm -rf $HOME/.macromedia/Flash_Player/#SharedObjects/*/*
```

You can also add this to your crontab to have it automatically run daily or
weekly. (See Chapter 8 for scheduling with cron.)

Adjusting the Security Settings

The Security tab allows you to change a few of the generic security
settings—not to be confused with the security settings under the Content,
Privacy, and Advanced configuration settings.

- **Enable warnings about add-ons.** Any time a web page tries to install
  something by itself, there is a good chance that you will be infected
  with malware. It is always good to be warned about sites that try to
  automatically install add-ons, plug-ins, and updates. By default, there
  are only two exceptions that can install anything: `addons.mozilla.org`
  and `updates.mozilla.org`. These are generally acceptable since Mozilla
  provides the Firefox web browser.

- **Warn about hostile sites**. Firefox 2.*x* introduced additional options to
  warn about suspected phishing (forgery) and malware sites. The options
  work by comparing URLs against a known blacklist of evil sites. On one
  hand, this does help mitigate some phishing and malware attacks. But
  it can also significantly slow the browsing experience—particularly on
  slow computers.

- **Storing passwords**. Firefox has the option to cache passwords for sites.
  This simplifies logins, particularly if you clear cookies every time you
  exit the browser. However, if you are going to store passwords in the
  browser, be sure to set a master password. The master password will
  encrypt your stored passwords and deter unauthorized access.

Tuning the Advanced Preferences

The Advanced category is a catchall for other Firefox options. The available
options under Ubuntu are different from the Firefox settings under Windows.
For example, you do not have the option to check for Firefox updates. This
is because the Synaptic's update manager will tell you if new updates are

available. You could choose to disable update checks for Installed Add-ons and for Search Engines—neither of these change often enough to require periodic update checks, but leaving the options enabled does not hurt either.

The Advanced category contains four tabs: General, Network, Update, and Encryption. The General tab covers accessibility, scrolling, and the spell checker. I usually make sure that the default browser check is disabled.

The Network tab allows you to set proxies and specifies the amount of disk space to devote to the web cache.

- **Configure proxies.** If you use a proxy instead of directly connecting to the Internet, Ubuntu gives you two choices. You can configure a systemwide proxy that will work for all network services (see Chapter 12), or you can give Firefox a special proxy setting through the Connection Settings button.

- **Limit cache size.** Cache files are stored on your hard drive for quick access to sites you commonly visit. The default is 50 MB of cache. I usually reduce it to 20 MB. Most sites that I visit have dynamic content that changes hourly (active web forums, news sites, and so on). Despite what advertisers may think, I usually don't *need* to cache 50 MB of banner ads on my system.

TIP If a web page does not show current information, then it is likely cached. Hold down the Ctrl key when you click on the Reload icon in order to forcefully refresh the page. You can also use Ctrl+F5 or Ctrl+Shift+R.

CACHE AND PRIVACY

The browser cache can lead to privacy concerns. Everything from web pages of online bank accounts to porn that you accidentally stumbled across gets stored in the cache. If your system is compromised or accessed by someone else, then everything in your cache becomes fair game. Reducing the cache size can also speed up system backups since less unnecessary data will be copied.

Keeping a small cache does remove the data from a typical user, but it won't stop the professionals. Even through a file is deleted, it can still be recovered through tools such as `e2undel` and `recover` (for ext2 file systems), or more complicated forensic tools such as The Coroner's Toolkit (tct), Sleuthkit, and Autopsy. Although these are not easy-to-use programs, they can recover most deleted files.

The best way to stay very safe is to completely disable caching, but that will lead to slow web pages. Every icon—regardless how small—must be down-loaded from the network every single time. In general, adjusting the cache size is done more for speed and disk space than for privacy, since anything saved to disk could potentially be recovered.

The Update tab manages automatic software and the Encryption tab manages SSL certificates. Unless you have special needs, you probably do not need to change anything under these tabs.

Fine-Tuning the Firefox Advanced Preferences

The Firefox Preferences menu shows you the most common things to tune, but those are not the only configurable items. There is a hidden configuration screen that you can access by entering `about:config` in the address bar (see Figure 6-3).

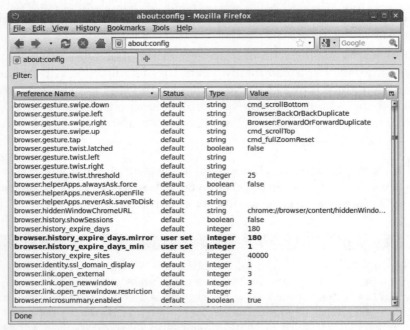

Figure 6-3: The advanced configuration menu

This configuration menu shows all of the configuration settings and their values. Default values appear with regular text, whereas bold text denotes modified settings. In this case, you can see that when I changed my history setting on the Preferences' Privacy menu, it changed the settings in the advanced configuration.

All items from the Preferences menu can be modified in the `about:config` area. To change a preference, double-click the item to change and enter a new value. Alternately, you can right-click the line to bring up a small menu.

Selecting the Modify or Toggle menu option is the same as double-clicking. For example, to completely disable saving files, web pages, and images to the disk cache, set the `browser.cache.disk.enable` option to `false`.

Beyond the common preferences, `about:config` gives you access to other settings. Some affect how the browser looks or how it displays items. For example, `browser.chrome.toolbar_tips` controls whether text appears when you hover the mouse over the toolbar icons. Other items impact functionality. For example, changing `layout.spellcheckDefault` to `2` applies the built-in spell checker to all text entry fields and not just multi-line text areas.

NOTE Modifying how HTML is displayed, such as turning off blinking text, only affects new web pages. You will need to reload pages that are currently being displayed in other browser windows or tabs.

Many configuration options manage performance. For example, the Hypertext Transport Protocol (HTTP) uses TCP for transferring data. TCP is not the fastest protocol and takes time to create and tear down network connections. To speed things up, HTTP allows you to make multiple requests over an established TCP connection. This way, when you need to request multiple pages or images from one server, you don't have the added delay from opening new connections. After a connection sits idle for a while, it is disconnected. You can adjust this timeout value using the `network.http.keep-alive.timeout` setting. The default value is 300 seconds (five minutes). If you use a home firewall (you have a home firewall, right?) then the timeout value on the firewall may be less than five minutes. For best performance, consider adjusting the Firefox timeout to match your firewall. Mine is set to 120 seconds (two minutes).

Since one TCP connection transfers one piece of data at a time, browsers use multiple connections for parallel downloads. You can alter the number of simultaneous connections by adjusting the `network.http.max-connections-per-server` and `network.http.max-connections` settings. The default settings are good for a cable modem or DSL users. But, if you have a faster network connection, you might want to increase these values (for example, 40 connections total and 10 per server), and if you are using a slow connection, such as a dial-up modem or 802.11b wireless network, then you might want to lower these values to 8 and 4 for dial-up, and 15 and 5 for wireless. The reason for this is to avoid bottlenecks: if you try to download too much data at once, it will all arrive at the same time. The resulting traffic will be interlaced and the network protocol may send flow-control packets back to the server, or the server may resend unacknowledged packets. As a result, having lots of parallel downloads can be slower than if you download the data one file at a time.

TIP If you can see the browser slowly loading many images, and frequently get broken or partially loaded images, then you probably have a slow connection. Lower the number of simultaneous connections and see if performance improves. In general, the total number of concurrent connections should be two to three times larger than the number of connections per server.

Fortunately, there is nothing in this advanced configuration menu that is dangerous—changing a setting will not corrupt anything (but may slow down performance) and can always be reset to the default value by right-clicking on the item and selecting Reset from the item's menu.

Managing Profiles

Firefox stores all settings in a profile. You don't need to use the same Firefox settings every time; you can create different profiles. For example, I use Ubuntu on a laptop that I carry between home and work. I have one profile configured to use a proxy for work and another to connect directly to the Internet for home.

NOTE You can also use profiles if you are using a shared machine. Ideally, everyone should have different user accounts on the system. This gives all users independent profiles. But sometimes it is easier for family members to just use the same account. You can easily give everyone (including your dog) different profiles.

To bring up the profile manager, you will need to run Firefox at a command prompt:

```
firefox -ProfileManager
```

This brings up the Profile Manager, where you can add, edit, or remove profiles (see Figure 6-4). The main profile is called *default*—don't delete this unless you want to lose all of your settings. After you create your new profile, you can select it and click the Start Firefox button. All preferences that you change now will only impact your new profile. Later, you can start Firefox with your new profile by specifying it on the command line. For example, in Figure 6-4, I created a profile called *SOCKS Proxy*. I can use this proxy by running: `firefox -P "SOCKS Proxy"`. Alternately, I can specify the default proxy by using `-P default`, or I can just use `-ProxyManager` to see the menu again.

Extreme Firefox Tweaks with File Configurations

The settings from the Edit ▷ Preferences menu are minimalistic, and the `about:config` menu allows you to control a lot of functionality but not everything. If you really want to tweak Firefox, you'll need to edit some configuration files.

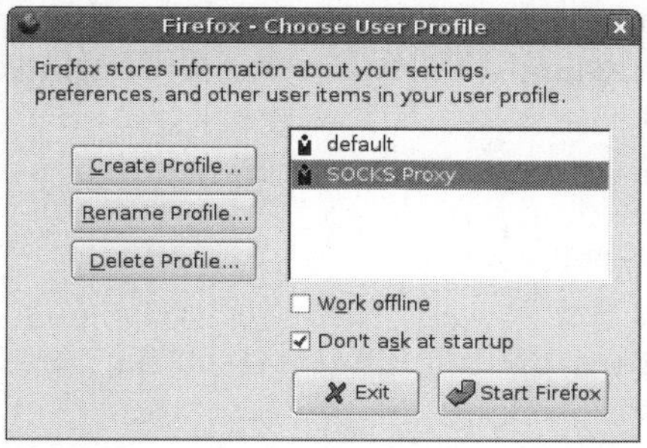

Figure 6-4: The Profile Manager window

Firefox stores all files in the $HOME/.mozilla/firefox/ directory. In this directory are subdirectories for each profile you created. These directories have a random eight-character string followed by the profile's name. In each profile directory are all of the configuration files. For example, the file prefs.js contains all of your modified configuration settings from the about:config menu.

Another cool directory is the chrome subdirectory (for example, $HOME/.mozilla/firefox/*.default/chrome/). This is where you can define what Firefox should actually *look* like. There are two sample files in this directory: userChrome and userContent. The former controls the display of Firefox and the latter controls the default rendering options.

1. At a command prompt, go into the chrome directory. In this example, you'll use the default profile, but you can really choose any profile.

   ```
   cd $HOME/.mozilla/firefox/*.default/chrome
   ```

2. If you have not already created customized files, then copy over the examples:

   ```
   cp userChrome-example.css userChrome.css
   cp userContent-example.css userContent.css
   ```

3. Edit userChrome.css. This allows you to alter what the browser looks like. The other file, userContent.css, is for customizing the default web page settings.

4. After modifying these files, save your changes. You will need to close all open browsers and then open Firefox to see the changes.

Here are some examples of cool things you can do with these configuration files:

▪ Stop scrolling text! While scrolling marquee text at the bottom of the browser's window can be informative, most web sites are just annoying.

Besides, I like to see the URL when I hold the mouse over a link. To disable marquee text, add the following to the `userContent.css` file:

```
marquee {
  -moz-binding: none !important;
  display: block;
  height: auto !important;
}
```

▪ While you can turn off blinking text in the `about:config` menu and `pref.js` file (set `browser.blink_allowed` to `false`), you can also set it in the `userContent.css` file:

```
blink {
    text-decoration: none ! important;
}
```

▪ By default, all tabs have a dull gray background color. If you use lots of tabs then you might find it convenient to highlight the active tab. In this case, I modified the `userChrome.css` file to change the active tab to a light green and the inactive tabs to dark red.

```
/* Change tab colors */
tab{
  -moz-appearance: none !important;
}
tab[selected="true"] {
  background-color: lightgreen !important;
  color: black !important;
}
/* Change color of normal tabs */
tab:not([selected="true"]) {
  background-color: darkred !important;
  color: white !important;
}
```

▪ You can specify any web color by name (for example, `lightgreen` or `white`) or by specifying the RGB values. For example, `rgb(128,255,128)` is a puke green color.

You will need to close all open browsers and then reopen Firefox to see the changes made to the `userChrome.css` and `userContent.css` files.

TIP The sample `userChrome` and `userContent` files contain few examples. They are mainly used to show formatting and offer a few simple examples. You can find larger lists of tunable items at `www.mozilla.org/unix/customizing.html`.

Adding Search Engines

When Firefox first starts, the top-left corner has a text entry field for doing searches on Google, Yahoo!, eBay, and a few other sites. There is no reason why you cannot add your own search engine. For example, if you work for a large corporation, then your company probably has its own search engine for the internal network. You can create your own search entry for performing internal company searches. As another example, you might want to add the search engines for SourceForge (`http://sourceforge.net`) or Google Linux (`www.google.com/linux`) to the menu so that you can quickly look for open source software.

1. Open a command prompt and go to the `/usr/lib/firefox-addons/searchplugins` directory. This is where the search engine plug-ins are defined.

WARNING Depending on your browser version, you may need to go into a different directory. Hardy Heron's Firefox 3.0 uses `/usr/lib/firefox-addons/searchplugin/`. Karmic Koala's Firefox 3.5 stores the global search addons under `/usr/lib/firefox-addons/searchplugin/en-US/`.

2. Create a new search engine. With Firefox 3.0, search engine addons are configured in XML files.

```
sudo gedit sourceforge.xml
```

TIP The `/usr/lib/firefox*` directories contain all of the system-wide default settings that will impact all users on the system. You can create a search engine that is only accessible to you by using the `$HOME/.mozilla/firefox/*.default/searchplugins/` directory instead. Initially you will need to create this directory, but you do not need root access to create any files in your home directory.

3. Edit the `xml` file to suit your needs. For example, I created an engine to search SourceForge for open source projects. I found the query values by typing **anything** into the search bar. What I saw was a search URL that said:

```
http://sourceforge.net/search/?type_of_search=soft&words=anything
```

This has a URL with two query fields (listed after the "?"). The first field is static and defined by SourceForge for software searches: `type_of_search=soft`. The second field holds the query. So, my `sourceforge.xml` file becomes:

```
<SearchPlugin xmlns="http://www.mozilla.org/2006/browser/search/">
<ShortName>SourceForge</ShortName>
<Description>SourceForge Search</Description>
<InputEncoding>UTF-8</InputEncoding>
<Url type="application/x-suggestions+json" method="GET"
  template="http://sourceforge.net/search/" />
<Url type="text/html" method="GET"
     template="http://sourceforge.net/search">
```

```
      <Param name="type_of_search" value="soft"/>
      <Param name="words" value="{searchTerms}"/>
   </Url>
</SearchPlugin>
```

4. Save the file, close all browsers, and restart Firefox. You should see your plug-in (for example, SourceForge Search) added to the list of search engines.

There are other options for the search plug-in file, but most are not needed. If your search engine uses a POST instead of a GET (you'll know because the search term will not appear in the URL), then you will need to find out the parameters. You can do this by viewing the source of the search engine's web page and seeing what fields are sent with the form (or jump to Chapter 12 and learn how to capture packets and see what is really being sent).

Playing with Plug-ins and Extensions

Plug-ins and extensions are small programs for Firefox that provide additional functionality. For example, the default Firefox installation cannot play SWF (Macromedia Flash) files. By adding in the Flash plug-in (see Chapter 5), you can add in an SWF player. To see the list of installed plug-ins, enter about:plugins in the address bar. While you cannot add, edit, or remove plug-ins from here, you can see what is installed.

> **TIP** Under about:config, set plugins.expose_full_path to true. This will display the full path to each plugin and not just the filenames.

Adding Plug-ins

When Firefox does not know how to handle a particular file type, it gives you a couple of options. First, it can save the file to disk. Although this doesn't run any programs, at least you can save it.

Another option is to search for an available plug-in at https://addons .mozilla.org/plugins/. You can also go to this URL and browse the list of available plug-ins. Another site that hosts plug-ins for Linux is located at http://plugindoc.mozdev.org/linux.html, but Firefox does not normally search this site.

A final option requires you to know the plug-in's name and install it using apt-get. Example plug-in packages include mozilla-helix-player, mozilla-mplayer, and totem-mozilla.

Removing Plug-ins

In the event that you add in a plug-in and it turns out not to be what you wanted, you need some way to remove it. Unfortunately, the Firefox menus offer no solution here. If you installed the plug-in using `apt-get`, then you can remove it (using, for example, `sudo apt-get remove totem-mozilla`). But if Firefox installed the plug-in, then you need to delete it by hand.

Plug-ins are stored in many different directories. The `$HOME/.mozilla/plugins/` directory stores plug-ins owned by you and that are only available to you; it is created when you install a plug-in without being root.

The other directories, `/usr/lib/firefox/plugins/`, `/usr/lib/mozilla/plugins/`, and `/usr/lib/firefox-addons/plugins/`, store systemwide plug-ins. Deleting files from these directories removes unwanted plug-ins from Firefox.

> **NOTE** Some plug-ins create multiple files in the plug-in directory. For example, the Helix plug-in creates `nphelix.so` and `nphelix.xpt`. Be sure to delete all files associated with the plug-in.

Helping Handlers

When a file is downloaded, it can be displayed in the browser window, saved to disk, or passed to another application. Web browsers have two ways to determine how to handle a downloaded file. The first method uses mime-types. For example, HTML pages are text/html, plain text is text/plain, and an image could be image/gif or image/jpeg. Each MIME type contains a general category (for example, text or image) and a specific format identifier (for example, gif or jpeg). The second method uses file name extensions. For example, a file named `ch06.doc` is a word processor document file, and `06-03.png` is a PNG image.

> **NOTE** Many Unix and Linux applications use a third method to determine file content. Called a *magic number file*, this method looks at the file's contents for identifying features. The file `/usr/share/file/magic` under Ubuntu lists the common magic values. Firefox uses this method when no MIME type is available, but not to identify unknown MIME types.

When you access data on a web site, the information is returned with a MIME type. The file name may be specified in the HTTP header, but is usually taken from the end of the URL. If the browser sees something it knows, such as text/html or image/gif, then it renders the file. However, if the browser does not recognize the MIME type (for example, application/binary-octet or video/x-ogm+ogg), then the options are limited: save the file or search for a plug-in. Although other web browsers allow you to associate helper applications to MIME types or file extensions, Firefox does not allow you to create your own helpers.

The solution to this limitation is a plug-in called `mozplugger`.

```
sudo apt-get install mozplugger
```

This plug-in creates a configuration file called `/etc/mozpluggerrc`, which allows you to associate a MIME type or file extension with a program on the computer. For example, if you want PostScript (`ps` and `eps`) files to open using Ghostview (`gv`), follow these steps:

1. Install the Ghostview PostScript viewer (if you have not already installed it):

   ```
   sudo apt-get install gv
   ```

2. As root, add the following lines to the end of `/etc/mozpluggerrc`:

   ```
   application/postscript:ps,eps:Postscript
    : gv $file
   ```

   The first line specifies the MIME type, extensions, and a description. Multiple extensions can be placed in a comma-separated list. The second line identifies the handler. The documentation for `mozplugger` (`man mozplugger`) explains many more options for this control file, including conditionals and special handling.

3. Remove the cached plug-in list generated by Firefox. Without this step, new handlers will not be recognized.

   ```
   rm $HOME/.mozilla/firefox/*/pluginreg.dat
   ```

4. Enter `about:plugins` in the address bar. Your new handler will be listed at the end of the `mozplugger` section.

When using `mozplugger`, you do not need to close your browser for changes to take effect.

Opening Remote Browsers

Firefox is an intelligent program. It knows how to communicate with other running instances in order to save memory. If you open two browsers and look at the process list for Firefox (`ps --ef | grep firefox`) you will see only one running process. This is because the second process detected the first and told it to open a new window rather than actually running a new, independent browser.

While reusing code is great for reducing memory requirements, it does have one undesirable side effect: you cannot run a browser remotely if you have one open locally. This situation happens often to system administrators. For example, you will log in to a remote host with X-Windows enabled, and want to run Firefox *on* that remote host, but with the browser's display shown on your local system. This is different from running the browser on your system because all web-network requests will originate from the remote system. Unfortunately, just running `firefox` on the remote host will tell your local browser to spawn a new window. Instead, use `firefox --no-remote -P`. This tells Firefox *not* to communicate through the X-Windows system in order to identify any running browsers. The result is that the remote browser will not see your local browser; it will start running on the remote system, and it will send its display over to your system.

WARNING Firefox 1.*x* was a simpler browser. You could `ssh` into a remote system and run `firefox --no-xshm`. This would start up the remote browser on local display, and it would use the default profile.

With Firefox 3.*x*, the simplicity was lost. You cannot have two browser instances using the same profile. Thus, if the remote host already has a browser open and is using the default profile, then you must specify -P (or -P *profile*) in order to use the remote browser.

There are other caveats as well. For example, Firefox under Hardy Heron (8.04 LTS) can be displayed on Dapper Drake (6.06 LTS) or Karmic Koala (9.10). However, the Firefox browser for Karmic cannot be displayed on Dapper Drake because it uses X-Windows extensions that are newer than Dapper. Depending on the X-Windows version of the local and remote systems, you may not be able to run Firefox remotely.

Using Other Web Browsers

Although Firefox is the default web browser, it is not the only one available. Many other browser packages can be installed, including `seamonkey`, `epiphany-browser`, `konqueror`, `lynx`, and `elinks`.

- **Seamonkey**—Previously called the Mozilla Application Suite, this is an all-in-one web browser, e-mail client, HTML editor, and more. Seamonkey is similar to the Mozilla Firefox browser because they stem from the same source.

- **Epiphany-browser**. This is the Gnome web browser. As such, it integrates very well with Ubuntu's Gnome desktop.

- **Konqueror**—Konqueror is the default browser for the KDE environment. If you choose to install Konqueror, you will need to install the entire KDE run-time environment.

- **Lynx**—Although Lynx is a text-based browser, I strongly recommend installing it and learning how to use it. When you crash X-Windows, lose the graphical display, or are simply using an Ubuntu server installation, you cannot use Firefox to search the web for help—*no graphics* means *no Firefox*. As primitive as Lynx may appear, it will allow you to search for help and download patches.

- **Elinks**—Similar to Lynx, this enhanced text-based browser handles frames, tables, and other web content that Lynx cannot display.

Why Use Different Browsers?

Although some web browsers are suited to special purposes, others just provide alternatives. Many web developers install an assortment of browsers in order to test their web pages. A page you design may look nice under one browser but can have serious problems with a different browser.

I sometimes use different web browsers in place of different Firefox profiles. Even if I give each profile a distinct color scheme, they can still look too familiar. For example, I use one browser for direct Internet use and a different browser for connections through a public proxy. The last thing I want to do is use the direct browser for things that should be done via proxy. If I use two different Firefox profiles at the same time, then I risk mistaking the two windows. But, if I use Firefox for direct access and the Epiphany browser for proxy access, then the browsers look completely different—I won't mistakenly use Firefox thinking it is using the proxy. (See the next section, "Securing Web Access with SSH," to understand why I'd want to use a proxy.)

Mitigating Crashes

Firefox is a pretty stable browser, but it has crashed on me in rare instances. When it crashes, all Firefox windows vanish. Even when using with multiple profiles, if one window crashes then all Firefox windows close—regardless of the profile. This can seriously impact productivity if you're like me and you heavily depend on web access for your work. A browser crash at an inopportune moment can cost me hours of searching that will need to be redone.

If you're going to access sites that occasionally crash your browsers (in 2006, www.cnn.com readily crashed Firefox), you can limit the risk from a crash by running different browsers. For example, one browser can be used to look at news and entertainment sites, and another can be used for work-related web access. Besides making a distinction between work and play, this also prevents a crash at a fun web site from impacting the work browser. (This is something your boss may care about, even if you don't.)

Securing Web Access with SSH

When you use the network from the comfort of your own home or small office, there is a degree of security because you are not sharing the Internet connection. You can access your favorite web sites or manage your bank account with relatively little risk of someone watching you. Although an evil hacker on the network between you and your bank can see your connection, the odds are very slim that someone is actually on the exact network route between you and your bank.

Unfortunately, the same sense of security does not apply to remote locations. Coffee shops, airports, bookstores, libraries, hotels, and other places that offer network access for free (or a fee) not only cannot protect you from eavesdropping, but they will happily offer the same free (or fee) connection to anyone—even an attacker. I've been in enough crowded coffee shops to realize that the chances of someone eavesdropping could be as high as 25 percent (and that's assuming that *I'm* not in the coffee shop with *my* laptop). Some people do it for fun or curiosity, but other people can be malicious—playing with connections or stealing passwords and accounts. Even using SSL and HTTPS cannot offer you much protection against an active attacker.

Since you don't know who might be listening, it is best to play it safe. If you want to access the network securely *and* want the freedom of browsing from anywhere, then consider using a Secure Shell (SSH) tunnel. SSH provides an encrypted connection between two computers, and can forward network traffic across the tunnel. To do this, you will need:

- **Two computers.** One will be your server at home (or at your trusted location), and the other will be your laptop, which you will take with you to the coffee shop.

- **SOCKS server proxy running on the server.** This is how you will relay your traffic from the coffee shop, over the SSH connection to your home, and proxy out to the network.

The goal is to use SSH to create a secure tunnel from your laptop at the coffee shop to your home. You will send all web traffic through the tunnel and relay the web requests through your own SOCKS server. This way, all your web traffic is encrypted as it passes through the coffee shop.

Although this approach is not foolproof, it is about as safe as accessing the network from your home. The basic steps are:

1. Install a SSH server at your home.

2. Open your home SSH server to the Internet. This way, you can access it from the coffee shop, library, or any other public location.

3. Install and configure a SOCKS server that is only accessible from your home.

4. Test the configuration before going to the public location.

5. Establish the full end-to-end tunnel and start relaying your web traffic.

6. Configure your SSH connection based on your speed requirements.

Installing the SSH Server

The first thing you will need to do is install the SSH server. The Ubuntu installation gives you an SSH client but not a server. To get the server, install the `openssh-server` package:

```
sudo apt-get install openssh-server
```

Besides installing the server, this package will also generate cryptographic keys, add itself to `/etc/init.d` for automatically starting at boot, and start the daemon. I usually check the default server's configuration found in `/etc/ssh/sshd_config`:

- Make sure that X11 forwarding is enabled (`X11Forwarding yes`). This way, if your laptop supports X-Windows, then you can run graphical applications from the remote system. For the SSH client (`/etc/ssh/ssh_config`), you will also want to enable `X11Forwarding`. If either the client or server does not support this option, then you cannot run graphical applications across the tunnel.

- Check to make sure `KeepAlive yes` is set. This prevents an idle SSH connection from being disconnected by an overzealous firewall.

- I like to enable a banner message (`Banner /etc/issue.net`). This way, people see a friendly greeting when they connect to the SSH server. This message is displayed before the user is prompted for a password. You will also want to edit the `/etc/issue.net` file. The default banner gives the operating system version and that could be a security risk. I changed mine so that it displays this happy message (see Figure 6-5):

  ```
  All connections and packets are being recorded.
  Unauthorized access attempts can and will be viewed as a network attack.
  Where unauthorized access is enforceable by law, it will be prosecuted.
  ```

After making any changes to the server's configuration, you will need to restart the daemon:

```
sudo /etc/init.d/ssh restart
```

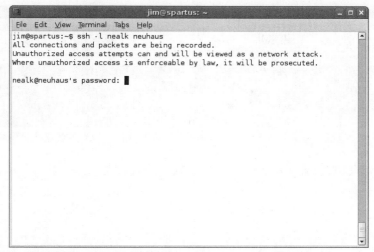

Figure 6-5: A SSH connection showing the /etc/issue.net message

Opening Ports

Since you will be accessing the SSH server from the Internet, you will need to open the SSH port to the world. If you have a firewall, it will need to allow traffic to enter on TCP port 22.

TIP For the cautious user, consider changing the SSH server to a different port (`/etc/ssh/sshd_config`, `Port` option). This way, worms and kiddies scanning for active SSH servers will be unlikely to find your server. Although this is security by obscurity, it is very effective against automated attacks.

Every firewall is different, so you will need to check how to open a port. If you are using a small home firewall and NAT system, then look for a setting for incoming connections. At minimum, you will need to supply the port (22) and the SSH server's IP address. Depending on your firewall, you may also need to supply the protocol (TCP). Figure 6-6 shows a home router (running the Linux-based DD-WRT firmware) that is configured to route SSH connections to an internal server. Other routers, including Linksys, D-Link, and Netgear all offer similar port forwarding options.

After you have the port opened, test it. Using the `ssh` command, connect to the server using your laptop. This will do two things: first, it will verify that the port is open and the SSH server is running properly. Second, it will transfer over the server's key to the laptop. This way, when you go to the coffee shop nobody will be able to hijack your SSH connection.

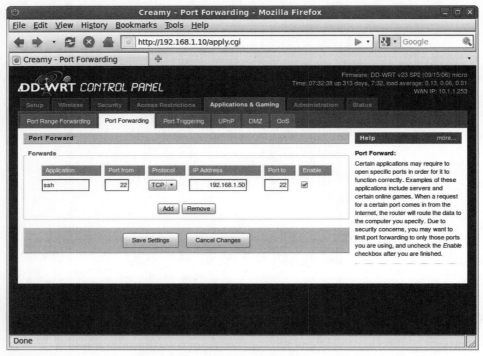

Figure 6-6: A home router running DD-WRT configured for routing port 22/tcp

Starting a Proxy

The second key component for creating a secured relay system is to install the proxy on your home system. There are two packages that provide this functionality: `socks4-server` and `dante-server`. Both servers provide SOCKS proxies and both are functionally equivalent, although `socks4-server` does require a little more configuration. In any case, you will only need to install one SOCKS server—do not install both. Since both servers use the same port (1080/tcp), only one can run at a time.

Using Socks4-Server

The `socks4-server` package provides a basic SOCKS version 4 proxy that is intended for use through `inetd`. To use this, you will need an `inetd` agent, such as `xinetd`. You will also need to edit `/etc/sockd.conf` to allow network traffic.

1. Install both server packages:

   ```
   sudo apt-get install xinetd socks4-server
   ```

2. As root, create a socks service for `xinetd`. The contents of `/etc` `/xinetd.d/socks` should look like this:

```
service socks
{
  disable = no
  socket_type = stream
  protocol = tcp
  wait = no
  user = daemon
  group = sys
  server = /usr/sbin/sockd
}
```

3. Restart `xinetd`: `sudo /etc/init.d/xinetd restart`. At this point, the SOCKS server is accessible from the network, but not configured.

4. Configure the SOCKS server to allow traffic relaying. The default configuration file, `/etc/sockd.conf`, forbids all connections. At bare minimum, you will want to remove the "deny all" command and replace it with permissions for the local host. If you want other systems to use this proxy, then you will need to permit additional hosts or subnets.

```
# deny  ALL  0.0.0.0   .my.domain  0.0.0.0
permit  localhost 255.255.255.255   ALL  0.0.0.0
```

WARNING Permitting *all* network traffic to relay through your box is a huge security risk for machines accessible from the Internet. If this computer is directly connected to the Internet, then spammers will likely use your open SOCKS server to relay e-mail. The time between making a SOCKS server public and relaying spam could be as little as a few hours. For this secure tunnel, we only allow the local host to use the SOCKS server, and the SOCKS server is not accessible from outside the firewall. As long as you only permit access to the SOCKS server from the local host (and not the entire Internet), you should be secure enough.

In case the SOCKS server does not appear to work right, look in the `/var/log/syslog` file for error messages. Both `sockd` and `xinetd` log their status to this file.

Using Dante-Server

The Dante server supports both SOCKS version 4 and version 5. Although Dante can run from `xinetd`, it is usually used as a standalone server.

1. Install the Dante server. When you install this, it will try to start the server and it will immediately fail since it is not configured:

```
sudo apt-get install dante-server
```

2. Configure the server by editing the `/etc/dante.conf` file. You will need to enable a port as well as connection rules. For example:

```
# log results to /var/log/syslog (for debugging)
logoutput: syslog stderr
# use 'ifconfig -a' to determine your network interface (e.g. eth0)
# in this case, lo is the loopback port so it only allows localhost
internal: lo port = 1080   # where to listen
external: eth0             # where to relay
# enable SOCKS connection methods
method: username none #rfc931
clientmethod: none
# configure which clients to relay; this only allows localhost
client pass {
   from: 127.0.0.1/32 to: 0.0.0.0/0
}
pass {
   from: 127.0.0.1/32 to: 0.0.0.0/0
   protocol: tcp udp
   log: connect error
}
# log all failed connections
block {
   from: 0.0.0.0/0 to: 0.0.0.0/0
   log: connect error
}
```

3. Restart the Dante server. Look at `/var/log/syslog` for any error messages:

```
sudo /etc/init.d/dante start
```

Testing the SOCKS Server

Regardless of which SOCKS server you installed, you will need to test it before you head to the coffee shop.

1. Open Firefox on the same host that has the SOCKS server.

2. Open the connection preferences: Edit ⇨ Preferences ⇨ Advanced ⇨ Network ⇨ Settings.

TIP If you do not want to modify your default Firefox settings, then create a new profile for this test.

3. Enable the SOCKS server. The server should be running on localhost port 1080 (see Figure 6-7). If you are using `socks4-server`, then specify SOCKS v4 as the protocol. If you are using Dante, then either SOCKS v4 or SOCKS v5 will work.

4. Use the browser to connect to a web site, for example, `www.google.com`.

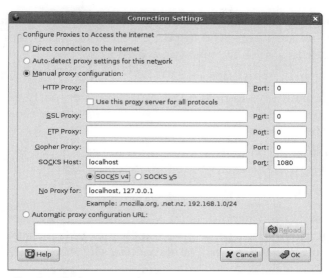

Figure 6-7: Configuring Firefox to use the proxy

If the connection works, you should see log entries in `/var/log/syslog` and the web page should be displayed. If the connection fails, look in `/var/log/syslog` for error messages or the reason for the failure.

Establishing the Tunnel

Now that you have working SSH and SOCKS servers, you can create a secure tunnel.

1. Find out your server's IP address. If you are doing this from home, then your ISP assigned you an IP address. If you have a stand-alone firewall, then connect to it and find out what its external (WAN) IP address is. On the other hand, if your computer is directly connected to the Internet, then you can run `ifconfig -a` to list your IP address (it is probably in

the `eth0` record). Without knowing your IP address, you will be unable to connect from the outside.

TIP If the IP address starts with 10., 192.168., 172.16. to 172.31. or 169.254., then you are looking at a private network address. You will need to identify the public address before you can access the server from outside your local network.

2. On your laptop, use SSH to create a tunnel to the server. The tunnel should forward the local port 8080 to port 1080 on the server. For example, if your IP address is 1.2.3.4, then you would use:

```
ssh 1.2.3.4 -L 8080:localhost:1080
```

This command says to relay local connections on port `8080` to the host and port `localhost:1080` on the server. The host name `localhost` will be resolved by the server.

3. On your laptop, configure your browser to use a proxy. In this case, you want to use `localhost` and port 8080 (not port 1080).

4. Test the connection by accessing a website.

If all goes well, you should see a web page. This means that all web connections go from your laptop to your local port 8080, where SSH securely tunnels all requests to the server. The server sends it to the local SOCKS server, which in turn sends the request to the Internet.

Although this path does not remove the risk from someone sniffing the network connection between your home and the Internet, it does prevent anyone at the coffee shop from spying on your bank accounts.

Changing Ciphers for Speed

SSH uses cryptographic ciphers for protecting data, but not all ciphers are equal. By default, SSH uses AES. While AES is a very strong algorithm, it is not as fast as others. If you plan to use the Web over a secure tunnel, consider using a different algorithm, such as Blowfish. This cipher is strong enough for everyday use and is much faster. As a result, you will see a speed enhancement for requests sent over this secure tunnel:

```
ssh -c blowfish 1.2.3.4 -L 8080:localhost:1080
```

NOTE As cryptography goes, AES is considered to be a very strong algorithm. However, it isn't the fastest cryptographic algorithm. The Blowfish algorithm isn't necessarily as strong, but it is much faster.

Depending on the type of network traffic, you may always want to enable or disable compression. For example, X-Windows traffic can be heavily compressed, while images (for example, GIF and JPEG) and multimedia files such as MP3 and MOV cannot. If you are browsing the Web or streaming audio, then do not use compression—this is the default setting. But, if you are doing remote administration over X-Windows, then enable compression with the -c parameter:

```
ssh -C -c blowfish 1.2.3.4 -L 8080:localhost:1080
```

Managing E-Mail with Evolution

The default e-mail reader for Ubuntu is called Evolution. This program is an open source clone of Microsoft Outlook. Besides viewing and composing e-mail, it also manages your calendar, task list, and contacts (see Figure 6-8). Evolution also enables you to manage multiple e-mail accounts. While it natively supports many different mail server configurations, it does have a couple of quirks.

Configuring an Account

The most powerful part of Evolution is its list of supported mail protocols. It natively supports the Post Office Protocol (POP, also called POP3) and Instant Message Access Protocol (IMAP or IMAP4), as well as Microsoft Exchange and Novell GroupWise. This means that you should be able to use Evolution at home and in most corporate and small office environments.

When you first run Evolution (by clicking the mail icon in the default top panel or by selecting Applications ➪ Internet ➪ Evolution Mail), it asks you to set up an account. You can later add or edit accounts by running Evolution and selecting Edit ➪ Preferences ➪ Mail Accounts. You will be asked to provide three main types of information.

- **Identity**—This specifies the e-mail address and the name of the person on the address.

- **Receiving options**—This identifies how you retrieve your e-mail. For example, if you use a POP mail server, then you will specify the server's address and your account name.

- **Sending options**—The way you receive mail is not necessarily the same as the way you send mail. For example, you may receive mail using POP, but send using SMTP.

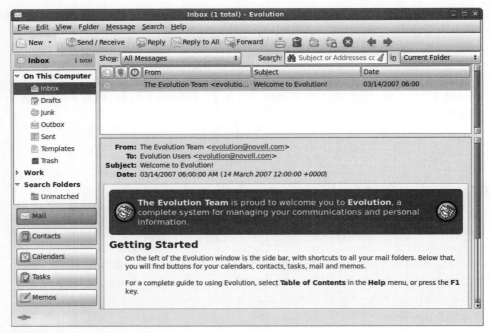

Figure 6-8: Evolution mailer

NOTE Your specific configuration will depend on your mail server. Most ISPs provide some type of mail server and instructions for configuring mail readers. Although they are unlikely to specify the configuration for Evolution, they should list the server's host name, protocol (for example, POP3 or IMAP4), and any required security steps, such as using SSL (or TLS) for encryption.

There are other options you can configure after creating a new account (select the Edit option under Mail Accounts). For example, you can specify how often to check for new mail and whether to save a copy of every outgoing e-mail message.

Besides using e-mail from your local ISP, you will probably want to manage your free e-mail accounts. Some of the most common free e-mail accounts are Google Gmail, Yahoo! Mail, and Microsoft MSN Hotmail. Knowing how to configure e-mail for these free mail services will help you configure mail for most other mail services.

Retrieving E-mail from Gmail

Of all the free e-mail account systems, Google's Gmail is the simplest to configure. Gmail offers a standard POP3 server that uses SSL for security.

Google provides a detailed list of supported POP3 configurations at `http://mail.google.com/support/bin/topic.py?topic=1555`. The mail configuration, including server, protocol, and security, is detailed at `http://mail.google.com/support/bin/answer.py?answer=13287`.

Preparing Your Gmail Account

Gmail is free mail system provided by Google. You can setup a new account by going to `mail.google.com`. All you will need to provide is a name (first and last), login name, password, and security question.

WARNING Google's Gmail has undergone many revisions. When it first came out in 2004, it was an invitation-only system. You could only get an account if a friend with an account invited you in. In August 2005, Gmail added an option to request an invite by sending a text message from your cell phone. (In an ironic twist, if you had a cell phone, then you didn't need friends.) In February 2007, Gmail became open to the public.

After you have your account, you will need to configure it for use with POP:

1. Open a web browser and connect to `www.gmail.com`. Log in using your Gmail account.

2. Select the Settings option in the top-left corner.

3. Select the Forwarding and POP/IMAP tab.

4. Enable POP (or IMAP) support (see Figure 6-9). You can either turn it on for all e-mail or only for all future e-mail.

5. Save your settings.

Adding a Gmail Account

To add your Gmail account to Evolution:

1. Open the account manager by selecting Edit ⇨ Preferences ⇨ Mail Accounts and click the Add button. This brings up the Mail Configuration helper.

2. The first information requested is your identity. Put in your name and Gmail e-mail address (*your_login*@gmail.com).

3. The second required information is for receiving e-mail. Gmail uses the POP protocol. The mail server is `pop.gmail.com` on port 995, so you should enter `pop.gmail.com:995` and select the SSL option. (For IMAP, use `imap.gmail.com:993`.) Figure 6-10 shows an example POP configuration. Although a password is needed to access the account, you

will be prompted for the password when you first try to send or receive e-mail. Selecting the Remember password option will save the password for you.

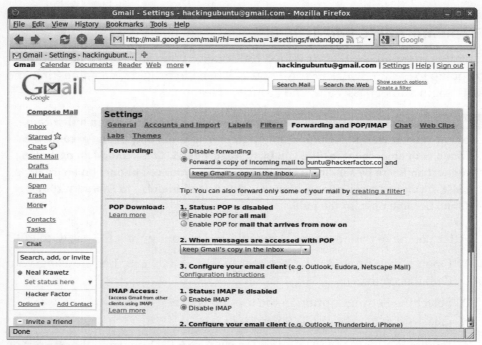

Figure 6-9: The Gmail settings for enabling POP support

4. On the Receiving Options page, I usually choose to leave messages on the server. This way, I always have a backup.

5. For the sending options, Gmail uses SMTP and the server is smtp.gmail.com. You need to specify a security protocol. Gmail supports SSL on port 465 (smtp.gmail.com:465) and TLS on port 587 (smtp.gmail.com:587).

6. Set the account name for Evolution. It defaults to the e-mail address.

7. Apply the new account. This completes the account creation.

8. Click the Send/Receive button. You will see a prompt for your password and a notice about the Gmail SSL/TLS certificate.

   ▪ You must approve the certificate. If you don't, then you cannot access your Gmail account. You will only see this prompt once.

   ▪ If you select the Remember password option, then you will not be prompted for your password again.

9. After entering your password, you should see the system checking your e-mail and retrieving any messages.

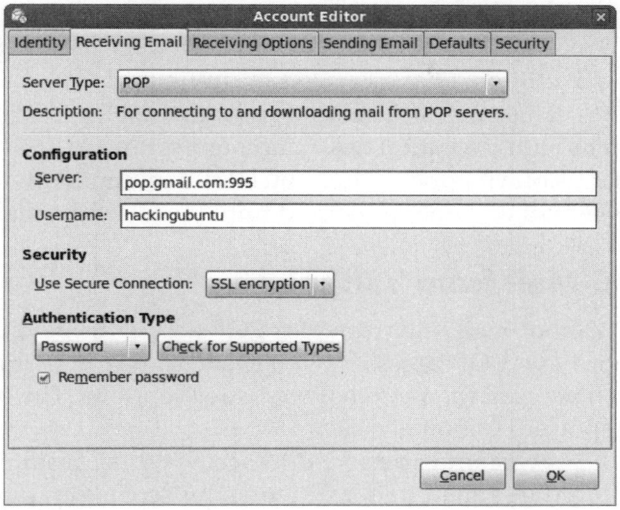

Figure 6-10: Configuring Evolution for receiving e-mail from Gmail

Fetching Mail

The command-line program `fetchmail` (`sudo apt-get install fetchmail`) is a standard component of most Unix mail systems. This program enables you to retrieve e-mail from a remote mail server using POP2, POP3, or IMAP4. While `fetchmail` cannot be used to send e-mail, it can be used to collect e-mail from multiple accounts.

NOTE To use `fetchmail`, you will also need to install a local mail delivery system. Chapter 13 shows how to install the Postfix mail system. The default Postifx installation (`sudo apt-get install postfix` and select any of the default configuration settings) is enough for `fetchmail` to work.

The `fetchmail` program looks for the configuration file `$HOME/.fetchmailrc`. Each line in this file specifies a different account. For example, to retrieve e-mail from `account@gmail.com`, you would have a line that says:

```
poll pop.gmail.com port 995 protocol POP3 username account
     password password ssl
```

Running `fetchmail` retrieves the e-mail and sends it to your local mail system. This should place it in your mail spool. If you configure Evolution to retrieve e-mail from a mail spool, you can read your e-mail from the `/var/mail/` directory.

> **TIP** The mail spool stores e-mail under your account name. If your account on the Ubuntu system is timb, e-mail will be stored in `/var/mail/timb`. The file is first created when you receive mail.

Harvesting e-mail with `fetchmail` can come in very handy if you are not always running Evolution. I have `fetchmail` configured to check for new mail every 10 minutes. This way, if Evolution is not running, new e-mail will be retrieved. Even though Evolution has an account setting to periodically check for new e-mail, this only happens after you start Evolution. If you reboot your computer, new e-mail will not be checked until you start the mail reader.

Retrieving E-Mail from Yahoo!

Unlike Gmail, Yahoo! Mail only provides POP access for paid accounts; free accounts do not have POP access. If you want to use Evolution with your free Yahoo! Mail account then you have very few options. The best (and only continually supported) option is `fetchyahoo`.

The `fetchyahoo` program is designed to access e-mail from a Yahoo! Mail account and store it in a mail folder. It works by screen-scraping the Yahoo! web interface and downloading mail.

Unfortunately, `fetchyahoo` is not a supported Ubuntu package. Instead, you will need to download and install the software from `http://fetchyahoo.twizzler.org/`. You may also need to update your Yahoo! account configuration, including changing the web interface.

> **WARNING** Yahoo! periodically changes its web interface. Since `fetchyahoo` reads the web pages, changes will cause it to stop working. If `fetchyahoo` stops working, then check the web site for an updated version.

1. Download `fetchyahoo` from `fetchyahoo.twizzler.org`. The file name will be something like `fetchyahoo-version.tar.gz`. For example, `fetchyahoo-2.13.7.tar.gz`.

2. Extract the code and enter the directory. For version 2.13.7, use:

   ```
   tar -xzvf fetchyahoo-2.13.7.tar.gz
   cd fetchyahoo-2.13.7
   ```

3. Make sure that the program is executable and copy it into your $PATH.

   ```
   chmod a+rw fetchyahoo
   sudo cp fetchmailyahoo /usr/local/bin/
   ```

4. Copy the `fetchmailyahoorc` configuration file to your home directory:

   ```
   cp fetchmailyahoorc $HOME/.fetchmailyahoorc
   ```

5. Edit $HOME/.fetchmailyahoorc. Be sure to set the username and password for your Yahoo! account. You will want to replace every instance of the variables yahoo-user-name, yahoo-password, and local-user-name.

TIP By default, **fetchmailyahoo** will deliver all e-mails to your local mail spool. However, the configuration file has options to forward e-mails using a mail relay, POP, or IMAP server.

When you are all done configuring your system, you can run fetchyahoo to retrieve your e-mail.

NOTE There are alternatives to **fetchyahoo**. Unfortunately, none are continuously maintained, and outdated versions are unlikely to work. For example, YahooPOPs (www.ypopsemail.com) actively supports Microsoft Windows, but Linux users need to wait for the community to port the software. Other programs, such as FreePOPs, Mechanoid, and SendYmail, have not been updated in years.

Addressing with LDAP

One of Evolution's biggest strengths is its integration with Lightweight Directory Access Protocol (LDAP) systems. In many large office environments, LDAP provides directory support, listing employee names, e-mail addresses, and other contact information. To enable LDAP support, simply add a new address book, File ➪ New ➪ Address Book, and change the type to On LDAP Servers (see Figure 6-11). After you enter your LDAP server's information, you can access the directory when composing an e-mail.

Crashing and Recovering Evolution

The Evolution mail reader used to have stability and usability issues. It could hang during network accesses, could crash while composing e-mails, and would have troubles importing meeting invitations from some Microsoft Outlook clients.

Fortunately, Evolution lives up to its name. With every new release, it evolves into something better. Unfortunately, newer versions of Evolution are not backported. While Karmic Koala (9.10) ships with Evolution 2.28, Hardy Heron (8.04 LTS) only has 2.22 and Dapper Drake (6.06 LTS) has 2.6. Even though newer software may exist and be stable, it may not be readily available for older Ubuntu versions—including the long-term support versions.

In rare cases, Evolution may still crash or close unexpectedly. When this happens, it may not kill all running processes. You will need to kill any running processes that became detached. To do this, use:

```
killall -r 'evolution'
```

This command will kill every running process from Evolution.

Figure 6-11: Adding an LDAP server

If you forget to kill all the old processes and just restart Evolution, you can expect to miss appointments, not retrieve e-mail, and to crash more often. This is because the dependent processes are no longer connected to the main Evolution process.

Using E-Mail with Thunderbird Mail

The Evolution mailer provides a full set of office services including e-mail management, calendar scheduling, and task lists. However, Evolution is only for Gnome. You may want to choose a mailing system that is supported on every platform, so moving between work and home does not require changing mail programs. If you only need e-mail access, you might want to consider Mozilla Thunderbird, since it is supported on every popular operating system:

```
sudo apt-get install thunderbird
```

This installation enables you to run `thunderbird` from the command line or select it from the menu: Applications ⇨ Internet ⇨ Thunderbird Mail. Unlike Evolution, this only runs one application and starts up a little faster.

In my opinion, Thunderbird is much more refined than Evolution, but not as full-featured. Table 6-1 shows a functionality comparison. Generally speaking, both systems are nearly equivalent when it comes to e-mail-only requirements. Although Evolution supports more protocols and non-e-mail features, Thunderbird currently offers more stability and usability.

Table 6-1: Comparison of Evolution and Thunderbird

Feature	Evolution 2.28	Thunderbird 2.0
Protocols	POP, IMAP, Exchange, Novell Groupwise, Files	POP, IMAP, Files
Security	SSL and TLS	SSL and TLS (available by Edit ⇨ Account Settings ⇨ Server Settings after creating account)
LDAP	Yes	Yes
Load Images	Can be disabled, enabled for all, or enabled for known contacts; default: enabled	Can be disabled, enabled for all, or enabled for known contacts; default: enabled
JavaScript	No	No
E-Mail Scam Detection	No	Yes
Antivirus Support	No	Yes; default: disabled
Missing Attachment Warning	Yes	Available as plug-in
Additional Functionality		
Address Book	Yes	Yes
Calendar	Yes	Available as plug-in
Task List	Yes	No
Memos	Yes	No

Instant Messaging with Ubuntu

The Web is great for one-way communications: someone posts a web page and someone else views it. Even in online forums, discussions may span days. E-mail is a faster communication method, and is bidirectional, but it is not instant. Instant messaging (IM) systems allow real-time communications with groups of people.

Internet Relay Chat (IRC) was one of the first IM protocols. (IRC predates most IM protocols by more than a decade.) There are plenty of IRC clients for Ubuntu, including the graphical xchat and text-based irssi. But IRC is only one type of IM protocol available today. Yahoo!, AOL, and MSN all have their own IM protocols. Beyond proprietary systems, the open source XMPP protocol is growing in popularity; XMPP is essentially IRC over an encrypted channel.

NOTE The Extensible Messaging and Presence Protocol (XMPP) is synonymous with *Jabber*. In 2007, the Jabber protocol was renamed XMPP. If you see anything that refers to Jabber, then it is actually talking about XMPP.

Although you could download a specific IM client for every protocol, it is much more convenient to have one client that supports them all. Empathy and Pidgin are two IM clients for Ubuntu. Which version is installed by default depends on your version of Ubuntu. For example, Karmic Koala (9.10) includes Empathy, Hardy Heron (8.04 LTS) has Pidgin, and Dapper Drake (6.06 LTS) has an older version of Pidgin called Gaim.

```
sudo apt-get install empathy telepathy-gnome
sudo apt-get install pidgin
```

NOTE From a functional viewpoint, Empathy and Pidgin are extremely similar. If you know how to use one of them, then there is virtually no learning curve for using the other. The only real reason to choose one over the other is personal preference and protocol support. As of this writing, Pidgin supports two more IM protocols than Empathy; Empathy lacks support for IRC and Apple's Bonjour.

Both Empathy and Pidgin support over a dozen of the most common IM protocols. You can find these programs listed under the Applications ⇨ Internet menu. Both of these IM clients will initially prompt you to add an account. Accounts specify IM servers and your identities on each server (see Figure 6-12). Each server protocol has different requirements that you will need to specify.

After creating an account, you can log in to the account—this connects to the server. From there, you can join chat rooms and communicate in real time. Although neither Empathy nor Pidgin allows you to bridge IM connections, both allow you to connect to many different servers at the same time.

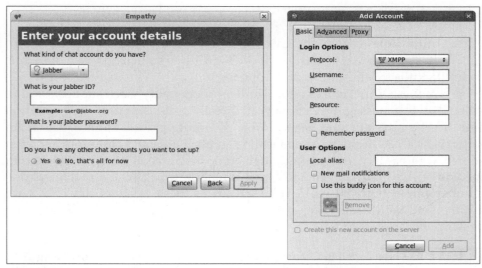

Figure 6-12: Adding an IM account to Empathy (left) and Pidgin (right)

Talking with VoIP

Ubuntu users are not restricted to the world of text and graphics. There are three different VoIP packages available for Ubuntu: Ekiga, Skype, and QuteCom. The default Dapper and Hardy desktops include Ekiga—formerly called *GnomeMeeting*. This is an open source VoIP system that supports SIP and H.323 protocols. This means you can use Ekiga to talk to other Ekiga users, as well as Microsoft NetMeeting, Skype, and QuteCom VoIP users.

TIP Karmic Koala (9.10) does not include a default VoIP client. You can add Ekiga using `sudo apt-get install ekiga`.

Although Ekiga is the open source favorite, Skype is the industry leader. Using Skype, you can call other SIP and H.323 VoIP users, or call landline and cell phones (nominal fees apply). However, you might be better off downloading Skype directly from `www.skype.com` rather than from the Ubuntu repositories; the repositories do not always keep up with the latest Skype version.

TIP If Skype does not exist for your Ubuntu version, then try installing an older one. For example, when Karmic was released, Skype did not exist for Ubuntu 9.10. However, the Ubuntu 8.04 version of Skype works just fine on Karmic.

The third VoIP option for Ubuntu is QuteCom (formerly *WengoPhone*; `sudo apt-get install qutecom`.) It offers features similar to those of Skype, including calls to land-line and cell phones.

Each of these VoIP choices offers similar functionality. Each supports audio, video, and text messaging, each can call directly or use a centralize registration and directory system, and each can handle multiple calls at once. The main differences are in licensing and land-line access: Ekiga and QuteCom are open source, whereas Skype is not (although an open sourced version of Skype is in the works), and only Skype and QuteCom allow you to call a real telephone number (for a nominal fee). Although all of these systems can chat with a Microsoft NetMeeting user, none of them can view a shared NetMeeting desktop.

NOTE As I mentioned in Chapter 3, Ubuntu does not support all video devices. But if Ubuntu supports the device, then Ekiga, Skype, and QuteCom can probably use it for video conferencing.

Summary

Ubuntu supports a variety of configurations. Although Ubuntu server is ideal for a standalone server, Ubuntu desktop enables you to reach out and communicate with other people. There are plenty of options for accessing the Web, e-mail, IM, and VoIP networks. While the default tools (Firefox, Evolution, Pidgin, and Ekiga) are very powerful, there are plenty of readily available alternatives such as Mozilla, Lynx, Thunderbird, xchat, irssi, QuteCom, and Skype. In the case of e-mail, there are even options for extending support to nonstandard and web-based mail systems.

With online communications come risks related to network security. There are options for securing web browsers, e-mail, and even off-site communications, but the topics listed in this chapter, such as tuning applications and using SSH tunnels, are just the tip of the iceberg. If you are interested in more information about network security, consider some of these other resources:

▪ *Steal This Computer Book*, by Wallace Wang, discusses threats from online forums.

- *Hacking Exposed: Network Security Secrets & Solutions*, by Stuart McCluer, Joel Scambray, and George Kurtz, covers many different network threats. Although this resource focuses on Windows, many of the threats are similar for Linux users.

- *Introduction to Network Security*, by Neal Krawetz, delves into many of the threats from online communications, regardless of the operating system.

Collaborating

What's In This Chapter?

Sharing files across the network
How to work on documents when everyone uses different operating systems
Collaborating on projects with remote users
Running operating systems in emulators

In today's always-connected world, few people work in isolation. In office environments, files and folders are shared with coworkers. In research groups, documents are passed back and forth. Even the hard-core hacker working alone in a dark basement isn't really alone—he's sharing files and projects with other people online. Teams of people collaborate on projects in real time while members are physically located around the world.

Incompatible operating systems do not work well in today's always-connected world. Collaboration includes working with people who don't run Ubuntu (let's call them "Windows users"). The default install of the Ubuntu desktop includes a wide variety of collaboration tools, and additional tools available in the standard repositories offer many more options.

Collaboration begins with sharing and compatibility. If you cannot share documents, then you cannot collaborate. And if your system and software cannot handle the files you need, then you won't be able to work with other people.

Unfortunately, some file formats lack strong support, and many applications demand specific operating systems. In order to work with others, you may need to share desktops or actually run programs designed for different operating systems. Fortunately, Ubuntu has many options for supporting both of these needs. In the best-case scenario, there are fully compatible applications. However, there are also options for linking your system with other computers and even using other operating systems in virtual machines. Running Ubuntu does not mean that you cannot run Windows *at the same time*.

Synchronizing the Clock

With the need to share files, file systems, desktops, and tools, where do you begin? You begin with the system clock. This may sound like a trivial piece of information, but if your clock is off by more than a little, then it can actually hamper collaboration efforts. E-mails won't be sorted in the right order, files won't have consistent timestamps, and time-sensitive applications become confused. For developers, timestamps are used to determine what files to compile—if your clock is way off, then source code may not compile correctly.

When you first installed Ubuntu (see Chapter 1), it asked you to set your time zone and choose whether the hardware clock should be in UTC. Everything else about the clock has been silently done behind the scenes.

Ubuntu sets the clock automatically each time the network interface is brought up. This happens in the script `/etc/network/if-up.d/ntpdate`. Ubuntu checks to see if the file `/etc/default/ntpdate` exists. This file should contain the hostname of the network time protocol (NTP) server. By default, this file specifies `ntp.ubuntu.com`. Here are some tips to make sure your clock is set correctly:

- If you cannot access the default server (`ntp.ubuntu.com`) from your network, then your clock will not be set at boot time and will likely drift, usually gaining or losing time by a few seconds per month. Edit `/etc/default/ntpdate` and specify an alternate NTP server.

WARNING NTP uses UDP packets. If your proxy or outbound firewall blocks UDP, then you will need to change the default NTP server to a system that is not filtered by the proxy or firewall. Alternately, you can configure a different network route or choose a different method for setting the system time.

- If your computer never reboots (and uptimes of over 100 days is common), then your clock can drift—usually by a few seconds per month. Consider adding `ntpdate` to your root's Cron entry so it runs weekly.

  ```
  sudo crontab -e
  ```

  Add this line to run `ntpdate` every Sunday at two minutes after midnight. (Cron is detailed in Chapter 8.)

  ```
  2 0 * * 0 /etc/network/if-up.d/ntpdate
  ```

TIP Clocks on virtual machines can significantly drift if the host operating system throttles the processor. You may want to resynchronize the clock on the virtual machine much more often.

- For Ubuntu systems that operate as network routers, tying the clock to a network interface can be a problem—particularly if the network connection continually bounces up and down. (Do you really need to synchronize the clock a few times each hour?) In these situations, you might consider removing `/etc/network/if-up.d/ntpdate` and creating an `/etc/init.d/ntpdate` command.

- If your clock is off by more than ±128 ms, then synchronizing can cause the system clock to jump and create problems for some applications (like the Gnome desktop). If this is an issue, then add `-B` to the NTPOPTIONS in `/etc/default/ntpdate`. This option will slowly adjust the clock to the correct time.

NOTE The boot scripts found in `/etc/init.d/` are discussed in Chapter 3. Actual sample scripts are in Chapters 11 and 12.

NTP is just one protocol for setting the date. Another option is `rdate` (`sudo apt-get install rdate`). By default, `rdate` uses TCP to query the network daytime service (port 13/tcp) of the timeserver. You will still need to create `/etc/init.d/rdate`, `/etc/network/if-up.d/rdate`, and Cron entries, but this command works through most proxies.

TIP The server ntp.ubuntu.com only supports the NTP protocol; `rdate` won't work with this server. If you use `rdate` and need a timeserver, consider one of the official atomic clock sites like `utcnist.colorado.edu`, `time-a.nist.gov`, or `time-b.nist.gov`.

PLAYS WELL WITH OTHERS

There is always a small, fanatical group who thinks *collaboration* means everyone should run the same operating system. Whether this is Linux people criticizing Windows users, BSD users criticizing Linux users, or Windows users trying to convert the world, the fringe groups are always shouting to be heard. In real life, a homogeneous network is neither realistic nor desirable. Although having one operating system for everyone does allow everyone to run the exact same software, it can lead to many other issues.

Some of the issues involve security. If everyone runs the same operating system, then everyone is vulnerable to the same weaknesses. Whether the risk comes from viruses, overflows, or unstable software, all computers

(continued)

> **PLAYS WELL WITH OTHERS** *(continued)*
>
> running the same configuration are vulnerable. (Windows may have more viruses today, but if everyone used Ubuntu then the virus writers would focus on Ubuntu instead. The lack of viruses for Linux is not due to a lack of opportunity but rather the lack of effort from virus writers.) Darwin called this "survival of the fittest"; there is safety in diversity.
>
> Other issues concern use models. An operating system is a tool—and nothing more. You should select the right tool for the right job. Windows offers excellent hardware support and many high-quality applications, but many applications lack collaboration support for non-Windows systems. BSD offers security from the ground up and a proven track record for stability but has minimal support from the community (compared to Windows and Linux). Linux has a wide variety of software (although quality varies dramatically) and excellent collaborative efforts. If you need an operating system that plays well with an assortment of other systems, then Linux is a terrific option and Ubuntu's long-term support commitments make it an ideal choice.

Sharing Files

When you collaborate on a project, you need some way to pass files between group members. The direct approach is to send the file as an e-mail attachment. Although this does give them a copy, it does not provide updates—people may pass around very old copies of files.

Sending files around also does not easily allow you to incorporate changes. In most cases, there will need to be an owner whose responsibility is to collect changes and incorporate them into a single document. This may work well with a few people, but it does not scale well to a dozen people working concurrently.

NOTE Other downsides to using e-mail for sharing files concerns disk space and convenience. Most corporations and service providers limit the mail queue size. If the queue fills, then nobody will receive any e-mails. Also, transferring large attachments can be time-consuming and searching for a specific attachment is usually inconvenient.

Another option is to place files on an FTP or web server. This gives a central source for distribution, allowing people to view recent changes to files. However, web servers don't readily allow feedback and active collaboration, and FTP servers are not known for their security.

The best option is to share a file system's directory among computers. This way, everyone can see all files in one common location. Everyone can also see all changes and everyone can make changes as needed. For Unix and Linux systems, there is NFS for file sharing, but for compatibility with Windows users, you'll probably want to use Samba.

Enabling NFS

Under Linux and most Unix operating systems, the network file system (NFS) is the common way to share directories. With other Unix and Linux operating systems, NFS is part of the core installation. But with Ubuntu, you need to install it as a package. There are three main components required by NFS:

- portmap—This package provides support for remote procedure calls (RPC) and is used by NFS. You don't need to install portmap by itself—the apt-get commands for the other two components will install portmap as a dependency.

- nfs-common—Although portmap provides *support* for the RPC function, this package actually *provides* the RPC functions for NFS. This package is required for NFS clients and servers. It provides basic RPC functions like file locking and status. If you only need to install an NFS client (meaning that you will mount a directory exported by some other server), then you can use: sudo apt-get install nfs-common.

NOTE Installing nfs-common may generate the error message "Not starting NFS kernel daemon: No exports." This is expected since it is not configured. To configure it, see the section titled "Acting as an NFS Server."

- nfs-kernel-server—This package adds kernel modules so that you can export a directory for use by a remote host; with this package, you get a server. You can install it using: sudo apt-get install nfs-kernel-server. This brings in portmap and nfs-common as dependent packages.

NFS is a great collaboration tool because entire file systems can be shared transparently. Everyone sees the same files and changes are immediately accessible by everyone. The main limitation is operating system support. Although NFS exists for Linux, BSD, HP-UX, AIX, Solaris, BeOS, Mac OS X, and even OS/2, Windows does not natively include it. If you need to share files with Windows users, skip to the next section on Samba.

TIP If you want to use NFS with Windows, consider installing the Windows Services for UNIX (SFU) or the Subsystem for UNIX-based applications (SUA). These free products from Microsoft include NFS server and client support. Another option is to install the Cygwin for Windows (www.cygwin.com).

Acting as an NFS Client

Mounting a remote file system with NFS is really easy. Just as the mount command can be used to access a hard drive, CD-ROM, or other block devices, it can be used to mount a remote file system. You just need three items: the server's name, the directory name on the server that is being exported, and the mount point on your local system (a directory) for the connection. For example, to mount the directory /home/project from the server sysprj1 and place it at /mnt/project on your local computer, you would use:

```
sudo mkdir -p /mnt/project # to make sure the mount point exists
sudo mount -t nfs sysprj1:/home/project /mnt/project
```

Now, all the files under /home/project on the host sysprj1 are access-ible from the local directory /mnt/project. The access is completely transparent—anything you can do on your local file system can be done over this NFS mount.

> **TIP** Access restrictions are set by the NFS server and follow the Unix permissions. If you find that you cannot access the directory after mounting it, check the permissions with ls -1. If you do not have permission, then talk to the administrator for the NFS server.

If you don't know the name of the exported directory, NFS enables you to browse the list of exported partitions by using the showmount -e command. This lists the exported directories and clients that can access it. The client list returned from the server can be an entire domain (for example, *.local.net) or a list of clients.

```
$ showmount -e sysprj1
/home/projects *.local.net
/media/cdrom *.local.net
```

When you are done with the mounted partition, you can remove it using sudo umount /mnt/project.

For short-term access, you will probably want to use mount and umount to access the directory as needed. For long-term collaboration, you can add the entry to /etc/fstab. For example:

```
sysprj1:/home/project   /mnt/project   nfs    defaults   0   0
```

Having the entry in /etc/fstab will make sure that the directory is mounted every time you reboot. You can also use sudo mount /mnt/project (specifying only the mount point) as a shortcut since mount consults /etc/fstab when determining devices.

WARNING NFS has one huge limitation. If the server goes down, then all file accesses to the network partition will hang—up to hours—before failing. The hang-up is due to network timeouts and retries. If your connection to the server is unstable, then don't use NFS.

Acting as an NFS Server

NFS servers export directories for use by NFS clients. This is a two-step process. First, you need to create a file called /etc/exports. This file contains a list of directories to export and clients that are permitted to access the directories. Special access permissions can also be specified such as ro for read-only, rw for read-write, and sync for synchronous writes. An example /etc/exports file is given in Listing 7-1.

TIP There are many more options besides ro, rw, and sync. See the man page for exports (man 5 exports) for the full list of options.

Listing 7-1: Example of an /etc/exports File

```
/home/project        *.local.net(rw,sync)
/home/solo_project   host.local.net(rw,sync)
/media/cdrom         *.local.net(ro,async)
```

TIP To get a Mac such as OS X 10.5 (Leopard) to mount a Linux partition, you need to add insecure to the export line on the Linux box. Otherwise, the Mac will not mount the partition on an insecure port (>1024/tcp) and you will see an error that the operation is not permitted.

```
mac$ mount linuxbox:/remote/path /local/path
mount_nfs: /local/path: Operation not permitted
```

When supporting NFS with a Mac, the Linux server's /etc/exports should look something like this:

```
/home/projects    *.local.net(rw,sync,no_subtree_check,insecure)
```

The NFS server will not start if /etc/exports is missing or contains no exported directories. The default file contains only a few comments, so the server will not start. After you create your first entries, you will need to start the server. The easy way is with the command sudo /etc/init.d/nfs-kernel-server start.

After modifying the /etc/exports file on a running server, you need to tell the NFS server to export the entries:

```
sudo exportfs -r  # re-export all entries in /etc/exports
```

The `exportfs` command can also be used for other tasks:

- **List the current export table**—Run `exportfs` without any parameters.

- **Export a specific directory once**—This is useful if the export is not intended to be permanent (`/etc/exports` is really for permanent mounts). You will need to specify options and the list of clients before the directory. For example:

  ```
  sudo exportfs -o ro,async '*.local.net:/media/cdrom'
  ```

- **Un-export directory**—If the entry is still listed in `/etc/exports`, then the removal is temporary; the mount will be re-exported the next time you reboot or restart the NFS server.

  ```
  sudo exportfs -u '*.local.net:/media/cdrom'
  ```

TIP Add **-v** to any of the `exportfs` commands (for example, `exportfs -v -r`) to verbosely list additional information.

You can export anything that is mounted. This includes CD-ROM drives, USB thumb drives, and even mounted NFS partitions from other servers! Although you cannot export single files or block devices, you can export the entire `/dev` directory (not that you would want to).

WARNING NFS offers no security, encryption, or authentication. Furthermore, established NFS connections can be easily hijacked. NFS is fine for most internal, corporate networks and for use within your home, but don't use it to share files across the Internet.

Exchanging Files with Samba

Although NFS is useful for collaborating with Unix and Linux systems, it is not ideal for sharing directories with Windows users. As mentioned in Chapter 3, Samba allows Linux to use the SMB protocol and communicate with Windows systems. Chapter 3 showed how to share printers, but Samba can also be used to share directories.

First, if you have not done it already, install the Samba server: `sudo apt-get install samba`. You will need to edit `/etc/samba/smb.conf` and configure your workgroup. This configuration file contains many other options that you will probably want to review. For example, you can bind the Samba server to a specific network interface, control client logging, and configure alternate login credentials—these are documented with comments found in the file. After configuring the server, restart it: `sudo /etc/init.d/samba restart`.

There are two ways to use Samba for collaboration. It can be a server that shares directories with Windows users, or a client that receives directories exported from Windows servers.

Sharing a Directory with Windows

The /etc/samba/smb.conf file comes with an entry that allows you to share every user's home directory. Search the configuration file for the [homes] section, and uncomment it (remove the ; before each line). The section should look like this:

```
[homes]
   comment = Home Directories
   browseable = no
```

This defines a Windows service (called a *share*) and is accessed using *server**username*, where *server* is the name of your Ubuntu system and *username* is an account found under /home/*username*. You can uncomment other options in order to restrict access (valid users = %S and writable = no) and set file permissions.

If you want to export a specific directory then you will need to create your own section in /etc/samba/smb.conf. Listing 7-2 gives an example for exporting the CD-ROM and a projects directory.

Listing 7-2: Sample Export Directories for /etc/samba/smb.conf

```
# Export the CD-ROM.
# The Windows system will use \\server\cdrom\ to access it.
[cdrom]
  comment = CD-ROM drive
  path = /media/cdrom
# Export a group project directory.
# The Windows system will use \\server\groupproject\ to access it.
[groupproject]
  comment = Group Project directory
  path = /home/project
  read only = no
  valid users = nealk, @team # nealk and group "team" have access
```

TIP Although the default Windows installation cannot access NFS partitions, Samba can export a mounted NFS partition to Windows users.

LEARNING TO SAMBA

Although Samba is very powerful, it is not very easy to manage if you are new to it. If Samba does not immediately share partitions, then be prepared to devote an hour or more to debugging. Common problems that I usually check (in order) before going into "Search the web for solutions" mode:

(continued)

LEARNING TO SAMBA *(continued)*

- Is the `smb.conf` file correct? Use the `testparms` (or `testparam.samba3`) program to check for problems. Not all problems are critical, but big problems will be identified. (Some warnings may come from default settings in the configuration file.)

- Is the share name spelled correctly? I have spent hours chasing down problems only to find typos in the `smb.conf` share name or on the Windows side.

- If you are using a "`valid user`" option for the share, you may need to use `smbpasswd` to create a user account. Samba does not consult `/etc/passwd`. Instead, it uses its own password database found in `/var/lib/samba/`. The command `sudo smbpasswd -a username` adds a new user to the database, and `smbpasswd` (as the user) changes the password.

- Older versions of Windows (for example, Windows 95, 98, and NT) use plain-text passwords. Later versions use encrypted passwords. Check the `encrypted password` value in `smb.conf`, and make sure that it matches the system you are supporting. Unfortunately, Samba cannot support old and new systems at the same time unless they all use the same encrypted (or unencrypted) password system.

- If the Windows system can read the partition but not write to it, then check the permissions on the directory. The Samba account may not have write access.

If all else fails, refer to the FAQ and HOWTO guides at `www.samba.org` and the Ubuntu Guide at `ubuntuguide.org`.

Accessing a Windows Directory

There are many different ways for Samba to access a Windows directory. The main things you need are the Windows system name and the share. The command `smbclient -L` lists the public shares on a system:

```
$ smbclient -L wserver
Password: [hit enter with no password]
Domain=[WSERVER] OS=[Windows 5.1] Server=[Windows 2000 LAN Manager]
    Sharename       Type        Comment
    _____           __          ____
    IPC$            IPC         Remote IPC
    print$          Disk        Printer Drivers
```

```
Big             Disk
Printer         Printer    Brother HL-1850/70N BR-Script3
ADMIN$          Disk       Remote Admin
```

The `smbclient` command can act as an FTP-like client for accessing the Windows share. For example, `smblclient //wserver/big` will open an FTP client for accessing the `big` share.

For remote backups, I prefer to use `smbtar`. This command enables you to remotely archive (or restore) files in a share. The backup is saved to a TAR file. For example, to back up the `big` share from host `wserver`, you can use either:

```
smbtar -t archive.tar -s wserver -x big              # regular archive
smbtar -t -s wserver -x big | gzip -9 > archive.tgz
        # compressed archive
```

For restores, add in the `-r` parameter:

```
smbtar -r -t archive.tar -s wserver -x big           # regular archive
zcat archive.tgz | smbtar -r -t -s wserver -x big    # compressed archive
```

WARNING This is good for backing up user files, but it is not necessarily a full system backup. For example, Windows XP and later versions will not allow SMB access to the system directory or registry.

Although `smbclient` and `smbtar` enable you to access files, they do not allow you to actually mount the share. For this, the `smbfs` package is needed:

```
sudo apt-get install smbfs
```

The `smbfs` package provides an SMB file system driver and the `smbmount` command. This allows you to transparently mount a share and use files concurrently with other people.

```
sudo mkdir /mnt/smb
sudo smbmount //wserver/big /mnt/smb
```

TIP The `smbmount` command is actually a wrapper around the `mount` command. You can also use `sudo mount -t smb`.

As with other mounted directories, `sudo umount /mnt/smb` will remove the mount.

NOTE Sharing files with a common directory can lead to problems from concurrent editing. One person may end up overwriting another person's work. See "Collaborating Over the Network" in this chapter for options that support concurrent edits.

Working with Open Office

In nearly every corporate environment, you will need to read and write Microsoft Word, PowerPoint, and Excel files. Although only Microsoft Office can handle all of these formats perfectly, Ubuntu includes OpenOffice.org—a set of open source tools that can read, write, and modify Microsoft Office documents. The OpenOffice.org tools include a word processor, presentation system, and spreadsheet application. Each of these is available under the Applications ⇨ Office menu.

Using the Word Processor

The OpenOffice.org word processor (`oowriter`) is an open source alternative to Microsoft Word (see Figure 7-1). Using this program, you can access most DOC files. This word processor has a number of benefits over Microsoft Word.

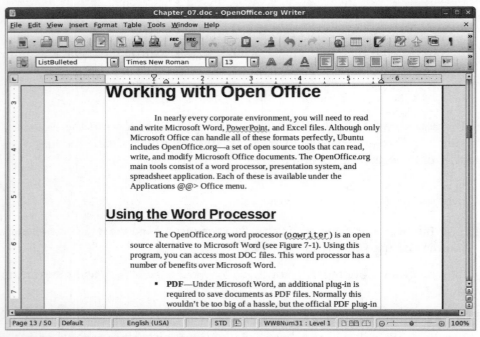

Figure 7-1: OpenOffice.org word processor

- **PDF**—Under Microsoft Word, an additional plug-in is required to save documents as PDF files. Normally this wouldn't be too big of a hassle, but the official PDF plug-in from Adobe is a resource-intensive application that can take a while to start up and frequently checks for updates. In contrast, every document in OpenOffice.org can be immediately exported to PDF by selecting File ➪ Export as PDF from the menu. This same menu option is available under all OpenOffice.org tools.

- **Security**—Microsoft Word embeds lots of unnecessary information in documents. This includes information about the author as well as deleted or edited text. The simple act of adding a character, deleting the character, and resaving the document can make the file larger. OpenOffice.org allows you to remove personal information and deleted text from saved documents. You can configure this option under the Tools ➪ Options ➪ OpenOffice.org ➪ Security settings (see Figure 7-2). The option is labeled "Remove personal information on saving."

NOTE With Microsoft Office 2003 and later, you have the option to exclude personal information—on a file-by-file basis. Under OpenOffice.org, this option is a default configuration that impacts all documents.

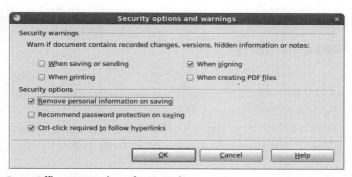

Figure 7-2: OpenOffice.org options for security

- **OpenDocument Standard**—Microsoft uses a proprietary format for storing documents. In contrast, OpenOffice.org defaults to the Open-Document standard. On the one hand, OpenDocument is much more portable. On the other hand, it is not supported by most versions of Microsoft Office. For compatibility, you will need to explicitly export the document for Microsoft Office. Alternatively, you can go to Tools ➪ Options ➪ Load/Save ➪ General and change the default file format.

As powerful as OpenOffice.org's word processor is, there are still some limitations.

- **Formatting**—Although it can view most Microsoft Office documents, the proprietary file format was reverse-engineered. As a result, complex formatting may look odd and may not save correctly. If the document has extremely complex formatting, it can actually crash the word processor.

- **Bullets, Numbers, and Headings**—This is a weakness in OpenOffice.org. If you just want a bulleted list, numbered list, or section heading, it can do it. If you want special formatting or characters, then you are better off initially creating the formats in Microsoft Office. OpenOffice.org can use formats included in a document, but cannot be easily used to create them. Although I expect this to change in later revisions, this is what you have to use today.

- **Macros**—As with formatting, OpenOffice.org does not handle Microsoft Word macros very well.

- **Annoying pop-ups**—When you save a document in the Microsoft Word format, OpenOffice.org may generate a pop-up warning you about the potential to lose formatting information.

Making Presentations

Either you love Microsoft Office PowerPoint or you hate it. Personally, it is one of my favorite presentation tools. The OpenOffice.org equivalent is called Impress (`ooimpress`). This presentation tool can read and write PowerPoint (PPT) documents. While the general look and feel of Impress is similar to that of PowerPoint (see Figure 7-3), there are some distinct differences:

- **Complexity**—As with the OpenOffice.org word processor, Impress may not display formatting correctly and can even crash if the PPT file is too complicated.

- **Animation**—Animated graphics, slides, and slide transitions do not always display properly.

- **Compatibility**—Some PPT files exported from Impress do not load under PowerPoint, and some PPT slides do not import properly into Impress. I have not seen this happen consistently, but it always happens when you need it most.

My general rule of thumb when working on presentations is to not change presentation tools. If the talk will be given using PowerPoint, then stick with real PowerPoint. If the talk will use Impress, then stick with Impress. Although

Impress is useful for viewing PPT files, the compatibility with PowerPoint is not complete enough for real collaboration.

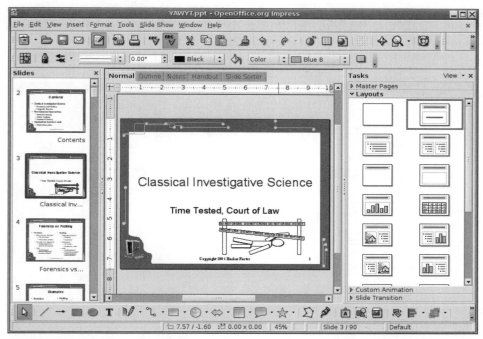

Figure 7-3: OpenOffice.org Impress—a presentation tool similar to Microsoft PowerPoint

Accessing Spreadsheets

Although `ooimpress` is an acceptable presentation tool and `oowriter` is a good word processor, Calc (`oocalc`) is an excellent spreadsheet application. Calc has a very similar look to Microsoft Excel and supports all of the standard functions and layouts (see Figure 7-4). There is virtually no learning curve between Excel and Calc. The only limitation I could find was the macro support; Calc won't run most Excel macros and does not support programmable shortcuts. For example, I have a large Excel spreadsheet where I mapped Ctrl+G to a specific macro. Under Calc, Ctrl+G does nothing and running the macro (Tools ➪ Macros ➪ Run Macros) generates errors about a missing parenthesis that is not missing.

Selecting Alternative Office Tools

OpenOffice.org includes many other useful tools. For example, `oobase` is the Open Office version of Microsoft Access, `oomath` is a powerful equation editor and `oodraw` is a very simple drawing tool for when you do not need the complexities of Gimp. These tools will help you be productive, even if they are not fully compatible with the equivalent Microsoft applications. Unlike word processors, spreadsheets, and presentation tools, lacking perfect compatibility between database interface front-ends, equation editors, and drawing tools usually does not impact collaborative efforts.

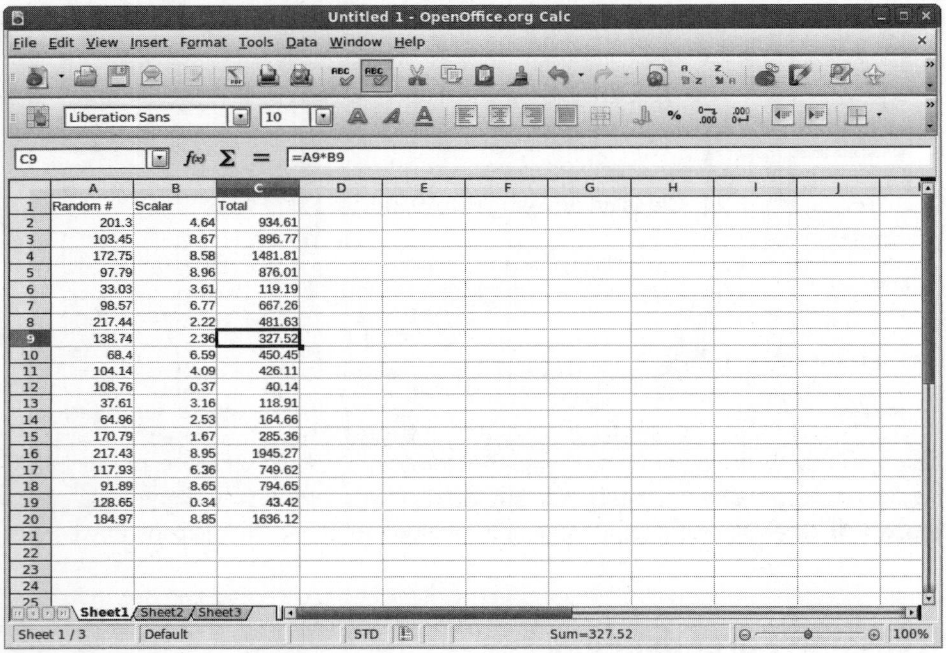

Figure 7-4: The OpenOffice.org Calc spreadsheet application

Although OpenOffice.org provides the flagship office tools for Ubuntu, they are not the only office tools available to Ubuntu. I believe that the best tool should be used for the task at hand, and that does not always mean using a word processor for viewing a Word document.

Alternate Document Viewers

One tool that I frequently use is `antiword` (`sudo apt-get install antiword`). This program converts a Microsoft Word document to plain text. This is so much easier than loading up a document and using File ➪ Save As to convert to text. It also comes in handy when you don't have a graphical login—you can use `antiword` to quickly see the text inside a Word file, even if fonts and graphics are excluded.

There is one other useful feature in `antiword`. As mentioned earlier, Microsoft Word documents can include hidden comments. Using `antiword -s`, you can see the hidden text. If you have ever wondered what information you were leaking, or what might be hidden inside a document, this tool will show you. To see what text was hidden in a document (for example, file.doc), I use these commands:

```
antiword file.doc > plain.text
antiword -s file.doc > hidden.text
sdiff plain.text hidden.text
```

The `sdiff` command shows the line-by-line, side-by-side differences between two files. Every line with a difference is flagged so you can immediately see where changes occur.

Another powerful tool is `wv` (formerly called WordView—`sudo apt-get install wv`). This program includes a suite of conversion tools, such as `wvPDF` for converting Word documents to PDF and `wvRTF` for converting them to RTF. This suite also contains forensic tools, such as `wvVersion` and `wvMime` for displaying a document's version and metadata information.

Other alternatives, such as `catdoc`, are also available for converting Word documents to text. In general, if you want to convert a Word document to any other format—especially text—you do not need the overhead of a full word processor.

If you need a full word processor and not a file converter, consider Abiword (`sudo apt-get install abiword`). This program can read and write Microsoft Word documents, including style formats and embedded images. It does have a few limitations, including display problems with embedded math equations and custom bullet formats, and no support for Word macros. However, Abiword offers similar functionality to OpenOffice without the massive overhead and slow startup time of `oowriter`.

Alternate Presentation Viewers

Although there are not many alternatives for presentation tools, there is `ppthtml` (`sudo apt-get install ppthtml`). This is a primitive program for extracting text from PPT slides and displaying them as HTML.

Alternate Spreadsheet Viewers

Besides OpenOffice.org's Calc, there is Gnumeric (`sudo apt-get install gnumeric`). At first glance, Gnumeric looks just like Calc and Excel. The difference is in the functionality: Gnumeric has many numerical analysis settings under the Tools ⇨ Statistical Analysis menu (see Figure 7-5). If you need a spreadsheet that makes numerical analysis easy, Gnumeric is a good choice. It is not that Gnumeric has functionality that is missing from Calc and Excel, but rather Gnumeric makes the functionality easier to access. Gnumeric also has a much faster startup time—Calc and Excel usually takes seconds to start up, and large spreadsheets can take a noticeably long time; Gnumeric usually starts up instantly, and large XLS files only take a few seconds.

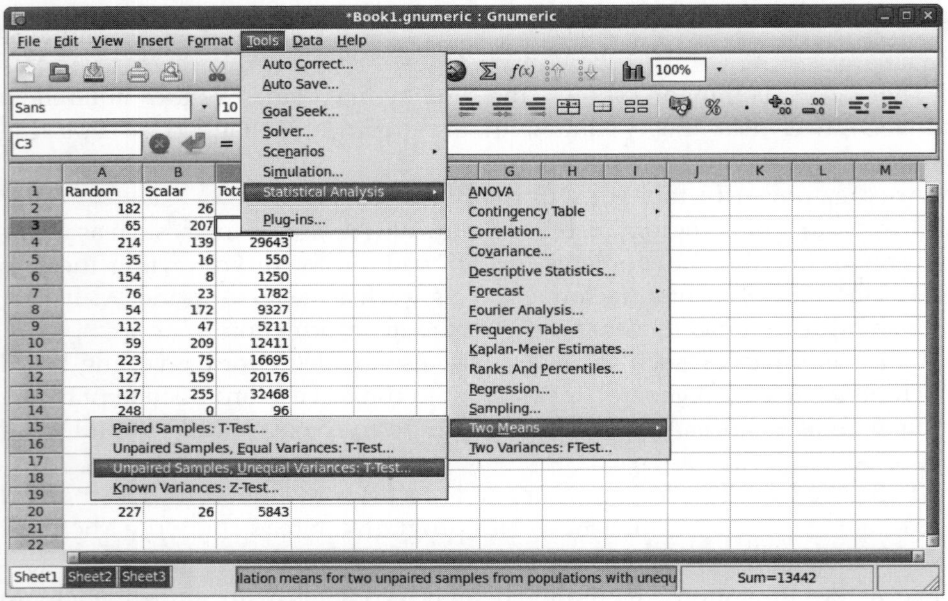

Figure 7-5: The Gnumeric spreadsheet application

Gnumeric is not perfect—it completely lacks programmable macro support and cannot display images and diagrams. But for spreadsheets that don't require these features, I find Gnumeric a better option than Calc or Excel.

Collaborating Over the Network

While sharing files allows people to work on different parts of large projects concurrently, everyone still works on independent pieces. For real productivity, nothing beats an occasional meeting. This allows people to identify problems, understand issues, and address details. Meetings can also be used as a teaching forum and used to spread knowledge.

NOTE Too many meetings can impede productivity. Lots of companies (and projects) get into situations where the project participants spend more time talking than actually doing work.

In today's online world, physically getting people together is not always practical. Some people work at home, some are in other countries, and some people are too lazy to walk across the hallway. VoIP and IM can provide real-time communication, but they don't let you see what is really going on. This is where sharing documents and desktops come in. It's one thing to describe a problem in an e-mail or over the phone; it's another to actually show it. When working together, a shared desktop and real-time file editing allows everyone to actually see what is going on.

Sharing Source Code

If you're a programmer, then you have probably worked on products with other programmers. When there is more than one programmer, or just one programmer with a really big project, then you have probably needed to track source code revisions. Ubuntu has many options for managing and tracking source code.

- **RCS**—The Revision Control System (RCS) is one of the oldest tracking systems. It is really intended for individual users. Using RCS, you can check out files (co to read, or co -l to check out and lock), and check in changes (ci). When you check in changes, you will be prompted for text to describe what modifications were made.

- **CVS**—The Concurrent Versions System (CVS) extends RCS, allowing projects to be accessed by multiple users and across the network.

- **Subversion (svn)**—This code control system is one of the most popular ones for open source projects. The functionality is very similar to that of RCS and CVS, except that the repository can be anywhere on the network. Moreover, you can use svn over HTTP or SSH if you need convenience or additional security.

- **Git**—Git was created by Linus Torvalds for managing the Linux kernel source code. (Git replaced Bitkeeper, which is a non-free source code management system.)

- **Mercurial**—This is the source control management tool used for projects hosted at code.google.com.

In my opinion, RCS is trivial to use, but outdated since few people today develop code in complete isolation. In contrast, Git is overly complex to configure and use. While Git is well suited for the needs of the Linux kernel group, it is overkill for most other projects. CVS is good for multiple users, but is not as popular as Subversion. In contrast, Subversion is difficult to configure but very easy to use and well suited to most collaborative projects.

NOTE There are other concurrent source code management systems. A few are free, like FreeVCS, and others are proprietary (Microsoft's SourceSafe immediately comes to mind). RCS, CVS, and Subversion are all readily available for Linux, BSD, Mac OS X, and even Windows. In contrast, Git has ports available for Mac OS X and Windows, but the ports may not be the latest-greatest versions. If you need to collaborate with people on different platforms, then Subversion is a great option (and CVS is a good alternate).

Configuring Subversion

Subversion tracks code changes and permits branching of the source code tree. This way, you can have a stable source code base (usually called *trunk*) and various branches where you can do serious modifications and changes without screwing up the main source code tree. If you like the changes made in a branch, then you can always merge it back into the trunk. Subversion also permits tagging certain releases with labels. The tags can be used to track major releases or milestones.

Installing Subversion is somewhat complicated because of the user configuration.

TIP Subversion has many more features and options than those discussed here. For more information, check out `subversion.tigris.org`.

1. Install Subversion.

```
sudo apt-get install subversion
```

2. Create the Subversion repository. This is where Subversion will store the source code, metadata, and configuration information. For example, if you want a project called `supercode`, then use:

```
mkdir $HOME/repos
svnadmin create $HOME/repos/supercode
```

TIP If you have many people on your server who will want their own Subversion repositories, then consider making a Subversion user (`useradd -m subversion`) and use that home directory as the root for the repository (instead of `$HOME/repos`, use `/home/subversion`). Then you can use `svnadmin` to create projects for each user. A simple script to do this is:

```
for i in $(cd /home; ls -1 | grep -v subversion); do
  svnadmin create $i
done
```

3. The repository configuration is stored in `$HOME/repos/supercode/conf/`
   `svnserve.conf`. The file contains plenty of comments and the options are
   very well documented. The default configuration permits anyone to read
   (check out) the files, but nobody can check in anything.

   Subversion files are always accessed using a URL. However, the type
   of URL depends on how you want people to access the repository. The
   options are:

   - `file://` only permits access from the local file system. No authoriza-
     tion files are used. Instead, the Unix file permissions restrict access.

   - `svn://` uses the native Subversion network protocol. This will use
     authorization files. Your `svnserve.conf` should look like this:

     ```
     # General settings for svn:
     [general]
     anon-access = read
     auth-access = write
     password-db = passwd
     authz-db = authz
     ```

   - `svn+ssh://` uses Subversion over Secure Shell. This is the most secure
     solution because `ssh` handles the authentication. However, every user
     must have an account on the server. To use this option, you must have
     the Secure Shell server installed and you must have authorization
     disabled (`anon-access = write`).

     ```
     # General settings for svn+ssh:
     [general]
     anon-access = write
     #auth-access = write
     #password-db = passwd
     #authz-db = authz
     ```

   If there are many users or you are in a corporate environment then you
   will probably want `svn:` or `ssh+svn:`. If your system is accessible from
   the Internet, then you'll want `svn+ssh:`. Make sure that the appropriate
   lines are uncommented under the general heading.

4. Subversion does not use `/etc/passwd` for accounts. For authorization, you will need to edit the repository's password file:
   `$HOME/repos/supercode/conf/passwd`. Each user needs a name and a
   password. For example:

   ```
   [users]
   user = password
   neal = mypassword
   rash = itchy
   ```

5. Edit the `authz` file and give the authorized users write permission. At minimum, you will need to create a new heading under `$HOME/repos/supercode/conf/authz` and list the users under it:

```
[/]
user = r
neal = rw
rash = rw
```

SUBVERSION PASSWORD SECURITY

Subversion passwords are stored in plain text. Anyone who can access this password file can see all of the passwords. Don't use your system login password for Subversion, and don't make it a string that insults the administrator because he will read it ("ToddSucks"). For better security, use `makepasswd` **(**`sudo apt-get install makepasswd`**) to generate random passwords for users.**

Subversion stores the plain text passwords in both the server's `repos/supercode/conf/passwd` **file, as well as the client's cached** `$HOME/.subversion/auth/` **directory.**

Beginning with version 1.6 (Karmic Koala 9.10 and later), Subversion includes options for storing the client's cached passwords in the Gnome Keyring or KDE Kwallet. Both of these options encrypt the client's cached password. To enable this option, edit `$HOME/.subversion/config` **and uncomment the line that says:**

```
password-stores = gnome-keyring,kwallet
```

The Subversion server can be started manually, as a standalone daemon, or as a network service. To start it one time by hand, use `svnserver -d -r $HOME/repos/`. The `-d` means to run it as a background process (daemon), and `-r` specifies the root of the repository.

To make Subversion start automatically, you can either create a script in `/etc/init.d/` (see Chapters 11 and 12 for some examples of startup scripts), or you can make it start as an as-needed network service using xinetd (`sudo apt-get install xinetd`). The xinetd service (`/etc/xinetd.d/svnserve`) should look like this:

```
# SVN server
# This is the tcp version.
# Be sure to set the root path to match your repository directory
service svn
{
        disable        = no
        id             = svn-stream
        socket_type    = stream
        protocol       = tcp
```

```
user            = root
wait            = no
server          = /usr/bin/svnserve
server_args     = -i --root=/home/user/repos
port            = 3690
}
```

Using Subversion

Unlike RCS, Subversion does not use file locks. Anyone can edit any file at any time. For tracking code changes, Subversion stores metadata in a bunch of .svn subdirectories. So before you begin, you will need to prepare a directory for your code. In this example, the SVN server is on a remote system named chai.

```
svn co svn://chai/supercode
svn co svn+ssh://chai/fullpath/supercode
```

For the local file system, you can use:

```
svn co svn://localhost/supercode
svn co svn+ssh://localhost/fullpath/supercode
svn co file:///fullpath/supercode
```

NOTE If you use svn: with authorization enabled, then you will need to specify the username and password. For example, svn --username user --password pass co svn://server/respository. The user and pass must match your entry in the passwd file. You may also see a warning about the password being stored unencrypted on your system.

This will create a supercode/ working directory and prepare it for use with Subversion. If there is any code in the supercode repository, then all of it is checked out. But if this is a new project, then only a .svn directory will be created.

NOTE The .svn directories are managed by Subversion. In a regular use scenario, you will never need to edit anything under the .svn directories.

The main operations you will use are the update, add, delete, and check-in. However, you may also want to see a file's history or differences.

- svn up—This command updates the copy of every file in the directory (and any subdirectories). You can also choose a specific file or directory to update (for example, svn up file). Use it to download the latest copies of whatever was checked in. If you don't periodically update your directory with svn up, then you will never receive new code that other people checked in.

- svn ci—This is the check-in command for committing changes. All modified files will be selected and sent to the server. You will be prompted for a human-readable description of the changes being made. In general, it is good to limit one type of change to each check-in. This way, if something needs to be removed (like a bad check-in), then you can narrow down the impact to a few files.

WARNING Subversion allows multiple people to edit the same file at the same time. If two people change the same area of the source code, then the second person will be blocked from checking in their code. Subversion will highlight the conflict in the code and not allow you to check it in until the conflict is resolved.

- svn add *file*—This is how you add new files into the project. If you specify a new directory, then everything under that directory will be added the next time you check in your code.

TIP While you will probably want to add source code, like svn add *.c, you probably do not want to add temporary files or binary objects that change with every build.

- svn del *file*—This deletes a file (or directory) from the repository. However, deletions do not take effect until you check in the changes.

- svn ren *old new*—Rename a file or directory from *old* to *new*.

- svn diff *file*—This command shows you the differences between your code and the copy in the repository.

- svn log *file*—This shows you the check-in history and the associated descriptions that you entered.

- svn status—This command lists any file conflicts and uncommitted changes.

- svn resolved *file*—On occasion, Subversion will forbid commits because it thinks there is a file conflict. If you are certain that there is no conflict (or managed to fix it), then use resolved to overwrite the conflict notification.

Every commit increments a revision number. You can specify the revision number to access the code from a specific time. For example, to compare my Makefile with the current top-of-tree, I would use svn diff Makefile. However, if I want to compare it with version 21, then I would use svn diff -r21 Makefile. Similarly, svn co retrieves the current code base, but svn co -r1280 will retrieve whatever code existed at revision 1280.

Branching and Merging with Subversion

A branch in Subversion is simply a copy of the source code. Before you use branching and merging, be sure that all of the code is in a subdirectory.

```
mkdir trunk
svn add trunk
svn ci trunk -m "Creating trunk"
# Move all files under trunk:
ls -1 | grep -v '^trunk$' | while read i; do svn ren "$i" trunk; done
svn ci -m "Populating trunk"
```

Use the `copy` command to copy `trunk` into your new branch. For example, I can copy my `supercode/trunk` on `chai` to an experimental branch called `branch/test123` using:

```
mkdir branch
svn add branch
svn ci branch -m "Creating parent directory for branches"
svn copy svn://chai/supercode/trunk/ \
      svn://chai/supercode/branch/test123 \
  -m "Experimental Test Branch"
svn up # check out the new branch
```

Eventually you will want to merge your branch back into the trunk. Both of these commands merge changes back into the trunk; the former merges a specific branch while the latter merges your current code directory.

```
svn merge svn://chai/supercode/branch/test123 \
      svn://chai/supercode/trunk/
svn merge --reintegrate svn://chai/supercode/trunk/ .
```

You can even merge specific revision changes from the test branch back into the trunk. For example, to merge all changes between revision 115 and 118, I would use:

```
svn merge -r 115:118 svn://chai/supercode/branch/test123 \
      svn://chai/supercode/trunk/
```

Sharing Documents in Real Time

While sharing source code is nice, it isn't the same as actively working on the same file at the same time. Now keep in mind, when I say "same time," I'm not talking about editing files on different systems or modifying web pages with a Wiki; I mean true multi-person real-time edits where you can see the other person type!

One of the best programs I have stumbled upon for concurrent edits is Gobby (`sudo apt-get install gobby`). Gobby is a real-time collaboration tool for editing text files. Using Gobby, one person starts up the server and everyone else connects as a client. (See Figure 7-6.)

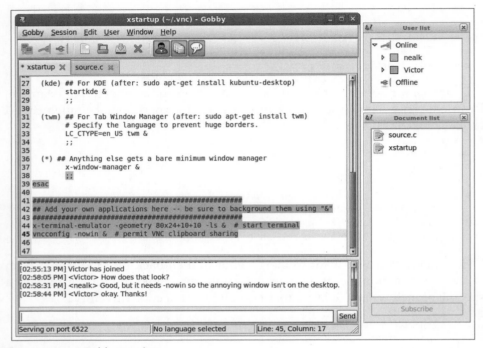

Figure 7-6: A Gobby session

Gobby permits anyone to open and share text files. Each person selects a name and a color. The names permit other people to identify who you are, and the color tells everyone what sections of the document you have modified.

Besides the shared documents, Gobby also includes a small chat window for sending text messages. The chat window looks and acts similar to other live text chat systems.

The thing that impresses me the most is that Gobby version 0.4 (found in Hardy Heron [8.04 LTS] and later Ubuntu versions) encrypts all network traffic. You can actually use Gobby safely over the Internet!

TIP For intense document collaboration, I usually use Gobby for sharing the file editing, and Skype for the free VoIP. While the chat window is nice, nothing beats talking for rapid communication.

There are a few alternatives to Gobby. For example, Abiword 2.6 includes an option to collaborate on Word documents. Unfortunately, Hardy Heron (8.06 LTS) only includes Abiword 2.4 in the repository. You will either need Jaunty Jackalope (9.04) or later to install it from the repositories, or you can compile the latest Abiword from source code. There is also DrawPile for sharing a drawing board (`http://sourceforge.net/projects/drawpile/`), but it can take hours to work out all of the compilation issues (they don't identify the dependent libraries for compilation).

Sharing Desktops with VNC

Under Ubuntu, Virtual Network Computing (VNC) is the best option for sharing desktops. VNC is supported on Unix, Linux, Mac OS X, and Windows operating systems. Rather than struggling with almost-compatible software, you can use VNC to provide access to remote desktops, where you can use software on its native platform. For example, I frequently find myself in phone conferences where Microsoft NetMeeting or LiveMeeting is used to shares slides. This is convenient for Windows users but not for Linux users. To get around this problem, we run a VNC server on one of the Windows clients. This way, Linux users can use VNC to watch the shared presentation.

VNC consists of two parts: a server and one or more clients (called *viewers*). The server shares the desktop, while the client creates a window to display the server's desktop.

> **WARNING** Under Microsoft NetMeeting, the server can choose which windows to share. Under VNC it is all or nothing; either the entire desktop is shared or nothing is shared. If you are sharing your desktop, don't forget that everyone can see you checking your e-mail.

REMOTE DESKTOPS

There are a couple of different ways to share desktops between Windows and other systems. Although VNC is very common and accessible, other options exist. For example, Microsoft offers the Remote Desktop Protocol (RDP) for sharing the desktop with a remote host. RDP is included by default on Windows 2003 and XP systems and is available from Microsoft for other Windows versions (`msdn.microsoft.com/library/en-us/termserv/termserv/remote_desktop_protocol.asp`). On the Linux and Unix side, tools such as `rdesktop` (part of the default Ubuntu desktop) allow access to the shared Windows desktop from non-Windows systems. To use this program, you just need to provide the name of the windows server—for example:

```
rdesktop winserver
```

(continued)

REMOTE DESKTOPS *(continued)*

> **Other RDP client packages for Ubuntu include** gnome-rdp **and** tsclient.
> **For the KDE desktop, there is also** krdc.
>
> **Although employing a native Microsoft protocol is useful for accessing a Windows desktop, there are two significant limitations. First, the RDP server (shared desktop) is not available for all versions of Windows; second, only Windows can be a server. Currently, you cannot use any of these Ubuntu RDP tools to share your Ubuntu desktop with a Windows system.**

Using the VNC Viewer

There are a couple of different VNC clients available for Ubuntu. Hardy Heron (8.04 LTS) and later Ubuntu releases include vinagre. However, I prefer the xvnc4viewer package (xvncviewer under Dapper Drake) since it has fewer prompts and is easier to use. To start the client, run: vncviewer. This pops up a small window that asks for the server's name.

TIP I usually add the VNC viewer as a launcher on the top panel. This way, clicking on an icon immediately prompts for the server's name. If you include the server's name as a launcher parameter, then **vncviewer** will immediately connect to the server.

VNC servers may require a password. If one is needed, you will be prompted to enter it. Then the viewer's window will appear, showing you the shared desktop (see Figure 7-7). When your mouse is over the viewer, your cursor will become a small square. If the server allows you to interact (and not just "view only"), then the server's cursor will follow you. Every keystroke and every mouse click will be transmitted from your system to the server.

Even more importantly, the clipboard buffers on the server and client are linked. This enables you to copy and paste text between applications on the client and everything on the server.

TIP If your remote Linux system does not support clipboard sharing, try running vncconfig (sudo apt-get install vnc4server).

NOTE If the server's desktop is larger than the client's window, then the viewer's window will have scrollbars. This can be inconvenient. Also, if the server's color palette differs from the client's, then colors may look wrong.

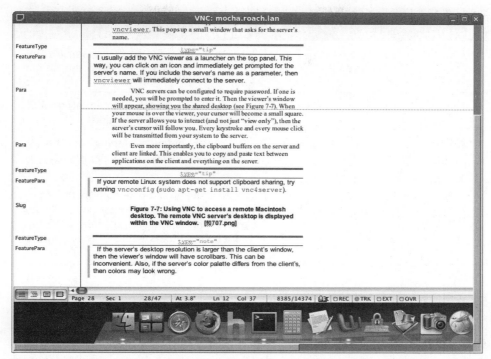

Figure 7-7: Using VNC to access a remote Macintosh desktop. The remote VNC server's desktop is displayed within the VNC window.

Sharing Your Desktop

For an Ubuntu VNC server, there are two options. First, you can share your own desktop. In this setup, every client sees everything you have. Although this is usually not a problem, it can sometimes hinder your own productivity. For example, you can't search the web or check e-mail privately if everyone can see your desktop. The second option is to share a virtual desktop, where clients only see what you want them to see.

Sharing Your Complete Desktop

To share your complete desktop, you will need to install the server, x11vnc.

```
sudo apt-get install x11vnc
```

To start the server, simply run x11vnc. The basic server uses no passwords, allows one client to fully interact with the server, and exits when the client disconnects. There are many other options for x11vnc. Table 7-1 shows some of the more useful ones. These options can be combined. I usually use something like x11vnc -forever -passwd SeCrEt.

Table 7-1: Command-line options for `x11vnc`

OPTION	EXAMPLE	PURPOSE
`passwd`	`x11vnc -passwd SeCrEt`	Assign a password to the server. It's not very secure, but it does keep the riff-raff out.
`viewonly`	`x11vnc -viewonly`	All clients can watch but cannot interact. This is useful for presentations.
`forever`	`x11vnc -forever`	The server continues running after the last client disconnects. The default setting is `-once`.
`clip`	`x11vnc -clip 600x400+0+25`	Restrict the desktop region. In this case, it is 600x400 pixels offset vertically 25 pixels—this is a region just below the top panel. Only items within this region are shared.

Sharing Independent Desktops

Although sharing your full desktop is useful, sometimes it is better to have a clean slate for sharing. X-Windows supports virtual desktops. These are desktops that exist in memory and do not conflict with your real desktop. The `tightvncserver` and `vnc4server` packages both provide a virtual desktop for sharing over VNC. However, only `vnc4server` provides shared clipboard support.

1. Install the VNC server.

```
sudo apt-get install vnc4server
```

2. Start the server. Be sure to specify the screen resolution (e.g., 800x600), color depth (e.g. 8, 16, or 32 bit), and the display number. Your normal desktop runs on display:0, so you will need to choose an alternative display.

```
vnc4server -geometry 800x600 -depth 16:9
```

TIP Although you can specify a desktop space that is larger than your real desktop and uses a higher resolution, don't. In most cases, it is more convenient to choose a geometry that is smaller than your desktop and has the same color depth (or less) to avoid scrollbars and ugly colors.

3. When you first start `vnc4server`, it will ask you for a password. Clients will need to provide this when connecting to the server. If you restart the server, you won't need to specify the password. If you want to change the password later, use `vncpasswd`.

4. Use `xvncviewer` to connect to the server. For the server's name, include the display. For example, if the server's hostname is `vserver` then type in `vserver:9`.

5. If you want to share the clipboard with the `vnc4server`, you will need to run `vncconfig`. This will pop up a small window asking if you want to send or receive the clipboard. I usually use the `-nowin` parameter to disable the window.

```
vncconfig -nowin &
```

The virtual desktop starts up in the background. To stop it from running, use the `-kill` option. For example, `vnc4server -kill:9`.

The default virtual desktop really depends on your version of Ubuntu. For example, Dapper Drake (6.06 LTS) and Hardy Heron (8.04 LTS) both default to a very simple configuration: one terminal window open, no menus, no icons, and no background beyond the default X11 "gray." With Karmic Koala (9.10), the VNC desktop uses your default Gnome desktop settings.

The desktop is defined in the `$HOME/.vnc/xstartup` script. You can change this in order to give it a real desktop. For example, Listing 7-3 shows my `xstartup`. It has options for many different desktops but currently starts up *my* Gnome desktop without showing any of the actual applications I have open (see Figure 7-8).

Listing 7-3: Sample $HOME/.vnc/xstartup with Different Desktops

```sh
#!/bin/sh
##################################################
# Set your desktop
# Options are: 'gnome', 'kde', 'twm', or 'plain'
##################################################
DESKTOP=gnome

# Load default settings
xrdb $HOME/.Xresources
xsetroot -solid grey

# Start the desktop
case "$DESKTOP" in
  (gnome) # This depends on your Ubuntu version
       # get primary version (e.g., 9.10 becomes 9)
       version=`lsb_release -sr | sed -e 's/[.].*//'`
       if [ "$version" -lt 9 ]; then
         # Older than Jaunty (e.g., Dapper or Hardy)
         gnome-session—sm-disable &
       else
         # Jaunty, Karmic, or later
         /etc/X11/Xsession
       fi
   ;;
```

(continued)

Listing 7-3: Sample $HOME/.vnc/xstartup with Different Desktops (*continued*)

```
(kde) ## For KDE (after: sudo apt-get install kubuntu-desktop)
      startkde &
      ;;

(twm) ## For Tab Window Manager (after: sudo apt-get install twm)
      # Specify the language to prevent huge borders.
      LC_CTYPE=en_US twm &
      ;;

(*) ## Anything else gets a bare minimum window manager
    x-window-manager &
    ;;
esac


####################################################
## Add your own applications here—be sure to background
## them using "&"
####################################################
x-terminal-emulator -geometry 80x24+10+10 -ls &  # start terminal
vncconfig -nowin & # permit VNC clipboard sharing
```

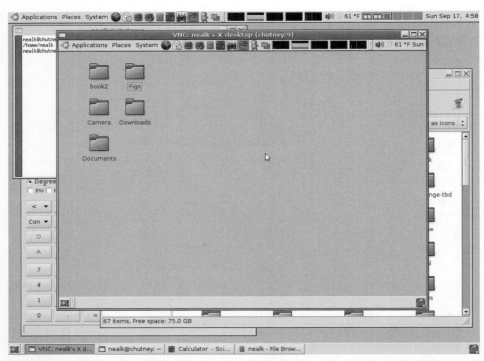

Figure 7-8: VNC server running the Gnome desktop. The real Gnome desktop has applications running that do not appear in the VNC server.

TIP When using Firefox on the VNC virtual desktop, you may see errors about Firefox already running or the profile being in use. Consider using an alternate profile to overcome this problem. See Chapter 6 for information on tuning Firefox.

Securing VNC Connections

The VNC password provides a basic level of security, but should not be trusted for safety over the Internet. Instead, you can tunnel VNC over an SSH connection. By default, the VNC server uses port 5900/tcp. Each VNC display increments this value. For example, if you are using Tight VNC and specify display:9, then the port is `5909/tcp`. Then, using SSH port forwarding, you can tunnel the VNC port. For example, to tunnel the local VNC port to the remote VNC server running on:9, do the following:

1. On the remote server, start the Tight VNC server on display:9. For example:

   ```
   vncserver:9
   ```

2. On your local system, use SSH to connect to the server and forward the local port `5900/tcp` to the server's port `5909/tcp`.

   ```
   ssh -L5900:localhost:5909 server
   ```

3. In a different window on your local system, start the VNC client with:

   ```
   xvncviewer localhost
   ```

This command tells the viewer to connect to the VNC server located on `localhost:5900`. However, `5900/tcp` is actually tunneled through the SSH connection to the remote server. The connection is tunneled to the server's port `5909/tcp`, where the VNC server is running.

By tunneling VNC over SSH, you prevent attackers from seeing your desktop and, more importantly, you do not need to have the VNC server and its weak password system accessible to the world.

TIP Tunneling VNC over SSH is not always fast. For better speed performance, enable compression (`-C`) and change the encryption selection to use the Blowfish algorithm: `ssh -C -c blowfish -L5900:localhost:5909 server`.

SEEING A SPEED DIFFERENCE

VNC transmits a lot of graphics and can be a bandwidth hog. If a dozen clients connect to a single server, then network traffic leaving the server can become a bottleneck and result in really slow updates for everyone.

(continued)

SEEING A SPEED DIFFERENCE *(continued)*

If you need to have lots of viewers, consider farming out the load. The main server should only share the desktop with a few clients (for example, one server shares to four clients). Each of the clients also runs a server and shares with more clients. You can continue spreading the network load among computers until everyone has access. It only takes three levels of this "one server to four clients" for over 200 people to see the same thing. Although the people at the end of this chain may need to wait a second before seeing updates, this is much faster than having 200 clients access the same VNC server.

Running Software in Emulators

Although nearly compatible software helps collaborators bridge a communication gap, nothing beats running the exact same application. For example, if you need to edit Word documents, then nothing does a better job than Microsoft Word. In the days of old, this true compatibility was accomplished with dual-boot systems. A single computer would have multiple operating systems installed and the user would reboot the computer into whatever operating system they needed. Although Ubuntu does support dual-boot environments (see Chapter 1), this is not as effective as being able to run applications from multiple operating systems at the same time. Today, people either run two separate computers with different operating systems and network connectivity (hardware is cheap), or they use hardware emulators.

A hardware emulator is an application that pretends to be an entire computer. Emulators replicate a computer in a virtual machine (VM): CPU, memory, devices (for example, hard drives), and even BIOS. A perfect emulator can run any operating system, and the operating system should not be able to tell that it is running in an emulator. For example, operating systems like Ubuntu and Windows expect standardized hardware. If the emulator mirrors the hardware, then either operating system will run without a problem. Most OSs do not need to know that the hardware is emulated.

There are many reasons to run an emulator, such as playing with hostile viruses, opening suspicious e-mails, or installing software without screwing up your main system. A true emulator is a perfect sandbox, where software can run without hurting the host operating system. But one of the main reasons to use an emulator is compatibility. Not all software can be used natively under Ubuntu, but an emulator running under Ubuntu can be installed with a non-Ubuntu operating system and used to run native applications. For example, if I really need to use Microsoft NetMeeting, then I can start a VM running Windows and use NetMeeting from within the emulation.

Choosing an Emulator

Emulators have three main components. The *host* operating system is where the emulator is running and the *guest* operating system runs in the emulator. For example, a Ubuntu host can run Windows 2000 as a guest within an emulator. The final component is a virtual hard drive. This is usually a file on the host system. I frequently install a guest operating system to a virtual hard drive (file), configure it just the way I like it, and make a backup of the file. Later, after playing with software in the guest system, I can copy back the image in order to reset the system. This is faster and cleaner than trying to remove undesirable software or perform a restore from a backup system.

TIP **If you want to see if a patch will make your system unstable, first install it in a VM. I have a VM installed with the same software as some of my critical computers. Before patching the real thing, I make sure the VM works after being patched.**

There are three main emulators for Ubuntu: Qemu, VMware, and Xen. Although each provides solid emulation, they are all different. Table 7-2 shows some of the differences. All three emulators offer the same basic features. They all support multiple drives, offer solid i386 emulation, and support network access. The main differences come from licensing, architecture support, and speed.

Qemu is the slowest of the emulators but offers the widest hardware support. Xen is arguably the fastest but only supports Linux or BSD systems. (Xen can support Windows if your CPU supports x86 virtualization. But most CPUs don't.) VMware offers a commercial-quality, fast emulation, refined interface, but it is proprietary and limited to Linux and Windows host systems.

There are two types of virtual machines: emulators and virtualizers. An emulator uses software to represent a computer system. A true emulator, such as Qemu and VMware, provides virtual hardware, BIOS, and even multiple CPUs. The benefit is that any operating system that is supported on the real hardware will work within an emulator. For example, if the emulator acts as an SMP Pentium Pro PC with 512 MB RAM, then it will support Windows, Linux, BSD, OS/2, E/OS, and any other PC operating system.

The biggest limitations with emulators are system resources and speed. If you configure an emulator to have 512 MB RAM but you actually have 128 MB RAM, then you can expect to spend time swapping RAM to disk. As speed goes, emulators interpret running opcodes. This means the guest operating system runs slower than if it were on a dedicated computer. The speed can be less than 25 percent of the actual operating system's clock speed. For example, a 2.8-GHz host system may have a guest that appears to run at 300 MHz. Systems can run even slower if they are performing hardware-intensive commands, and the detection of attached peripherals may take a very long time. To overcome some of the speed limitations, kernel modules are available for boosting performance. These modules allow the emulator to directly link some functions into the host operating system. Drive, memory, and video access can all be performed faster with a kernel module. In the best case, a kernel module can give you a nearly 1-to-1 performance ratio.

Table 7-2: Comparison of Hardware Emulators

FEATURE	QEMU 0.11.0	VMWARE 3.0	XEN 3.24
Licensing	GPL	Commercial	GPL
Open Source	Yes	No	Yes
VM Type	Emulator	Emulator	Virtualizer
Host Architectures	32- and 64-bit x86, PowerPC, Sparc; Linux, BSD, Windows, Solaris, MacOS X; portable to other host systems	32- and 64-bit x86; Linux and Windows	32- and 64-bit x86; Linux and BSD; Windows with appropriate hardware
Guest Platforms	32- and 64-bit x86, PowerPC[1], ARM, MIPS, Sparc, and more	32- and 64-bit x86	32- and 64-bit x86[4]
Kernel Boost Module	Yes[2]	Yes	Yes
Ubuntu Support	Universe repository[3]	Generic Linux binary	Download source or Debian binary; Ubuntu repository for Hardy Heron and later
Installation and Removal	`apt-get` for install and remove[3]	Install script; manual removal	Manual install and removal

[1] Qemu only supports Linux as a guest OS on a PowerPC.
[2] Qemu includes a kernel boost module, but it does not work consistently under Ubuntu.
[3] The Ubuntu universe repository usually does not have the latest version of Qemu available and usually does not include all of the different emulated platforms.
[4] Xen virtualizes hardware, so it can only run multiple instances of the host's hardware.

In contrast to emulators, *virtualizers* do not emulate hardware. Instead, they manage the existing host hardware and allow different guest systems to share the same resources. Xen is an example of a virtualizer. Xen allows multiple guest operating systems to run independently on the same hardware. Although Xen won't allow you to run different applications for collaboration, it can assist in dividing workloads, testing networked applications, and even benchmarking software. Xen is often used for security. Each independent operating system performs a specific task. If one Xen VM is compromised, it will not impact other VMs.

Understanding Virtual Disks

In general, there are a few types of virtual drives you can use with emulators. The first is a disk image of an actual hard drive. After installing the guest OS, this image will contain a partition table, boot loader, and the guest OS—similar to the block device /dev/hda. This is the most flexible option. Unfortunately, this option is not always desirable since you cannot easily copy files off of the disk image. (Linux does not allow you to mount a file containing a partition table.)

The second option is a plain disk partition. This is a file (or device) missing the partition table and boot loader—similar to the block devices /dev/hda1 and /dev/hda2, which are partitions under /dev/hda. This option allows you to mount the file as a loopback device. If you want to share files between the guest and host OSs, you can mount the partition image. For example, if the partition file is called disk.img, then you can use:

```
sudo mkdir /mnt/img   # make sure the mount point exists
sudo mount -o loop disk.img /mnt/img  # mount the disk
```

By mounting the partition, you can copy any files you need to and from the VM.

A third option is to use an existing directory. The directory is used by the VM and treated as a disk partition. While not supported by all emulators, this does make it easier to copy files between the host and guest systems.

Differences between VNC and VM

All of these emulators have the ability to grab the mouse. This means that the mouse's input is completely used by the VM. This is different from VNC, where the remote mouse is separate from the local mouse, and moving the mouse outside the window allows you to leave the remote window. To release the mouse from the emulator, press Control and Alt at the same time.

> **NOTE** For Qemu, only the Ctrl+Alt keys on the left side of the keyboard release the mouse. The ones on the right are sent to the guest operating system. With VMware, any combination of Ctrl and Alt keys will release the mouse.

The other big difference concerns the clipboard. Under VNC, you can cut and paste between the remote (guest) and local (host) operating systems. Qemu does not support this feature—the host and guest do not share a clipboard. Xen and VMware do offer shared clipboards if the guest OS kernel is modified.

Emulating with VNC

The coolest feature provided by all three emulators is the ability to use VNC *as the display*. Normally when a VM is started, a window appears that acts as the display for the operating system. Qemu, VMware, and Xen allow you to specify a VNC display instead of a normal window. For example, under Qemu you would use `qemu -vnc 2` to start the display on the VNC server `localhost:2`. Now, if you want to collaborate, you can use any application on any supported guest operating system—you are not limited to sharing your Ubuntu desktop.

Using VMware (Commercial)

VMware is a commercial emulator. It is very fast and very configurable. However, it is not open source and not available for every hardware platform.

1. Go to `www.vmware.com`. VMware offers three different types of emulators: VMware Player, VMware Server, and VMware ESXi.

> **TIP** If you plan to install VMware Server, get your serial number code *first*! While you can re-run the installer, the server will not run until you enter your serial number. VMware Workstation offers a short trial period but then must be registered to be used.

2. Install the software. For example, if you downloaded `VMware-Player-3.0.0-203739.i386.bundle`, then you would install it using:

   ```
   sudo sh ./VMware-Player-3.0.0-203739.i386.bundle
   ```

3. Start VMware Player by running `vmplayer`.

The `vmplayer` window has everything you need to create a new virtual machine instance, install on a hard drive, and even change virtual hardware configurations.

VMware provides lots of options for using peripherals and networking virtual machines. You can easily create a virtual subnet with lots of virtual machines. This is really useful for testing network software.

Using Qemu (Open Source)

The Q-Emulator (Qemu) is the most flexible emulator option because it supports a wide variety of host and guest architectures. Although it is very portable, Qemu is not as fast as VMware, nor does it support peripherals as well as VMware.

While Qemu is available from the Ubuntu repositories, you will probably want to compile Qemu from scratch since the Ubuntu package does not always contain the most recent code release.

NOTE You will need to have a developer's environment installed. See Chapter 5 for Programming with C.

1. Download the latest source code from `http://www.qemu.org/`.
2. Follow the installation instructions. They should be as simple as:
   - Extract the source code and `cd` into the source code directory.
   - Configure the build files with `./configure`.
   - Compile Qemu using `make clean; make`.
   - Install it using `sudo make install`.
3. You will need to do one manual configuration step to specify the keyboard mapping for the Qemu VNC server:

```
sudo ln -s /usr/share/rdesktop/keymaps /usr/local/share/qemu/keymaps
```

Installing a Qemu VM

To get started using Qemu, you first need a virtual disk. There are many options for doing this:

- **Use** `qemu-img`—The program `qemu-img` creates a blank file that will act as a disk image. To create a 2-GB file called disk.img, use:

```
qemu-img create disk.img 2G
```

- **Create a blank disk**—You can use `dd` to create a blank disk. For example, `dd if=/dev/zero of=big1 bs=512 count=4194304`. This will do the same thing as using `qemu-img` (but is not as fast).

- **Copy a working drive**—Use `dd` to make a copy of a working hard drive. This is much faster than installing a guest OS within the VM. If the disk is located at `/dev/hdb`, then you can copy it to `disk.img` using:

```
dd if=/dev/hdb of=disk.img
```

- **Use a real hard drive**—If the disk is installed as `/dev/hdb`, then you will just need read/write access to `/dev/hdb`.

WARNING Do not use the same boot device as your host system! If your host OS is using /dev/hda, do not tell the VM to use /dev/hda. The drive may become corrupted if two operating systems use it at the same time.

If you have configured a blank disk, then you will need to install an operating system on it. This is usually done using a CD-ROM drive or ISO image. For example, if you downloaded the Ubuntu server ISO, then you can burn it to a CD-ROM or install directly from the ISO:

```
qemu -hda disk.img -cdrom /dev/cdrom -boot d  # run from real DVD
qemu -hda disk.img -cdrom ubuntu-9.10-server.iso -boot d
     # run from image
```

Both of these commands will start the Qemu i386 VM and begin installing Ubuntu. The main options for Qemu specify the images for hard drives (-hda and -hdb for the primary and secondary IDE drives), CD-ROM (-cdrom), and floppy drives (-fda and -fdb). By default, Qemu boots from the first hard drive (-boot c). If you want, you can specify booting from the floppy (-boot a) or CD-ROM (-boot d). There are other options for supporting USB devices, network cards, and video.

Installing Ubuntu under Qemu can take a very long time. Although a real Ubuntu installation may complete in under a half-hour, a Qemu-based installation may take two hours or longer. You can usually speed up VMs by increasing the amount of emulated RAM. Qemu defaults to 128 MB for each VM. With this default setting, I do not recommend booting off the Ubuntu Live Desktop CD-ROM—you may grow old and die before the desktop loads (it can take over four hours). If you increase the VM's RAM to 512 MB (-m 512), then it should come up fully in a few minutes.

Running a Qemu VM

Although installations usually take a long time, installed operating systems are fast enough for real-time use. After you have installed the operating system, you can boot from the image drive using:

```
qemu -hda disk.img
```

The only limits to the number of operating systems you can run simultaneously are the speed of the host system and the amount of shared memory. Although you can increase the shared memory size (see Chapter 8), you cannot increase your computer's speed. On a dual 2.8-GHz computer with 1-GB RAM, I would not recommend running more than two graphical operating systems (or four text systems) at one time. Since the boot sequence for most guest systems consumes the most resources, I would also recommend booting them one at a time. After booting, it is very easy to run two emulators at once. Figure 7-9 shows two Qemu sessions running. One VM is running E/OS (a BeOS clone) with a VNC display. The other is running Windows 98 with the Firefox web browser. The host operating system is Ubuntu's Dapper Drake.

TIP If Qemu's mouse is overly sensitive or not correctly aligned under the host's mouse, try adding **-usbdevice tablet** to the list of command-line parameters. This will change the virtual mouse to emulate a properly aligned drawing tablet.

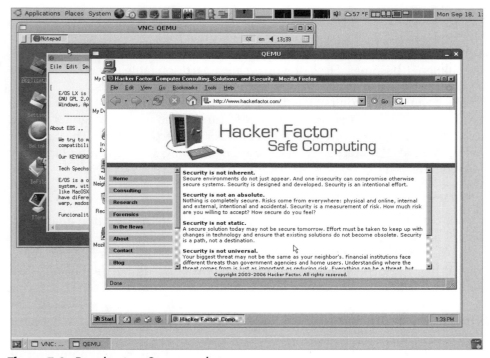

Figure 7-9: Running two Qemu sessions

NETWORKING WITH QEMU

Qemu predefines a few IP addresses for virtual network connectivity. The default IP address for the guest operating system is 10.0.2.15. The virtual firewall, DHCP server, and optional TFTP server are at 10.0.2.2. 10.0.2.3 is the DNS server, and 10.0.2.4 is the Qemu SMB server.

Qemu virtualizes all of these network addresses. For example, DNS queries from the guest OS to 10.0.2.3 are forwarded to the host OS's DNS server.

(continued)

NETWORKING WITH QEMU (continued)

And if the guest OS needs an IP address, then the virtual DHCP server will supply one.

Finally, if your guest OS needs to connect to the host operating system, you can use `ssh`, `ftp`, or direct a web browser to `10.0.2.2`. (Just be sure that the host operating system is running an SSH, FTP, or web server—see Chapter 13 for information on enabling network services.)

Creating Partitions

Although having a disk partition for a file is great for loopback mounts, Qemu and VMware cannot use a disk image as a drive unless it has a partition table. The challenge becomes: How do you create a partition table when all you have is a partition? The answer involves the `dd` and `fdisk` commands.

Let's assume that you have a disk partition in a file (for example, `part.img` created from `/dev/hda1`) and you want to turn it into a disk image for Qemu (`disk.img`). First, you need to allocate space for the partition table. The partition table consumes the first 63 sectors of the drive. Using `dd`, you can replace your partition file (`part.img`) with a disk image (`disk.img`):

```
dd if=part.img of=disk.img bs=512 seek=63
```

Your disk file (`disk.img`) is 32,256 bytes larger than the partition image and has space for a partition table.

The next step is more complicated. Disks have sectors, heads, and cylinders. While old drives had a direct correlation between heads and physical read-write heads, newer drives simply use it as a numerical offset. Groups of sectors are grouped into cylinders. The maximum sizes are 63 sectors per cylinder, 255 heads, and 16,383 cylinders. For disks larger than 125 GB, sector sizes greater than 512 bytes are used.

Take a look at the size of your `disk.img` file and compute the number of cylinders. For example, let's say the size of `disk.img` is 1,073,774,080 bytes (a 1-GB partition plus partition table). Qemu prefers 16 heads and 63 sectors: 1,073,774,080 bytes ÷ (512 bytes per sector × 63 sectors × 16 heads) = 2080.5704 cylinders. Since you cannot have a fractional cylinder, round up to 2081. Now you can use `fdisk` to create the partition table:

```
fdisk -C 2081 -H 16 -S 63 disk.img
```

TIP The `fdisk` command works on both block devices and files. You don't need to be root to modify a file, but `fdisk` will still try to synchronize disks. If you see errors about `ioctl()`, don't worry—only root has permission to call it and your changes are still saved.

Create one partition that spans the entire disk, from cylinder 1 to 2081. The final partition table should look like this:

```
Device Boot       Start      End      Blocks    Id  System
disk.img,         1          2081     1048823+  83  Linux
```

NOTE Based on the type of partition, you may need to change the system identifier in the partition table. If you plan to boot from this drive, you will also need to make the partition active.

Your saved disk image is now usable as a disk by Qemu. Even though it may not be bootable (since there is no boot manager for Linux), you can boot from a live CD-ROM and set up a boot manager.

Converting Between Qemu and VMware

VMware and Qemu use different disk image formats. Qemu supports a variety of formats but is usually used with either a copy-on-write disk (cow or qcow) or a raw disk image. In contrast, VMware uses the vmdk format, which includes metadata along with the disk. Fortunately, you can easily convert between formats using qemu-img. To convert a raw Qemu image (for example, disk.img) to VMware disk (disk.vmdk), use:

```
qemu-img convert disk.img -O vmdk disk.vmdk
```

Similarly, you can convert a VMware disk to a Qemu disk using:

```
qemu-img convert -f vmdk disk.vmdk disk.img
```

Using this approach, you can use any Qemu disk under VMware and vice versa. Even though VMware Player cannot be used to create a virtual disk, Qemu can! And the Qemu disk can be quickly converted for use with VMware.

Using Xen (Open Source)

Xen is an operating system virtualizer designed for speed. This application replaces the host operating systems. While not available from the repositories for Dapper Drake (6.06 LTS), it is available for Hardy Heron (8.04 LTS) and later Ubuntu versions.

WARNING Installing Xen requires you to change your kernel and boot loader (Grub) configuration. If you screw up the installation, then you can really hose your system. If you are not comfortable with a lot of manual configuration and troubleshooting, then don't try Xen. You might want to wait until the project matures a little more.

Before you begin, check your system requirements. Xen only supports 32-bit and 64-bit x86 architectures. If you are using a PowerPC system or other host architecture, then you cannot use Xen.

While there are many different ways to install Xen, the instructions at `https://help.ubuntu.com/community/Xen` are very helpful and detailed.

NOTE Why are the instructions not in this book? Xen is undergoing a lot of development and the installation instructions frequently change. It is likely that any instructions listed here would become outdated quickly. The best instructions are found on the Ubuntu Community's Xen web page.

After you install Xen and reboot your system to use the Xen kernel, you can use the xm command to create a new VM, launch a VM, and remove a running VM.

WINE OR VINEGAR?

When people talk about emulators, the topic almost always turns to Wine. (*Wine* is a recursive acronym: Wine Is Not an Emulator.) Wine was created before most hardware emulators. It provides converted Windows libraries, enabling Windows applications to run under Linux. This is different than an emulator: emulators provide an entire system, whereas Wine provides support for Windows applications under Linux.

Wine's support is very good for most Windows programs. In fact, it is so complete that it even permitted some Windows viruses to spread! (In `http://www.linux.com/archive/feature/42031`, **Matt Moen reported that Klez, Sobig, and a few other viruses worked under Wine.)**

While many applications can be used with Wine (for example, Microsoft PowerPoint and Word), other applications are hit or miss. Even newer versions of supported programs do not always work because of changes in the Microsoft libraries. Wine is also a mostly unsupported application—it had no updates between August 2005 and August 2006, and serious development interest did not resurface until 2008. Even though it was created in 1993, it was beta software for 15 years. (The formal 1.0 release came out in October 2008.)

Although Wine was an acceptable solution a few years ago, true emulators and virtualizers such as Qemu, VMware, and Xen provide better compatibility.

Sharing Files with Emulators

Regardless of your choice of emulator, you will need some way to exchange files between the guest and host systems. There are a variety of choices—you should choose the one(s) that best fit your needs.

- **FTP**—You can run an FTP server on the host OS and use the guest to connect and transfer files. This can also be done using Secure Shell's `scp` command. This option is almost universally supported by all guest operating systems.

- **NFS**—The host OS can export a partition to the guest OS. This works well if the guest is running a version of Linux or Unix.

- **Samba**—You can export a partition from the host OS using Samba. The guest OS must either be Windows or a system with Samba installed.

- **Port forwarding**—Qemu and VMware allow you to forward ports between the host and guest operating systems. For example, the Qemu parameter `-redir tcp:10022:22` will redirect port `10022/tcp` on the host to the SSH server (`22/tcp`) on the guest. Port forwarding allows the host to communicate with the guest OS using whatever server you require.

- **HGFS**—If you install the VMware Tools (VM ⇨ Install VMware Tools), VMware can map host directories to a guest Linux OS under `/mnt/hgfs/`.

NOTE All of these options require network access. Although network access is supported by each of these hardware emulators, you may want to disable the emulator's network access if you are evaluating viruses, performing disk forensics, or installing questionable software. If the network is disabled then there is no easy way to get data off of the virtual system.

Other Collaboration Tools

There are other collaboration tools beyond office applications, shared desktops, and virtual machines. Most common file formats, such as PDF and PostScript have plenty of support under Ubuntu. Tools like `evince`, `xpdf`, Ghostscript, and Ghostview can show you the contents of these common file types. With regard to networking, there are plenty of peer-to-peer applications. Packages like `amule` and `peercast` are available from the Ubuntu repositories.

Developers also have options for collaboration. The Concurrent Versioning System (`cvs`) and Subversion (`svn`) file management systems are readily available and not too difficult to configure. Both `svn` and `cvs` support sharing source code across the network and are secure enough to use over the Internet (especially when they are tunneled over SSH).

Summary

Ubuntu offers plenty of options for collaboration. The available tools enable you to work with other people, regardless of operating system configuration. If you can't find a compatible tool, you can access a remote system where the tool is supported or run a virtual machine where the needed application runs natively.

Improving Performance

In This Part

Tuning Processes

What's In This Chapter?

Identifying and tuning system resources
Discovering when processes are launched and what starts them
Shorting startup times

The default Ubuntu installation includes some basic processes that check devices, tune the operating system, and perform housekeeping. Some of these processes are always running, while others start up periodically. Occasionally you might see your hard drive start up or grind away for a few minutes—what's going on? On mission-critical servers, serious gaming boxes, and other real-time systems, unexpected processes can cause huge problems; administrators should know exactly what is running and when. The last thing a time-sensitive application needs is a resource-intensive maintenance system starting at an unexpected time and causing the system to slow down.

In order to fine-tune your system, you will need to know what is currently running, which resources are available, and when processes start up. From there, you can tweak configurations: disable undesirable processes, enable necessary housekeeping, and adjust your kernel to better handle your needs.

Learning the Lingo

Everything that runs on the system is a *process*. Processes are programs that perform tasks. The tasks may range from system maintenance to plug-and-play device configuration and anything else the user needs. *System processes* keep the operating system running, whereas *user processes* handle user needs.

Many processes provide *services* for other processes. For example, a web server is a service for handling HTTP network requests. The web server may use one or more processes to perform its task. Some services are critical to the system's operation. For example, if the system must support graphics but the X-Windows service is unavailable, then a critical service is missing.

Although most system processes are services, most user processes are *applications*. Applications consist of one or more processes for supporting user needs. For example, the Firefox web browser is an application that helps the user browse the web. In general, services start and end based on system needs, while applications start and end based on user needs.

These definitions—programs, processes, applications, and services—are not very distinct. For example, the Gnome Desktop Environment (GDE) consists of programs and processes that provide services to other programs and supports user needs. GDE can be called a set of programs, processes, applications, or services without any conflict.

TIME TO CHANGE

Different versions of Linux (including Ubuntu) use different startup scripts and run different support processes. Knowing how one version of Linux works does not mean that you know how all versions work. For example, one of my computers has a clock that loses a few minutes after every reboot. (It's an old computer.) When I installed Ubuntu Dapper Drake (6.06), I noticed that the time was correct after a reboot. I looked around to find out how it did that and which timeserver it was using. The first thing I noticed was that there was no script in /etc/init.d/ for setting the time. Eventually I tracked down the network startup scripts and found that the ntpdate script was moved from /etc/init.d/ (in previous Ubuntu releases) to /etc/network/if-up.d/. This script allowed me to find the network time protocol (NTP) configuration file (/etc/default/ntpdate).

A similar problem came up when I started running Ubuntu Hoary Hedgehog (5.04). Periodically the hard drives would grind when I was not doing anything. At other times it happened when I was running processes that were impacted by disk I/O—when the drives began to grind, the critical process would detect a processing problem. I quickly narrowed the disk grinding to updatedb—a caching program that works with slocate for quickly finding files. What I could not find was how this program was being started. Eventually I discovered that updatedb was started by anacron, an automated scheduler.

While it is important to know what is running, it is even more important to know how to track down running processes and tune them to suit your needs.

When I talk about processes, I refer to anything that generates a running process identifier (see the next section, "Viewing Running Processes"). Programs are the executable files on the system that generate one or more processes. Users directly use applications, while the operating system uses services.

Viewing Running Processes

The only things that consume systems' resources are running processes. If your computer seems to be running slower than normal, then it is probably because of some process that is either misbehaving or consuming more resources than you have available.

There are a couple of easy ways to find out what is running. From the command line, you can use `ps` and `top` to show applications, dependencies, and resources. For example, `ps -ef` shows every (-e) running process in a full (-f) detailed list (see Listing 8-1). The columns show the user who runs the process (UID), the process ID (PID), the parent process ID (PPID) that spawned the process, as well as when the process was started, how long it has been running, and, of course, the process itself.

Listing 8-1: Sample Listing of Running Processes from ps -ef

```
% ps -ef
UID        PID  PPID  C STIME TTY          TIME CMD
root         1     0  0 Sep28 ?        00:00:01 init [2]
root         2     1  0 Sep28 ?        00:00:00 [migration/0]
root         3     1  0 Sep28 ?        00:00:00 [ksoftirqd/0]
root         4     1  0 Sep28 ?        00:00:00 [watchdog/0]
root      2406     1  0 Sep28 ?        00:00:00 [kjournald]
root      2652     1  0 Sep28 ?        00:00:00 /sbin/udevd—daemon
root      3532     1  0 Sep28 ?        00:00:00 [shpchpd_event]
root      4219     1  0 Sep28 ?        00:00:00 [kjournald]
daemon    4370     1  0 Sep28 ?        00:00:00 /sbin/portmap
root      4686     1  0 Sep28 ?        00:00:00 /usr/sbin/acpid

nts -s /var/run/acpid.socket
root      4857     1  0 Sep28 ?        00:00:00 /bin/dd bs 1

ar/run/klogd/kmsg
klog      4859     1  0 Sep28 ?        00:00:00 /sbin/klogd

sg
root      5174     1  0 Sep28 ?        00:00:00 /usr/sbin/gdm
hplip     5213     1  0 Sep28 ?        00:00:00 /usr/sbin/hpiod
hplip     5217     1  0 Sep28 ?        00:00:00 python /usr/sbin/hpssd
```

(continued)

Listing 8-1: Sample Listing of Running Processes from ps -ef (*continued*)

```
nobody     5303      1  0 Sep28 ?        00:00:00 /usr/sbin/danted -D
nobody     5304   5303  0 Sep28 ?        00:00:00 /usr/sbin/danted -D
nobody     5306   5303  0 Sep28 ?        00:00:00 /usr/sbin/danted -D
nobody     5308   5303  0 Sep28 ?        00:00:00 /usr/sbin/danted -D
```

ALL IN THE FAMILY

There are two main branches of Unix: BSD and System V. BSD is the older branch and provides a standard that is used by operating systems such as FreeBSD, OpenBSD, SunOS, and Mac OS X. The BSD standard defines process management, device driver naming conventions, and system directory layouts. The younger branch, System V (pronounced "System Five"), includes operating systems such as HP-UX, AIX, Solaris, and IRIX. System V follows the POSIX standards and differs slightly from the BSD family. For example, BSD places all device drivers in /dev—this directory may contain hundreds of devices. POSIX defines subdirectories in /dev, so all disks will be in /dev/disk (or /dev/dsk, /dev/rdsk, and so on) and all network drivers are located in /dev/net. This makes /dev a cleaner directory.

These differences also show up in the ps command. Typing ps -ef on System V generates output similar to that of ps -aux on BSD.

Not every operating system is strictly in the BSD or System V camp. Linux, for example, supports both BSD and POSIX. Under Linux, hard drives are usually listed in /dev/ (for example, /dev/hda and /dev/hdb) and in /dev/disk/. There are a few places where the standards conflict (for example, what goes in specific directories); in these cases, the Linux selection seems almost arbitrary. For example, the /sbin directory under BSD contains system binaries. Under POSIX, they contain statically linked executables. Under Linux, they contain both.

The Linux ps command actually supports two different output formats: BSD and POSIX. Options that begin with a dash (for example, -e, -f, or combined as -ef) follow the POSIX standard. Without the dash (for example, ps aux) ps acts like BSD. Under Linux, the POSIX output from ps -ef looks similar to the BSD results from ps aux, and nothing like ps ef (without the hyphen, e includes the entire runtime environment and f shows the process hierarchy).

The top command shows all running processes and orders them by memory or CPU resource usage. Unlike ps, which provides a single snapshot of the currently running applications, top refreshes every few seconds to show you what is actively running. Processes that are spawned but not active will appear farther down the top listing. You can interact with top in order to change the refresh rate (type **s** and then enter the refresh rate in seconds) or ordering (use **<** and **>** to select the order-by column). You can also press **h** to see a full list of the supported commands.

The graphical System Monitor (System ⇨ Administration ⇨ System Monitor) also enables you to see the list of running processes (see Figure 8-1).

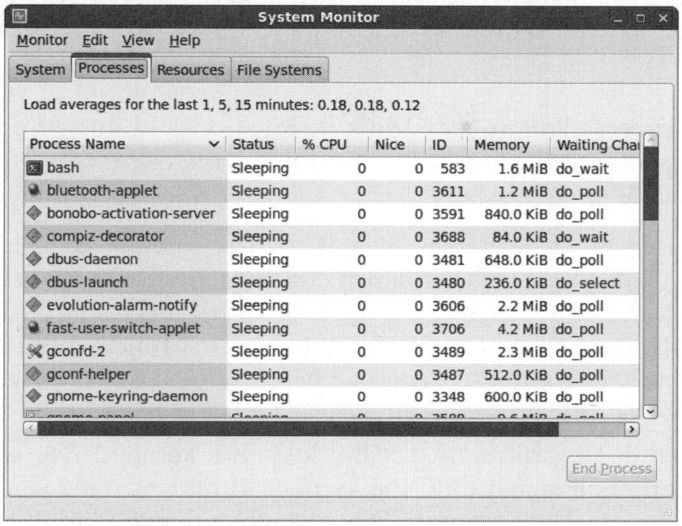

Figure 8-1: The System Monitor showing processes

Killing Processes

Under Linux, there are a maximum of 65,536 different PIDs—you cannot have more than 65,536 processes running at once. Under Ubuntu, the default maximum is 32,768 PIDs. (See "Tuning Kernel Parameters" later in this chapter; this parameter's name is `kernel.pid_max`.) Any new process is assigned the next available PID. As a result, it is possible to have a new process start with a lower PID than some older process. You can use the PID to kill processes using the `kill` command. For example to kill PID 123 use `kill 123`. The `kill` command can also be used to suspend processes (`kill -STOP 123`) and continue paused processes (`kill -CONT 123`). However, some processes do not die immediately.

NOTE Technically, PIDs are *handles* to processes and not actual processes. A multi-threaded process may have one handle for all threads or one handle per thread. It all depends on how the process creates the threads.

Every process is assigned a dynamic PID, but there are two exceptions: kernel and `init`. The kernel uses PID 0 and is not listed by `ps`, `top`, or the System Monitor. You cannot kill the kernel (with the `kill` command). The `init` process (briefly discussed in Chapter 1) is the master parent process. Every process needs a running parent (PPID) to receive return codes and status from children. If a process's parent dies, then `init` becomes the parent.

WARNING While you can kill `init` (`sudo kill -9 1`), you don't want to do this! Killing `init` will eventually crash the system since `init` is used to clean up dead processes.

Killing a process kills it *once*; the kill signal does nothing to prevent the process from being started up again. In addition, there are some processes that cannot be killed.

- **Zombies**—When a process dies, it returns an error code to its parent (PPID). A dead PID whose return code has not yet been received by its parent becomes a zombie. Zombies take up no CPU resources, but do take up a PID. For programmers, calling the `wait()` function retrieves return codes and kills zombies. In contrast, sending a kill signal to a zombie does nothing since the process is already dead.

- **I/O Bound**—A process that is blocked on a kernel driver call may not process the kill signal until the kernel call returns. This is usually seen with Network File System (NFS) calls when the network is down or on disk I/O when the drive is slow or bad. For example, if you are using an NFS mounted directory and run `ls`, the command may hang if the network mount is bad. Sending a kill signal to the `ls` process will not immediately kill it. I've also experienced these hangs when using `dd` to copy a disk that was in the middle of a head-crash, and when trying to stop a `dd` or `rm` on a RAID drive.

- **Interception**—Some kill signals can be intercepted by applications. For example, programs can intercept the default signal (`kill`, `kill -15`, or `kill -TERM`). This is usually done so that the program can clean up before exiting. Unfortunately, some programs don't die immediately. Other kill signals, such as `kill -KILL` or `kill -9`, cannot be intercepted.

TIP If you really want to kill a process, first use `kill` *PID* (e.g., `kill 1234`). This sends a TERM signal and allows well-behaved processes to clean up resources. If that does not get the result you want, try `kill -1` *PID*. This sends a hang-up signal, telling the process that the terminal died. This signal is usually only intercepted by well-behaved processes; other processes just die. If that does not kill it, then use `kill -9` *PID*. This is a true kill signal and cannot be intercepted by the process. (The `kill -9` command always reminds me of Yosemite Sam shouting, "When I say whoa, I mean WHOA!")

SIGNALS: NIGHT OF THE LIVING DEAD

Each signal is associated with a long name, short name, and number. The most common signals are:

- **SIGHUP, HUP, 1** — This is a hang-up signal that is sent to processes when the terminal dies.

- **SIGINT, INT, 2** — This is an interrupt signal. It is sent when the user presses Ctrl+C.

- **SIGKILL, KILL, 9** — The true kill signal. This cannot be intercepted and causes immediate death.

- **SIGTERM, TERM, 15** — This request sends a terminate signal and is the default signal sent by the `kill` command. Unlike KILL, TERM can be intercepted by the application.

- **SIGSTOP, STOP, 19** — This signal stops the process but does not terminate it. This is sent when you press Ctrl+Z to halt the current process.

- **SIGCONT, CONT, 18** — This resumes a process that is suspended by SIGSTOP. For a process paused at the command line (Ctrl+Z), typing `fg` will continue the process in the foreground and `bg` will continue the process in the background.

- **SIGCHLD, CHLD, 17** — Programmers who write spawning applications use this signal. CHLD is sent to the parent whenever any child dies.

The full list of signals is in the man page for `signal` (`man 7 signal`). Any of these representations can be used by the `kill` command. Typing `kill -9 1234` is the same as `kill -KILL 1234` and `kill -SIGKILL 1234`.

Signals are flags; they are not queued up. If you send a dozen TERM signals to a process before the process can handle them, then the process will only receive one TERM signal. Similarly, if a program spawns six children and all die at once, then the parent may only receive one CHLD signal. If the parent fails to check for other dead children, then the remaining children could become zombies.

Killing All Processes

Every developer I know has, at one time or another, created a spawning nightmare. Sometimes killing a process only makes another process spawn. Since spawning happens faster than a user can run `ps` and `kill`, you won't be able to kill all of the processes. Fortunately, there are a couple of options.

▪ **Kill by name**—If all the processes have the same name, you can kill them all at once using `killall`. For example, if my process is called `mustdie`, then I can use `killall -9 mustdie` to end all running instances of it.

▪ **Kill all user processes**—There is a special `kill` command that will end all processes that you have permission to kill: `kill -9 -1`. As a user, this kills all of your processes, including your graphical display and terminals. But it will definitely kill any spawning loops you may have running.

NOTE Technically, the process ID -1 is a special case for the `kill` command. This means kill everything except the `kill` command (don't kill yourself) and `init` (don't kill the default parent).

WARNING Never use `kill -9 -1` as root! This will kill every process—including shells and necessary system applications. This will crash your system before you can take your finger off the Enter key. If you need to kill all processes as root, use the power button or use the `reboot` or `shutdown` commands—don't use `kill -9 -1`.

▪ **Stop processes**—Infinite spawning loops usually happen because one process detects the death of another process. Instead of killing the processes, use the stop signal: `kill -STOP PID` or `killall -STOP Name`. This will prevent further spawning and enable you to kill all the sleeping processes without them respawning.

Identifying Resources

Your system has a lot of different resources that can be used by processes. These resources include CPU processing time, disk space, disk I/O, RAM, graphic memory, and network traffic. Fortunately, there are ways to measure each of these resources.

Accessing /proc

Linux provides a virtual file system that is mounted in the `/proc` directory. This directory lists system resources and running processes. For example:

```
$ ls -F /proc
1/      3910/   4133/   4351/   bus/          iomem      partitions
1642/   3930/   4135/   4352/   cmdline       ioports    pmu/
1645/   3945/   4137/   4363/   cpuinfo       irq/       scsi/
1650/   3951/   4167/   4364/   crypto        kallsyms   self@
1736/   3993/   4220/   4382/   devices       kcore      slabinfo
1946/   4/      4224/   5/      device-tree/  key-users  stat
2/      4009/   4237/   54/     diskstats     kmsg       swaps
20/     4027/   4250/   55/     dma           loadavg    sys/
3/      4057/   4270/   56/     driver/       locks      sysrq-trigger
```

```
3310/   4072/   4286/   57/     execdomains  mdstat    sysvipc/
3333/   4073/   4299/   6/      fb           meminfo   tty/
3335/   4081/   4347/   651/    filesystems  misc      uptime
3356/   4091/   4348/   apm     fs/          modules   version
3402/   4092/   4349/   asound/ ide/         mounts@   vmstat
3904/   4127/   4350/   buddyinfo interrupts  net/      zoneinfo
```

The numbered directories match every running process. In each directory, you will find the actual running command line and running environment. Device drivers and the kernel use non-numeric directories. These show system resources. For example, /proc/iomem shows the hardware I/O map and /proc/cpuinfo provides information about the system CPUs.

Although /proc is useful for debugging, you should be careful about allowing applications to depend on it. In particular, everything is dynamic: process directories may appear and vanish quickly and some resources constantly change.

The /proc directory actually provides an active view of the running operating system. Changes made to /proc alter the running system. For example, if you want to disable all network ping packets, then you can use:

```
echo 1 | sudo tee /proc/sys/net/ipv4/icmp_echo_ignore_all
```

This change takes effect immediately and will last until you either change it back (changing 1 to 0), some other process changes it, or you reboot. (See "Tuning Kernel Parameters" later in this chapter if you want to make this permanent. This parameter's name is net.ipv4.icmp_echo_ignore_all.)

WHAT'S UP, /PROC?

The /proc **directory is a real-time view of the system. Don't be surprised if the results change each time you look in the directory. Also, while some items under** /proc **can be modified directly, others cannot. For example, even as root you cannot modify the CPU information in** /proc/cpuinfo, **memory usage in** /proc/meminfo, **or the environment of a running process (e.g.,** /proc/1234/environ**).**

Measuring CPU

The CPU load can be measured in a couple of ways. The uptime command provides a simple summary. It lists three values: load averages for 1 minute, 5 minutes, and 15 minutes. The load is a measurement of queue time. If you have one CPU and the load is less than 1.0, then you are not consuming all of the CPU's resources. A load of 2.0 means all resources are being consumed and you need twice as many CPUs to reduce any wait time. If you have two CPUs, then a load of 1.0 indicates that both processors are operating at maximum capacity. Although a load of 1.0 won't seem sluggish, a load of 5.0 can be noticeably detectable because commands may need to wait a few moments before being processed.

While uptime provides a basic metric, top gives finer details. While running top, you can press 1 to see the load per CPU at the top of the screen and you can see which processes are consuming the most CPU resources. The command ps aux also shows CPU resources per process.

Measuring Disk Space

The commands df and du are used to identify disk space. The disk-free command (df, also sometimes called *disk-full* or *disk-file system*) lists every mounted partition and the amount of disk usage. The default output shows the information in blocks. You can also set the output to a human-readable form (-h) and see the sizes in kilobytes or megabytes: df -h. The df command also allows you to specify a file or directory name. In this case, it will show the disk usage for the partition containing the file (or directory). For example, to see how much space is in the current directory, use:

```
$ df .      # default output
Filesystem          1K-blocks       Used Available Use% Mounted on
/dev/hda1           154585604   72737288   73995748  50% /
$ df -h .  # human readable form
Filesystem           Size  Used Avail Use% Mounted on
/dev/hda1            148G   70G   71G  50% /
```

You can also use the System Monitor (System ➪ Administration ➪ System Monitor) to graphically show the df results (see Figure 8-2).

The disk-usage (du) command shows disk usage by directory. When used by itself, it will display the disk space in your current directory and every subdirectory. If you specify a directory, then it starts there instead. To see the biggest directories, you can use a command like du | sort -rn | head. This will sort all directories by size and display the top 10 biggest directories. Finally, you can use the -s parameter to stop du from listing the sizes from every subdirectory. When I am looking for disk hogs in my directory, I usually use du -s * | sort -rn | head. This lists the directories in size order. I can then enter the biggest directory and repeat the command until I find the largest files.

TIP The du command looks at every file in every subdirectory. If you have thousands of files, then this could take a while. When looking for large directories, consider the ones that take the longest to process. If almost every directory takes a second to display and one directory takes a minute, then you can press Ctrl+C because you've probably found the biggest directory.

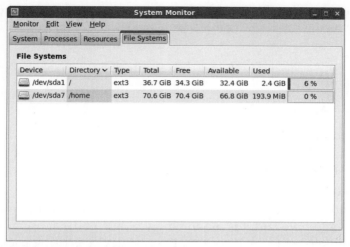

Figure 8-2: System Monitor showing available disk space

Measuring Disk I/O

All processes that access a disk do so over the same I/O channel. If the channel becomes clogged with traffic, then the entire system may slow down. It is very easy for a low-CPU application to consume most of the disk I/O. While the system load will remain low, the computer will appear sluggish.

If the system seems to be running slowly, you can use iostat (sudo apt-get install sysstat) to check the performance (see Listing 8-2). Besides showing the system load, the I/O metrics from each device are displayed. I usually use iostat with the watch command in order to identify devices that seem overly active.

```
watch—interval 0.5 iostat
```

Listing 8-2: Installing and Using iostat

```
$ sudo apt-get install sysstat   # install iostat
$ iostat
Linux 2.6.24-24-generic (lindt)        09/13/2009
avg-cpu:  %user   %nice %system %iowait  %steal   %idle
           6.53    0.01    0.47    1.10    0.00   91.89

Device:           tps   Blk_read/s   Blk_wrtn/s   Blk_read   Blk_wrtn
sda              2.35        40.25       107.24    7301369   19451016
sdb              5.68       300.10         1.88   54433418     340824
sdc              5.52       297.05         1.88   53880280     340824
sr0              0.00         0.00         0.00        672          0
md0             16.82       597.13         1.78  108310698     323256
```

After finding which device is active, you can identify where the device is mounted by using the mount command:

```
$ mount
/dev/hda1 on / type ext3 (rw,errors=remount-ro)
proc on /proc type proc (rw)
/sys on /sys type sysfs (rw)
varrun on /var/run type tmpfs (rw)
varlock on /var/lock type tmpfs (rw)
udev on /dev type tmpfs (rw)
devpts on /dev/pts type devpts (rw,gid=5,mode=620)
devshm on /dev/shm type tmpfs (rw)
```

Now that you know which device is active and where it is used, you can use lsof to identify which processes are using the device. For example, if device hda is the most active and it is mounted on /, then you can use lsof / to list every process accessing the directory. If a raw device is being used, then you can specify all devices with lsof /dev or a single device (for example, hda) by using lsof /dev/hda.

NOTE Unfortunately, there is no top-like command for disk I/O. You can narrow down the list of suspected applications by using lsof, but you cannot identify which application is consuming most of the disk resources.

Measuring Memory Usage

RAM is a limited resource on the system. If your applications consume all available RAM, then the kernel will temporarily store chunks of memory to the disk in order to free up space. The disk space used for storing RAM is called *swap space*. Although swap space can allow you to run massively large applications, it is very slow compared to using RAM.

There are a couple of ways to view swap usage. The command swapon -s will list the available swap space and show the usage. There is usually a little swap space used, but if it is very full then you either need to allocate more swap space, install more RAM, or find out what is consuming the available RAM. The System Monitor (System ➪ Administration ➪ System Monitor) enables you to graphically view the available memory usage and swap space and identify if it is actively being used (see Figure 8-3).

To identify which applications are consuming memory, use the top or ps aux commands. Both of these commands show memory allocation per process. In addition, the pmap command can show you memory allocations for specific process IDs.

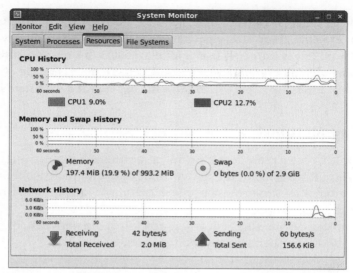

Figure 8-3: The System Monitor displaying CPU, memory, swap, and network usage

Measuring Video Memory

The amount of memory on your video card will directly impact your display. If you have an old video card with 256 KB of RAM, then the best you can hope for is 800x600 with 16 colors. Most high-end video cards today have upwards of 128 MB of RAM, allowing monster resolutions like 1280x1024 with 32 million colors. More memory also eases animation for games and desktops. While one set of video memory holds the main picture, other memory sections can act as layers for animated elements.

There is no simple way to determine video memory. If you have a PCI memory card, then the command lspci -v will show you all PCI cards (including your video card) and all memory associated with the card. For example:

```
$ lspci -v | more
0000:01:00.0 VGA compatible controller: nVidia Corporation NV18
                                        [GeForce4 MX 400
0 AGP 8x] (rev c1) (prog-if 00 [VGA])
        Subsystem: Jaton Corp: Unknown device 0000
        Flags: bus master, 66MHz, medium devsel, latency 248, IRQ 177
        Memory at fa000000 (32-bit, non-prefetchable) [size=16M]
        Memory at f0000000 (32-bit, prefetchable) [size=128M]
        Expansion ROM at fbee0000 [disabled] [size=128K]
        Capabilities: <available only to root>
```

This listing shows an NVIDIA NV18 video card with 128 MB of video RAM.

TIP On large supercomputers, `lspci` not only shows what is attached but also where. For example, if you have eight network cards then it can identify which slot each card is in. This is extremely useful for diagnostics in a mission-critical environment with fail-over hardware support. One example is to use (`lspci -t; lspci -v`) | `less` to show the bus tree and each item's details.

Measuring Network Throughput

Just as disk I/O can create a performance bottleneck, so can network I/O. While some applications poll the network for data and increase the CPU load when the network is slow, most applications just wait until the network is available and do not impact the CPU's load.

If the computer seems sluggish when accessing the network, then you can check the network performance by using `netstat -i inet`:

```
$ netstat -i inet
Kernel Interface table
Iface   MTU Met   RX-OK RX-ERR RX-DRP RX-OVR    TX-OK TX-ERR TX-DRP TX-OVR Flg
eth0   1500 0  25415143      0      0      0 46521403      0      0      0 BMRU
lo    16436 0     25629      0      0      0    25629      0      0      0 LRU
vnet0  1500 0         0      0      0      0       93      0      0      0 BMRU
```

This shows the amount of traffic on each network interface as well as any network errors, dropped packets, and overruns. This also shows the name of the network interface (for example, eth0). When checking network usage, I usually use `netstat` with the `watch` command so I can see network usage over time:

```
watch—interval 0.5 netstat -i inet
```

TIP The `netstat -i inet` command shows the number of packets from every interface. You can use `ifconfig` (for example, `ifconfig eth0`) to see more detail; `ifconfig` shows the number of packets and number of bytes from a particular network interface.

The `netstat -t` and `netstat -u` commands allow you to see which network connections are active. The -t option shows TCP traffic, and -u shows UDP traffic. There are many other options including--`protocol=ip`, for showing all IP (IPv4) connections, and IPv6 connections are listed with--`protocol=ip6`.

To identify which processes are using the network, you can use `lsof`. The -i4 parameter shows which processes have IPv4 connections, -i6 displays IPv6, -i `tcp` lists TCP, and -i `udp` displays applications with open UDP sockets:

```
$ sudo lsof -i4 -n # show network processes and give IP addresses

COMMAND  PID  USER   FD   TYPE DEVICE SIZE NODE NAME
ssh  8699 mark   3u   IPv4 120398   TCP 10.3.1.5:41525->10.3.1.3:ssh
(ESTABLISHED)
ssh  8706 mark   3u   IPv4 120576   TCP 10.3.1.5:41526->10.3.7.245:ssh
(ESTABLISHED)
```

NOTE When run as root, `lsof -i4` shows all processes using IPv4. Without the sudo, it only shows processes that are running as the current user. The same applies to all other `lsof` command-line parameters.

Finding Process Startups

While the `ps` command can list what is running now, and other tools show what resources are being used, there is no good tool for telling how something started in the first place. Although `ps` can identify the PPID, in many cases the PPID is 1—indicating that `init` owns it. Instead, there are plenty of places where a process can be started, including boot scripts, device configuration scripts, network changes, logins, application initialization scripts, and scheduled tasks.

Inspecting Boot Scripts

The directory `/etc/init.d/` contains scripts for starting and stopping system services (these are detailed in Chapter 3). These scripts are activated by links in the different `rc` directories (`/etc/rc0.d`, `/etc/rc1.d`, and so on). As `init` enters each run level, the appropriate S links are executed. For example, at run level 1, all S links in `/etc/rc1.d/` are started. This includes `S20single` for single-user mode configuration. When the system changes levels, all K (for kill) scripts are executed before changing run levels. To find the current run level, you can either use `who -r` or the `runlevel` command.

NOTE The `runlevel` command displays the previous and current run levels. Usually the previous one is not defined (since you probably booted into the current level) and is displayed as an N (for not defined).

```
$ who -r
      run-level 2  2009-09-12 20:32                  last=
$ runlevel
N 2
```

During booting, all output from the init scripts is sent to /var/log/messages. You can use this log file to identify which processes were executed.

Inspecting Upstart

Under Dapper Drake and earlier Ubuntu versions, init was the topmost process and critical for managing running processes. Starting with Edgy Eft (Ubuntu 6.10), the System V init was replaced with Upstart—an event-driven process manager.

With init, the configuration file /etc/inittab defined what applications started at each runlevel. It also defined how to handle certain system signals, such as Ctrl+Alt+Del and power failures.

Later Ubuntu versions use Upstart. With Upstart, runlevels and power changes are treated as events. Each event handler is defined as a script in /etc/event.d/. Each script identifies when it should run, when it should not run, and an action. The action can run either a single program or complex script.

An example of a script for runlevel 2 (rc2) is shown in Listing 8-3. This script only operates at runlevel 2. It sets the runlevel state, saving both the current and previous runlevels, and then executes the script /etc/init.d/rc with the current runlevel. The overall startup flow becomes:

1. The Upstart program /sbin/init runs at boot.

2. Upstart runs /etc/event.d/rc-default which changes the runlevel to 2.

3. The runlevel change causes /etc/event.d/rc2 to execute.

4. The rc2 script sets the system's runlevel and then executes the /etc/init.d/rc script.

5. The rc script runs all of the boot scripts found in the /etc/rc2.d/ directory that begin with an "S". (See Inspecting Boot Scripts.)

6. Each of the "S" scripts are links to scripts in /etc/init.d/.

Listing 8-3: The /etc/event.d/rc2 Script for Runlevel 2

```
# rc2—runlevel 2 compatibility
#
# This task runs the old sysv-rc runlevel 2 ("multi-user") scripts.
# It is usually started by the telinit compatibility wrapper.

start on runlevel 2

stop on runlevel [!2]
```

```
console output
script
        set $(runlevel—set 2 || true)
        if [ "$1" != "unknown" ]; then
            PREVLEVEL=$1
            RUNLEVEL=$2
            export PREVLEVEL RUNLEVEL
        fi

        exec /etc/init.d/rc 2
end script
```

You can query the list of Upstart scripts, as well as their status, with the `sudo initctl list` command:

```
$ sudo initctl list
control-alt-delete (stop) waiting
logd (stop) waiting
rc-default (stop) waiting
rc0 (stop) waiting
rc1 (stop) waiting
rc2 (stop) waiting
rc3 (stop) waiting
rc4 (stop) waiting
rc5 (stop) waiting
rc6 (stop) waiting
rcS (stop) waiting
rcS-sulogin (stop) waiting
sulogin (stop) waiting
tty1 (start) running, process 6893
tty2 (start) running, process 5429
tty3 (start) running, process 5431
tty4 (start) running, process 5426
tty5 (start) running, process 5427
tty6 (start) running, process 5433
```

NOTE With `init`, the system will always start in single-user mode (runlevel S) and then move to another runlevel (e.g., runlevel 2). With Upstart, the system goes directly to the desired runlevel, so scripts in single-user mode are not executed when the system boots.

For example, what if you want disable the Ctrl+Alt+Del sequence on your system? You would edit the Upstart event script /etc/events.d/control-alt -delete and comment out the exec line by adding a # to the start of the line.

```
# exec /sbin/shutdown -r now "Control-Alt-Delete pressed"
```

Similarly, if you want the system to boot into something other than runlevel 2, then edit the /etc/event.d/rc-default script. Change the telinit 2 lines to the desired runlevel.

Currently Upstart only replaces the init process. However, in the future Upstart will likely replace time-based process schedulers, such as cron, at, and anacron. (See "Inspecting Schedulers: at, cron, and anacron.")

Inspecting Device Startups

Dynamic device configuration is managed by udev (see Chapter 3). The udev process watches and manages plug-and-play devices. Based on the configuration in /etc/udev/rules.d/, different applications may be launched.

Inspecting Network Services

New network interfaces are managed by a couple of different systems. First, udev identifies the network interface (/etc/udev/rules.d/85-ifupdown. rules). This rule runs the interface startup command (/sbin/ifup).

NOTE Under older Ubuntu versions, such as Dapper Drake (6.06), the udev script was 25-iftab.rules and it called a helper script, iftab_helper. Later versions of Ubuntu changed the script's location and replaced the helper code with the executables /sbin/ifup and /sbin/ifdown.

There are four directories of scripts for managing network interfaces:

■ /etc/network/if-pre-up.d/—This contains steps that must be completed before (pre) the interface is brought up. For example, the scripts may need to load wireless drivers.

■ /etc/network/if-up.d/—These scripts are used after bringing up the configured network interface. For example, this is where the system clock is set—every time any network is brought up, the computer's clock is set.

■ /etc/network/if-down.d/—These scripts are used to remove any running configuration. For example, if you have the Postfix mail server running, then there is a script that tells Postfix to reload its configuration when an interface is taken down.

■ /etc/network/if-post-down.d/—This directory contains any cleanup stages that are needed after (post) the interface is taken down. For example, unnecessary wireless drivers can be unloaded.

TIP The /etc/network/ scripts are used when an interface is brought up and down. The /etc/init.d/networking script is used to actually bring the

interfaces up and down. Interfaces are configured according to the `/etc/network/interfaces` **file, described in Chapter 12.**

Although `/etc/network/` is used only when interfaces are brought up or down, other programs, such as `xinetd`, can run applications based on network connections. If you installed `xinetd` (`sudo apt-get install xinetd`), the configuration file `/etc/xinetd.conf` and the `/etc/xinetd.d/` directory contain the list of executables that can be started by `xinetd`.

Inspecting Shell Startup Scripts

Each time you log in, log out, or create a new shell, configuration scripts are executed. Each of these scripts run processes. You are likely to use the configuration scripts in Table 8-1.

The default shell, `/bin/sh`, is a link to the real shell. Under Dapper Drake (6.06 LTS), it linked to `/bin/bash`. Beginning with Edgy Eft (6.10), the default shell changed to `/bin/dash`. Bash is a very feature-rich shell, but it is also very large. In contrast, Dash is a minimal shell that lacks some of Bash's features, but loads and runs much faster. Many scripts that specified `/bin/sh` broke when they assumed the shell was bash and it changed to become dash. If your

Table 8-1: Shell Startup Scripts

INITIALIZATION SCRIPT	PURPOSE
`/etc/profile`	Used by every login shell, system-wide.
`/etc/bash.bashrc`	Every interactive shell runs this system-wide configuration script. Under Ubuntu, `/etc/profile` calls `/etc/bash.bashrc` for backwards compatibility when using Dash.
`$HOME/.profile`	Each user can have a personalized login script.
`$HOME/.bash_profile`	With Bash, each user can have a personalized login script. Under Ubuntu, `$HOME/.profile` calls `.bash_profile` for backwards compatibility when using Dash.
`$HOME/.bashrc`	Every interactive Bash shell runs this user-specific configuration script. This is not used by Dash.
`/etc/bash.logout`	If you create it, this system-wide script is executed by Bash every time a user logs out. This is not used by Dash.
`$HOME/.bash_logout`	User-specific Bash script that is used during logout. This is not used by Dash.

shell script does not work, consider changing the first line from `#!/bin/sh` to `#!/bin/bash`.

> **WARNING** There are three different ways to create user accounts: `useradd`, `adduser`, and the graphical System ⇨ Administration ⇨ Users and Groups applet. While the default user shell from the `useradd` is `/bin/sh`, the other methods default to `/bin/bash`.

> **TIP** If you really want to use the Bash shell, you can run `bash` on the command-line for as-needed use. You can also use `chsh` to change your default shell, or change the system-wide symbolic link:
>
> `sudo ln -f -s /bin/bash /bin/sh`

All of these scripts are divided into two situations: login/logout and interactive shells. Whenever you log into your Ubuntu system, the login and interactive shell scripts are executed. When you open a terminal window, only the interactive scripts are used.

> **TIP** The default user-specific shell scripts are stored in `/etc/skel/`. Use `ls -la /etc/skel/` to list all of the default files. Changing these defaults will give all new user accounts the modified configuration files, but you will still need to modify existing user accounts. For systemwide changes, consider creating scripts under `/etc/profile.d/`, modify `/etc/profile`, or edit `/etc/bash.bashrc` instead.

Inspecting Desktop Scripts

Beyond user-level shell scripts, the graphical desktop run scripts. First, X-Windows runs. This starts up applications by running the scripts `/etc/X11/xinit/xinitrc`, `/etc/X11/Xsession`, and `/etc/X11/xinit/xserverrc`. Each of these scripts set environment variables and can run applications. There are also startup scripts in `/etc/X11/Xsession.d/` that are started after a user logs in, and individual users can have a `$HOME/.xsession` script for running applications at startup.

After X-Windows, the desktop starts. Under Ubuntu, this is Gnome. Gnome runs lots of applications that, in turn, can run many more applications. The main places to look for automatically running Gnome processes are in the `/etc/gdm/` directory (`/etc/X11/gdm/` on older Ubuntu systems), in the file `$HOME/.gnomerc`, and under System ⇨ Preferences ⇨ Startup Applications (or Sessions under older Ubuntu versions). The `/etc/gdm/` directory contains systemwide startup scripts. The `$HOME/.gnomerc` script enables you to configure your own startup applications, and the graphical session configuration tool (see Figure 8-4) enables you to easily customize nonstandard startups.

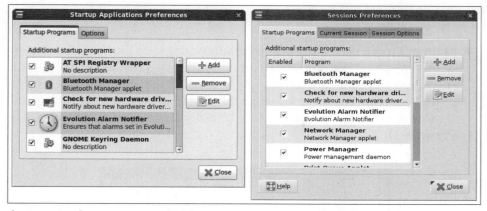

Figure 8-4: The Gnome graphical startup application preferences (left is from Ubuntu 9.04, right is from 8.04)

Having all of these startup options can be very confusing. For example, if you want to automatically start Firefox on login, then you can add it to `/etc/X11/Xsession`, `/etc/gdm/Xsession`, `/etc/gdm/PostSession/Default`, `/etc/X11/Xsession.d/99start_firefox`, `$HOME/.xsession`, `$HOME/.gnomerc`, or use the graphical Gnome Session editor to add a startup applications. The main question to ask is, "who will want this?"

- **Everyone running X-Windows?**—Use `/etc/X11/Xsession` or place the startup script under `/etc/X11/Xsession.d/`.

- **Just you running X-Windows?**—Use `$HOME/.xsession`.

- **Everyone running Gnome?**—Use `/etc/gdm/PostSession/Default`. This will work for Gnome users, but not KDE or other desktops. KDE, XDM, and other desktops have their own configuration directories and files.

- **Just you running Gnome?**—Use `$HOME/.gnomerc` or the graphical session editor.

NOTE These are not all of the possible startup hooks. There are plenty of places where code can be told to start running. If you are trying to find where an application starts, look here first or use `ps` and start tracking down parent processes. Most graphical processes use configuration files and any of those files can potentially run applications.

Inspecting Gnome Applications

Just as udev watches for plug-and-play devices, so does Gnome. The Gnome desktop can identify some devices and automatically run applications. Finding the default settings can be tricky since they vary according to the version of Ubuntu. For example:

- **Dapper Drake (6.06 LTS)**—The default settings are found under System ⇨ Preferences ⇨ Removable Drives and Media. The tabs show you the items you can change. For example, to change the default action when a digital camera is connected, select the Cameras tab, and the Storage tab defines what happens when a new USB drive or CD-ROM is added (see Figure 8-5).

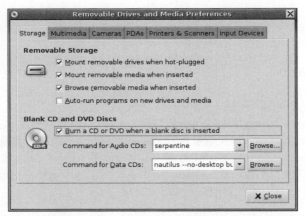

Figure 8-5: The Removable Drives and Media preferences from Ubuntu 6.06 (Dapper Drake), showing drive handlers

- **Hardy Heron (8.06 LTS)**—As with Dapper, there is a Removable Drives and Media menu. However, it is missing the Storage and Multimedia tabs (See Figure 8-6). This functionality has moved under the Nautilus (file browser) tab.

  1. Open any File Browser window. An easy way is to go to Places ⇨ Computer, or run `nautilus` at a command prompt.

  2. Select Edit ⇨ Preferences from the File Browser's menu.

  3. The new popup window has a tab called Media. This contains settings for the default applications when different media types are connected (see Figure 8-7).

- Unfortunately, this menu does not provide options for auto-mounting and auto-running applications. For those, you need `gconf-editor`. The settings are found under `/apps/nautilus/preferences/` (see Figure 8-8).

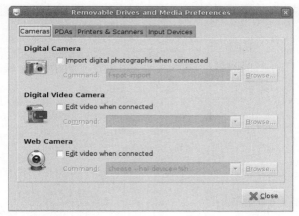

Figure 8-6: The Removable Drives and Media preferences from Ubuntu 8.06 (Hardy Heron)

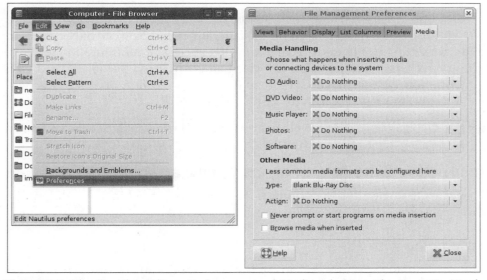

Figure 8-7: The Nautilus Edit ⇨ Preferences and Media tab from Ubuntu 8.06 (Hardy Heron) and later versions

▪ **Jaunty Jackalope (9.04) and Karmic Koala (9.10)**—If you did a clean install (and not an upgrade from Hardy), then the Removable Drives and Media menu is gone. You will need to use the Nautilus file browser's Edit tab, and `gconf-editor`, just as under Hardy Heron.

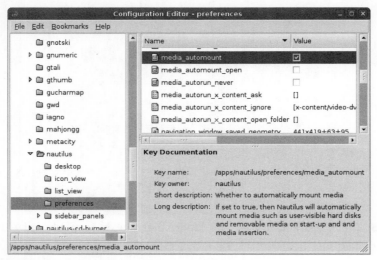

Figure 8-8: Nautilus settings in the Configuration Editor

Although other spawning subsystems, such as udev and /etc/init.d/, are configurable and extendable, Gnome is fairly inflexible. You can only configure auto-run settings for items listed in the applet or Gnome configuration settings. If you have a new plug-and-play device that is not listed (for example, a GPS system), you cannot make Gnome spawn an application. Instead, you will need to configure udev to run the application.

TIP Configuring udev to run programs is covered in Chapter 3. See the section on "Associating Applications with USB."

Inspecting Schedulers: at, cron, and anacron

Programs that should run periodically are usually placed in a scheduler. The three common schedulers are at, cron, and anacron.

Scheduling with at

The at command specifies that an application should run at a specific time. This is used for run-once commands. For example, to start xclock in 15 minutes, you could use:

```
echo "DISPLAY=:0 xclock" | at now + 15 minutes
```

The at command takes one or more command-line statements as input. The time format can either be in an HH:MM with am or pm (for example, 3:45 pm or 3:45 PM), a date format (for example, 09/15/09), or as an offset (for example, noon + 3 hours or 8am + 6 days). Scheduled at jobs are stored in the /var/spool/cron/atjobs/ directory. You can query them by using atq and remove jobs using atrm. After the process runs, any text output is e-mailed back to the user.

Scheduling with cron

While `at` is used for one-time applications, `cron` is used for repeated tasks. Each user has a `crontab` entry where processes can be scheduled. For example, mine has this entry:

```
3,18,33,48 * * * * fetchmail -U -n --invisible > /dev/null 2>&1
```

Each `cron` entry has six elements per line. The first five specify when to run, and the last element is a single command line to actually execute. The time fields are:

- **Minute**—The minute to run. This can be a single value (`0-59`) or a comma-separated list of times (for example, `3,18` means run at 3 and 18 minutes after the hour). A star can also be used to mean *every minute*.

- **Hour**—The hour to run. This can be a single value (`0-23`), a range (for example, `9-17` means hourly from 9 am to 5 pm), a comma-separated list, or a division indicating how often. For example, `9-17` means hourly from 9 am to 5 pm, but `9-17/3` means every 3 hours between 9 am and 5 pm (9 am, 12 pm, and 3 pm). A star means *every hour*, and when combined with a divisor, `*/4` means every four hours.

- **Day**—Day of the month to run. As with the other fields, this can be a single value (`1-31`), a range, or a list and can use a divisor. A star means *every day*.

- **Month**—Month of the year to run. This can be a single value (`1-12`), a range, or a list and can use a divisor. A star means *every month*.

- **Day of week**—You can specify which weekday to run on. The days are numbers: `0-6` for Sunday through Saturday (`7` can also mean Sunday). Again, this can be a value, list, or range and may include a divisor.

Usually the date specification is simple. For example, `0 12 * * 0` means to run every Sunday at noon. But it can be very complex: `*/3 */3 */3 */3 */3` says to run every three minutes, every third hour of every third day in every third month but only when this corresponds with every third day of the week.

> **TIP** Try to space `cron` jobs so that they do not all run at once. Although I could use `*/15` to run `fetchmail` four times per hour, I use the list `3,18,33,48` instead. This prevents lots of applications from all trying to start on the hour.

To schedule a `cron` task, use `crontab -e`. This edits your `crontab` file (found in `/var/spool/cron/crontabs/`). You can also use `crontab -l` to list your `crontab` entries. A `#` at the beginning of a `crontab` line indicates a comment. I usually put the following comment at the start of my file just so I can remember what the time fields mean:

```
# mm ss DD MM WW command
```

As with at, every text output from the cronjob is e-mailed back to the user. If you don't want to receive e-mail, then add > /dev/null 2>&1 to the end of the command. This directs all output to /dev/null.

Scheduling with anacron

While cron runs tasks repeatedly, it makes no distinction as to the system state. The anacron service is similar to cron but allows tasks to be run based on a relative period rather than an absolute date. For example, the default anacron installation runs updatedb (to update online man-page indexes) daily, starting at five minutes after the computer first boots up.

The configuration schedule for anacron is found in the /etc/anacrontab file. The default scripts are located in /etc/cron.d/, /etc/cron.daily/, /etc/cron.weekly/, and /etc/cron.monthly/.

If you run a mission-critical system, or a computer with limited resources, then you should seriously consider looking at these configuration settings and tuning them to suit your needs. For example, if your system is a deployed server, then you probably do not need updatedb running daily. In fact, you could disable anacron completely and move any required functionality into root's crontab (sudo crontab -e). This way, tasks such as log file rotation will happen on a predictable schedule.

TIP A clean install includes all three schedulers: anacron, cron, and at. However, all default system tasks are stored in anacron; there are no default cron or at jobs.

Tuning Kernel Parameters

Many of the tunable performance items can be configured directly by the kernel. The command sysctl is used to view current kernel settings and adjust them. For example, to display all available parameters (in a sorted list), use:

```
sudo sysctl -a | sort | more
```

NOTE There are a few tunable parameters that can only be accessed by root. Without sudo, you can still view most of the kernel parameters.

Each of the kernel parameters is in a *field* = *value* format. For example, the parameter kernel.threads-max = 16379 sets the maximum number of concurrent processes to 16,379. This is smaller than the maximum number of unique PIDs (65,536). Lowering the number of PIDs can improve performance on systems with slow CPUs or little RAM, since it reduces the number of simultaneous tasks. On high-performance computers with dual processors, this value can have a large default value. As an example, my 350-MHz iMac is set to 2,048, my 2.8-GHz dual-processor PC is set to 16,379, and my 2.3-GHz quad-processor PC is set to 65,536.

TIP The kernel configures the default number of threads based on the available resources. Installing the same Ubuntu version on different hardware may set a different value. If you need an identical system (for testing, critical deployment, or sensitive compatibility), be sure to explicitly set this value.

There are two ways to adjust the kernel parameters. First, you can do it on the command line. For example, `sudo sysctl -w kernel.threads-max=16000`. This change takes effect immediately but is not permanent; if you reboot, this change will be lost. The other way to make a kernel change is to add the parameter to the `/etc/sysctl.conf` file. Adding the line `kernel.threads-max=16000` will make the change take effect on the next reboot. Usually when tuning, you first use `sysctl -w`. If you like the change, then you can add it to `/etc/sysctl.conf`. Using `sysctl -w` first allows you to test modifications. In the event that everything breaks, you can always reboot to recover before committing the changes to `/etc/sysctl.conf`.

Computing Swap

The biggest improvement you can make to any computer running Ubuntu is to add RAM. In general, the speed impact from adding RAM is bigger than the impact from a faster processor. For example, increasing the RAM from 128 MB to 256 MB can turn the installation from a day job to an hour. Increasing to 1 GB of RAM shrinks the installation to minutes.

There is an old rule of thumb about the amount of swap space. The conventional wisdom says that you should have twice as much swap as RAM. A computer with 256 MB of RAM should start with 512 MB of swap. Although this is a good idea for memory limited systems, it isn't practical for high-end home user systems. If you have 1 GB of RAM, then you probably will never need swap space for running applications—and you are very unlikely to need 2 GB of swap unless you are planning on doing video editing or audio composition.

WARNING Laptop and desktop users usually suspend their systems rather than turn them off. The suspend/resume mode saves all memory to swap space. If you plan to suspend your system, make sure that your available swap space on the drive is at least as large as your available RAM.

When it comes to memory, Linux systems have historically had two key limitations. First, they could only access up to 4 GB of RAM. This was a limitation due to the Intel 32-bit architecture. The second limitation came from the kernel: it could only access 1 GB of RAM, and used the rest for swap. The default kernel that ships with the 32-bit version of Ubuntu can only access 3 GB of RAM. To access more, you will need to install a different kernel.

```
sudo apt-get update
sudo sudo apt-get install linux-headers-server \
  linux-image-server linux-server
sudo reboot
```

WARNING After installing the new kernel, you may need to reinstall any additional drivers, such as the restricted drivers for your video driver (see Chapter 10).

Swap can be configured either as an independent partition or as a file on the file system. The default install allocates a swap partition on the disk. Unfortunately, if you do run out of swap space, it will probably happen at an inconvenient time when you cannot repartition the disk. The following steps can be used to create a swap file.

1. Allocate the swap space. For example, to allocate 1 GB of swap, use:

   ```
   sudo dd if=/dev/zero of=/swapfile bs=1G count=1
   ```

   Be sure that the destination partition (e.g., /) has enough free space for the swap file.

2. Format the file for use as swap space:

   ```
   sudo mkswap /swapfile
   ```

3. Turn on the swap space. This way you will have it turned on until the system reboots.

   ```
   sudo swapon /swapfile
   ```

4. To make the change permanent, add the swap file to /etc/fstab. The configuration line is:

   ```
   /swapfile swap swap defaults 0 0
   ```

You can check the amount of memory on your system with the free command. This lists the amount of RAM as well as the amount of swap space.

```
$ free
             total       used       free     shared    buffers     cached
Mem:       3369464    2200988    1168476          0     156860    1738152
-/+ buffers/cache:     305976    3063488
Swap:      9871900      40840    9831060
```

Modifying Shared Memory

Some sections of virtual memory can be earmarked for use by multiple applications. Shared memory allows different programs to communicate quickly and share large volumes of information. Applications such as X-Windows, the Gnome Desktop, Nautilus, X-session manager, Gnome Panel, Trashcan applet, and Firefox all use shared memory. If programs cannot allocate or access the shared memory that they need, then programs will fail to start.

The interprocess communication status command, `ipcs`, displays the current shared memory allocations as well as the PIDs that created and last accessed the memory (see Listing 8-4).

TIP There are many other flags for `ipcs`. For example, `ipcs -m -t` shows the last time the shared memory was accessed, and `ipcs -m -c` shows access permissions. In addition, `ipcs` can show semaphore and message queue allocations.

Listing 8-4: Viewing Shared Memory Allocation

```
$ ipcs -m
---Shared Memory Segments---
key         shmid      owner    perms    bytes     nattch    status
0x00000000 327680      nealk    600      393216    2         dest
0x00000000 360449      nealk    600      393216    2         dest
0x00000000 196610      nealk    600      393216    2         dest
0x00000000 229379      nealk    600      393216    2         dest
0x00000000 262148      nealk    600      393216    2         dest
$ ipcs -m -p
---Shared Memory Creator/Last-op---
shmid      owner      cpid     lpid
327680     nealk      7267     7307
360449     nealk      7267     3930
196610     nealk      7182     7288
229379     nealk      7265     3930
262148     nealk      7284     3930
393221     nealk      7314     3930
425990     nealk      7280     3930
458759     nealk      7332     3930
$ ps -ef | grep -e 3930 -e 7280   # what processes are PID 3930 and 7280?
root      3930  3910  0 09:24 tty7     00:00:02 /usr/bin/X:0 -br -audit
                        0 -auth /var/lib/gdm/:0.Xauth -nolisten tcp vt7
nealk     7280     1  0 15:22 ?        00:00:01 update-notifier
```

Programs can allocate shared memory in two different ways: temporary and permanent. A temporary allocation means the memory remains shared until all applications release the memory handle. When no applications remain attached (the `ipcs nattch` field), the memory is freed. In contrast, permanent allocations can remain even when no programs are currently using it. This allows programs to save state in a shared communication buffer.

Sometimes shared memory becomes abandoned. To free abandoned memory, use `ipcrm`. You will need to specify the shared memory ID found by using `ipcs` (the `shmid` column).

More often than not, you will be more concerned with allocating more shared memory rather than with freeing abandoned segments. For example, databases and high-performance web servers work better when there is more shared memory available. The `sysctl` command shows the current shared memory allocations:

```
$ sysctl kernel | grep shm
kernel.shmmni = 4096
kernel.shmall = 2097152
kernel.shmmax = 33554432
```

In this example, there is a total of 33,554,432 bytes (32 MB) of shared memory available. A single application can allocate up to 2 MB (2,097,152 bytes), and the minimal allocation unit is 4096 bytes. These sizes are plenty for most day-to-day usage, but if you plan to run a database such as Oracle, MySQL, or PostgreSQL, then you will almost certainly need to increase these values.

Changing Per-User Settings

Beyond the kernel settings are parameters for configuring users. The `ulimit` command is built into the bash shell and provides limits for specific application. Running `ulimit -a` shows the current settings:

```
$ ulimit -a
core file size          (blocks, -c) 0
data seg size           (kbytes, -d) unlimited
max nice                        (-e) 20
file size               (blocks, -f) unlimited
pending signals                 (-i) unlimited
max locked memory       (kbytes, -l) unlimited
max memory size         (kbytes, -m) unlimited
open files                      (-n) 1024
pipe size            (512 bytes, -p) 8
POSIX message queues     (bytes, -q) unlimited
max rt priority                 (-r) unlimited
stack size              (kbytes, -s) 8192
cpu time               (seconds, -t) unlimited
max user processes              (-u) unlimited
virtual memory          (kbytes, -v) unlimited
file locks                      (-x) unlimited
```

These setting show, for example, that a single user-shell can have a maximum of 1,024 open files and core dumps are disabled (size 0). Developers will probably want to enable core dumps, with `ulimit -c 100` (for 100 blocks). If you want to increase the number of open files to 2,048, use `ulimit -n 2048`.

The user cannot change some limits. For example, if you want to increase the number of open files to 2,048 then use `ulimit -n 2048`, but only root can increase this value. In contrast, the user can always lower the value.

NOTE Some values have an upper limit defined by the kernel. For example, although root can increase the number of open file handles, this cannot be increased beyond the value set by the kernel parameter **fs.file-max** (**sysctl fs.file-max**).

On a multi-user system, the administrator may want to limit the number of processes that any single user can have running. This can be done by adding a `ulimit` statement to the `/etc/bash.bashrc` script:

```
# Only change the maximum number of processes for users, not root.
if [ $(/usr/bin/id -u) -ne 0 ]; then
  ulimit -u 2048 2>/dev/null # ignore errors if user set it lower
else
  ulimit -u unlimited # root can run anything
fi
```

Speeding Up Boot Time

The default init scripts found in `/etc/init.d/` and the `/etc/rc*.d/` directories are good for most systems, but they may not be needed on your specific system. If you do not need a service, then you can disable it. This can reduce the boot time for your system. In some cases, it can also speed up the overall running speed by freeing resources. Use `sysv-rc-conf` (`sudo apt-get install sysv-rc-conf`) to change the enable/disable settings. Some of the services to consider disabling include:

- `anacron`—As mentioned earlier, this subsystem periodically runs processes. You may want to disable it and move any critical services to `cron`.

- `atd` and `cron`—By default, there are no `at` or `cron` jobs scheduled. If you do not need these services, then they can be disabled. Personally, I always leave them enabled since they take relatively few resources.

- `apmd`—This service handles the advanced power management (APM) events and is primarily used by laptops. It monitors the battery and runs programs when APM events are received. If you do not need APM support, then this can be disabled.

- bluetooth or bluez-utiles—This provides support for Bluetooth devices. If you don't have any, then this can be disabled.

- cupsys—This is the Common Unix Printing System and provides printing support. If you don't need a printer then this can be disabled.

- dns-clean, ppp, and pppd-dns—These services are used for dynamic, dial-up connections. If you do not use dialup, then these can be disabled.

- hplip—This optional package provides Linux support for the HP Linux Image and Printing system. If you do not need it, then it can be disabled. Without this, you can still print using the lpr and CUPS systems.

- mdadm, mdadm-raid, and lvm—These provide file system support for RAID (mdadm and mdadm-raid) and Logical Volume groups (lvm). If you do not use either, then these can be disabled.

- nfs-common, nfs-kernel-server, and portmap—These are used by NFS—they are only present if you installed NFS support. If you do not need NFS all the time, then you can disable these and only start them when you need them:

```
sudo /etc/init.d/portmap start
sudo /etc/init.d/nfs-common start
sudo /etc/init.d/nfs-kernel-server start
```

- pcmcia and pcmciautils—These provide support for PCMCIA devices on laptops. If you do not have any PCMCIA slots on your computer, then you do not need these services.

- powernowd and powernowd.early—These services are used to control variable-speed CPUs. Newer computers and laptops should have these enabled but older systems (for example, my dual-processor 200-MHz PC) do not need it. You could also replace powernowd with cpufreqd for more configuration options:

```
sudo apt-get install cpufreqd
```

- readahead and readahead-desktop—These services are used to preload libraries so some applications will initially start faster. In a tradeoff for speed, these services slow down the initial boot time of the system and consume virtual memory with preloaded libraries. If you have limited RAM, then you should consider disabling these services.

- rsync—This is a replacement for the remote copy (rcp) command. Few people need this—it is used to synchronize files between computers.

TIP There is a System ⇨ Administration ⇨ Services applet for enabling and disabling some services. However, this applet only knows of a few services; it does not list every available service. The **sysv-rc-conf** command recognizes far more services and offers more management options.

The `sysv-rc-conf` command shows most of the system services. However, it does not show all of them. If the service's name ends with `.sh`, contains `.dpkg`, or is named `rc` or `rcS`, then it is treated as a non-modifiable system service. To change these services, you will need to manually modify the `/etc/init.d/` and `/etc/rc*.d/` directory contents.

LEAVE IT ON!

Although there are many services that you probably do not need, there are a few that are essential. You should not turn off these essential services unless you really know what you are doing:

- `dbus`—**Provides messaging services.**
- `gdm`—**This is the Gnome desktop. Only disable this if you do not want a graphical desktop.**
- `klogd`—**This is the kernel log daemon. Removing it disables system logging.**
- `makedev` **and** `udev`—**These create all device nodes.**
- `module-init-tools`—**Loads kernel modules specified in** `/etc/modules`.
- `networking` **and** `loopback`—**These start and stop the network. Disabling removes the network configuration at boot.**
- `procps.sh`—**Any kernel tuning parameters added to** `/etc/sysctl.conf` **are processed by this service.**
- `urandom`—**This seeds the real random number generator that is used by most cryptographic systems. You should leave it enabled.**

As a rule of thumb, if you do not know what it is, then leave it on. Also, if the service only runs in single-user mode (`rcS`), it is usually smart to not change it. Single-user mode is where you should go when everything fails, in order to repair the system.

Profiling the Boot Sequence

While each version of Ubuntu seems to boot faster than the last, you can usually make it even faster with boot profiling. When the operating system boots, it can be told to track the needed files. Then, it will preload files during boot. This cuts down on random access seeks and, depending on your system, may dramatically shorten the boot time.

1. Reboot the computer.
2. During the Grub boot loader screen, you will have about 3 seconds to press the Escape key. If you don't press Esc, then the computer will boot

normally. If you press Esc, then you will see a text menu listing the kernels installed on the system.

3. Press **e** to edit the current kernel settings.

4. Select the line that starts with "kernel" and press **e** to alter the kernel parameters.

5. You should see a long line that ends with parameters like `ro quiet splash`. Add to the list `profile`. You may optionally remove the `quiet` and `splash` parameters so that you can see what it is doing.

6. Press **Enter** to temporarily save the change. This is a one-time change that will not be there on your next reboot.

7. Press **b** to boot the kernel with the profile parameter.

The first time you do this, the system will take a little longer to start up. However, subsequent boots will take less time. My clean-install laptop went from taking 38 seconds to boot Jaunty (9.04) to taking 7 seconds.

Summary

Ubuntu is designed for the average computer user. As a result, there are some running processes that may not be needed and some resources that are not used optimally. Using a variety of commands, you can see what is running, what resources are available, and what resources are being used. The system can be tuned by adjusting kernel parameters, shell parameters, and settings for specific applications.

Multitasking Applications

What's In This Chapter?

Maximizing multitasking
Customizing application windows
Creating quick-start launchers
Automating tasks
Enabling quotas
Tracking projects

Twenty years ago, computers did one thing at a time. You either used a word processor *or* used a spreadsheet *or* printed a document—but not all at once. Today, people rarely use computers for just one thing. While using a spreadsheet, you may be modifying a document in a word processor, watching the stock market, reading news, and checking the weather—all at the same time! In my experience, the only times a computer does one dedicated task today is when (a) it is an embedded system, (b) it is devoted to a game that consumes all resources, (c) it is solving some computationally complex formula (for example, cracking passwords, modeling, or data mining) and needs all of the system's computing power, or (d) it's a *really* old computer.

Multitasking does not just mean running two programs at once. The definition encompasses your ability to switch between programs, communicate between applications, and find running programs. In the corporate world, it also means accountability: you need to be able to say how much time was spent on each project. Fortunately, Ubuntu has many options for addressing these needs.

Switching Applications

Starting up an application on the Ubuntu desktop can be as easy as clicking an icon or choosing from a menu. However, after you have a few dozen programs running, it can be a challenge to find the right program again. Without a good application management scheme, I frequently find myself clicking through windows before finding the right one. The worst is when I select text from one application and cannot find the right window to paste into, and after finding the right destination, discover that I have lost the selection buffer. After a couple of times, this becomes frustrating.

Fortunately, Ubuntu has many options for finding the right application. These include the Window List, Window Selector, and keyboard for switching between applications.

Using the Window List and Window Selector

The two most common window management tools are the Window List and the Window Selector (see Figure 9-1). By default, the Window List appears in the display's bottom panel. It opens a new button every time you start a new application window. To switch between applications, simply click on the button. You can also right-click a button in the Window List to see a menu for maximizing, minimizing, moving, or closing the window.

The Window Selector provides a drop-down menu of all windows on the desktop. To set up the Window Selector, you will need to add it to the panel.

1. On an empty space on the top (or bottom) panel, right-click to bring up the panel menu.

2. Select Add to Panel from the menu. This will bring up the Add to Panel applet.

3. Near the bottom of the list of applets is the Window Selector. Drag this applet to the top panel. Releasing the mouse button will place the applet on the panel.

NOTE Earlier versions of Ubuntu installed the Window Selector in the top-right corner of the panel. If you upgraded from Hoary or Breezy to Dapper, then you probably have the Window Selector already on the top panel. However, if you did a clean install of Dapper, then you will need to add it to the top panel.

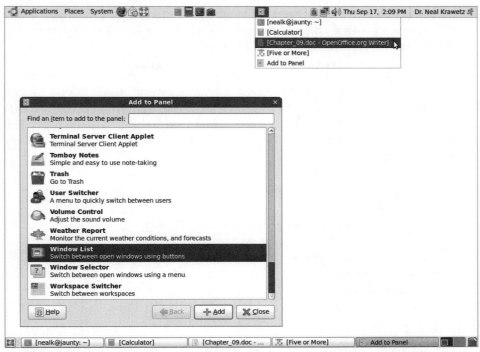

Figure 9-1: The Window List is visible on the bottom panel. The Window Selector has been added to the top panel and is open, showing five processes.

Another method of switching between applications uses Alt+Tab. When you press the Alt and Tab keys at the same time, a small window manager appears in the middle of the screen (see Figure 9-2). This window manager shows the icons for each open window. As long as you hold down the Alt key, this window manager will remain up. By holding down the Alt key and repeatedly pressing Tab, you can select different windows. Releasing the Alt key selects the window.

Using Alt+Tab

Another method to switch between applications uses Alt+Tab. When you press the Alt and Tab keys at the same time, a small window manager appears in the middle of the screen (see Figure 9-2). This window manager shows the icons for each open window. As long as you hold down the Alt key, this window manager will remain up. By holding down the Alt key and repeatedly pressing Tab, you can select different windows. Releasing the Alt key selects the window.

> **TIP** Each selected window shows the window title in the window manager and highlights the window on the screen using a black rectangle. If the window is partially covered, then you can see where it will appear.

The icons in this window manager are ordered from left to right by usage; the leftmost icon represents the window that was just used. If you switch between two windows, then the two icons on the left will represent them. An infrequently used window will be shuffled to the right. Pressing Alt+Tab moves the selector from left to right; pressing Alt+Shift+Tab moves the selector from right to left.

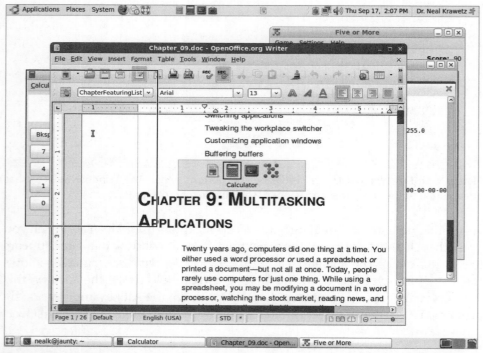

Figure 9-2: The Alt+Tab window manager. The calculator is selected but partially covered by another application.

Navigating the Desktop without a Mouse

Let's say that your mouse stopped working or did not work when the computer came up. What do you do? How do you navigate the graphical desktop?

The main keys to remember for mouseless navigation are Alt+F1, Alt+F2, and F10.

- Alt+F1 opens the top menus. From the top menus, you can open a terminal for debugging or repairing the system, or shut down the computer.

- Alt+F2 opens a prompt for running any application. In the worst case, you can run a program like xterm to open a command-line terminal.

- Many applications contain their own graphical menus. The F10 key opens the local menus for any application.

There are two other key combinations similar to Alt+F1 for selecting the top and bottom panels from the keyboard. However, the Ctrl+Alt+Tab and Ctrl+Alt+Esc sequences are unreliable for keyboard-only navigation. Don't use them if your mouse does not work.

WARNING When navigating the desktop without a mouse, use Alt+F1 to access the top menus. Do not use Ctrl+Alt+Tab or Ctrl+Alt+Esc.

The Ctrl+Alt+Tab and Ctrl+Alt+Esc sequences are supposed to allow you to select between the top panel, bottom panel, and (depending on your Ubuntu version) the desktop for keyboard-only navigation. However, the sequence became buggy around the time Hardy Heron (8.04 LTS) was released. With Hardy, the menus at the top may catch the focus and prevent you from ever leaving the menus, even if you start an application. The problem got worse with Jaunty (9.04)—It became possible to completely lose the user's focus, making navigation without a mouse virtually impossible. However, Alt+F1 Alt+F2, and F10 are still reliable for accessing the top menus, running applications, and navigating menus—in case you don't have a mouse.

Switching Between Tabs

Some applications also enable you to have multiple windows within the application and then switch between the windows. With most applications, Ctrl+PgUp and Ctrl+PgDn are used to navigate between application tabs. This works for common applications like Firefox and the Gnome terminal.

Applications may also define their own tabs. Firefox, for example, also recognizes Ctrl+Tab and Ctrl+Shift+Tab for switching between web page tabs.

The tab management in programs like Firefox and the terminal has two big differences from the desktop's Alt+Tab. First, the applications do not display a dialog in the middle of the screen. Instead, watch the tabs to see which one is highlighted. Second, the tabs are ordered from left to right, not based on last usage. If you want to change the order of the tabs, grab a Firefox (or terminal) tab by right-clicking it and drag it left or right to reposition it.

Tweaking the Workplace Switcher

It does not take long before you have a desktop with dozens of open windows. When this happens, no amount of Alt+Tab combinations will help you become organized. Fortunately, there is the Workplace Switcher. This applet gives you multiple desktops—you can put all work windows on one workplace, games on another, short projects on a third, and so on. By default, the Workplace Switcher is placed in the right corner of the bottom panel—I usually move mine to the top right so that the Window List has more room. If you don't have the Workplace Switcher, you can add it by opening the Add to Panel menu and dragging the applet to your panel.

Switching Workspaces with Ctrl+Alt+Arrows

The Workplace Switcher gives you a tiny view of each desktop (see Figure 9-3). Although you cannot see icons or window titles, you can see the general layout—there are gray boxes that represent each window on each desktop. To switch between desktops, you can either click on the Workspace Switcher or use the Ctrl+Alt+Arrow keys. For example, Ctrl+Alt+LeftArrow switches the workspace to the left, and Ctrl+Alt+RightArrow moves to the workspace on the right.

TIP If you open the Workspace Switcher's Preferences, then you can add more desktops and change their layout. The default has a few desktops arranged in one row. If you add more rows, then you can use Ctrl+Alt+UpArrow and Ctrl+Alt+ DownArrow to navigate between them.

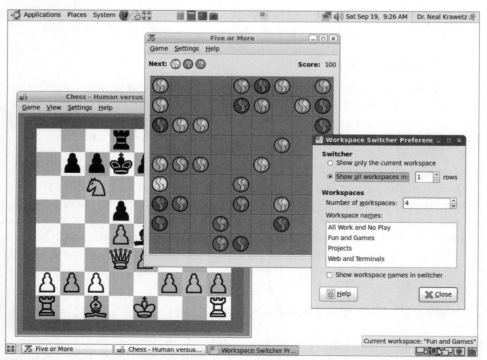

Figure 9-3: The Workspace Switcher in the lower-right corner, showing four distinct desktops

Managing Workspaces

By default, there are either two or four workspaces available (depending on your Ubuntu version). You can add additional workspaces by right-clicking the Workspace Switching and selecting Preferences (see Figure 9-3). From here, you can name workspaces, adjust the layout, or add more workspaces (you can also remove workspaces, but who would want to do that?). For example, I usually name my middle workspace *Games*—I can always go to this workspace when the boss is not around. (And if he suddenly shows up, I can use Ctrl+Alt+LeftArrow to quickly hide my games and show real work-in-progress.)

Applications do not need to stay in one workspace. Your active window appears highlighted in the Workspace Switcher. You can drag an application's window onto any other desktop in the Workplace Switcher. I usually do this when one window becomes cluttered, or when popup windows come from a different application. For example, when the Evolution mailer pops up a To Do list alert, I'll drop it in the appropriate window. (There is no reason to have "Write Status Report" appear in the middle of my Games workspace.)

Some application windows are small and may be hard to grab in the Workspace Switcher. Another way to move windows is to click on the top-right corner of any window. This will open a menu that displays options such as Move to Workspace Right and Move to Another Workspace followed by a list of workspaces. You can also pull up this menu by right-clicking any of the buttons in the Workspace List.

Finally, some application windows may be very important. These are ones that you will want to appear on every workspace, not just one workspace. In the window's top-left corner menu is an option titled "Always on Visible Workspace." If you select this, the window will be visible regardless of the selected workspace. I find this option to be very handy for important online conversations (for example, IRC and Jabber), and when using xawtv (watching TV while working—see Chapter 3). This way, I won't miss any communications when I switch workspaces. Without this option, something may happen in a window and I won't notice it until I switch back to that workspace.

Customizing Application Windows

When graphical applications start up, the X-Windows system sets elements such as the placement and dimensions (geometry), whether the window is visible or hidden, maximized or minimized, and always on top or bottom. Usually the application defaults are fine, but sometimes they need to be tweaked. For example, xawtv (discussed in Chapter 3) always seems to get buried under other windows—that makes it hard to watch *MythBusters*. If I want it to always start on top, I either need to press t (an interactive command to the program) to tell xawtv to always be on top, create an X-resource file to specify properties, or use a program like Devil's Pie (see the section on this tool) to automatically set the graphical properties.

Creating X-resources

Many X-Windows applications support a set of externally configurable parameters. These resources enable you to customize everything from a program's startup position to its size, fonts, and colors. The type of resource depends on the type of executable. There are Gnome Toolkit (Gtk) resources, used by most applications that start with a "g" like gedit and gnobots2. There is the Qt library, used by many KDE applications that start with a "k" (like kate, konqueror, and konsole), and there is the X Toolkit (Xt), which is used by most applications that start with an "x" (for example, xedit, xman, and xterm).

Most Gtk and KDE applications get their resource configurations from application-specific configuration files. For example, gedit uses $HOME/.gnome2/gedit-2, $HOME/.gnome2/accels/gedit, and other files in the .gnome2/ directory. Unfortunately, the location, name, format, and contents of these configuration files are application-specific (if they exist at all).

In contrast to Gtk and Qt, most Xt applications follow a standard configuration format: *application*resource: value*. For example, xterm*scrollBar: true sets the scrollBar resource for the xterm application to true (the default is false). This way, all new xterm windows will start with a scrollbar. To create a set of Xt X-resources:

1. Identify the application name. If you run the program from the command line, then this is the program's name. If you click an icon or menu item to run the program, then use xprop to identify the name of the program. The xprop program will turn your cursor into crosshairs. By clicking the window, you will see the running application's name in the WM_CLASS string.

   ```
   xprop | grep WM_CLASS
   ```

   TIP There may be multiple class strings for an application. Some are specific, while others are general. Any will work as a resource name. However, if you choose a specific string, then keep in mind that the resource must match the specific string. This can be very useful if you want one set of properties for the general xterm and another for the specific xterm (remote via TELNET).

2. Identify the name of the resource. Unfortunately, there are few standards here. Sometimes you can find the resource names and properties in the

man pages for your particular application, but not always. For example, `man xterm` and `man xman` lists lots of X-resources, while `man xeyes` provides no information. The few almost universal resources include:

- `geometry`—Specifies the dimension and location for an application. For example, `80×42+150+180` creates a window that is 80×42, with the top-left corner located at the screen coordinates 150×180.

NOTE The dimensions are application-specific. `80×42` for `xterm` means 80 columns wide and 42 characters tall, while `80×42` for `xeyes` specifies 80 pixels wide and 42 pixels tall.

- `font`—Specifies the font name to use. This can be a short name, such as `serif` or a long name that describes the exact font, such as `-*-serif-medium-r-normal-iso9241-*-*-75-75-p-*-iso8859-1` for a regular serif font at 75 dpi. You can use the program `xfontsel` to browse the available fonts and determine the exact font name.

- `background`—Specifies the background color. This can be a standard color name (for example, `yellow` or `black`) or a set of three hex values representing the red, green, and blue components (for example, `#ff0010` for red with a little bit of blue).

- `foreground`—Specifies the foreground color.

3. Add your resource to the X-resource file. By default, the resource file is `$HOME/.Xdefaults` (create it if it does not exist). For example, my `$HOME/.Xdefaults` specifies the dimensions of the default `xterm` window and turns on the scrollbars:

```
xterm*VT100*geometry: 80×42+150+180
! this line is a comment (! denotes a comment)
!xterm*scrollBar: false
*scrollBar: true
```

4. Load the resource file. The command `xrdb` is used to load the X-resources. There are many options for this, but I usually use: `xrdb -merge $HOME/.Xdefaults`. This says that all values should be lexically sorted and then loaded into memory. Existing values are replaced and new values are added. Alternately, you can use `xrdb $HOME/.Xdefaults`, which will load the file in order (unsorted) and replace existing values.

TIP Under other window managers, changes to `.Xdefaults` are loaded automatically. Under Gnome, you will need to explicitly run `xrdb`. To automatically load your defaults, add `xrdb -merge $HOME/.Xdefaults` to your `$HOME/.profile` script. This way, it will run every time you log in.

While individual users can have a $HOME/.Xdefaults file for personalizing applications, there are also systemwide configurations. The directory /etc/X11/app-defaults/ contains a file for every application and the default X-resource values. Changing these defaults will impact the entire system. Also, you don't need to use xrdb for the systemwide defaults—changes take effect immediately because applications know to look here for default configuration information.

Using Devil's Pie

Some applications don't use X-resources, and configuring other applications can be inconvenient. An alternative configuration method is to use a tool called Devil's Pie (sudo apt-get install devilspie). This program watches for new X-Windows applications and configures them as they appear. Unlike the Xt X-resources, Devil's Pie works with all X-Windows applications (Xt, Gtk, and Qt).

Devil's Pie uses a configuration file that describes what to look for and how to modify the X-resources.

1. Make a $HOME/.devilspie/ directory. Any file in this directory will become a resource for Devil's Pie.

2. Create a resource file. For example, I have a file called $HOME/.devilspie/games.ds that opens all games on workspace #4:

```
(begin
(if (is (window_class) "Gnobots2") (begin (set_workspace 4)) )
(if (is (window_name) "Iagno") (begin (set_workspace 4)) )
(if (is (window_name) "same-gnome") (begin (set_workspace 4)) )
)
```

Similarly, I have an xawtv.ds configuration file that says:

```
(if (is (window_class) "xawtv") (above) )
```

3. Run devilspie. As long as it is running, it will monitor new windows and adjust their X-resources as needed.

> **TIP** If you like Devil's Pie, consider adding it to your startup: System ⇨ Preferences ⇨ Sessions ⇨ Startup Programs. Alternately, you can use devilspie & to run this command in the background.

Each clause in the configuration file contains a condition (is, contains, or matches), item to match against (window_name, window_role, window_class, or application_name), and one or more actions. Table 9-1 lists the set of available actions and associated values (if any).

The window_name is the text that appears in the window's title bar. Applications may change this on the fly. For example, OpenOffice and Gimp both set the title bar to the name of the open file. Devil's Pie may perform an action each time the window name changes. In contrast, the `window_class` represents the application and usually does not change.

TIP Not every window has every property. If the `application_name` does not work for you, try the `window_class` or `window_role`. See the Devil's Pie man page (`man devilspie`) for the full list of items to match and possible actions.

Table 9-1: List of common actions for Devil's Pie

ACTION	VALUE	EXAMPLE	PURPOSE
Geometry	width×height+ xpos+ypos	geometry 80×42+100+20	Start the application with the specified dimensions
Fullscreen	n/a	fullscreen	Make full-screen
Focus	n/a	focus	Give the application focus
Center	n/a	center	Center the application on the desktop
maximize	n/a	maximize	Maximize the window
minimize	n/a	minimize	Start the window minimized
above	n/a	above	The window should always be on top of other windows
below	n/a	below	The window should always be below other windows
set_workspace	workspace number	set_workspace 4	Place the window on a specific workspace

Devil's Pie can match an X-Windows application based on the window's name, role, or class. To identify these values, use:

```
xprop | grep -E "^(WM_NAME)|(WM_WINDOW_ROLE)|(WM_CLASS)"
```

This will list any or all of the available values for any given window. Using Devil's Pie, you can automatically make windows appear in the right place on the right workspace and with the right settings. You can even handle dynamic popup windows like those created by Firefox (web), Evolution (mail), and Pidgin (chat client). For example, to have Pidgin's chat window start maximized in a different workspace, you can use:

```
(if
  (and
    (contains (window_class) "Pidgin")
    (contains (window_role) "conversation")
  )
  (begin (set_workspace 3) (maximize))
)
```

Buffering Buffers

I don't think there is anybody who uses a graphical interface without periodically cutting and pasting information between windows. Under some operating systems (for example, Microsoft Windows), there is only one commonly used clipboard. This clipboard can be used to share information between applications. Under Ubuntu, X-Windows and the Gnome Desktop provide *two* clipboards for common use. The first is the selection clipboard. Whenever you highlight any text, it gets placed in this buffer. Using the middle mouse button, you can paste the contents.

The second clipboard (called the *primary clipboard*) is used when you use Ctrl+C to copy, Ctrl+X to cut, and Ctrl+V to paste. Word processors (for example, OpenOffice) and graphic editors like Gimp usually use this second buffer. Also, some text applications, such as gnome-terminal, change cut-and-paste to use Shift+Ctrl instead of Ctrl (for example, Shift+Ctrl+C to copy) because Ctrl+C on the command-line is commonly used to stop running applications.

NOTE X-Windows provides a couple of different clipboard buffers. *Clipboard* is used for selection, *primary* is used by Ctrl+C and Ctrl+V, and *secondary* is usually not used.

I usually come across two problems with the default clipboards. First, the selection clipboard loses information too quickly. Simply clicking in a window to bring it forward could accidentally select a space or other character, wiping out the current selection. Although you could click the title bar to bring the window forward and prevent clipboard changes, other windows usually cover my title bars. Second, when doing a lot of development or editing, I sometimes need more than just two clipboards. I usually end up pasting text into a temporary file and then grabbing the temporary data when I need it.

Fortunately, there is a better way to manage clipboards. The program `xclip` (`sudo apt-get install xclip`) enables you to manipulate the clipboard contents. You can dump the clipboard contents to a file or load a file into the clipboard. Using `xclip`, you can easily give yourself one or more additional clipboards. You can even save clipboard contents between system reboots! Think of it like a calculator with a memory button—do you want one storage area, or many? Do you want to lose the memory when the calculator shuts off, or retain the memory?

The basic `xclip` usage specifies whether you want to write out (`-o`) or read in (`-i`) clipboard data, and which clipboard to use (`p` for primary, `s` for secondary, and `c` for the selection clipboard). For example:

- To store the primary clipboard to a file, use:

  ```
  xclip -o -selection p > buff
  ```

- To load a file into the secondary clipboard, use:

  ```
  xclip -i -selection s < buff
  ```

- To copy the selection clipboard into the primary clipboard, use:

  ```
  xclip -o -selection c | xclip -i -selection p
  ```

These commands can be mapped to keys. For example, Listing 9-1 creates three additional clipboards. Ctrl+F1 copies the primary clipboard into the first storage area, Ctrl+F2 uses the second storage area, and Ctrl+F3 creates the third storage area. To recall these buffers, use Ctrl+Shift+F1, Ctrl+Shift+F2, or Ctrl+Shift+F3. Using this hack, you can copy text into the primary clipboard (Ctrl+C) and then move it into the second storage area (Ctrl+F2). Later, you can recall this buffer by using Ctrl+Shift+F2 and paste it by using Ctrl+V.

TIP This hack also enables you to inspect and easily replace the contents of the clipboard. The storage buffers from the hack (see Listing 9-1) are in `$HOME/.xclip/`. You can view, edit, or replace the contents and then use the Ctrl+Shift keys (for example, Ctrl+Shift+F1) to load them into the clipboard buffer.

A similar hack can be used to exchange the contents of the selection and primary buffers (Listing 9-1, mapped to Ctrl+F4). This way, if you press Ctrl+C to copy a buffer and then use Ctrl+F4 to swap clipboards, you can use the middle mouse button to paste the contents, rather than using Ctrl+V.

TIP Swapping the clipboards may sound overly complicated or unnecessary, but some applications use specific clipboards. For example, `xterm` uses only the primary buffer. Anything copied into the clipboard buffer (e.g., using Ctrl+C in a word processor) cannot be pasted into an `xterm` window. Using Ctrl+F4, you can now paste the content.

Listing 9-1: Using xclip to Create Three Additional Clipboards

```
mkdir ~/.xclip  # create space for the clipboard buffers
# Map commands to actions
## Map the save commands
gconftool-2 -t str-set /apps/metacity/keybinding_commands/command_1 \
   'bash -c "xclip -o -selection p > ~/.xclip/clip.1"'
gconftool-2 -t str-set /apps/metacity/keybinding_commands/command_2 \
   'bash -c "xclip -o -selection p > ~/.xclip/clip.2"'
gconftool-2 -t str-set /apps/metacity/keybinding_commands/command_3 \
   'bash -c "xclip -o -selection p > ~/.xclip/clip.3"'
## Map the recall commands
gconftool-2 -t str-set /apps/metacity/keybinding_commands/command_4 \
   'bash -c "xclip -i -selection p < ~/.xclip/clip.1"'
gconftool-2 -t str-set /apps/metacity/keybinding_commands/command_5 \
   'bash -c "xclip -i -selection p < ~/.xclip/clip.2"'
gconftool-2 -t str-set /apps/metacity/keybinding_commands/command_6 \
   'bash -c "xclip -i -selection p < ~/.xclip/clip.3"'
# Map keys to commands
gconftool-2 -t str-set /apps/metacity/global_keybindings/run_command_1 \
   '<Control>F1'
gconftool-2 -t str-set /apps/metacity/global_keybindings/run_command_2 \
   '<Control>F2'
gconftool-2 -t str-set /apps/metacity/global_keybindings/run_command_3 \
   '<Control>F3'
gconftool-2 -t str-set /apps/metacity/global_keybindings/run_command_4 \
   '<Control><Shift>F1'
gconftool-2 -t str-set /apps/metacity/global_keybindings/run_command_5 \
   '<Control><Shift>F2'
gconftool-2 -t str-set /apps/metacity/global_keybindings/run_command_6 \
   '<Control><Shift>F3'
# Make Control+F4 swap the primary and selection clipboards
# Do this by using the secondary clipboard as a temporary buffer
gconftool-2 -t str-set /apps/metacity/keybinding_commands/command_10 \
   'bash -c "xclip -o -selection p | xclip -i -selection s;
            xclip -o -selection c | xclip -i -selection p;
            xclip -o -selection s | xclip -i -selection c"'
gconftool-2 -t str-set /apps/metacity/global_keybindings/run_command_10\
      '<Control>F4'
```

Automating Tasks

There are some tasks that we end up doing over and over by hand. For example, I frequently convert DOC and PDF files to text. Rather than opening a command prompt and running pdftotext or antiword every time I need to convert a file, I created an automated conversion directory.

The dnotify program watches a specified directory for any change. A change may be a file creation, update, renaming, deletion, permission modification, or all of the above. When a change happens, `dnotify` can run a script. I have a script that converts DOC and PDF files to text, and the directory being monitored is on my desktop. Using `dnotify`, I can convert files by simply dropping them into a directory on my desktop.

1. Install `dnotify` as well as any conversion tools you need. In this example, `pdftotext` and `antiword` will perform text conversions.

```
sudo apt-get install dnotify
sudo apt-get install poppler-utils  # provides pdftotext
sudo apt-get install antiword
```

2. Create a small script to convert all files in a directory. Listing 9-2 shows my `convert2text` script. This script takes a directory name on the command line and scans the directory for all DOC and PDF files. Any file not already available as text is converted.

Available for download on Wrox.com

Listing 9-2: Simple convert2text Script to Convert Files to Text

```
#!/bin/sh
# Be sure to make this executable: chmod a+x convert2text
# Be sure to place it in your $PATH
# (e.g., sudo cp convert2text /usr/local/bin/)
if [ "$1" = "" ]; then
  echo "Usage: $0 directory"
  exit
fi
# Get list of files in the directory
find "$1" -type f |
while read filename; do
# Based on the file name, perform the conversion
  case "$filename" in
    (*.pdf) # convert pdf to text
      filenameTxt="${filename%.pdf}.txt"
      if [ ! -f "${filenameTxt}" ]; then
        pdftotext "${filename}" "${filenameTxt}";
      fi
      ;;
    (*.doc) # convert doc to text
      filenameTxt="${filename%.doc}.txt"
      if [ ! -f "${filenameTxt}" ]; then
        antiword "${filename}" > "${filenameTxt}";
      fi
      ;;
  esac
```

3. Create a directory to monitor:

```
mkdir $HOME/Desktop/convert2text
```

4. Run the `dnotify` program. Specify the `convert2text` script and the directory to monitor. In this case, the action to watch for is file creation (`-C`). The `dnotify` program changes the `'{}'` string to the directory name.

```
dnotify -C $HOME/Desktop/convert2text -e convert2text '{}'
```

Now, dragging or pasting any PDF or DOC file into this folder will create a text file. The text file will have the same name as the original document but will end with the .txt extension. For example, `ch09.doc` will generate `ch09.txt`. If you are using the command line then you can copy (`cp`) or move (`mv`) files into `$HOME/Desktop/convert2text/` for automatic conversion. Figure 9-4 shows a sample conversion directory.

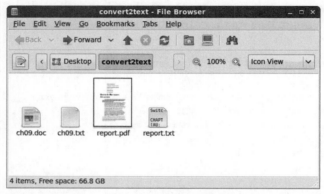

Figure 9-4: Automatic file conversion using dnotify and the convert2text directory

TIP If you are like me and frequently use the `convert2text` directory, then you can add the `dnotify` command to your Gnome startup (System ➪ Preferences ➪ Sessions ➪ Startup Programs or System ➪ Preferences ➪ Startup Applications). This way, the automatic conversion will be enabled immediately after you login. Also, you can use the `-b` option to run it in the background.

```
dnotify -b -C $HOME/Desktop/convert2text -e convert2text '{}'.
```

Besides modifying text, you might want to modify graphics. The `netpbm` package (`sudo apt-get install netpbm`) provides support for manipulating JPEG, GIF, PNG, and other image formats. For example, Listing 9-3 is a `dnotify` script that will convert all JPEG, PNG, and GIF images to thumbnails that are 64 pixels wide.

Listing 9-3: Simple Script to Convert Images to Thumbnails

```
#!/bin/sh
# Be sure to make this executable: chmod a+x convert2thumbnail
# Be sure to place it in your $PATH
# (e.g., sudo cp convert2thumbnail /usr/local/bin/)
if [ "$1" = "" ]; then
  echo "Usage: $0 directory"
  exit
fi
# Get list of files in the directory that do not
# begin with "thumbnail-".
cd "$1"
find . -type f ! -name thumbnail\* |
while read filename; do
# Based on the file name, perform the conversion.
# The output filename becomes thumbnail-$filename.
filename="${filename#./}"  # remove the ./ from the filename
if [ ! -f "thumbnail-$filename" ]; then
  # only process files that have no thumbnail.
  case "$filename" in
    (*.jpg|*.jpeg) # convert files ending in jpg or jpeg
      jpegtopnm "$filename" | pnmscale -xsize 64 | \
      pnmtojpeg > thumbnail-"$filename"
     ;;
    (*.gif) # convert gif
      giftopnm "$filename" | pnmscale -xsize 64 | \
      ppmtogif > thumbnail-"$filename"
     ;;
    (*.png) # convert png
      pngtopnm "$filename" | pnmscale -xsize 64 | \
      pnmtopng > thumbnail-"$filename"
     ;;
    esac
fi
done
```

Tracking Projects

Many corporate and government environments require employees to keep track of their time. For example, when consulting, I usually track my time in 15-minute intervals. I once had a job where the employer required account-ability down to every 6-minute interval. With today's operating systems, multitasking becomes a blessing and a curse. The good news is that you can do many things at once. The bad news is that tracking billable time on projects can get very confusing when you're multitasking (and double-billing clients is a definite no-no). If the accounting people require you to track your work, then Ubuntu is definitely what you want.

Tracking Time on Projects

There are a variety of packages that enable you to track your time on projects. Some examples include gnotime, gtimer, gtimelog, wmwork, and worklog. Each of these packages allows you to create a project, start, and stop a work-time clock, and easily switch between projects. They also allow you set the accumulation interval (from one minute to hourly) and display total time spent summaries.

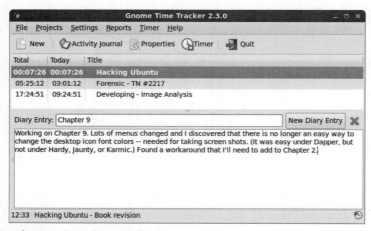

Figure 9-5: The Gnotime Time Tracker

My personal preference is the GnoTime Time Tracker (sudo apt-get install gnotime). After installing it, you can run the GnoTime Time Tracker from Applications ➪ Office ➪ GnoTime Tracking Tool. Besides being able to add projects and diary entries, it allows you to specify billable rates on a per-project basis. You can also mark projects with a priority and urgency level. Figure 9-5 shows the main window for gnotime. Simply double-click any task to start the clock. Diary entries can be added to help track what work was being done.

GnoTime can generate a variety of reports, including a journal of time spent (see Figure 9-6) and a billing list (see Figure 9-7). Each report includes clickable items with menus, so you can add more diaries, annotations, adjust times, change rates, and so on. Reports can be saved as HTML, exported to a web server or FTP site, or e-mailed.

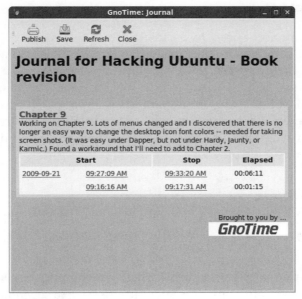

Figure 9-6: The work journal

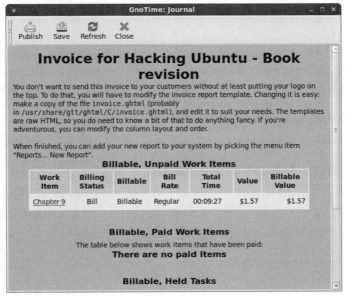

Figure 9-7: Invoice report showing billable hours. (Wow! $1.57 in just 9 minutes!)

GnoTime isn't perfect. It cannot merge times from multiple people or export information to a spreadsheet. However, it is more than enough for tracking the work from a single individual. For group tracking, consider a collaborative project-tracking system, such as `gforge`.

Tracking CPU Usage

In some cases, projects need to be tracked by the resources they consume. The two most common billable resources are CPU time and disk space. Unfortunately, there are no nice GUI applications for tracking a project's CPU consumption. Instead, this is done by using the `time` command. This keeps track of the real elapsed time, time spent in user-space, and system time (time spent in the kernel). For example, `time bash` monitors the command `bash` (a shell) and every process created by `bash`. When the shell finally exists, a run-time summary is displayed:

```
$ time bash
# run some commands
$ exit
real    1m12.428s
user    0m0.292s
sys     0m0.588s
```

The sample summary shows that the shell was running for a little more than a minute, but most of the time was spent idling—0.588 seconds were spent in the kernel and 0.292 seconds were spent in user-space. If you need to know for how long a process was running, preface the command with `time`. When the process exits, you will know how much time was spent.

WARNING The `time` command has trouble monitoring spawned processes. If the program being timed kicks off a CPU-intensive process, then `time` will only see the total duration, not the kernel or user-space times. Also, if a process is separated from its parent (for example, scheduled to run using `at`), then `time` will not measure the spawned application.

Tracking Disk Usage and Quotas

Disk space is much easier to compute. The `df` command (discussed in Chapter 8) shows you the current disk usage, but this is usually inadequate for billing. Another way to track disk usage is to install the `quota` package. Enabling quotas is not the easiest system, but the command-line tools allow you to specify how much disk space a user can have on a specific file system.

NOTE When using `df` to determine disk space, be aware that this is only a snapshot. There may have been a time between snapshots when the disk space exceeded the current allotment.

Although quotas may seem unnecessary for the average home user, they can be very useful for project tracking. Quotas enable you to track disk use, bill by the megabyte, and identify when a project dramatically increases in size. Quotas can also stop runaway processes from filling your hard drive. For example, the default installation for Ubuntu places all files in one partition. If you are running a mail server then you might want to enable quotas for the e-mail system. This prevents a massive e-mail (or flood of small e-mails) from filling your disk.

Understanding Your Limits

Under Ubuntu, the quota system enables you to specify limits for files, links, and disk space per user. There are soft limits and hard limits, and an allotted grace period. These limits can be set for users or groups. This way, a group can share files within a given quota.

- **Hard limits**—A hard limit specifies the maximum allocation for a user or group. For example, if you are allotted 10,000 files, then you cannot create any new files if you are over your quota. The only ways to get under your quota is to either delete files or have the administrator increase your limit.

- **Soft limits**—Soft limits are used to provide a warning to users. If they go over their soft limit quota, then the grace time kicks in. The grace time says how long they have to remove files and get under their quota. If the grace time is set to seven days, then users have seven days to get under their quota. After the grace period, the soft limit is treated as a hard limit and the user is blocked from creating or updating new files. Soft limits are really useful since sometimes you might go a little over your quota for a short duration.

- **Disk limits**—Soft and hard limits can be set based on disk space. For example, a user may be allocated a 100-MB soft limit and a 110-MB hard limit. Small systems may have limits set in the megabyte range, while large systems may use gigabyte or larger quotas.

- **File limits**. This limit allows you to specify how many files a user (or group) can have. Files are anything that consumes an inode—this includes real files, device files, and links to other files. Small systems, such as local e-mail servers, may be limited to a few hundred or a few thousand files. In contrast, large file repositories may be allowed hundreds of thousands of files, or have no limit at all.

NOTE The file system uses *inodes* to store meta-data information about files. This includes the actual file name (since it is not found inside the file contents), permissions, timestamps, and directory information.

Enabling Quotas

1. Install the quota package:

   ```
   sudo apt-get install quota
   ```

2. Quotas are set on a per-file-system basis. Edit /etc/fstab and add the mount options usrquota and grpquota to your file system. In my case, I have added user quotas to my Ubuntu file system (/dev/hda1) and both user and group quotas to a second hard drive (/dev/hdb4). My /etc/fstab file looks like this:

   ```
   # /etc/fstab: static file system information.
   # device   mount        fs         options                          dump    pass
   proc       /proc        proc       defaults                          0       0
   /dev/hda1  /      ext3   defaults,errors=remount-o,usrquota 0       1
   /dev/hda5  none         swap       sw                                0       0
   /dev/hdc   /media/cdrom0 udf,iso9660 user,noauto                     0       0
   /dev/hdb4  /mnt/disk    ext3       defaults,usrquota,grpquota 0       0
   ```

   TIP Don't enable quotas on read-only devices such as CD-ROM drives. Since a user has no way to add or remove files, quota information provides no value. Similarly, removable devices such as floppy disks and USB thumb drivers usually should not have quotas enabled.

3. Since the partitions are already mounted, you will need to remount each of the quota-enabled file systems in order to load the new mount flags. Since the changes are in /etc/fstab, you won't need to do this after a reboot. Since I added quotas to / and /mnt/disk, I can remount using:

   ```
   $ sudo mount -o remount /
   $ sudo mount -o remount /mnt/disk
   $ mount | grep quota   # check results
   /dev/hda1 on / type ext3 (rw,errors=remount-ro,usrquota)
   /dev/hdb4 on /mnt/disk type ext3 (rw,usrquota,grpquota)
   ```

4. Before quotas can be enabled, you need to check for existing problems (even through there shouldn't be any problems). This is done using the quotacheck command. The parameters -augmv means "all file systems, all user and group quotas, and don't remount the partitions." For large disks, this check might take a few minutes. If you don't have user quotas, then you do not need -u, and -g is only used when group quotas are enabled. Specifying the -g without the grpquota mount option will generate a warning but won't cause problems.

   ```
   $ sudo quotacheck -augmv
   quotacheck: Scanning /dev/hdb4 [/mnt/disk] quotacheck: Cannot stat
   old user quota file: No such file or directory
   quotacheck: Cannot stat old group quota file: No such file or
   ```

```
directory
quotacheck: Cannot stat old user quota file: No such file or
directory
quotacheck: Cannot stat old group quota file: No such file or
directory
done
quotacheck: Checked 10254 directories and 228748 files
quotacheck: Old file not found.
quotacheck: Old file not found.
```

The first time you run `quotacheck -augmv`, you will see a bunch of warnings about files not existing. This is because the system has not been checked before. After it is checked, the quota version 2 files `/mnt/disk/aquota.user` and `/mnt/disk/aquota.group` (or `quota.user` and `quota.group` if you are using the older quota version 1 system) will be created, and these errors should not appear again.

NOTE Even if you are not enabling both user and group quotas on a file system, you should create both files. Otherwise some quota commands may generate warnings.

5. Now quotas can be turned on:

```
sudo quotaon -augv
```

TIP Running `sudo /etc/init.d/quota start` will perform the quota check (Step 4) and turn on quotas (Step 5).

Editing Quotas

After quotas are enabled, you can edit them using `edquota`. Using `edquota -u`, you can edit the quota for any particular user. Similarly, `edquota -g` edits group quotas.

```
sudo edquota -u bill
sudo edquota -g users
```

The `edquota` command opens an editor that allows you to specify the soft and hard limits for disk space (blocks) and files (inodes). Each partition where quotas are enabled is listed. The current values are also displayed. For example, my quota settings look like this:

Filesystem	blocks	soft	hard	inodes	soft	hard
/dev/hda1	68866148	0	0	247947	0	0
/dev/hdb4	31153944	0	0	238603	0	0

This says that I am currently using about 65 GB on `/dev/hda1`, and using 247,947 inodes. On `/dev/hdb4`, I am using about 30 GB and 238,603 inodes.

This also says that I have no quota limits. Changing and saving the soft and hard values will immediately enable quotas. If I am over quota, then the soft and hard limits are immediately enforced.

The grace times default to seven days, but they can be edited using `sudo edquota -t`. This brings up an editor that displays the current settings per device and allows you to change the values.

```
Grace period before enforcing soft limits for users:
Time units may be: days, hours, minutes, or seconds
  Filesystem                Block grace period      Inode grace period
  /dev/hda1                      7days                   7days
  /dev/hdb4                      7days                   7days
```

TIP Don't worry about maintaining the correct column spacing when editing with edquota. The system only checks the number of columns separated by spaces, not the actual number of spaces. Saving changes and then running edquota again will reformat the columns.

Reporting Quotas

After enabling quotas, you can generate periodic reports using the `repquota` command. These can either be in the raw system format or in a human-readable form (`-s`).

```
$ sudo repquota -a
*** Report for user quotas on device /dev/hda1
Block grace time: 7days; Inode grace time: 7days
                        Block limits                 File limits
User            used    soft    hard   grace    used  soft  hard  grace
----------------------------------------------
root        -3953944       0       0          189921     0     0
nealk      -68866148       0       0          247947     0     0
postfix -       56         0       0              41     0     0
test    -       28         0       0               8     0     0
*** Report for user quotas on device /dev/hdb4
Block grace time: 7days; Inode grace time: 7days
                        Block limits                 File limits
User            used    soft    hard   grace    used  soft  hard  grace
----------------------------------------------
root    -      36628       0       0             192     0     0
nealk  -31153944 41153944 51153944          238603 59153944 61153944
postfix -        4         0       0               1     0     0
test    -      32472       0       0             207     0     0
```

```
$ sudo repquota -as
*** Report for user quotas on device /dev/hda1
Block grace time: 7days; Inode grace time: 7days
                        Block limits               File limits
  User            used   soft    hard  grace     used  soft  hard  grace
  ---------------------------------------------------
  root       —   3862M      0       0          190k      0     0
  nealk      —  67253M      0       0          248k      0     0
  postfix    —      56      0       0            41      0     0
  test       —      28      0       0             8      0     0
*** Report for user quotas on device /dev/hdb4
Block grace time: 7days; Inode grace time: 7days
                        Block limits               File limits
  User            used   soft    hard  grace     used   soft    hard  grace
  ---------------------------------------------------
  root       —   36628      0       0           192      0       0
  nealk      —  30424M  40190M  49956M         239k 59154k  61154k
  postfix    —       4      0       0             1      0       0
  test       —   32472      0       0           207      0       0
```

You can also generate quota e-mails by using `warnquota`. By default, e-mails are sent to each user when they are over quota, and root also receives a copy of each e-mail. You can change the e-mail sender's information by editing /etc/warnquota.conf.

When I need to track projects by disk space, I usually create a user account just for the project and enable a `cron` job to generate a nightly (or hourly) report for the project's user (`sudo repquota -a | grep` *projectusername*).

Summary

Ubuntu provides many different options for managing concurrent applications. Whether your needs are for task switching, window management, or project tracking, there are plenty of options available. Using simple scripts, you can enhance clipboard usage and create directories that automate tasks. And best of all, you can literally budget your time.

## CHAPTER 10

Getting Graphical with Video Bling

What's In This Chapter?

Tips and tricks to troubleshoot and tune the display
Changing screen savers and animating the desktop
How to widen your desktop with multiple monitors

When you install the Ubuntu desktop, the video display becomes the single most important system. If the mouse doesn't work, you can use the keyboard. If the keyboard does not work, then you can remotely login. However, if the display does not work, then you cannot see what you are doing and are completely out of luck.

Some Linux versions install very basic VGA or SVGA graphics support. It is up to the user to upgrade the driver to something other than the default low resolution (for example, 800x600 with 256 colors).

Ubuntu takes the next step. During the installation of the graphical desktop, it tries to detect your video card. In most cases, you will end up with at least 1024x768 and 24-bit color (16 million colors). Although this is good for getting started, it might not be the best you can do.

> **NOTE** If you start off with 800x600 and 256 colors, then you probably have an unsupported video card. Video cards have really come down in price—you can get a decent one that can do 1024x768 (or higher resolution!) with true color for under $30. See `https://wiki.ubuntu.com/HardwareSupport` for a list of supported video cards.

With graphics come customizable elements such as screen savers and animated backgrounds. I've seen some people spend hours selecting and tuning screen savers. Other customizations that are becoming really common are dual-monitors and cross-desktop systems. With Ubuntu (and a little tweaking), you can enable two monitors on the same computer, or use a second computer as a second monitor.

Troubleshooting the Display

Each version of Ubuntu updates functionality. Following Dapper Drake (6.06 LTS), there has been a strong emphasis on updating the display, desktop, and user interface. The updated X-server does a much better job at auto-configuration, more video cards are supported, and adding multiple displays to one computer no longer requires manually editing configuration files.

Hacking Around Troublesome Areas

As newer versions of Ubuntu are released, some things have changed. Menus have moved and some applets have different functionality. Unfortunately, some features broke. Most notably, xvidtune (for turning the video display), Xdmx (for connecting desktops over the network), and Nautilus (the desktop and graphical file manager system) have each introduced some serious defects that have been known for years, yet have not been corrected.

It is important to recognize that these problems are not specific to Ubuntu. Ubuntu is a collection of open source software. Every Linux operating system that uses the X.Org X Server version 1.4 (2007) and later will have broken versions of xvidtune and Xdmx. Similarly, every Gnome desktop since at least Gnome 2.24 (2008) will have the broken Nautilus file browser. This includes Fedora, Suse, Debian, and Ubuntu; they all have these same issues.

The hacks in this chapter do not just introduce new features. They also identify some of the problem areas and provide workarounds, so the defects do not become showstoppers.

Patching Nautilus

Many of the hacks in this chapter modify settings used by the file manager, Nautilus. While this normally isn't a problem, there was a bug introduced after Dapper Drake (6.06 LTS). If the Nautilus configuration option show_desktop changes, then Nautilus crashes. For example, the following command will kill Nautilus on Hardy Heron (8.04 LTS)—but only if you don't have an open file folder:

```
gconftool-2 -s -t bool /apps/nautilus/preferences/show_desktop false
```

The problem got worse under Jaunty Jackalope (9.04) and Karmic Koala (9.10). On these systems, Nautilus auto-restarts, causing it to respawn and crash ad infinitum. To disable the infinite spawning, add the following line to the end of the /usr/share/applications/nautilus.desktop file:

```
AutostartCondition=GNOME /apps/nautilus/preferences/show_desktop
```

TIP You may need to log out and log back in for this change to take effect.

If Nautilus does crash on you, or the desktop does not automatically refresh, then you can restart Nautilus by opening any file folder, running the file manager, or executing nautilus in a terminal window.

Enabling X11

Ubuntu does a good enough job of selecting a viable video driver. However, it may not default to settings that match your needs. In order to tweak your video configuration, you may need to enable some X11 components.

Enabling Ctrl+Alt+Backspace

The key sequence Ctrl+Alt+Backspace restarts the X-server. During normal computer operating, you will probably never need this key sequence. However, when debugging or changing video drivers, you will constantly need to restart the X-server in order to enable changes. This key sequence becomes a great timesaver.

Early versions of Ubuntu had this sequence enabled by default. However, beginning with Jaunty (9.04), the Ctrl+Alt+Backspace sequence is disabled. The decision was made because some users would accidentally hit this odd three-key combination. (As an aside, I don't know anyone who has accidentally pressed this three-key combination.)

For playing with video drivers and the X-server configuration, you are going to want it enabled. On Jaunty and earlier systems, use the dontzap program.

```
sudo apt-get install dontzap
sudo dontzap—disable
sudo reboot # or logout and restart the X-server
```

TIP Older systems also have a dontzap package. Install it and use dontzap—enable to disable the Ctrl+Alt+Backspace sequence.

With Karmic Koala (9.10), `dontzap` is no longer available. Instead, the option is buried under the System ➾ Preferences ➾ Keyboard menu. Select the Layout tab and click on the Layout Options button, then enable the Key Sequence to kill the X server (see Figure 10-1).

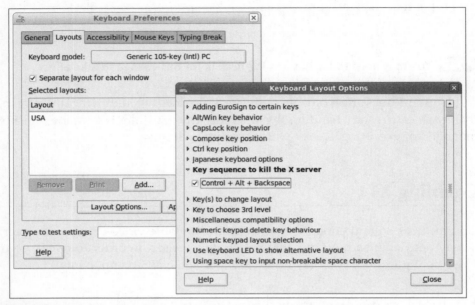

Figure 10-1: The Keyboard Layout Options under Karmic Koala (9.10)

Editing xorg.conf

Most manual video modifications require changes to the `/etc/X11/xorg.conf` file. Before you begin, you will want to make a backup of this file.

As mentioned in Chapter 4, starting with Karmic Koala (9.10), the `xorg.conf` file is not created during the installation. Instead, the server relies on built-in defaults. If `xorg.conf` exists, then Ubuntu will use it. But for editing, it first needs to exist. To do this, you need to stop the X-server, create `xorg.conf`, move it into place, and then restart the server.

1. Press Control+F2 to get to a text prompt.

2. Login to the text console.

3. Stop the X-server.

   ```
   sudo stop gdm     # Karmic Koala use Upstart
   ```

4. Create the default `xorg.conf` file. It will be placed in your current directory and named `xorg.conf.new`.

   ```
   Xorg -configure
   ```

5. Move the configuration file into place for the X-server.

```
sudo cp xorg.conf.new /etc/X11/xorg.conf
```

6. Restart the X-server.

```
sudo start gdm       # Restart using upstart
```

Tuning Graphics

During the installation, Ubuntu detects the graphics card and installs a usable driver. The detection is done using the ddcprobe and xresprobe commands. For example, to list all of the resolution information about my video card and monitor, I can use:

```
$ sudo apt-get install xresprobe
# The xresprobe package is installed
$ sudo ddcprobe -?
vbe: VESA 3.0 detected.
oem: NVIDIA
vendor: NVIDIA Corporation
product: NV18 Board—p160nz Chip Rev A4
memory: 131072kb
mode: 640x400x256
mode: 640x480x256
mode: 800x600x16
mode: 800x600x256
mode: 1024x768x16
. .
$ sudo xresprobe any
id: L1780U
res: 1280x1024 1024x768 800x600 720x400 640x480
freq: 30-83 56-75
disptype: crt
```

NOTE For xresprobe, you may need to specify the type of driver. For example, sudo xresprobe ati works for the ATI driver. Other drivers include vesa, nvidia, nv, intel, and i810.

These commands identify the video card and monitor. During the desktop install, they are used to identify the maximum resolution and to configure the /etc/X11/xorg.conf file.

Unfortunately, ddcprobe and xresprobe do not always know about your monitor, especially if you are using old equipment. If your graphics card supports a resolution of 1280x1024, but your monitor supports only 1024x768, then you won't be able to see the display at 1280x1024. Unless you have a really old CRT monitor, your display probably supports 1024x768. Thus, this is usually the default resolution. To change the default resolution, use System ⇨ Preferences ⇨ Display applet (see Figure 10-2). From here, you can select the desired resolution and refresh rate. You can also choose to set a new resolution for your login account or make it a systemwide change.

NOTE Older Ubuntu systems, such as Hardy Heron and Dapper Drake, call the menu options System ⇨ Preferences ⇨ Screen Resolution instead of Display.

Figure 10-2: The Screen Resolution applet from Hardy Heron (8.04)

Changing Screen Resolution (xrandr)

The System ⇨ Preferences ⇨ Display applet may not list all of your available screen resolutions and settings. The full list of supported screen resolutions can be found with the X-Windows rotate and reflection command: xrandr. For example, the command xrandr -q lists the screen resolutions supported by the video driver:

```
$ xrandr -q
Screen 0: minimum 320 x 200, current 1280 x 1024, maximum 1280 x 1280
VGA1 disconnected
DVI0 disconnected
VGA2 connected 1280x1024+0+0 338mm x 270mm
   1280x1024     60.0 +   75.0*    59.9
   1152x864      75.0
   1024x768      74.9     75.1     60.0
   832x624       74.6
   800x600       75.0     74.9     60.3
   640x480       75.0     74.8     60.0
   720x400       70.1
```

In this example, my video driver supports seven different screen resolutions and up to three different refresh rates. These resolutions are not necessarily the same as the ones listed in /etc/X11/xorg.conf (for X-Windows), and some resolutions may not be supported by your monitor.

WARNING Your video card, video driver, and monitor may not support the same resolutions. The xrandr command shows your video driver resolutions and allows you to set a screen resolution that is *not* supported by your monitor. This could damage your monitor and video card!

You can use xrandr to change resolutions by specifying one of the listed sizes. Using the example, you can set the screen to 1024x768 with any of these commands:

```
xrandr -s 2              # screen size 2 is 1024x768 (0 is 1280x1024)
xrandr -s 1024x768       # specify by dimensions
xrandr -s 1024x768 -r 60 # for 60 Hz (default listed is 75 Hz)
xrandr -s 2 -r 60        # screen size 2 at 60 Hz
```

Thinking Safety

When the Display applet makes changes, it gives you 20 seconds to undo the change. This way, if the resolution is not supported and the display becomes dark or unreadable, you just need to wait 20 seconds for it to switch back. Unfortunately, with xrandr, you do not have that luxury. The xrandr command will change the resolution immediately, and it assumes that you know what you are doing.

If you want to test a screen change with xrandr, use a small script (see Listing 10-1) to save the current resolution, change the screen, and then change back. If you like the resolution, you can press Ctrl+C to kill the script, or run xrandr without the test script to set the resolution.

Listing 10-1: Script to Test a Screen Resolution

```
#!/bin/bash
# Temporarily change resolutions (great for testing)
# Example usage: ./testres -s 1 (set to xrandr screen setting #1)
#
# xrandr output changes with xrandr version.
version=$(xrandr -v | sed -e 's/^[^0-9]*//')
resolution=""
rate=""
if [ "$version" = "1.2" ]; then
    resolution=$(xrandr -q | grep '*' | awk '{print $1}')
    rate=$(xrandr -q | grep '*')
    rate=${rate%\**} # remove everything after the current rate
```

(continued)

Listing 10-1: Script to Test a Screen Resolution (*continued*)

```
    rate=${rate##* } # remove everything before the rate
fi
if [ "$version" = "1.1" ]; then
    resolution=$(xrandr -q | grep '*' | \
        sed -e 's/ x /x/g' | awk '{print $2}')
    rate=$(xrandr -q | grep '*')
    rate=${rate##*\*} # remove everything before the rate
    rate=${rate%% *}  # remove everything after the current rate
fi
if [ "$resolution" = "" ]; then
  echo "Unknown xrandr version."
  exit
fi

echo "Old: Resolution: $resolution  Refresh rate: $rate Hz"
# Set the resolution using the command-line options.

xrandr $*
if [ "$1" == "" ]; then
  echo -e "\nSelect a resolution. For example: $0 -s 1024x768"
  exit
fi
echo "New: $(xrandr -q | grep '*')"
# Wait 20 seconds, then change back
echo "Waiting 20 seconds.."
sleep 20
xrandr -s $resolution -r $rate
echo "Switching back"
echo "Current: $(xrandr -q | grep '*')"
exit
```

Flipping Cool!

Some video drivers support flipping the screen. If your video driver supports this, then you can use xrandr -x to flip the screen horizontally, making a mirror reflection. The xrandr -y command flips the screen vertically, and xrandr -x -y flips both. Similarly, the -o option can change the orientation from normal (-o normal) to rotated 90 degrees (-o right), 180 degrees (-o inverted), and 270 degrees (-o left).

However, not every video driver supports flipping and rotation. If your driver does not support these commands, then xrandr will give you a cryptic error message such as:

```
    X Error of failed request:  BadMatch (invalid parameter attributes)
    Major opcode of failed request:  155 (RANDR)
    Minor opcode of failed request:  2 (RRSetScreenConfig)
    Serial number of failed request:  12
    Current serial number in output stream:  12
```

Practical Uses for xrandr

By now you're probably thinking, "xrandr is cool, but it has no long-term practical use." Most people set the display and that's it. However, sometimes there is a need to switch between display resolutions. For example, web designers may want to quickly switch screen resolutions to see what their web pages look like with different settings. This is important since not everyone uses 1280x1024. On the laptop that I use for presentations, I use xrandr to quickly change the display to something that will work with the overhead projector; I've seen too many conferences where people spend more time fighting with the projector rather than actually presenting. And for this book, I used a quick script (see Listing 10-2) to change the screen resolution, and set the background, colors, and so forth to match the publisher's guidelines for screen shots. This script ensures that every screen shot is taken the same way.

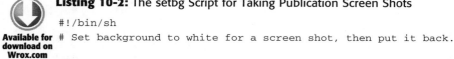

Listing 10-2: The setbg Script for Taking Publication Screen Shots

```
#!/bin/sh
# Set background to white for a screen shot, then put it back.

# Config Paths
gnomeBG="/desktop/gnome/background"
gnomeSC="/desktop/gnome/screen/default/0/resolution"
nautilus="/apps/nautilus/preferences"

# Save current settings
RES=$(gconftool-2 —get $gnomeSC)
BG1=$(gconftool-2 —get $gnomeBG/primary_color)
BG2=$(gconftool-2 —get $gnomeBG/secondary_color)
BG=$(gconftool-2 —get $gnomeBG/draw_background)
BF=$(gconftool-2 —get $gnomeBG/picture_filename)
SD=$(gconftool-2 —get $nautilus/show_desktop)

# Set change
gconftool-2 -t str—set $gnomeSC "1024x768"
gconftool-2 -t str—set $gnomeBG/primary_color "#ffffff"
gconftool-2 -t str—set $gnomeBG/secondary_color "#ffffff"
gconftool-2 -t boolean—set $gnomeBG/draw_background "false"
gconftool-2 -t str—set $gnomeBG/picture_filename ""
xrandr -s "1024x768"
# Bug introduced Post-Dapper: nautilus dies when show_desktop
# changes. So, wait a few seconds for everything else to take
# effect, then let nautilus die.
sleep 4
gconftool-2 -t boolean—set $nautilus/show_desktop "false"
# Poof: Nautilus crashed, but desktop is gone so I can take
# screen shots.
```

(continued)

Listing 10-2: The setbg Script for Taking Publication Screen Shots (*continued*)

```
# Wait for the user
echo "Use Control+Alt+D to hide all windows (and later restore)"
read key

# Put it back
xrandr -s "$RES"
if [ "$RES" != "" ]; then
  gconftool-2 -t str-set $gnomeSC "$RES"
fi
gconftool-2 -t str-set $gnomeBG/primary_color "$BG1"
gconftool-2 -t str-set $gnomeBG/secondary_color "$BG2"
gconftool-2 -t boolean-set $gnomeBG/draw_background "$BG"
gconftool-2 -t str-set $gnomeBG/picture_filename "$BF"
gconftool-2 -t boolean-set $nautilus/show_desktop "$SD"

# Bug introduced Post-Dapper: nautilus dies if show_desktop changes
nautilus 2>/dev/null &
exit
```

Changing Video Drivers

X-Windows supports dozens of graphics cards. For a quick list, use
apt-cache search video driver. Most of these video drivers are installed
on the system during the default Ubuntu installation and are found in
/usr/lib/xorg/modules/drivers/. The enabled graphic card is listed in the
/etc/X11/xorg.conf file, under the Device section. For example:

```
Section "Device"
        Identifier      "ATI Technologies, Inc. Rage 128 RL/VR AGP"
        Driver          "ati"
        Option          "UseFBDev"              "true"
EndSection
```

This specifies the use of the ati driver found in /usr/lib/xorg/modules/
drivers/ati_drv.so. If you want to change the driver, then you
will need to change the xorg.conf configuration and restart the
X-server.

Enabling OpenGL

The Open Graphics Library (OpenGL) provides a set of extensions for accelerated 2D and 3D rendering. Without this extension, some graphics must be
explicitly drawn by each application, leading to slower graphic rendering.

Some video card drivers support OpenGL without any additional steps.
For example, if you have an Intel, SiS, or Matrox video card, then OpenGL

may already be supported and enabled. However, if you have an NVIDIA or ATI video card, then you might get lucky with a standard package install; otherwise, you will need to change drivers and install the accelerated graphics extensions.

To tell if you need to enable OpenGL, use the `glxinfo` command and you'll see the output identifying whether OpenGL's direct rendering is enabled:

```
$ glxinfo | grep "direct rendering"
direct rendering: No
```

If it says yes, then OpenGL is already enabled. However, if it says no, then either OpenGL is not supported, or you need to enable it.

Automated Driver Selection

Beginning with Hardy Heron (8.04), the Envy package has been available for automating ATI and NVIDIA driver installation. To run Envy, use the following commands:

```
sudo apt-get install envyng-gtk
sudo envyng -g
```

Envy allows you to automatically select the correct drivers for your video card. The good news is that it works for most ATI and NVIDIA cards. The bad news is that, when it fails, either you need to manually install the drivers, or you have an unsupported configuration.

WARNING Some NVIDIA drivers do not work with some default Ubuntu kernels. For example, the generic Desktop kernel does not support more than 3 GB of RAM, but it works well with the NVIDIA GeForce 8500 GT video card. However, if you install the Ubuntu server kernel for accessing more than 3 GB of RAM (see Chapter 8), then you also get a Xen-enabled kernel for virtual machines. The NVIDIA GeForce 8500 driver does not work with Xen-enabled kernels. As a result, you can either access your entire RAM, or you can take advantage of your video card, but you can't do both unless you recompile your kernel from scratch—with the physical address extension (PAE) for extended RAM support and without Xen.

Manually Enabling OpenGL

1. To enable OpenGL, make sure that your video card is either NVIDIA or ATI. Use the `lspci` command to list your video cards. If the result does not say "nVidia" or "ATI" (in lowercase, uppercase, or mixed case), then you do not need these steps.

```
$ lspci | grep -i -e Display -e VGA   # on an iMac
0000:00:10.0 Display controller: ATI Technologies Inc Rage 128
RL/VR AGP
```

```
$ lspci | grep -i -e Display -e VGA   # on a PC
0000:01:00.0 VGA compatible controller: nVidia Corporation NV18
[GeForce4 MX 4000 AGP 8x] (rev c1)
```

Not every ATI and NVIDIA card is supported. Make sure that the model listed by the `lspci` command matches a supported card:

- ATI must be a 9*xxx* series (or higher), or have TV-out support. Your monitor must also support at least 60 Hz.

- NVIDIA supports most GeForce, nForce, and Quadro models with AGP, TV-out, and flat panel displays.

- NVIDIA supports older TNT, TNT2, and GeForce models with legacy drivers.

NOTE The two example `lspci` commands show an ATI Rage 128 video card in an iMac system that is not supported, and a NVIDIA GeForce4 MX 4000 card in a PC system with AGP that is supported.

2. Back up your `xorg.conf` file. If anything does not work you'll need this backup copy to return to a working display:

```
sudo cp /etc/X11/xorg.conf /etc/X11/xorg.conf.bak
```

3. Regardless of your video card, you will need to install the restricted drivers for your kernel (if they are not already installed):

```
sudo apt-get install linux-restricted-modules-`uname -r`
```

At this point, you must perform some card-specific configurations.

If You Have an ATI Video Card . . .

1. Install the ATI drivers:

```
sudo apt-get install xorg-driver-fglrx fglrx-control
```

2. Run these commands to configure your `xorg.conf` file:

```
sudo aticonfig—initial
sudo aticonfig—overlay-type=Xv
```

3. Reconfigure the X-server:

```
sudo dpkg-reconfigure xserver-xorg
```

This auto-detects your video card. Be sure to select fglrx and not ATI. For the remaining prompts (and there are a lot of prompts), you can just press Enter and select the default values. (Since you're already running the X-server, the default values work.)

4. Check the `/etc/X11/xorg.conf` settings and make sure that the driver in the Device section says: `Driver "fglrx"`.

5. Restart your X-server. You can do this by rebooting or by logging out and then pressing Ctrl+Alt+Backspace.

If all goes well, then your display will start. Otherwise, you should be stuck at a text prompt—skip to the "Debugging X-Windows" section for resolving the problem.

If You Have an NVIDIA Card . . .

1. Install the NVIDIA drivers for the current or legacy card. *Do not install both.* (Actually, `apt-get` will not allow you to install both.)

   ```
   sudo apt-get install nvidia-glx nvidia-kernel-common
   ```

   If you have a legacy card, use:

   ```
   sudo apt-get install nvidia-glx-legacy nvidia-kernel-common
   ```

2. If you previously made changes to your `xorg.conf` file, then make sure it is archived:

   ```
   md5sum /etc/X11/xorg.conf | sudo tee /var/lib/x11/xorg.conf
   ```

   NOTE While archiving `xorg.conf` is always a good thing, the NVIDIA configuration script will not continue if it is not archived.

3. Configure the driver:

   ```
   sudo nvidia-glx-config enable
   ```

4. Edit `xorg.conf` and check the Device section. There are two types of NVIDIA drivers. The "nv" driver is provided by the open source community. The "nvidia" driver is the manufacturer's official driver. To enable OpenGL, the driver should be `nvidia`, not `nv`. If it says `nv`, then change it to `nvidia`.

5. When you are editing `xorg.conf`, add the following line to the Device section to disable the NVIDIA splash screen (and speed up the boot time):

   ```
   Option "NoLogo" "true"
   ```

   The full Device section should look something similar to this example (although your video card model and BusID may be different):

   ```
   Section "Device"
       Identifier  "NVIDIA Corporation NV18 [GeForce4 MX 4000 AGP 8x]"
       Driver      "nvidia"
       BusID       "PCI:1:0:0"
       Option      "NoLogo"        "true"
   EndSection
   ```

6. Restart your X-server. You can do this by rebooting or by logging out and then pressing Ctrl+Alt+Backspace.

If all goes well, then your display will start. Otherwise, you should be stuck at a text prompt—skip to the next section, "Debugging X-Windows," for information on resolving the problem.

Debugging X-Windows

When X-Windows fails, it either drops you at a text prompt, or leaves the screen blank. In the worst case, X-Windows will hang and ignore the keyboard; you will need to reboot the computer in order to get to a text login prompt. The X-Windows system logs everything—including cryptic error messages—in `/var/log/Xorg.0.log`. Check the log for a place to start debugging. Fortunately, problems usually fall into one of four categories:

1. Human error. Make sure you didn't type something wrong. The `xorg.conf` file is not very forgiving of typographical errors.

2. Your card is not supported.

3. You installed multiple, conflicting drivers.

4. Your card was not recognized properly.

The first problem can be resolved by checking everything that you entered into the `xorg.conf` file. The other items are a little more complicated and are covered in the next subsections.

Putting Things Back

If your card is not supported or your changes were not correct, then put back your `xorg.conf` file. You should be able to run `startx` from the command line. This will start the graphics system and let you know if you put it back correctly.

> **TIP** Hopefully, you made a backup of `/etc/X11/xorg.conf`. If you didn't, then all is not lost. Some drivers make backups automatically when they install. Look in the `/etc/X11/` directory for files like `xorg.conf~` and `xorg.conf.backup`. These are probably functional configuration files. In the worst case, you can run `sudo dpkg-reconfigure xserver-xorg` to generate a new configuration file.

Although `startx` is good for running the server and debugging the `xorg.conf` file, it runs the server from your text login. This means that logging out or shutting down from the graphical desktop will return you to your text command prompt; it will not actually log you out or reboot the system. To get the automatic login working, use:

```
sudo stop gdm
sudo start gdm
```

On older systems that don't use Upstart, like Dapper Drake (6.06 LTS), use:

```
sudo /etc/init.d/gdm restart
```

Debugging the Wrong Driver

Usually people will blindly install one driver and, if it does not work, then try the other. (OK, I admit that I've done that.) If you're going to do this, be sure to remove the unused driver first; otherwise, neither driver will work.

- To remove the ATI drivers, use:

  ```
  sudo apt-get remove xorg-driver-fglrx fglrx-control
  ```

- To unconfigure the NVIDIA drivers, use:

  ```
  sudo /usr/bin/nvidia-installer—uninstall
  sudo apt-get remove nvidia-glx        # for current cards
  sudo apt-get remove nvidia-glx-legacy # for legacy cards
  ```

- To copy back your `xorg.conf file`, use:

  ```
  sudo cp /etc/X11/xorg.conf.bak /etc/X11/xorg.conf
  ```

- Restart your X-Windows system by either rebooting or logging out and pressing Ctrl+Alt+Backspace.

Forcing Drivers to Install

For ATI, some cards are claimed to be unsupported even though they will work. You can change the PCI ID and try to fake the driver into thinking the card is supported. For example, the Radeon Mobility 9600 (found in laptops) is reported as unsupported by the ATI drivers. This card uses PCI ID 4e53 (found using the `lspci -n` command). You can add a line to the `xorg.conf` Device section to specify a supported ID (for example, 4e50—the Radeon 9600 M10—is supported and seems to be compatible with the 4e53). For example:

```
Section "Device"
  Identifier "ATI"
  Driver     "fglrx"
  ChipID     0x4e50
  ..
EndSection
```

The full list of PCI IDs is found in `/usr/share/misc/pci.ids`. Vendors usually follow a consistent ID convention, so the 4e50, 4e51, 4e52, and 4e53 are all ATI Radeon cards. If one does not work, try another. However, forcing an ATI ID onto a non-ATI card (for example, Cirrus GD 5440) has virtually no chance of working.

Adjusting Video Position

Many newer computers come with flat LCD displays. This means that the picture is usually centered. (And if it isn't, then there should be an auto or manual adjustment setting.) However, CRT monitors are not always centered. The desktop may appear slightly cut off at the top, bottom, left, or right. (In the case of some monitors, more than a little may cut off.) Some video card and monitor combinations permit the X-server to adjust the screen—shifting the width, height, and position.

As of this writing, xvidmode is broken and has been so for over two years, since the Xorg 1.4 server. X-Windows is moving to a newer, automated system but xvidmode has not been updated. One way to check this is with xrandr. If xrandr -v reports version 1.2 or later, then your X-server is newer than xvidmode, which only supports version 1.1. In order to align the screen, you'll need an ugly hack that uses the broken xvidmode and the new xrandr.

The video screen is adjusted by altering the scan-line frequencies. The xvidtune program allows you to adjust the screen's width, height, and position by tuning the horizontal and vertical scan frequencies.

The xvidtune program does not actually perform the system changes (although it does allow you to test the settings). Instead, it generates code that can be inserted into /etc/X11/xorg.conf for adjusting the monitor automatically.

1. Open a terminal and run the xvidtune program. This will display a warning about possible damage to your monitor (see Figure 10-3). Take this warning seriously, then smile, and click OK.

NOTE You will need to run **xvidtune** from a terminal window (for example, Applications ➪ Accessories ➪ Terminal). This is because the final output from **xvidtune** will be printed in the terminal window.

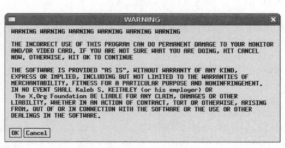

Figure 10-3: The xvidtune warning screen

2. The xvidtune menu may not be pretty, but it is functional (see Figure 10-4). At the top of the window are the actual horizontal and vertical scan synchronization values used to denote the start of an analog video scan. I usually ignore these. The more important items are the buttons. These enable you to adjust the screen.

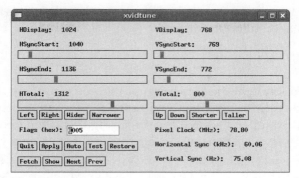

Figure 10-4: The xvidtune configuration settings

The xvidtune adjustment options are:

- **Left, Right, Up, Down**—These options shift the screen's position.

- **Wider, Narrower, Shorter, Taller**—These options adjust the screen's width and height.

- **Test**—This temporarily applies the changes to the screen, so you can see what it looks like.

- **Auto**—Rather than making adjustments and clicking Test, you can click Auto to automatically apply the changes as you make them. These changes are not permanent, but they allow you to see what they will look like.

- **Restore**—If you think you really screwed up, you can click this button to return to the current settings.

- **Show**—This displays the current settings in the text console where you started running xvidtune.

- **Quit**—This exits the program. You can also type q to quit.

3. Make your adjustments. Use Test or Auto to view your changes. If the Test and Auto buttons work to view the settings, then you can skip to Step 8. Otherwise, continue on to the ugly hack (Steps 4–7).

TIP On some monitors, clicking Left or Right may really swing the display over to the side. Before making adjustments, move the xvidtune window into the middle of the screen. This way, it will not accidentally go out of view.

4. Since the "Test" or "Auto" buttons display an error about an unsupported configuration, you will need to test the scan-line frequencies by hand. This requires xrandr. In the xvidtune window, click Show. This will

display a line in your terminal window that describes the frequency settings. It should look similar to:

```
"1280x1024"  135.00  1280 1288 1432 1688  1024 1025 1028 1066
                                      +hsync +vsync
```

5. The quoted string at the beginning of the frequency line is just a unique name. Change it to be something unique, and not just the screen resolution. For example, I shifted the screen right and renamed the string to "1280x1024_shift". Then use xrandr to add this as a new video mode.

```
xrandr—newmode "1280x1024_shift"  135.00  1280 1288 1432 1688  \
1024 1025 1028 1066 +hsync +vsync
```

If you run xrandr with no parameters, then it will list the new mode at the end of the listing.

```
$ xrandr
Screen 0: minimum 320 x 200, current 1280 x 1024, maximum 1280 x 1280
VGA1 disconnected
DVI0 disconnected
VGA2 connected 1280x1024+0+0 338mm x 270mm
   1280x1024      60.0 +   75.0*     59.9
   1152x864       75.0
   1024x768       74.9     75.1      60.0
   832x624        74.6
   800x600        75.0     74.9      60.3
   640x480        75.0     74.8      60.0
   720x400        70.1
1280x1024_shift (0x59)   135.0MHz
    h: width  1280 start 1288 end 1432 total 1688 skew   0
        clock  80.0KHz
    v: height 1024 start 1025 end 1028 total 1066
        clock  75.0Hz
```

6. Assign the mode to a video display. The displays are provided by xrandr at the beginning of the list, with capital letters. In the example, my displays are VGA1, VGA2, and DVI0; only VGA2 is currently connected. The addmode option assigns the new mode to the display.

```
$ xrandr—addmode VGA2 "1280x1024_shift"
$ xrandr
Screen 0: minimum 320 x 200, current 1024 x 768, maximum 1280 x 1280
VGA1 disconnected
DVI0 disconnected
VGA2 connected 1024x768+0+0 338mm x 270mm
   1280x1024      60.0 +   75.0      59.9
   1152x864       75.0
   1024x768       74.9*    75.1      60.0
   832x624        74.6
```

```
800x600        75.0    74.9    60.3
640x480        75.0    74.8    60.0
720x400        70.1
1280x1024_shift    75.0
```

7. Now you can enable the mode to test it. I like to use a small delay and then put the screen back to a known-good video mode, just to make sure I don't screw up the display.

```
$ xrandr -s "1280x1024_shift"; sleep 10; xrandr -s "1280x1024"
```

If this is not a good enough adjustment, then you can repeat Steps 4–7. Just be sure to give each mode a new name every time you try it.

8. After finding a good adjustment setting, click Show in xvidtune. The terminal window should display a line with your settings. It should look similar to:

```
"1280x1024"  135.00   1280 1288 1432 1688   1024 1025 1028 1066
                                         +hsync +vsync
```

This line lists the resolution (in quotes) and the scan line settings.

9. Edit /etc/X11/xorg.conf and scroll down to the Monitor section. Add a ModeLine option that includes the output from xvidtune. The PreferredMode option tells the server to enable this mode first. For example, mine (including a very long line that wraps on the screen) looks like:

```
Section "Monitor"
    Identifier "MyDisplay"
    ModeLine   "1280x1024_shift"  135.00   1280 1288 1432 1688   1024
    1025 1028 1066 +hsync +vsync
    Option "PreferredMode" "1280x1024_shift"
EndSection
```

10. Save your changes, log out, and restart the X-server by using Ctrl+Alt+Backspace.

TIP If you use multiple screen resolutions, then run xvidtune *after* changing each resolution. You can have multiple ModeLine entries in the xorg.conf file—as long as they all have different resolutions.

Improving Performance

When you have a slow display, everything else seems slower. Much of this may be because the display is consuming CPU, delaying commands, and monopolizing memory resources. Fortunately, there are a few things you can do to improve the display's performance.

■ **Install the accelerated drivers**—The OpenGL video cards, including the NVIDIA and ATI accelerated 3D drivers mentioned in the Enabling OpenGL section, significantly improve performance. If you have the option to install either of these, then do it!

■ **Disable the Nautilus background**—Nautilus is used to place icons on the background (see Chapter 2). If this is disabled, then memory and CPU resources are freed up. Otherwise, Nautilus may need to redraw the background every time something on the screen changes. To disable it, use:

```
gconftool-2-type bool \
 -set /apps/nautilus/preferences/show_desktop FALSE
```

■ **Disable Gnome background images**—Drawing a background takes time and memory. If you don't need a background image, then turn it off. This can be done either by the background applet (System ⇨ Preferences ⇨ Desktop Background, select No Wallpaper) or with gconftool-2.

```
gconftool-2-type string \
 -set /desktop/gnome/background/picture_options none
```

■ **Disable thumbnails**—Nautilus can generate thumbnail icons and preview audio. If Nautilus opens a directory with lots of images in it, the overhead from creating thumbnails can be very noticeable (especially on slow systems). To disable previews, use:

```
gconftool-2-type string \
 -set /apps/nautilus/preferences/show_image_thumbnails never
```

TIP If you want some thumbnail icons, use `local_only` instead of `never`. This gives you icons in local folders but disables them for networked file systems. This way, you don't need to wait for the network to transfer all of the images—an action required for making thumbnail images.

■ **Disable icons in menus**—By default, every menu item includes an icon. While these icons are cached, they can take time to load (especially on a slow system). You can disable the icons by using:

```
gconftool-2-type bool \
 -set /desktop/gnome/interface/menus_have_icons FALSE
```

ACCESSIBILITY

Not everyone optimizes the display for cool graphics and speed. People with sight disabilities can optimize the display for their own needs. By default, Ubuntu includes many themes for addressing accessibility. For example, under System ⇨ Preferences ⇨ Appearance (or Theme), you can select many different high- and low-contrast configurations. Even without my glasses, I can read the screen using the large print themes, without being inches from the monitor.

For people who have little or no sight, the default Ubuntu installation supports text readers and Braille displays. The Gnome-Orca package is installed by default and includes text-to-speech and other accessibility options.

1. Configure Orca. At a terminal, run `orca`. It will ask you questions such as:

   ```
   Use key echo? Enter y or n:
   ```

   Orca supports some text-to-speech systems and can use your sound card.

2. After it is configured, Orca will finish tuning Gnome and create a `$HOME/.orca` directory. You will need to log out and log back in for the changes to take effect.

Switching Screen Savers

Ever since Dapper Drake, the default screen saver has been `gnome-screensaver`. (Prior to Dapper, Ubuntu Hoary and Breezy used `xscreensaver`.) Although `gnome-screensaver` does the basic job of preventing the screen from being burned in, it has some serious limitations. For example:

- The Gnome Screensaver is missing many of the options found in other screen savers. For examples, many screen savers have options for changing the size, number, and complexity of elements found in the screen saver. The Gnome Screensaver offers no options.

- The Gnome Screensaver sometimes fails to start. For example, if you leave the mouse on a pull-down menu, then the screen saver won't activate. But if you return after 30 minutes and move the mouse off the menu, then it will start.

- The Gnome Screensaver also has the bad habit of turning on while applications are running full-screen. When I first upgraded to Dapper, I started playing my favorite game: `bzflag`. This is a full-screen networked tank game. Ten minutes into the game, the screen would fade to black! At first, I thought it was the game, then I realized that it was the screen saver. The game was intercepting all keyboard and mouse inputs. As a result, the screen saver thought the computer was inactive.

While I could write a script around these problems, I opted for a better solution: replace `gnome-screensaver` with `xscreensaver`. This gives me all the missing functionality, as well as a screen saver that was game-aware. This change requires a couple of steps:

1. Install `xscreensaver`:

```
sudo apt-get install xscreensaver
```

2. Stop the running `gnome-screensaver`:

```
sudo killall gnome-screensaver
```

3. Disable the Gnome Screensaver:

```
gconftool-2—type boolean \
  —set /apps/gnome_settings_daemon/screensaver/start_screensaver false
```

WARNING With Dapper Drake, uninstalling `gnome-screensaver` was bad: it had dependencies that would remove the entire desktop! With Hardy, Jaunty, and Karmic, `sudo apt-get remove gnome-screensaver` works, but it does not remove all of the Gnome hooks. I recommend leaving it installed but deactivated.

4. Configure `xscreensaver` to start when you log in. Go to System ➪ Preferences ➪ Startup Applications (or System ➪ Preferences ➪ Sessions ➪ Startup Programs). Click Add and enter:

```
xscreensaver -nosplash
```

Then click Close. This makes the new screen saver start when you log in.

5. Change the menu preferences so that they use `xscreensaver`:

- Right-click the System menu and select Edit Menus. This brings up the Menu Editor applet.
- In the Menu Editor, scroll to the bottom of the left window, and click Preferences.
- In the right window, scroll down and right-click Screensaver (see Figure 10-5). Select Properties from the item menu.
- If you only see one Screensaver item listed, then change the command from `gnome-screensaver` to `xscreensaver-demo`. (See Figure 10-6).
- If you see two Screensaver items listed, then check the Properties on each and disable (uncheck) the `gnome-screensaver` item. Only `xscreensaver` should be checked.
- Close all of the Menu Editor windows.

6. As root, edit the file `/usr/share/applications/gnome-screensaver -preferences.desktop`. Near the bottom you will see the line, `Exec=gnome-screensaver-preferences`. Change this line to `Exec= xscreensaver-demo`. Also, comment out (or delete) the following lines:

```
X-GNOME-Bugzilla-Bugzilla=GNOME
X-GNOME-Bugzilla-Product=gnome-screensaver
X-GNOME-Bugzilla-Component=general
X-Ubuntu-Gettext-Domain=gnome-screensaver
```

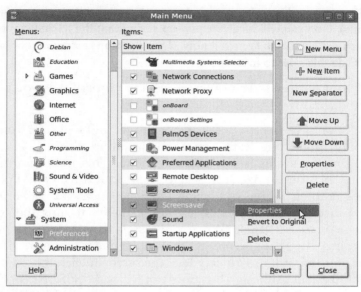

Figure 10-5: The Menu Editor properties for the Screensaver item

Figure 10-6: The properties for the Screensaver menu item

WARNING If you use `sudo apt-get upgrade` (or the automatic upgrade) and refresh the screen saver package, then you may need to make this change again.

7. Make the screen saver daemon run when you login. Open the startup application list (under System ➪ Preferences as Startup Applications or Sessions). If a screen saver exists, remove or disable it. Add a new screen saver that runs `xscreensaver -nosplash`.

8. Open the screen saver preferences (System ➾ Preferences ➾ Screensaver), and deselect all of the grayed-out Screensaver options. If you do not disable them, then the default random screen saver may try to run missing screen savers, resulting in errors.

NOTE If you open the preferences before starting the screen saver (per these instructions), then you will receive a pop-up saying that the XScreenSaver daemon is not running. Click OK to launch it now. If the daemon is already running, then you won't see this pop-up message.

9. Select your desired screen saver, adjust the properties as you see fit, and close the window.

Now, `xscreensaver` is your default screen saver and will start from bootup. I have only found one limitation from installing `xscreensaver`: it does not work from the system's Lock Screen menu. This menu normally contains options including Log Out, Restart, and Shutdown. The Lock Screen option does nothing when you install `xscreensaver`. To get around this limitation, I installed an applet on the top panel that runs the command: `xscreensaver-command -lock`. (When you install `xscreensaver`, it even gives you an icon in `/usr/share/pixmaps/` that looks like a monitor with a flame coming out of it.) In order to quickly lock the screen, I click the `xscreensaver` icon on my top panel. Although this does not fix the Lock Screen option in the system menu, I find it is more convenient to click-and-lock rather than drill down through menus in order to lock the screen.

Adding New Screen Savers

The default Ubuntu installation includes some screen savers that are not installed under `xscreensaver`. For example, Lattice (my favorite GL screen saver) is not installed by default. To install Lattice, you'll need an OpenGL video driver (see the section on "Enabling OpenGL"). However, non-GL screen savers can also be added with the following steps:

1. As root, edit `/etc/X11/app-defaults/XScreenSaver`. This file lists all of the screen savers that `xscreensaver` knows about.

2. Search for `fliptext`—this is another screen saver that *does* exist. You'll use it as a template.

3. Duplicate the line and change `fliptext` to `lattice`. Keep the `GL:` since Lattice is a GL screen saver.

```
GL:                     fliptext -root              \n\
GL:                     lattice -root               \n\
```

4. Search further down for `fliptext` (there will be a second line). Duplicate this line and change `fliptext` and `FlipText` to `lattice` and `Lattice`:

```
*hacks.fliptext.name:        FlipText
*hacks.lattice.name:         Lattice
```

5. Save your changes.

When you are all done, log out and restart the desktop by using Ctrl+Alt+Backspace. When the graphics comes back up, it will be using your new screen saver and Lattice will be installed. You can select this screen saver by using System ➪ Preferences ➪ Screensaver. If you followed the instructions in the previous section on installing `xscreensaver`, then this will run `xscreensaver-demo` and allow you to select Lattice—the interlocking rings.

Animating the Desktop Background

The default Ubuntu desktop can either be a solid color or a static image. With a few simple scripts, you can change the background image or color (see Chapter 2), but this isn't real animation. The secret to really animating the desktop is to run an X-Windows application that draws the background. Here's an example where the background is drawn by a screen saver:

1. You'll need to tell Nautilus to not draw the desktop. This means that you will lose all your desktop icons, but who needs icons when you can animate the desktop!

   ```
   gconftool-2 -s -t bool /apps/nautilus/preferences/show_desktop false
   ```

2. Start the X-application that will draw the background. In this case, I'll use the Lattice screen saver, tell it to draw the full background (`-root` window), render rings that look like circuits (as opposed to doughnuts, brass, etc.), and consume fewer CPU cycles (`-n` and `nice`). The other options specify the rendering rate (20 frames per second), motion speed (`-e 1`), field of view (`-o 10`), and a background fog (`-f`). All of these options are detailed in the man page for `lattice`.

   ```
   nice /usr/lib/xscreensaver/lattice—root—circuits -x 20 -e 1 -o 10 -f
   ```

This creates an animated background with moving rings (see Figure 10-7).

NOTE Lattice is a GL screen saver. If your video driver does not have GL support, Lattice will not work. In addition, if your OpenGL video driver does not have direct rendering enabled, then Lattice will consume all of your CPU resources, making the system sluggish. You can always choose a different screen saver that is better supported by your display.

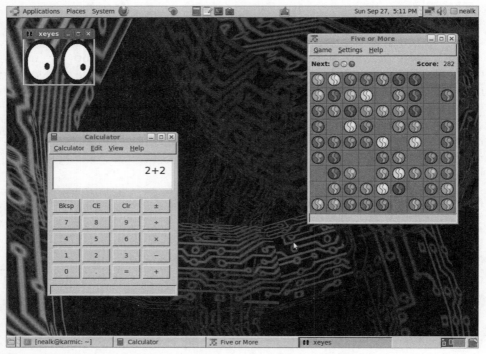

Figure 10-7: An animated background using the Lattice screen saver

Any application that can render content to the root window can be used as a background image. However, there are a few caveats:

- **Applications do not store the images behind them**—As a result, a background that does not redraw the screen (for example, /usr/lib/xscreensaver/sonar -root) can have large gaps when a window is moved or closed. The best backgrounds render the entire screen at least 5 times per second—20 times per second is better.

- **Some background applications consume lots of resources**—For example, running /usr/lib/xscreensaver/colorfire-root can noticeably slow down your system. Good backgrounds consume few resources, and many screen savers have options to lower their resource consumption.

- **As funny as it may sound, moving backgrounds can give some people a sense of motion sickness**—Although sonar probably won't cause a problem, the constant motion from `lattice` can be both fun and not so fun. Consider testing the background before you make it permanent.

Disabling Animated Backgrounds

If you decided to turn off the animated background, you'll need to follow a few steps:

1. Kill the background animation. For example, if you are running `lattice`, then use `killall lattice`. This will stop the background from being drawn. However, it won't put back your default background and moving windows will start erasing parts of the background.

2. Tell Nautilus that it is OK to draw the background.

   ```
   gconftool-2 -t bool /apps/nautilus/preferences/show_desktop -s true
   ```

3. Even though Nautilus now has permission to draw the background, you still need to force it to redraw the background once. You can do this by logging out and logging back in, or running: `nautilus -q; nautilus`. This will quit Nautilus and—if it does not automatically restart—start it.

Configuring Dual Monitors

The graphical display has a limited amount of screen real estate. As more windows are opened, space on the desktop becomes an issue. Using the Workplace Switcher (see Chapter 9) is a good start, but eventually you will find yourself rapidly switching back and forth between desktops as you try to use two applications at once. For serious power users, one monitor is usually not enough. Ubuntu offers a couple of different options for adding multiple monitors:

■ **Two-headed systems**—One computer can have multiple graphics cards. This is an ideal solution for people with extra hardware. Alternately, some graphics cards are capable of driving more than one monitor.

■ **Shared desktops**—There is no reason why all of the desktops need to run the same operating system. This is a must-have for anyone with a need to use Windows, Mac OS X, and Linux at the same time.

In previous Ubuntu versions (Dapper Drake and earlier), there was a third option: networked desktops. Using Xdmx, the same desktop could span multiple computers over the network. While two-headed systems and shared desktops work very well with all versions of Ubuntu, the same cannot be said for networked desktops. Networked desktop support broke in 2007 because of an incompatibility between Xdmx and X Server 1.4 (and later). You can find your X-server version at the beginning of `/var/log/Xorg.0.log`.

Using Two Heads

If your computer has multiple video ports, then you can frequently use them to drive two different monitors. Although most workstation computers don't have multiple video cards installed, you can always plug in an extra one. However, many laptops include two video sources: one for the LCD display and one for an external monitor. In some cases, these video ports can be configured to work together, forming one large display, while other laptops must display the same thing on both ports.

> **NOTE** The computer display is commonly called a *head*. A computer with two displays is a *dual-headed* system. Many servers are *headless*, since they have no display attached.

There are three ways to configure a dual-headed system. The first is with the graphical display setting (available since Hardy Heron). The second combines monitors by using TwinView. However, TwinView is strictly limited to NVIDIA video cards. The more universal option is Xinerama.

Using the Graphical Display Configuration

With early versions of Ubuntu, such as Dapper Drake (6.06 LTS), there were only manual options for configuring multiple heads. However, Hardy Heron (8.04 LTS) and later releases have an intelligent X-windows server and graphical monitor configuration option. This makes setup trivial. As long as the second display already has video drivers loaded, you can just plug in the second monitor and it will work.

1. Run xrandr and see if there are multiple monitors listed. They will be labeled "connected" (a monitor is attached) or "disconnected" (no monitor . . . yet). To use the graphical configuration, there must be multiple video adapters listed. In this example, there are two: VGA1, DVI0, and VGA2.

   ```
   $ xrandr
   Screen 0: minimum 320 x 200, current 1280 x 1024, maximum 1280 x 1280
   VGA1 disconnected
   LVDS1 connected 1280x800+0+0 286mm x 179mm
   ```

2. Connect the second monitor.

3. Open the Display configuration applet. It will be under the menu System ⇨ Preferences menu as either Display or Screen Resolution. (See Figure 10-8.) If you have a Display icon in your top panel, then you can also use it to configure displays.

TIP Newer Ubuntu versions, such as Jaunty and Karmic, also display the screen's name in the top corner of each monitor. This way, you can quickly tell which real monitor corresponds to which icon.

WARNING Don't be surprised if the screen flashes for a moment and some of your open applications suddenly vanish. As soon as the monitor is detected, it is used and the desktop is extended. Applications are moved to the leftmost monitor, which may be the new monitor.

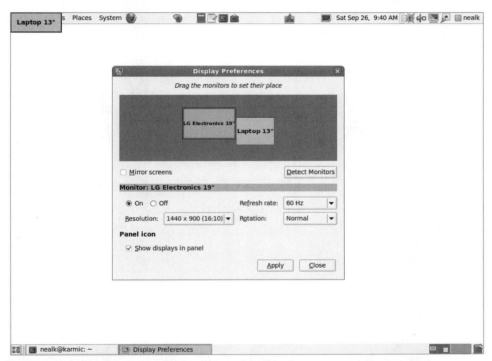

Figure 10-8: The Display configuration applet, showing two monitors attached

4. Two monitors should be displayed in the applet. You can drag them around to configure their relative positions (left, right, top, etc.).

5. When you are all done, click Apply and close the configuration window.

Monitors do not need to be the same sizes or even perfectly aligned. This can make screen shots very interesting. Screen shot portions that are not covered by the desktop appear as black rectangles. (See Figure 10-9.)

Using Two Heads with TwinView

If you have an NVIDIA graphics card *and* it supports two monitors, then you can use TwinView to combine both monitors into one desktop. TwinView is an NVIDIA-specific graphics extension for managing multiple monitors.

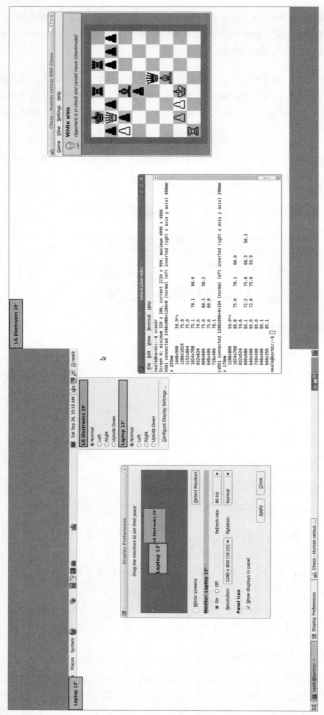

Figure 10-9: A full-screen screen shot from Karmic Koala shows offset monitors, top-corner monitor labels, and black regions with no desktop

1. Create a backup of your working `xorg.conf` file:

```
sudo cp /etc/X11/xorg.conf /etc/X11/xorg.conf.orig
```

2. Tell X-Windows about the second monitor. In the file `/etc/X11/xorg.conf` is a section titled `Device`. This contains the video card attributes. Add in TwinView options for the second monitor. For example:

```
Section "Device"
    Identifier   "NVIDIA Corporation NV18 [GeForce4 MX 4000 AGP 8x]"
    Driver       "nvidia"
    BusID        "PCI:1:0:0"
    Option       "TwinView"
    Option       "MetaModes"  "1280x1024,1280x1024; 1024x768,1024x768"
    Option       "TwinViewOrientation"    "RightOf"
    Option       "ConnectedMonitor"       "CRT,CRT"
    Option       "SecondMonitorHorizSync"         "UseEdidFreqs"
    Option       "SecondMonitorVertRefresh"       "UseEdidFreqs"
#   Option       "SecondMonitorHorizSync"         "24-80"
#   Option       "SecondMonitorVertRefresh"       "50-75"
EndSection
```

These options include pairs of video resolutions (one for each monitor), the location of the second monitor (right of the first), and the monitor scan rates (either using defaults or specifying range).

3. Save your new `xorg.conf` file and restart the X-server. Log out and use Ctrl+Alt+Backspace to restart the server. If it does not come up, then refer to the section "Debugging X-Windows" earlier in this chapter. (If it does come up, then you're done and you should have two working displays.)

Using Two Heads with Xinerama

If your system has two different video ports, then you can use Xinerama to link them into one virtual display. Before you can use two monitors, you will need to make sure that the computer actually has two video devices. Use the `lspci` command to list all display devices:

```
lspci -x | grep -i -e VGA -e DISPLAY
```

If only one display controller is listed, then you won't be able to use this option. However, if you see multiple controllers, then you can configure your X-server to use both cards. This requires editing the `/etc/X11/xorg.conf` file.

1. Create a backup of your working `xorg.conf` file.

```
sudo cp /etc/X11/xorg.conf /etc/X11/xorg.conf.orig
```

2. Tell X-Windows about the second monitor. In the file `/etc/X11/xorg.conf` is a section titled `Monitor`. This contains a unique identifier and monitor attributes. Create a second one for your second monitor. For example:

```
Section "Monitor">
        # Default monitor
        Identifier      "LCD"
        Option          "DPMS"
EndSection
Section "Monitor"
        # Second monitor that I added
        Identifier      "CRT"
        Option          "DPMS"
        HorizSync       31.5—57.0
        VertRefresh     50-100
        # You may want to add ModeLine items later
EndSection
```

3. Each monitor in the `xorg.conf` file may display different desktop screens. You need to tell X-Windows about the second screen. In the file `/etc/X11/xorg.conf` is a section titled `Screen`. This contains a unique identifier and information about the graphics modes. Create a second screen section with a different identifier for the second monitor. For example:

```
Section "Screen"
  # Define the first screen
  Identifier     "Default Screen"
  Device         "NVIDIA Corporation NV18 [GeForce4 MX 4000 AGP 8x]"
  Monitor "LCD"
  DefaultDepth  24
  BusID          "0000:1:0:0" # optional for distinguishing cards
  SubSection "Display"
    Depth        24
    Modes        "1024x768"
  EndSubSection
EndSection
Section "Screen"
  # Define the second screen
  Identifier     "Second Screen"
  Device "ATI Technologies, Inc. M9+ 5C63 [Radeon Mobility
9000 (AGP)]"
  Monitor        "CRT"
  DefaultDepth  24
  SubSection "Display"
    Depth        24
    Modes        "1280x1024"
  EndSubSection>
EndSection
```

NOTE Be sure the labels in your `Screen` section's `Monitor` lines match the unique identifiers from the `Monitor` sections. The `Device` name and option `BusID` value should match the results from the `lspci -x` command.

TIP Use the `BusID` option when you have two of the same type of video card in one computer. This distinguishes one card from the other.

4. In the `/etc/X11/xorg.conf` file is a section titled `ServerLayout`. This is where you will specify the geometry of the desktop. Using the screen identifiers, you need to specify the X-display number (for example, 0 for `DISPLAY=:0`, 1 for `DISPLAY=:1`, and so on) and their relationship in forming the desktop: Above, Below, LeftOf, or RightOf. For example, if my CRT monitor is located to the right of the LCD monitor, then I can use:

```
Section "ServerLayout"
        Identifier "Default Layout"
        Screen 0 "Default Screen"
        Screen 1 "Second Screen" RightOf
"Default Screen"
        InputDevice "Generic Keyboard"
        InputDevice "Configured Mouse"
        InputDevice "stylus"
"SendCoreEvents"
        InputDevice "cursor"
"SendCoreEvents"
        InputDevice "eraser"
"SendCoreEvents"
        InputDevice "Synaptics Touchpad"
EndSection
```

5. (Optional) If you want to have the displays linked as one desktop, rather than being treated as individual displays, then you will need to add a Xinerama option. This can be done by creating a section titled `ServerFlags` and setting the `Xinerama` option to true:

```
Section "ServerFlags"
        Option "Xinerama" "true"
EndSection
```

Alternately, you can add the `Option` line to the ServerLayout section.

6. If you have everything in place, then you should be able to save your new `xorg.conf` file and restart the X-server. Log out and use Ctrl+Alt+Backspace to restart the server. If it does not come up, then you'll need to go to the section in this chapter titled "Debugging X-Windows." (If it does come up, then you're done and you should have two working displays.)

XINERAMA

The big trick to making a multi-display desktop is the Xinerama extensions to X-Windows. This library is installed by default and allows you to chain multiple X-Windows displays into one large, virtual desktop. Without the flag, multiple displays can be used, but they do not appear as one coherent desktop.

How can you tell if you need the flag?

- If you cannot drag a window across the desktop, from one monitor to the other, then you need the Xinerama flag.

- If your graphical desktop (Gnome or KDE) replicates the background image and panels in every window, then you need the Xinerama flag.

Without the flag, each display is treated independently. With the flag, they are linked into one large desktop. However, as one large desktop all panels will only appear in the first display. This allows the secondary displays to be used for presentation projectors and not be cluttered with panels and widgets.

Using Two Computers with Different Desktops

In the corporate world, few Linux users work strictly with other Linux users. Usually you need to interact with a wide variety of Windows, Linux, and Unix users (and the rare OS/2 fanatic). I know plenty of people who run two computers, one Linux and one Windows, for full compatibility. The problem is that they spend a lot of time either transferring files or using shared hard drives. Taking output from a Linux program and pasting it into a Microsoft Outlook e-mail is definitely a multi-step solution. While Part II of this book (and Chapter 7 in particular) covered many of the ways to share information between different operating systems, there is another option.

Using a tool called Synergy, you can connect the desktops from completely different operating systems. Although you cannot drag applications off desktops, you can use one mouse and keyboard to navigate the linked desktops. And most importantly, you can share the clipboard. This way, you can copy text from a Linux application and paste it into a Windows program without a dozen steps.

Installing and configuring Synergy is much simpler than using Xdmx.

1. Install Synergy on each of the virtual desktop systems. Under Ubuntu, this is simply `sudo apt-get install synergy`. For other operating systems, you will need to visit `http://synergy2.sourceforge.net/`. They have precompiled binaries available for Windows (from Windows 95 to Windows XP and Windows ME), Linux, and Mac OS X (10.2 and higher). If you need other platforms, then you can download and compile the source code.

TIP The original Synergy project, found in the Ubuntu repositories, is functional but has not been updated since 2006. A revised project called Synergy+ has picked up where the original project left off (`code.google .com/p/synergy-plus`). This new project includes bug fixes and better support for today's operating systems. However, Synergy+ is not currently available from the Ubuntu repositories.

2. Synergy uses a central server as the primary system, and one or more clients for the shared desktops. The server is the system that has the mouse and keyboard, and this system uses a configuration file to manage the screen relationships. Synergy can even handle nonrectangular relationships and loops where, for example, moving off the far left takes you to the far right.

   ■ For an Ubuntu Synergy server (and Mac OS X server), the configuration consists of a text file that contains hostnames and relationships. My configuration file (Listing 10-3) has three hosts: a Windows client named willy, a Mac OS X named matt, and an Ubuntu system named udo. The computers are arranged with the Windows box (willy) sitting above the Ubuntu system (udo), and the Mac (matt) is to the right of the Ubuntu system.

   ■ For Windows systems, the Synergy server uses an application for specifying systems and relational positions (see Figure 10-10).

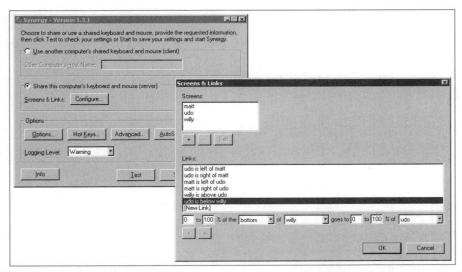

Figure 10-10: The Microsoft Windows Synergy server configuration window showing the same relationships as Listing 10-3

Regardless of the server's platform, the configuration has three main components. First, all of the possible clients are listed. Second, the links between the displays are defined. Finally, any special options can be listed. The links form the most complicated part; they define what happens when the mouse goes off the edge of a screen. You can specify left, right, above, and below relationships. Only defined relationships exist—nothing is assumed.

TIP Synergy links do not have to be symmetrical. For example, my system named matt may be located to the right of udo, but udo may not be left of matt. You can also create loops. For example, moving right from udo goes to matt, and continuing to the right can cycle back to udo.

WARNING Be sure to define both directions of a link. If I only define matt as being right of udo without specifying the return link (for example, udo is left of matt) then I will not be able to move the cursor back.

Listing 10-3: A Sample Synergy Configuration File (synergy.conf) with Three Systems

```
# The layout:
#    willy          —is above udo
#    udo    matt —matt is right of udo

section: screens
  # List every known client by name, and any special mappings
  udo:
  matt:
    meta = super  # this is a Mac and uses the command/super key
  willy:
end

section: links
  # Define every link relationship.
  # It does not need to by symmetrical!
  udo:
    right = matt
    left = matt # make a horizontal loop
    up = willy
  matt:
    left = udo
    right = udo # make a horizontal loop
  willy:
    down = udo
end

section: options
  # Make all screensavers turn on at the same time
  screenSaverSync = true
end
```

3. Check your client configuration. Synergy supports pretty much any Windows, Mac OS X, Linux, and Unix system. For X-Windows systems, be sure to have the XTEST extension enabled. You can check this with `xdpyinfo | grep XTEST`. This should display the word `XTEST`. For Windows and Mac systems, no special configurations are needed.

4. Start the client. Each client requires two elements. First, it needs to know the hostname of the server. Second, it needs a unique name that is listed in the server's configuration (in the `screens` section). By default, the name is the client's hostname. However, you can specify an alternate client name.

   ■ Under Linux, Unix, and Mac OS X, the client is `synergyc`. The server's name is specified on the command line. You can also include an optional name for the client. Following the preceding example, I used this command to connect my Mac (`matt`) to my Ubuntu server (`udo`).

   ```
   synergyc—name matt udo
   ```

   ■ Under Windows, use the Synergy client to specify the server's name and optional client's name (see Figure 10-11).

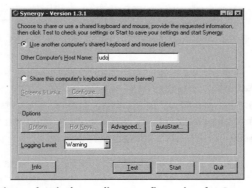

Figure 10-11: The Microsoft Windows client configuration for Synergy

5. Start the server. On Ubuntu, Mac OS X, and other Unix and Linux systems, the command is `synergys`. You specify the configuration file using:

   ```
   synergys—config synergy.conf
   ```

   On Windows systems, open the Synergy application, "select Share this computer's keyboard and mouse (server)," and click Start.

   TIP By default, `syngergys` and `synergyc` detach from the console and run in the background. To prevent the process from becoming a daemon, use `-f`. For example, `synergys -f --config synergy.conf`.

Although the server and clients all need to be started, the order does not really matter. Clients regularly poll the server until a connection is achieved.

As each system connects, the rules for the links are applied. Following the example, the cursor will be unable to move off the right side of udo until matt connects. When matt connects, the movement to the right will follow the established link.

NOTE Under Synergy, systems are either clients or a server. You do not need to run a server on the client.

When all of the clients connect to the server, you can start sharing desktops. Moving the mouse between windows allows you to set the focus for the keyboard. And most importantly: if you copy text from any desktop, then you can paste it into application on any other desktop.

TIP Synergy allows clients to connect and disconnect without notice. If you have systems that crash or reboots often, Synergy is definitely a good productivity solution since you can continue working while one part of the desktop is down.

Dual heads and Synergy do not need to be independent solutions. You can actually run two displays on one computer (a dual-headed solution) *and* use Synergy to link in desktops from other operating systems. The only limitation to your virtual desktop size becomes your physical desktop. Just how many monitors can your desk hold?

TIP Consider installing a Synergy client in a virtual machine, such as Qemu (see Chapter 7). This enables you to cut and paste between the virtual computer and the real desktop. In many cases, this is much more convenient than transferring data across a network or through a shared partition.

Summary

Although the basic Ubuntu desktop is good for beginners, its flexibility enables you to change it from good for most things to excellent for your specific requirements. Whether you simply want a different screen resolution, display adjustment, or something more complicated, there are hacks for customizing the system to fit your needs. Using these tweaks, you can enable cool screen savers, animated backgrounds, and even massively large desktops that span multiple screens and operating systems.

Securing Your System

In This Part

Locking Down Ubuntu

What's In This Chapter?

Understanding the default security model
How to encrypt files, directories, and disks
Making backups and removing temporary files

From a fresh install, Ubuntu starts as a very secure operating system. Without applying any security patches, it poses few risks from external and remote attackers. However, maintaining security after the installation is *your* responsibility. There are a couple of tricks you can do to keep your files and data secure. These include using Sudo for root privileges, GPG to encode messages, enabling encrypted files systems, and even log file and cache management. The basic Ubuntu system is safe enough, but with a few hacks, it can be made even safer.

Outside of the security field, many people view encryption and cache removal as a sign of guilt. The basic feeling is usually, "why are you covering your tracks if you have nothing to hide?" Just because you are encrypting data and cleaning temporary files does not mean you are doing anything illegal. Consider it like closing the curtains on your bedroom window—it means you want privacy, not that you're doing anything wrong. Privacy is also preventative. If your laptop gets stolen, do you want the thief to see all of your bank account information in your web cache? How about the source code from some big project you're working on? The same goes for your computer(s) at home. Thieves are just as likely to steal your desktop workstation as they are your TV and stereo.

Locking down your system limits the amount of damage a bad guy can cause. Furthermore, many of these preventative steps require no additional work beyond installation and initial configuration.

Understanding Ubuntu Security Defaults

Ubuntu installs using a basic security model that consists of no network accessible services, and no root logins. These basic principles ensure that a clean install cannot lead to a remotely compromised host. If you need a network service, then you will need to explicitly install it (see Chapter 13). Even after installing the network services, it usually takes a couple of steps to fully enable it.

There are a few basic steps to maintaining a secure Ubuntu system:

- **Don't use root**—The default Ubuntu installation does not assign a root password and you cannot log in as root. Instead, the default user account can use Sudo (see the next section) to run commands as root. Additional user accounts cannot even run Sudo unless they are given explicit permission. Restricting root access limits your ability to accidentally (or intentionally) screw up the entire operating system.

- **Limit network services**—Only enable services that you need. If you don't need a mail server, then don't install one. If you do not host web pages, then don't install a web server. Attackers can only exploit network services that are running on your system.

- **Use trusted software sources**—Chapter 5 describes how to modify `/etc/apt/sources.list` in order to change the supported repository list. The default repositories come from a trusted location: the four official Ubuntu repositories. However, there are literally hundreds of unofficial repositories. Installing software from an unknown and untrusted repository could result in the installation of hostile software. Don't change the default repository settings or install software from untrusted providers unless you know what you are doing. Remember: just because *they* say it is safe does not mean it really is safe.

- **Limit scripts**—web browsers, chat room software, and other programs can transfer potentially hostile software from the network, download files, and run programs. If you don't need this functionality, then disable it. For example, if you don't need Java in your web browser, then disable it (see Chapter 6).

TIP I used to recommend disabling JavaScript, but most popular web sites today require JavaScript for content and navigation. Instead, consider installing the

Firefox NoScript plugin. This plugin restricts which sites can use JavaScript and other web plugins.

- **Use strong passwords**—If you are the only person with physical access to your computer and you do not allow remote network access, then you can probably get away with having *abcd* or your pet's name as your password. (One of my home computers is usually logged in and the screen saver does not demand a password—this is as effective as having no password.) However, if you are in a corporate environment with many users, or enable remote access, or are at home with young kids (or cats) who like to press the delete button, then consider a strong password. Remote access and physical access attacks can use brute force approaches that include:

  - **Dictionary words**—If your password is found in a dictionary (English, French, Chinese, and so on) then it can be easily guessed.

  - **Words with numbers**—Simple word-number combinations, like *apple12* or *288cereal* can be easily guessed. The same goes for punctuation (*hello!* and *?what?*).

  - **Keyboard patterns**—Sequences like *asdfghjk* (adjacent keys on the keyboard) are very easy to guess.

  - **Common data**—License plates, dates (birthday, anniversary, and so on), kids names, and other types of public information are very easy to guess.

  - **Common letter substitutions**—Many people replace letters with similar shaped characters. For example, a zero (0) looks like an oh (o), one (1) replaces ell (l), three (3) is a backwards 'E', and ampersand has a lowercase 'a' in the middle. Passwords like "p@ssw0rd" and "N3@1" (Neal) can be easily guessed.

- **Don't compromise your security**. Telling people "I have a really cool password—it's my student ID number from high school and nobody will guess that!" is a huge hint to an attacker. Don't hint at your password, don't e-mail it, and don't tell it to anyone in public. If you think that somebody might have a clue about your password, then change it immediately. Remember: the only person inconvenienced by a password change will be you. Beyond passwords, don't give accounts with Sudo access to everyone, don't install software from strangers, and don't run with scissors. Your security is as strong as its weakest link, and that is often the user.

WARNING Don't use your Ubuntu system's password anywhere else. Many people use the same password for their Yahoo!, Gmail, and eBay accounts as well as other online services. If you use your password everywhere, then one compromised site will compromise all of your accounts. Most people underestimate the blackhat hacker's ability to find your other accounts. I'm a good guy (whitehat) and I spend a lot of time tracking people online—believe me, finding your other accounts is easy.

SECURE BY DEFAULT

The default Ubuntu server and desktop installations do not include any remote network services. This way, a clean install can be patched and prepared without the risk of an external attacker compromising the system. You can place a clean install of Dapper Drake, Karmic Koala, or any other Ubuntu system on the Internet without a firewall and not risk any remote compromises. (You cannot compromise a network service when no network services exist.)

After the installation, you can update the system (`sudo apt-get update; sudo apt-get upgrade`) and begin adding in services and user accounts. This minimizes the risk from remote exploitation.

The basic idea of "no default network services" is a concept that could benefit other operating systems. For example, Microsoft Windows, HP-UX, and RedHat Fedora Linux all enable some basic network services during the installation. This leads to big problems. For example, if you work for a large company that has a few infected Windows systems, then installing a new Windows system on the network becomes a problem: the new system may be infected over the open network services before the first security patch is applied.

Locking Down Passwords

Many organizations have rules about using strong passwords and regularly changing them. However, having a rule is not the same as enforcing it.

You can force users to change passwords with `passwd -w` to warn and `-x` to expire, forcing a password change at the next login. You can even use `-i` to disable an inactive account. For example, `sudo passwd -w 30 -x 35 -i 60 joe` will warn `joe` to change his password after 30 days, expire his password after 35 days, and lock his inactive account after 60 days. To disable expirations, set the values to zero.

Programs like John the Ripper (`sudo apt-get install john`) are designed to crack passwords through dictionary attacks and common password patterns like the ones listed in the previous section. In my experience, John can crack about 20 percent of user-chosen passwords in the first few minutes, and up to 80 percent in a few hours. The best passwords will not be based on dictionary words or simple patterns, and will be memorable. Good passwords should make sense to only you and not anyone else.

If you are an administrator with lots of users on your system, consider using John the Ripper to look for weak passwords. It is much safer if you find the weak ones and ask the users to proactively change their passwords than wait for a hostile user to find them and exploit the accounts.

Of course, there are different things that you can do when you find a weak password. The polite thing is to inform the user. I once called a faculty member and informed him that his password was a city in Texas. (I didn't know that his son was named Austin.) Other options include forcing a password change at the next login (sudo passwd -e *username*), blocking the offending account (sudo passwd -l *username* to lock and -u to unlock), or posting their names on a Wall of Shame. While this may inconvenience users, you'll virtually guarantee that they will only choose a bad password once.

Hacking with Sudo

Throughout this book we have used sudo for running commands as root. Sudo allows you to run a command with root privileges. The default installation of Ubuntu includes the Sudo command (sudo) and gives the default user account access to this command. If you need something to run as root, you can use sudo. A related command, sudoedit, allows you to edit a file as root. For example, to edit the root-only file /etc/fstab, you can use either of the following commands:

```
sudo vi /var/spool/anacron/cron.daily
sudoedit /var/spool/anacron/cron.daily
```

TIP The sudoedit command uses the editor defined in the $EDITOR environment variable. If this editor is not defined, the nano editor is used. See "Tuning the Shell" in Chapter 2 for setting the $EDITOR variable.

When Unix was young (circa 1970), administrators needed a way to change between user access privileges. This was accomplished with the su command. Although originally designed to switch user access, it was mainly used to change privileges from a regular user to root. (The su command is sometimes called the super-user command for this reason.)

There are a couple of huge risks with using su to run commands as root. Most notably, all commands are executed with root privileges. Many times, only one command within a long list of commands really needs root access. Also, when a terminal is logged in as root, users may forget which user they are running as. The potential for accidentally deleting important user and system files as root is much greater than doing so as a regular user.

Sudo was created to limit the commands that can run as root. Rather than changing all privileges, only the privileges for a specific command are changed. Sudo has other benefits over su that include limiting which commands a user can run as root, and not needing to share the root password. Sudo also keeps track of when you last authenticated. While `su -c cmd` will run a specific command, it will always prompt you for a password; this isn't useful for iterative scripts. In contrast, `sudo cmd` only needs to authenticate the first time, so you can easily use it in a script.

When the Sudo command completes, you are back to your regular user access. This way, only the required steps run as root, and you won't accidentally leave a terminal logged in a root.

Although very old Unix systems still rely on `su` to change access levels, it is being forcefully replaced by `sudo`. Furthermore, in most BSD and Linux distributions (including Ubuntu), Sudo has become standard for enabling root privileges. Although the `su` command is included with the Ubuntu installation, you cannot use it to run commands as root unless you first set a root password using `sudopasswd root`.

Adding Users to Sudo

The configuration file for `sudo` is `/etc/suders`. This lists who can run commands as root, which commands they can run, and any configuration preferences. Listing 11-1 shows the default `/etc/sudoers` file from Hardy Heron (8.04 LTS).

NOTE Different Ubuntu versions have slightly different default `/etc/suders` files. While the comments differ, they all contain the same default restrictions: only root and members of the group *admin* have Sudo privileges. And since the root user has no password and cannot log in, it really means that only users in the *admin* group have access.

Although the sudoers file can be edited using `sudo vi /etc/sudoers` or `sudoedit /etc/sudoers`, this is not recommended. Instead, the command `sudovisudo` (short for `vi sudo`) is the preferred approach. The `visudo` command ensures that only one person edits the file at a time. It also checks for syntax errors before installing the new file. (The last thing you need is to corrupt `/etc/sudoers` and lose the ability to run `sudo` for fixing the problem.)

The default `/etc/sudoers` file gives access to everyone who is part of the `admin` group. Non-`admin` users are blocked from running commands as root. If you want to add someone to the `admin` group, use the following steps:

1. Use the `vigr` command to edit the `/etc/groups` file.

   `sudovigr`

2. The `/etc/groups` file lists each group name, group ID number, and a comma-separated list of users. Search for the line that begins with `admin`.

It should list one account name (your default Ubuntu account). For example, my default account name is *neal* and the line says:

```
admin:x:112:neal
```

3. Add the new user name to this line. Use a comma to separate usernames. For example, if I want to add the user *marc* to this line, I would have:

```
admin:x:112:neal,marc
```

4. Save your changes and quit the editor.

NOTE Changes to `/etc/groups` do not propagate to running applications. If the user is currently logged in, he or she will need to log out before noticing the group changes.

If you want to give a user Sudo access without adding them to a group, then you can add them as a privileged user.

1. Edit the `/etc/suderers` file using `sudovisudo`.

2. Look for the line that says `root ALL=(ALL) ALL`.

3. Create a similar line with the user's account name. For example, if I want to give the account *marc* access, I will use:

```
root    ALL=(ALL) ALL
marc    ALL=(ALL) ALL
```

This addition says that the users *root* and *marc* can use `sudo` and can run any command with root privileges.

4. Save your changes and exit the `visudo` command.

Listing 11-1: The Default /etc/sudoers File from Hardy Heron (8.04 LTS)

```
# /etc/sudoers
#
# This file MUST be edited with the 'visudo' command as root.
#
# See the man page for details on how to write a sudoers file.
#

Defaults        env_reset

# Uncomment to allow members of group sudo to not need a password
# %sudo ALL=NOPASSWD: ALL

# Host alias specification

# User alias specification
```

(continued)

Listing 11-1: The Default /etc/sudoers File from Hardy Heron (8.04 LTS) (*continued*)

```
# Cmnd alias specification

# User privilege specification
root    ALL=(ALL) ALL

# Members of the admin group may gain root privileges
%admin ALL=(ALL) ALL
```

Tweaking other Sudo Options

The sudoers file includes default options that are applied to every `sudo` command. You can add or change these options. Under Dapper Drake (6.06 LTS), the default options are `!lecture`, `tty_tickets`, and `!fqdn`. Later versions of Ubuntu, including Hardy (8.04 LTS), Jaunty (9.04), and Karmic (9.10), the default is `env_reset`.

These options are flags—the `!` in front of any flag disables the option. Other options can be added that include values. All the options belong on the `Defaults` line in the `/etc/suders` file (use `sudovisudo` to edit this file). Some command options that you might want to tweak include:

- `env_reset`—This flag clears the environment variables. Only `$LOGNAME`, `$SHELL`, `$USER`, `$USERNAME`, and a few other variables are kept.

> **WARNING** Many commands require environment variables to run properly. For example, if you need to use a SOCKS server for accessing the network (see Chapter 6), then you will probably need a `$SOCKS_SERVER` environment variable. The env_reset command will remove this variable from all Sudo environments. If you want to keep your environment for a specific command, use `sudo -E command`. The `-E` option preserves environment variables.

- `lecture`—When this flag is enabled, the `sudo` command will display a warning about running commands as root. This can be useful if there are lots of administrators on a system. However, people usually ignore the warning. The default installation disables the message: `!lecture`.

- `timestamp_timeout`—This option lists the number of minutes before `sudo` requires you to re-enter your password. If you are running many `sudo` commands in a row, then it can become very inconvenient to re-enter your password after every command. The default configuration is 15 minutes (`timestamp_timeout=15`)—if your last `sudo` command was executed more than 15 minutes ago, then you will need to re-enter your password to run `sudo`. Setting the value to zero will always prompt for a password; setting the value to a negative number disables the timeout.

If you are in a very sensitive environment, then you may want to lower this value (or set it to zero).

- `tty_tickets`—If you have lots of windows open, then you will notice that you need to enter your password the first time you run `sudo` in each window. This is due to the `tty_tickets` flag—every terminal (`tty`) has its own `sudo` environment. If you disable this flag (`!tty_tickets`), then entering your password for `sudo` in one window will stop the `sudo` password prompts in all other windows.

- `fqdn`—When host names are used in the sudoers file, this flag specifies the use of fully qualified domain names (fqdns).

- `passwd_tries`—This sets how many password attempts the user gets before `sudo` fails. The default is `passwd_tries=3`.

- `insults`—This is a fun flag. If the user enters in a bad password, then `sudo` will generate a random message. (The default is `!insults`.) For example:

```
$ sudo id
Password: [wrong]
Just what do you think you're doing Dave?
Password: [wrong]
It can only be attributed to human error.
Password: [wrong]
My pet ferret can type better than you!
sudo: 3 incorrect password attempts
```

TIP There are many other advanced configuration options including logging and user-based restrictions. If you have specific needs, look at the manual for sudoers (`man sudoers`).

Becoming Root

Although the Ubuntu security model has all administrative commands issued through `sudo`, there are some times when you really would be better off with a command prompt as root. Fortunately, there are many ways to accomplish this with `sudo`. A few examples:

```
sudo -s          # run a shell as root
sudo bash -o vi  # run a shell as root with vi-style command-line edits
sudo -i          # set root's initial login environment
sudosu-root      # become root and run root's login environment
```

In the first two cases, the shell runs as root, but other environment variables, like $HOME, are inherited. In the other two cases, the environment is replaced with root's real environment settings.

If you *really* need to be able to log in as root, then you can use sudopasswd root to give the root account a password. As soon as you set the password, the root account can log in. You can always undo this change with sudopasswd -l root to lock the account.

WARNING Enabling root logins is usually a bad idea. Logins give a trail of accountability. If someone logs in without a personalized account, then there is no way to identify the person who really logged in. sudo gives an audit trail in /var/log/auth.log (even though users with sudo access have the ability to blow away the logs).

Encrypting Data

There are many different ways to encrypt information, and Ubuntu provides plenty of options. You can encrypt individual files, specific directories, your whole home directory, or even the entire hard drive. More importantly, these options are independent. You can have an encrypted file in an encrypted directory within your encrypted home directory that is located on an encrypted disk partition! Each of these options are discussed in the next sections.

- Encrypt files. If you want to encrypt specific files, use GPG or a text editor like vi. With GPG, a copy of the decrypted file will still exist on your file system and may be recoverable if you delete it. In contrast, the vi editor's encryption (vi -x *file*) does not save decoded text to the hard drive, but it really only works well with plain text files.

TIP If vi -x does not work, then you likely have the basic vim package installed. Install the full version using sudo apt-get install vim.

- Encrypt directories. If you want to have a single directory with multiple encrypted files, use EncFS.

- Encrypted user directory. Using eCryptfs, you can encrypt your entire home directory. The rest of the system will be accessible to anyone who can access the hard drive, but your home directory will be encrypted until you log in. This is a good option for privacy, but may prevent cron and at jobs from running correctly when the user is not logged in.

- Encrypt the entire drive. For the truly paranoid, the entire disk is encrypted. You cannot even boot without a password. This is not an ideal solution for remote-access servers since you cannot remotely enter the password.

Using Gnu Privacy Guard (GPG)

Security and encryption are frequently used in the same sentence. If you want to keep something private, use cryptography. In 1991, Phil Zimmerman made public a cryptographic system called *Pretty Good Privacy* (PGP). This became the basis of his company, PGP, Inc. The PGP system was rewritten and licensed under the Gnu Public License (GPL). This new system, the Gnu Privacy Guard (GnuPG or GPG), has become a de facto standard for file and e-mail encryption among Linux and Unix systems. As such, it is included in the default Ubuntu installation.

TIP Many people use the names GPG and PGP interchangeably. Both systems use the same encryption method and the tools have similar use models. A file encrypted with PGP can be decrypted with GPG. The most significant differences are licensing and availability; GPG is open source, GPL, and more widely used.

GPG is included with every Ubuntu installation, even a minimal install. GPG enables you to create public and private keys, securely exchange keys, and encrypt and decrypt messages. Many e-mail programs either natively integrate with PGP (and GPG) or have plug-ins available. For example, the Evolution mailer natively supports GPG. The `mutt` text-based mailer also supports PGP, and even Microsoft Outlook users can get a plug-in for PGP encryption.

There are many required parts for using GPG:

- Key generation
- Searching keys
- Exchanging keys
- Defining trust for keys
- File encryption and decryption
- Cryptographic signatures
- E-mail integration

Creating Keys

GPG uses asymmetrical key cryptography. This means that one key is used to encrypt the data, and a different key is required to decrypt the data. The two keys are called *private* and *public*. Basically, the private key is never passed out (it is kept private), while anyone and his dog can have a copy of the public key. Messages that are encrypted with the private key can only be decrypted with the public key.

Creating keys under GPG is pretty painless: `gpg --gen-key`. This provides a series of text prompts for creating a private-public key pair (see Listing 11-2).

All users have their own set of keys (called a *key ring*) that are stored in $HOME/.gnupg/. The main key rings are $HOME/.gnupg/pubring.gpg and secring.gpg. The former stores public keys, whereas the latter stores private keys.

Although giving out your public keys is expected, your private keys should be kept as secret as possible. During the generation of your key pair, GPG prompts you for a password. Although this password is not used during the cryptography (only the keys are used for that), it *is* used to encrypt your private keys while they are on the hard drive. This deters some other user on the system from stealing your private keys and using them to access your encoded data (or impersonating you—see the section on Signing Data).

TIP Passwords are not required. Many automated tools use GPG, so it can be very desirable to not use a password at all. If you leave the password blank (just hit enter when generating the key), then you will never be prompted for a password.

Listing 11-2: Generating GPG Public and Private Keys

```
$ gpg --gen-key
gpg (GnuPG) 1.4.9; Copyright (C) 2008 Free Software Foundation, Inc.
This is free software: you are free to change and redistribute it.
There is NO WARRANTY, to the extent permitted by law.

Please select what kind of key you want:
   (1) DSA and Elgamal (default)
   (2) DSA (sign only)
   (5) RSA (sign only)
Your selection? 1
DSA keypair will have 1024 bits.
ELG-E keys may be between 1024 and 4096 bits long.
What keysize do you want? (2048) 2048
Requested keysize is 2048 bits
Please specify how long the key should be valid.
         0 = key does not expire
<n>  = key expires in n days
<n>w = key expires in n weeks
<n>m = key expires in n months
<n>y = key expires in n years
Key is valid for? (0) 2y
Key expires at Thu 06 Oct 2011 10:56:08 AM MDT
Is this correct? (y/N) y
You need a user ID to identify your key; the software constructs the
user IDfrom the Real Name, Comment and Email Address in this form:
```

```
"Heinrich Heine (Der Dichter) <heinrichh@duesseldorf.de>"
Real name: John Travolta
Email address: travolta@discomania.tv
Comment:
You selected this USER-ID:
"John Travolta <travolta@discomania.tv>"
Change (N)ame, (C)omment, (E)mail or (O)kay/(Q)uit? O
You need a Passphrase to protect your secret key.
Enter passphrase: *******
Repeat passphrase: *******
We need to generate a lot of random bytes. It is a good idea to perform
some other action (type on the keyboard, move the mouse, utilize the
disks) during the prime generation; this gives the random number
generator a better chance to gain enough entropy.
++++++++++.++++++++++.+++++.+++++++++++++++++++++++++++++++++++.+++++++
+++.++++++++++++++++++++++++++++++++++++++++++.++++++++++.++++++++++
>+++++..................+++++
gpg: key 7B88C50D marked as ultimately trusted
public and secret key created and signed.

gpg: checking the trustdb
gpg: 3 marginal(s) needed, 1 complete(s) needed, PGP trust model
gpg: depth: 0  valid: 1  signed: 0  trust: 0-, 0q, 0n, 0m, 0f, 1u
gpg: next trustdb check due at 2011-10-06
pub   1024D/7B88C50D 2009-10-06 [expires: 2011-10-06]
Key fingerprint = 10B6 1C42 92AC AC29 2D87  E79C 5308 470A 7B88 C50D
uid                  John Travolta <travolta@discomania.tv>
sub   2048g/71D990B6 2009-10-06 [expires: 2011-10-06]
```

CAN YOU REPEAT THAT?

Private keys are supposed to be unique, and GPG uses some of the strongest cryptographic algorithms available. If you lose your password, delete your private key, or corrupt your key ring without a backup available, then you are out of luck. You will not be able to recover the data.

Similarly, don't delete private keys unless you are positive that you will never need them ever again. Since they are unique, there is no going back after you make this decision. My key ring contains many old and expired keys because they are needed to decode some old messages and verify signatures.

When sending GPG-encoded e-mails, be sure to send a copy to yourself. Otherwise, you won't be able to decode your sent mail. Simply saving a copy of the sent message is not enough since your key is not added to the encryption. I occasionally receive e-mails where the sender asks me to send them back the e-mail so they can have a copy of their own text.

Searching Keys

After you create the keys, you can view them using the `list-keys` option. The `gpg --list-keys` command will list every public key in your key ring. You can also specify filter words for searching the key ring. For example, `gpg --list-keys 7B88C50D` returns the key matching this unique identifier. You can also specify words, like `gpg --list-keys disco` to list every key where the string *disco* appears in the person's name or e-mail address.

> **TIP** Since keys contain e-mail addresses, I use `gpg --list-keys` as a cheap Rolodex. For example, if I need to remember Marc See's e-mail address, then I use `gpg --list-keys marc` and his entry (Marcus T. See <msee@test.lan>) comes right up.

Other search options include `gpg --list-secret-keys` and `gpg --finger print`. The former lists all of your private keys and the latter shows key-unique hashes that can be used to validate keys. Since anyone can create any key with anyone's name and e-mail address, the unique fingerprint allows you to make sure the key is from the right person (see Transferring Keys).

> **NOTE** You can delete keys using `—delete-key` and `—delete-secret-key`. However, you probably will never need to delete keys, and deleting a secret key is irreversible unless you have a backup.

Searching for keys based on name, e-mail address, or unique ID is used by most of the GPG operations. For example, when encrypting a message you will be asked to provide a list of keys for the encryption. These can be found by searching names, e-mail addresses, or IDs.

> **TIP** You can specify multiple search terms on the `gpg` command line. These terms form a logical OR—any key that matches any of the terms will be displayed.

Transferring Keys

After you create your keys, you will need to pass around your public key. Only people with your public key can encrypt messages to you. To do this, you will need to export the public key from your key ring. The command `gpg --export -a` will export *all* of your private keys. You can use the search strings to narrow down the keys being exported. For example, `gpg --export -a travolta` will export my public key for John Travolta. The result from this command is an ASCII-encoded text block that can be e-mailed or passed to other people. The block should look similar to this one:

```
-----BEGIN PGP PUBLIC KEY BLOCK-----
Version: GnuPG v1.4.9 (GNU/Linux)
```

```
mQGiBErLdqgRBADHF2uphafC8vHj4q5xLUVI7BNjD8DVfX0I+PvIvgfCLy0FFJz7
XBvPVGzHF3VPT9/hVolunNvsZyCOp5ztpJV/7YmKIU+QxSlrFr57jJUTvHs+RUtm
iIbFUoXp5yrpg7rmTHPIE62C1eiizymwQYXQEr1jmvhky9/VSI04m0eNmwCg4zk+
O8s1fQuNDVR4M/YiTFTB58ED/iTbCjFJfbJ8Pq1x3aLhFT75LoJSEiAHPsC4LUcU
RzEOsEQtimfCakcB2Pm8SWVdEJ7gXtl6a2qg3mP4Qi6X8VlQ+M1EJ73w6srNyz7K
mwl5Y3GmeTfWWxGV4wPeeUzkhI+LY6E9+KV7QZK9lFaGAqVHZJaWwgbVQaZEG5DU
NZUgA/0TT0PimOpgGG3fDnKJRIHWyE74OOUujYia0ElgTbhT4OoYX+MTvNIjk+Csk
ocLCxWxfJdG3AGzUgKHOz3INnEmHBhKxkQCrPwr3LHM0gya6S/I/RoW921GMj3ez
R4WzEdbbboxK17B3I9e0eBBmkT0AY6q3nZQDM2Rgd72EPuNRRLQmSm9obiBUcmF2
b2x0YSA8dHJhdm9sdGFAZGlzY29tYW5pYS50dj6IZgQTEQIAJgUCSst2qAIbAwUJ
A8JnAAYLCQgHAwIEFQIIAwQWAgMBAh4BAheAAAoJEFMIRwp7iMUN59YAnRy4SWCW
yMXcHIuVhuPTg7FEdhR+AKCTuEBpwMN5PBJk9OOVnWpRlfgRI7kCDQRKy3aoEAgA
97A8EYW3Tt9UHJmQY+sOyq2IibuK+gvfF8m/70HuWhlqNY7N/+NswRTOV4V8mrpB
ZF6HTY6bDeuOUdT1g0E+jV2tUpE++vMApnvpuH4a3VIR7UulEhTVtTWsw8XQIoc5
coWquJYGwoySkks8r6S54t7GbqohlyVPzZqU9TmbSBW1scNSfOch3ut7tkSYoRq1
ZCCfUiwZbWQTNY6nMzne3Pi0t8gcQGFSYQwyF7jpjrgMyZWBJsA9bkKITaradPtG
wNky9ig2NrPmjGlZ2QKg0BNw1Vzuku7NqBnf0bnxA5QWsDeyO+5Erpk7t3kwxcO9
1K6CauG3Ai0lzupCRpjVjwADBQf8Diq1RrdsUAlfZNo1XCI/MgaDULEHySu8kWBw
kbSZKT9+zGstc5Qx+kYCUw2f1eELP2v9GKaznWinNKSgbBZLtC75hB3yHyTNnoIT
x1OrAKGnm0cXkAdF2qzNoArVeW/Xt4Te9GJ0diACvVgf1WNB1xgX/zi9zAAirgZL
MMR5Lz6TC1q70qyieQA0lhb+uNce9QPgUH/+wUOZgGketo2+ORt3KwA5LGLCXnTx
cMuSaXkKko2np2Xi0vCtoK1Sp/Y8NNJ9FOf18Ck/jcnei78RgWn2MeECfLM5u0B4
Srv2KfL41qfd3xdIDaBu+rCRmnXxQp4HpCurL/na5oG3IWVaS4hPBBgRAgAPBQJK
y3aoAhsMBQkDkDwmcAAAoJEFMIRwp7iMUN0W0AoMHmpx5m1hiiH+DZXuwrE/k7jnIy
AKC8c5oFooIV3kPivqr0z6lSL+57iA==
=Rp14
```

```
-----END PGP PUBLIC KEY BLOCK-----
```

When you receive a message like this, you can import it using gpg --import. For example:

```
gpg --export -a travolta > travolta.pub # export public key
gpg --import travolta.pub                # import public key
gpg --import < travolta.pub              # inline import public key
```

The import command looks for the BEGIN and END markers, so you don't even need to separate it from the rest of the file before doing the import. For example, if you have a bunch of keys in an e-mail file (such as, email.mbox), then you can import all of them using:

```
gpg --import email.mbox
```

Defining Trust

GPG has a well-defined notion of trust. Although a new key that you import can be used to decode a message, you shouldn't communicate with keys you do not trust. Using the gpg command, you can set an explicit trust level for a key. The basic levels are:

- **Undefined**—You can use the key to decode messages, but probably shouldn't use it for encryption.

- **Do not trust**—This key is a known forgery or is otherwise evil.

- **Marginal trust**—The key is probably authentic.

- **Fully trust**—You know the key is valid. Most likely, you were given a hash fingerprint and have compared it using gpg --fingerprint and you know it is correct.

- **Ultimately trust**—This usually means it is your own key.

Listing 11-3 shows an example for setting the trust level on the example Travolta key.

NOTE Few programs that use GPG actually use the trust level. The main one that I have found is Evolution. If a public key is not explicitly trusted, then you cannot send an encrypted e-mail to that user.

Listing 11-3: Setting the Trust Level

```
$ gpg --edit-key travolta trust
gpg (GnuPG) 1.4.9; Copyright (C) 2008 Free Software Foundation, Inc.
This is free software: you are free to change and redistribute it.
There is NO WARRANTY, to the extent permitted by law.

Secret key is available.

pub  1024D/7B88C50D  created: 2009-10-06  expires: 2011-10-06  usage: SC
                     trust: ultimate      validity: ultimate
sub  2048g/71D990B6  created: 2009-10-06  expires: 2011-10-06  usage: E
[ultimate] (1). John Travolta <travolta@discomania.tv>

pub  1024D/7B88C50D  created: 2009-10-06  expires: 2011-10-06  usage: SC
                     trust: ultimate      validity: ultimate
sub  2048g/71D990B6  created: 2009-10-06  expires: 2011-10-06  usage: E
[ultimate] (1). John Travolta <travolta@discomania.tv>

Please decide how far you trust this user to correctly verify other
users' keys
(by looking at passports, checking fingerprints from different
sources, etc.)

  1 = I don't know or won't say
  2 = I do NOT trust
  3 = I trust marginally
  4 = I trust fully
```

```
    5 = I trust ultimately
    m = back to the main menu

Your decision? 4
pub  1024D/7B88C50D   created: 2009-10-06   expires: 2011-10-06   usage: SC
                      trust: full          validity: ultimate
sub  2048g/71D990B6   created: 2009-10-06   expires: 2011-10-06   usage: E
[ultimate] (1). John Travolta <travolta@discomania.tv>
Please note that the shown key validity is not necessarily correct
unless you restart the program.

Command> q
```

Encrypting Files with GPG

GPG has two ways to encrypt files. The first way, `gpg -e file`, will prompt you to select all of the public keys that should be use to encrypt the data. If you select three public keys, then any of those three people (with the private keys) can decrypt the data. The output from this command is a binary file with the `.gpg` extension. If you use `file`, then the output becomes `file.gpg`, and if you use `cow.txt`, then the output is `cow.txt.gpg`. Because this is a binary file, the contents will look like random gibberish. When you transfer the file, be sure to use a system that can transfer binary files—pasting `file.gpg` into an e-mail will likely corrupt the data.

> **WARNING** If you have a file encrypted with GPG and you lose the keys, then the file will be unreadable.

A second encryption method uses ASCII armoring. In this approach, the binary data is encoded using text characters. The content is wrapped with BEGIN and END labels and is ready for e-mailing. Using `gpg -e -a file` or `gpg -e --armor file` will create `file.asc`, containing the ASCII armored encrypted message. An armored message should look like a random jumble of characters within the BEGIN and END labels:

```
-----BEGIN PGP MESSAGE-----
Version: GnuPG v1.4.9 (GNU/Linux)

hQIOAyi9T1Zx2ZC2EAgA0tLhXZxZZfJ7v9v9ZS9bcPo/FMrQ+yWc+qrD5w8Yavir
cALFR/87mjMBuaDyWoSoLzlZe7kVvgm6XQ5/OXnut5GblSHi1nC+zJi9NIn/ir4P
LqGrOJTZ6F8Rp5T0Wtl1ehpqEYf4VMERI3CpVoPB0Ig7zAzA/gpGLZVhkW/m7byx
8+Eyr2Rt3QUq136WMah39MMjCkIpKdhS8RMdaf0nbAPOzEVZPxrDSSzhaO72bW7d
wZhIJOitv+eaai7QwHvXmpdRJ1rdxXTsyoF3nUPismBnoNoAjxaGLUEIV9ISAo11
qSyXTGNFQSLxvJ4waC7gs+JG4+gpS4PSkHJVq/poKggAtdUt5ynf5zYveQ4p4iWv
UE9C8V87uDKS9LkfIwDn3zpGcZCkWNFFEtDLHmHKmA5x9KkHTe5sbkQsgtlnLgOg
XWstrn5wYiOTs97oauaoFRI1JzTbvANObFt/4JRcbVA6ewg7P7y/M0vg1/iKZZM4
```

```
RXW0UVIyx2Hbr5LmMEgxnjULeMzDzIMaz80diNmzoJU8SYCcMz7au+Gx6JLnYk/9
7A/HxtQ/dVg8DMI7ox8is0LPjCYFjcaci2T76fUTzzOJ8MZJICld2ftK51097nJd
vlMitcuVoVLL7XXdeoBO83iYSUzLzwLIPKuA2bCjPgdh8m4clMCnwCyzL6WaQN5v
FtJdAQA4TEPmVL3RjvfP8WS1YIa3PlFO/ns5VSCd68h+X6liQ63/I43W8sLr/nla
2wGl2AkyfYzHKVICwy/a8e5u4a2xwt4IkbiXVRxcLP4QJohkaFzTG+ci/+621YiU
=FyU2
-----END PGP MESSAGE-----
```

WARNING Don't modify anything between the BEGIN and END markers or you will corrupt the data.

Decoding a GPG message is a snap. The -d parameter means *decode* and the command-line specifies the file to decrypt. The decoded contents are sent to standard-out.

```
gpg -d file.gpg > file  # decoding a binary GPG file
gpg -d file.asc > file  # decoding an ASCII armored GPG file
```

During the decryption, you will be asked to provide your private key's password.

Signing Data

Usually public keys are used to encrypt data, so only the private key can decrypt the file. This way, anyone can encrypt a message and only you can decrypt it. However, GPG does allow you to reverse the process. GPG can be used to sign messages using the private key—anyone with the public key can validate the cryptographic signature. This allows recipients to know that the data has not been tampered with and that it is authentic. To sign a file, use:

```
gpg -s file       # creates a signed binary file.gpg
gpg -a -s file    # creates a signed ASCII armored file.asc
gpg -e -a -s file # creates a signed and encrypted ASCII armored
                    file.asc
```

When signing a file, you will be asked to provide your private key's password. During the decoding process (gpg -d), the signature will be tested and validated.

TIP Even if you don't have a copy of the public key, you can still view the signed contents using gpg -d. However, you will not be able to authenticate the signature without the public key, and if the file is encrypted then you will not even be able to view the contents.

Although signing data may sound like a neat idea, it serves a critical purpose. In some jurisdictions, a digital signature is legal and binding. If you are sending contracts or making business agreements, consider using GPG to digitally sign a document. Doing this will prevent forgeries and is much more secure than faxing your signature on a piece of paper. (Be sure to first check with your legal council to make sure a digital signature is binding.)

Integrating with e-mail

PGP and GPG are most commonly used for encrypted e-mail. The Ubuntu mail program, Evolution, natively supports GPG (although it calls it PGP). When composing an e-mail, select the PGP options from the Security menu (see Figure 11-1).

Evolution has one big limitation when using PGP: you will only be able to send encrypted e-mail when the trust level is defined on the public key. If the trust for a key is not defined, or a public key is unavailable for the recipient, then you will be unable to send an encrypted e-mail. (See the section on "Defining Trust" earlier in this chapter.) This can become a big problem if the key is associated with one e-mail address, but the user has a couple of different e-mail addresses.

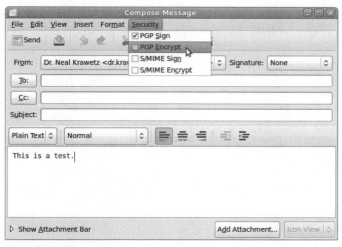

Figure 11-1: Enabling PGP encryption and digital signatures

Evolution is not the only e-mail program that supports PGP. I frequently use mutt (see Figure 11-2). This is a text-only mail program (sudo apt-get install mutt). This program enables me to easily send my public key to other people (by pressing **Esc**, then **k**) and I can enable encryption or signing by pressing **p**. Unlike Evolution, if mutt cannot find the appropriate keys, then it allows me to search for alternate keys. However, mutt is not a graphical application—HTML contents and images cannot be viewed using this tool.

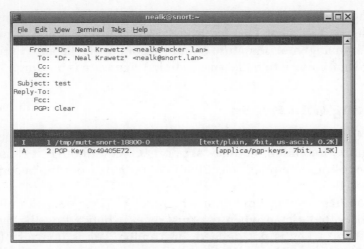

Figure 11-2: Sending an e-mail using mutt. In this example, a public key is being forwarded as an attachment

PGP does have one large limitation when used with e-mail: different e-mail programs may be incompatible. A PGP e-mail sent with Microsoft Outlook may not be immediately readable with mutt or Evolution. This is because different mailers use different mail headers to identify an encrypted message. With mutt, you can usually resolve incompatible formats by pressing **Ctrl+E** and changing the Content-Type to application/pgp. In contrast, with Evolution you will need to save the e-mail to a file and decrypt it by hand.

Using Other File Encryption Options

There are a few other common encryption options for files. Both the emacs and vi editors have options for encrypting files. With emacs, you will need to install EasyPG; EasyPG is a GPG plugin for emacs.

1. Install EasyPG with sudo apt-get install easypg. If you have not already installed emacs, this will install it.

2. Add the following line to $HOME/.emacs. (Create the file if it does not already exist.)

   ```
   (require 'epa-file) (epa-file-enable)
   ```

3. If you run emacs on any file that has a .gpg suffix, it will prompt you for the key to decode it.

4. When saving to a file with a .gpg suffix, you will be given a choice of keys from your GPG key ring for encrypting. Scroll down the list and type **m** to mark each key for encryption, then click on **OK**.

In contrast to emacs, vi does not use GPG. Instead, it uses a different algorithm called *crypt*, which is based on the Data Encryption Standard (DES) algorithm. While DES is considered weaker than that PGP, it is usually strong enough for text files, as long as you use a good (and preferable long) password.

To encrypt a file with vi, use `vi -x file`. This will prompt you for the initial password. After that, you just need `vi file` to edit. The editor will detect the encryption and prompt you for the password.

Encrypting with a text editor is good for encrypting text files. However, it is not ideal for encrypting binary data. For binary data, consider using Mcrypt (`sudo apt-get install mcrypt`). Mcrypt allows you to encode a file using a variety of cryptographic algorithms. For example, to encrypt a file using the Blowfish algorithm, you can use: `mcrypt -a blowfish myfile`. This will create *myfile*.nc. To decrypt, use `mcrypt -d myfile.nc`.

Encrypting File Systems

Early versions of Ubuntu did not provide any built-in support for cryptographic file systems, but you could add it in. Dapper Drake (6.06 LTS) supported encrypted directories using the encrypted filesystem. EncFS encrypts files and directories. Hardy Heron (8.04 LTS) introduced full disk encryption with the Linux Unified Key Setup (LUKS), and Jaunty Jackalope (9.04) introduced eCryptfs for encrypting home directories. Each type of encryption has a specific use model and tradeoffs.

Installing and Configuring EncFS

EncFS is not an independent file system. Instead, it is a file system plug-in that encrypts and decrypts files on the fly. It uses the existing file system for storing data, but all data is encrypted on a file-by-file basis. File names are also cloaked to ensure that the encrypted directory has limited usefulness to someone without the password.

1. Install EncFS if it is not already installed. This will also install the FUSE (Filesystem in Userspace) utilities.

   ```
   sudo apt-get install encfs
   ```

2. Make sure the command `fusermount` can run as root.

   ```
   sudochmodu+s /usr/bin/fusermount
   ```

3. Each user who will need to use EncFS must be added to the `fuse` group. Use `sudovigr` to add users to this group. Find the line that starts with `fuse` and add user names to the end of the line.

4. Changes to /etc/groups do not impact current logins. Make sure the user is in the group fuse by running the command groups. If the group fuse is not listed, then the user must log out and log back in for the change to take effect.

5. Make sure the FUSE kernel module is loaded. You may also want to add fuse to /etc/modules so it is always loaded after a reboot.

   sudomodprobe fuse

6. Using the encfs command, create the encryption and decryption directories. For example, I use encrypt/ and decrypt/. If the directories do not exist, then you will be prompted to create them. You will also be prompted for a password.

NOTE The encfs command tries to run in the background. To do this, you must use absolute paths. If you specify a relative path, then you will need to use the -f option and it will not run in the background.

```
encfs $(pwd)/encrypt $(pwd)/decrypt
The directory "/../encrypt/" does not exist.
Should it be created? (y,n) y
The directory "/../decrypt" does not exist.
Should it be created? (y,n) y
Creating new encrypted volume.
Please choose from one of the following options:
 enter "x" for expert configuration mode,
 enter "p" for pre-configured paranoia mode,
 anything else, or an empty line will select standard mode.
?> [enter]
Standard configuration selected.
Configuration finished.  The filesystem to be created has
the following properties:
Filesystem cipher: "ssl/blowfish", version 2:1:1
Filename encoding: "nameio/block", version 3:0:1
Key Size: 160 bits
Block Size: 512 bytes
Each file contains 8 byte header with unique IV data.
Filenames encoded using IV chaining mode.
Now you will need to enter a password for your filesystem.
You will need to remember this password, as there is absolutely
no recovery mechanism.  However, the password can be changed
later using encfsctl.
New Encfs Password: [password]
Verify Encfs Password: [password]
```

WARNING Do not forget your password! There is no way to recover a lost password.

Now you have two directories: decrypt/ contains the decoded file system, and encrypt/ contains the real encrypted files. If you copy files into the `decrypt/` directory, then you will see encrypted counterparts in the `encrypt/` directory.

> **NOTE** An attacker who views the `encrypt/` directory can see the number of files, owner's name, permissions, and timestamps. He can also see the approximate file sizes. However, he cannot see the actual file names or file contents.

Maintaining EncFS

When you are all done with the decrypted directory, you un-mount it using `fusermount -u decrypt`. Although the encrypted files still exist in the `encrypt/` directory, the `decrypt/` directory will appear empty (because it is not mounted). Later, when you need to access the encrypted files, you can use: `encfs $(pwd)/encrypt $(pwd)/decrypt`. This will only ask you for your password. The files will only appear in the `decrypted/` directory if you enter the correct password.

If you ever need to change the password, you can use the `encfsctl passwd encrypt/` command. This will prompt you for your old and new passwords.

> **NOTE** You do not need to un-mount the directory in order to change the password. The password is only used during the initial file mounting. However, if you change the password, then you will need the new password in order to re-mount the encrypted files.

Using EncFS

EncFS is great for storing files if you are worried about someone stealing the media or accessing the stored data. Here are some sample situations where you might want to use EncFS:

- **Encrypt an entire directory**—If you have a directory that you don't want people to access, then you can encrypt it. For example, I have a source code repository containing sensitive information. The actual files are stored using EncFS. If you are worried about your web cache, consider encrypting `$HOME/.mozilla/`.

- **Encrypt a CD-ROM**—Rather than burning a regular directory to a CD-ROM, you can burn an encrypted directory. The CD-ROM will appear to have garbage file names and random data in each file. However, you can then use `encfs` to mount it and access the decrypted data. If you are worried about someone stealing a CD-ROM that contains sensitive information, then this is an excellent solution. The CD-ROM is as secure as your password.

- **Encrypt a USB drive**—You can specify a USB thumb drive for storing the encrypted files. This is similar to the CD-ROM solution, except you can read and write to the drive.

- **Encrypt a networked file system**—NFS does not offer encryption, and SMB provides few security options. Rather than exporting unprotected files, you can export the encrypted file system. Network clients can mount the NFS (or SMB) partition containing the encrypted files, and then use `encfs` to access the decrypted files. This way, the file system's data is encrypted as it is passed along the network. (See Chapter 7 for configuring NFS and Samba.)

Knowing EncFS Limitations

EncFS is very flexible and supported by a variety of file systems. You can download EncFS for Windows and other versions of Linux. However, there are some limitations with this type of encrypted file system.

- **Supported platforms**—EncFS is not supported on every operating system. BSD and Mac OS X are just two examples. If you need EncFS on these platforms, consider running a supported platform using a virtual machine like Qemu (see Chapter 7) and exporting the decrypted directory to the host operating system.

- **EncFS does not un-mount when you log out**—Unmounting needs to be a conscious effort. Consider placing `fusermount -u -z decoded/` in your `$HOME/.bash_logout` script. This will un-mount the directory after all processes end.

- **EncFS does not protect the decrypted directory**—If you successfully run `encfs` and can access the decrypted files, then anyone on the system can access the decrypted files.

- **EncFS is not for automated systems**—Some people have tried to configure EncFS to mount automatically, when the system boots (or when a user logs in). Doing this defeats the security. For example, if the encrypted file system is mounted when the system powers up, then a thief who steals the system only needs to power up the computer in order to access the sensitive files.

Encrypting Home Directories

Beginning with Jaunty Jackalope (9.04), there is an easy way to make home directories encrypted. This is done using the Linux Unified Key Setup (LUKS) for partition (block) encryption, and eCryptfs for file and directory encryption.

1. Install eCryptfs and LUKS.

   ```
   sudo apt-get install ecryptfs-utils cryptsetup
   ```

2. When you create a new user account, use the command-line `adduser` program and include the parameter to encrypt the home directory.

   ```
   sudo adduser --encrypt-home username
   ```

3. The `adduser` command will ask you for the password and use it to encrypt the account's home directory.

When the user is not logged in, the directory is encrypted. Even root cannot see the decrypted files. However, when the user logs in, all files are decrypted and accessible.

TIP eCryptfs works in a similar fashion to EncFS. Your actual directory is located in `$HOME/.Private`. Every file is located there, but it is encrypted. An attacker can see how many files you have, the approximate file size, and timestamp when it was last modified. But they cannot see the real name or content.

There are some important warnings about encrypting your home directory.

■ Anyone with root access can reset the account's password with `sudo passwd` *username* in order to gain access to the encrypted files. Moreover, anyone with access to the physical hard drive can reset the root password by booting from a recovery disk. eCryptfs only protects your data from other (non-root) users on the system. Consider using full disk encryption for additional protection. (See the next section.)

■ Your home directory is actually encrypted with a randomly generated password. Use `ecryptfs-unwrap-passphrase` to see the password. For very important data, you might want to record this someplace other than on the computer system.

■ Automated processes, such as background tasks and schedule commands such as `cron` or `at` jobs, will be unable to access your directory if you are not logged in. The commands may fail to run.

■ If you are going to encrypt your home directory, then disable automatic logins. (Automatic logins to an encrypted home directory defeat the purpose.) Go to System ➪ Administration ➪ Login Window, select the Security tab, and uncheck the Enable Automatic Login option.

■ If any of your files get pushed out to swap space, then the data will be accessible in an unencrypted location. Consider either disabling swap, or encrypting it with `sudo ecryptfs-setup-swap`. Unfortunately, disabling swap prevents suspending the computer. And you can only suspend with an encrypted swap space if you run Karmic Koala (9.10) or later versions of Ubuntu.

▪ There is no option for encrypting an existing unencrypted user account, or for permanently decrypting an encrypted home directory. Instead, create a new account with the appropriate permissions, move over the files, and then delete the undesirable account.

Encrypting the Entire Disk

Beginning with Hardy Heron (8.04 LTS), you have the option to encrypt the entire disk using LUKS. However, this requires a fresh installation using the Alternate or Server CD image.

1. Follow the text-based installation screen, but stop at the disk partition screen.

2. Select the option for an encrypted logical volume (LVM). (See Figure 11-3.)

3. After the drives are formatted, you will be prompted for an encryption passphrase. This will be used to encrypt the drive. (See Figure 11-4.)

4. Continue with the installation.

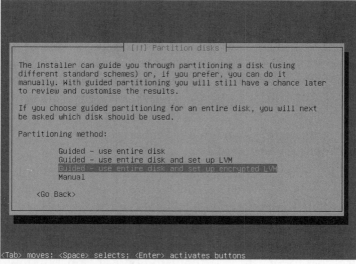

Figure 11-3: Enabling an encrypted file system.

Each time the system boots, you will be prompted to enter the partition's passphrase. The system will not boot until the correct passphrase is entered.

WARNING Do not enable partition encryption on remote servers or systems that may boot automatically. With nobody at the terminal to enter the passphrase, the system will never boot.

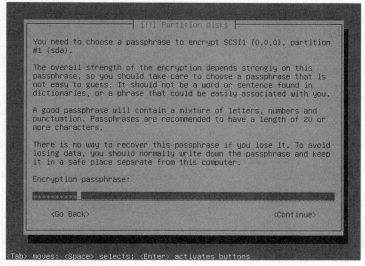

Figure 11-4: Setting the passphrase.

Changing the disk's password is not as straightforward as changing a user's password. LUKS supports up to eight passwords for unlocking the drive. Each password is stored in a *slot*. To change passwords, you'll need to add a new password, and then delete the old one.

1. Find the encrypted partition. It will be one of the `crypt` partitions listed in `/dev/mapper/`. In this example, `/dev/sda1` is encrypted and listed as `/dev/mapper/sda1_crypt`.

   ```
   $ ls /dev/mapper/
   control  cryptswap1  sda1_crypt  ubuntu-root  ubuntu-swap_1
   ```

2. Add a new password using `luksAddKey`. This will prompt you for the new passphrase.

   ```
   $ sudo cryptsetup luksAddKey /dev/sda1
   Enter any LUKS passphrase: [oldpassword]
   key slot 0 unlocked.
   Enter new passphrase for key slot: [newpassword]
   Verify passphrase: [newpassword]
   Command successful.
   ```

3. Remove the old password with `luksRemoveKey`.

   ```
   $ sudo cryptsetup luksRemoveKey /dev/sda1
   Enter LUKS passphrase to be deleted: [oldpassword]
   Key slot 0 selected for deletion.
   Enter any remaining LUKS passphrase: [newpassword]
   key slot 1 verified.
   Command successful.
   ```

TIP You can enable multiple passwords to the hard drive. This way, different administrators can use different passwords. And if you happen to forget one password, you can always use another.

Managing Logs and Caches

Backups are essential for security, but not everything needs to be backed up. For example, cache files and really old logs probably do not need to be archived. Some files, like logs, also need to be maintained. Without the occasional pruning, logs may expand to fill all available disk space.

Besides consuming unnecessary disk space and slowing down backup systems, temporary files and cache files can pose a security risk. Cache files allow someone to look at a history of your activities and possibly recover sensitive information. While deleted files may be recoverable with forensic tools, this is usually more effort than a simple attacker can manage. Deleting an unnecessary cache file is better than leaving it around.

Clearing Temporary Files

Many applications need to use temporary files for storage. Although some programs write to the current directory, others write to /tmp or /var/tmp. Without periodic maintenance, these directories can become cluttered. In addition, because /tmp is usually part of the / partition, temporary files can consume all available space on the root partition.

By default, Ubuntu flushes files from /tmp during boot. The variable TMPTIME is defined in /etc/default/rcS and set to the number of days to keep files in /tmp. By default, the value is zero (0), meaning all files 0 days or older are removed. Setting TMPTIME to -1 prevents cleaning /tmp.

There are a couple of problems with TMPTIME. First, it only cleans files in /tmp, and not /var/tmp. Second, and more importantly, it blows away *everything* in /tmp. This includes directories like lost+found (in case /tmp is a standalone partition), disk quote configurations (for when you want to limit user consumption in /tmp), and all files owned by root.

Instead, I set TMPTIME=-1 to disable it, and use my own cleaning script (see Listing 11-4). This script deletes all temporary files from /tmp and /var/tmp, except for root-owned system files.

Available for download on Wrox.com

Listing 11-4: /etc/init.d/cleantmp for Cleaning Temporary Directories

```
#!/bin/sh

PATH=/bin:/usr/bin:/sbin:/usr/sbin
. /lib/lsb/init-functions
```

```
cleantmp()
{
  # EXCEPT list for system files
  for i in /tmp /var/tmp; do
  EXCEPT="! ( -path $i )
          ! ( -path $i/lost+found -uid 0 )
          ! ( -path $i/quota.user -uid 0 )
          ! ( -path $i/aquota.user -uid 0 )
          ! ( -path $i/quota.group -uid 0 )
          ! ( -path $i/aquota.group -uid 0 )
          ! ( -path $i/.journal -uid 0 )
          ! ( -path $i/.clean -uid 0 )
          ! ( -path '$i/..security*' -uid 0 )"
    # Find everything in the directory (except the exceptions)
    find $i -maxdepth 1 $EXCEPT -exec rm -rf "{}" \;
  done
}

case "$1" in
  start|stop|restart|reload)
    log_begin_msg "Cleaning tmp directories..."
    cleantmp
    ;;
  *)
    log_success_msg "Usage: /etc/init.d/cleantmp" \
      "{start|stop|restart|reload}"
    exit 1
esac

exit 0
```

To make the `cleantmp` script run during boot and shutdown, I added it to `/etc/rcS.d/`, `/etc/rc2.d/`, and `/etc/rc0.d/`.

```
sudo chmod a+rx /etc/init.d/cleantmp
cd /etc/rcS.d
sudo ln -s ../init.d/cleantmp S36cleantmp  # for startup
cd /etc/rc2.d
sudo ln -s ../init.d/cleantmp S36cleantmp  # for startup
cd /etc/rc0.d
sudo ln -s ../init.d/cleantmp K78cleantmp  # for shutdown
```

Erasing Web Caches

Web browsers store lots of cache files. The default setting for Firefox is 50 MB per profile per user! (See Chapter 6 for managing profiles and configuring browsers.) Most of the time, these cache files do not need to be kept by backup systems. For a list of the Firefox cache files, use:

```
sudo ls -d /home/*/.mozilla/firefox/*/Cache
```

Most of the time, you can safely blow away (or not back up) these files. However, you should leave the empty cache directory so that Mozilla won't need to re-create it next time you start the browser.

> **NOTE** If you installed Konquerer (part of the Kubuntu desktop), then look for user-owned cache files in **/var/tmp/kdecache*/**.

Firefox stores a history of every URL accessed. This can also become a very big file and is usually not critical to system operation. All history files can be found using:

```
sudo ls -d /home/*/.mozilla/firefox/*/history.dat   # Firefox 1.x and 2.x
sudo ls -d /home/*/.mozilla/firefox/*/places.sqlite # Firefox 3.x
```

If you want to remove the cache files during boot, you can add them to the `find` command in the `/etc/init.d/cleantmp` script (see Listing 11-4) by changing the `for`-loop to:

```
for i in /tmp /var/tmp /home/*/.mozilla/firefox/*/Cache; do
```

You may also want to add lines to zero-out history files. For example:

```
for i in /home/*/.mozilla/firefox/*/history.dat ; do
  cat /dev/zero > $i
done
for i in /home/*/.mozilla/firefox/*/places.sqlite ; do
  cat /dev/zero > $i
done
```

Cleaning APT Cache

The APT command can be another source of large, unnecessary files. For example, if you install some software and then remove it, the installation files may still be on the system. By default, APT does not automatically remove these files. However, the command `sudo apt-get autoclean` will remove these residues.

You can also configure APT to periodically remove old files by editing: `/etc/apt/apt.conf.d/10periodic`. For example, you can tell APT to periodically remove old files by adding different command directives:

- Set the auto-clean interval to once a week (the interval is specified in days).

    ```
    APT::Periodic::AutocleanInterval "7";
    ```

- Tell APT to remove cache packages older than seven days.

    ```
    APT::Periodic::MaxAge "7";
    ```

■ If you disabled the periodic Synaptic update check (or installed the minimal Ubuntu server and don't have Synaptic installed), then you can enable a weekly (seven days) check for new packages:

```
APT::Periodic::Update-Package-Lists "7";
```

These changes are processed by `anacron` in `/etc/cron.daily/apt`. (See Chapter 8 for configuring `anacron`.)

Rotating Logs

There are many different system log files. Some are rotated daily, others are rotated weekly, and some are never rotated. If you don't manage your log files, then they can grow indefinitely. And since most log files are stored in `/var/log`, filling the disk can lead to system failures.

The basic command for rotating a log file is `savelog`. This will rename the log file. So, `savelog test.log` will move `test.log` to `test.log.0` (or `test.log.0.gz` if it is big enough to compress), and any old `test.log.0` will become `test.log.1`, `test.log.1` becomes `test.log.2`, and so on. The default settings keep seven levels of backups (`test.log.0` to `test.log.7`). Anything older is deleted. You can change the number of rotated copies with the `-c` parameter. For example, `savelog -c 20 test.log` will keep 20 rotations.

If you want to create your own log file then you should add it to a rotation system. The main rotation system is `logrotate`, and is called by `anacron` (see `/etc/cron.daily/logrotate`). This command consults a directory of rotation command scripts: `/etc/logrotate.d/`. In this directory are a bunch of files that define log files and rotation schedules. For example, `/etc/logrotate.d/acpid` on Hardy Heron (8.04 LTS) looks like:

```
/var/log/acpid {
    weekly
    rotate 4
    compress
    missingok
    postrotate
        pkill -SIGUSR1 acpid > /dev/null
    endscript
}
```

This specifies four log rotations of `/var/log/acpid` on a weekly basis. After rotating the log, the service `/etc/init.d/acpid` is restarted. Everything between the `postrotate` and `endscript` lines form a script that will be executed. For some processes, you may need to use `prerotate...endscript` to stop a process before rotating the logs.

Some log files don't always need to be rotated. In the `logrotate` configuration file you can add a `size` parameter. For example, `size 10M` will only rotate the log if it is bigger than 10 MB. You can also use other sizes such as `50k` or `1G`. The single letters *k*, *M*, and *G* are recognized as kilobytes, megabytes, and gigabytes. If no size modifier is specified, bytes are assumed.

If you run a high-volume service, like a web server that gets millions of hits per day, then you will probably want to rotate logs more often than daily or weekly. I'd suggest putting the `logrotate` command in your `crontab` (see Chapter 8) so it runs more often. For example, to rotate logs hourly (at 1 minute after the hour):

```
1 * * * * logrotate /etc/logrotate.d/mylog
```

Alternately, you can use `savelog`:

```
1 * * * * savelog -c 48 /var/log/mylogfile  # save last 48 hours as 0..47
```

If you notice a log that is growing too large, or never being rotated, then look for log configuration files in `/etc/logrotate.d/`. If it does not exist, consider adding it. If it does exist, then maybe it needs to be rotated more often.

Summary

The default Ubuntu installation is a good start for a secure system. Although it does reduce risks from remote attackers, it is vulnerable to local data exposure. Restricting root access, encrypting files and directories, and removing unnecessary files all provide additional security. Tools such as Sudo, GnuPG, EncFS, and LUKS help protect files and access, while `savelog` and `logrotate` manage files that would otherwise grow without bounds.

## CHAPTER 12

Advanced Networking

What's In This Chapter?

How to configure, debug, and tune your network driver
Enabling wireless network connections
Managing network firewalls
Creating secure network tunnels
Configuring your own proxy servers
Enabling smart proxy servers for parental control
Setting up a secure network connection

Most of the time, people will install Ubuntu, configure the network during the installation, and not need to change it again. However, there are some situations where you will want to configure the network. This can happen if you have a laptop and frequently move between different networks, if you add in a second network card, or if you need more security than the default settings.

In many cases, changing the network configuration can be as simple as using a GUI. In other cases, you'll need to edit some configuration files in order to properly configure some adapters.

As mentioned in Chapter 11, the default Ubuntu desktop installation is pretty secure because no network services are enabled. However, your network traffic is probably still being sent unencrypted across the network. There are a couple of different ways you can enable encryption, authentication, and anonymity when accessing the network.

If you start turning on network services (see Chapter 13), you will need to make sure that your network is hardened. Tools like `iptables` can definitely help lock down a system.

Finally, when everything goes wrong, you will need to know how to debug the network. This is where tools like `tcpdump`, `snort`, and Wireshark come in handy.

Using the Network Manager

The simplest way to configure the network is through the graphical network manager. How you start this applet depends on your version of Ubuntu. For example:

- **Dapper Drake** (6.06 LTS). The application is called `network-admin` and can be started from the System ⇨ Administration ⇨ Networking menu.

- **Hardy Heron** (8.04 LTS). The `network-admin` program be started from the System ⇨ Administration ⇨ Network menu.

- **Jaunty Jackalope (9.04) and Karmic Koala** (9.10). While `network-admin` can be installed (`sudo apt-get install gnome-network-admin`), it isn't the default application. Instead, `nm-connection-editor` is used. It can be found under the System ⇨ Preferences ⇨ Network Connections menu, or by right-clicking on the network icon in the top panel and selecting Edit Connections.

WARNING The menus appear in a clean installation. If you upgraded to Jaunty or Karmic, then your account may not have these menus. Also with Jaunty and Karmic, the icon changes based on the network's status. It may look like two computers (Jaunty has a wired connection), a network connector (Karmic wired connection), some bars indicating wireless signal strength (Karmic and Jaunty wireless connection), or two dots with an animated swirl (establishing connection).

Regardless of the Ubuntu version, the graphical network manager shows each of the available network adapters and enables you to configure them. You can enable or disable interfaces, and set addresses statically or through DHCP. For modems, you can enter the ISP's phone number, login credentials, and whether to reconnect after any disconnects.

With each Ubuntu release, network configuration becomes easier. Under Dapper Drake, you really needed to know about networking. The `network-admin` tool required you to know about adapters, IP addresses, subnets, and DNS (see Figure 12-1). Configuring wireless networks required some complex hacks.

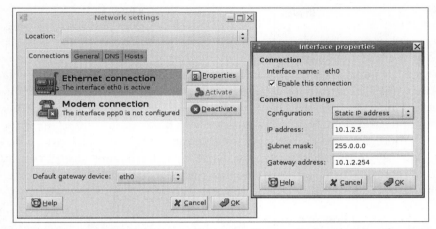

Figure 12-1: The Network Settings applet under Dapper Drake, showing the properties for eth0

Beginning with Jaunty Jackalope, the network manager has become trivial to use. While you can use the GUI to create or edit new network connections, you can also just left-click on the Network Panel icon and select from the list of auto-detected networks. (See Figure 12-2.)

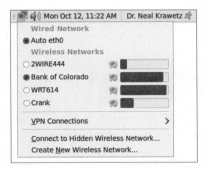

Figure 12-2: The auto-detected network options under Jaunty Jackalope

Configuring Networks from the Command Line

The current Ubuntu development efforts have been centered on GUI-based configurations. What if you installed the Ubuntu Server and don't have a GUI?

What if you are remotely administrating the system? What if your graphical desktop is not working? In these cases, you can still configure networking, but it isn't as straightforward. You will need to manually configure each network interface.

The command `ifconfig -a` lists all known network interfaces. There are three common network devices: `lo`, `eth0`, and `sit0`. The `lo` device is the local loopback, `eth0` is usually the first wired Ethernet adapter, and `sit0` is used to bridge IPv4 and IPv6. Your system may have additional network interfaces and they may be enumerated, such as `eth1` and `eth2` for two additional Ethernet cards.

The configuration for each device is stored in file `/etc/network/interfaces`. This is where you can define static or dynamic configurations, and whether they start up automatically or only as needed. For example, my computer has two Ethernet cards, but only the first one is automatically configured (see Listing 12-1).

Listing 12-1: Sample /etc/network/interfaces

```
# This file describes the network interfaces available on
# your system and how to activate them. For more information,
# see interfaces(5).
# The loopback network interface
auto lo
iface lo inet loopback
# The primary network interface is eth0
auto eth0
iface eth0 inet static
address 10.1.2.30
netmask 255.0.0.0
gateway 10.1.2.254
# The second network interface is eth1
auto eth1
iface eth1 inet dhcp
```

Table 12-1 shows some of the common fields for `/etc/network/interfaces`. For additional information, see the online manual (`man 5 interfaces`).

After configuring the `/etc/network/interfaces` file, you can load the settings using:

```
sudo /etc/init.d/networking restart
```

For interfaces that are not brought up automatically, you can use `ifconfig` to bring them up and down. For example, `sudo ifconfig eth1 up` and `sudo ifconfig eth1 down`. You can only use an interface when it is up.

Table 12-1: Common Fields for /etc/network/interfaces

FIELD NAME	EXAMPLE	PURPOSE
iface	iface eth0 inet dhcp	Defines an interface. The parameters are the interface name (for example, eth0), protocol (inet for IPv4 or inet6 for IPv6), and whether the configuration is static, dhcp, ppp, or bootp.
address	address 10.1.2.5	Static IP or IPv6 address.
netmask	netmask 10.255.255.255	Static subnet mask.
gateway	gateway 10.1.2.254	Static default gateway.
hostname	hostname myhost.local.lan	When using DHCP, this is the hostname to request.
auto	auto eth0 lo	Set one or more interfaces to automatically come up configured. If you want an interface to *not* come up automatically, then leave it off the auto field.
wireless -essid	wireless-essid home	For wireless networks, specifies the Service Set Identifier (SSID) to connect to (for example, "home").
wireless-key	wireless-key 0123456789abcde f0011223344	For wireless networks that use WEP for security, this string specifies the WEP key as 10 or 26 hex digits (for 64-bit or 104-bit encryption, respectively).
pre-up	pre-up /usr/local/ bin/myscript	Run this script before bringing up the network interface.
post-up	post-up /usr/local/ bin/myscript	Run this script after bringing up the network interface.
pre-down	pre-down /usr/local/ bin/myscript	Run this script before taking down the network interface.
post-down	post-down /usr/local/ bin/myscript	Run this script after taking down the network interface.

Configuring Wireless Networks

Beginning with Jaunty Jackalope (9.04), most supported wireless network cards are automatically recognized. The wireless network just needs to be configured through the GUI or command line.

Unfortunately, if your wireless card is not automatically identified, then you've got some work cut out for you. In the worst case, many wireless cards only include Windows drivers, not Linux. Without drivers, there is no way to use the hardware. Fortunately, `ndiswrapper` enables you to use some Windows drivers under Ubuntu!

Assuming you have a working wireless network card, configuring new wireless network configurations is not always automatic. Also, WEP, WAP, and other wireless security protocols can be hard to configure.

Installing Wireless Devices the Easy Way

With Hardy Heron (8.04 LTS) and later versions of Ubuntu, you can go to System ▷ Administration ▷ Hardware Drivers. If the hardware is recognized by the operating system, then there is a good chance that you can simply enable any proprietary drivers and have a working system. (See Figure 12-3.) Unfortunately, my luck is rarely that good. I usually have to go looking for drivers.

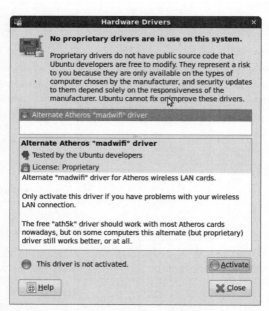

Figure 12-3: The auto-detected hardware, Jaunty Jackalope

Looking for Drivers

Wireless network drivers can come from many different sources and use different hardware components (*chipsets*). Some network interface cards (NICs) are identified during the Ubuntu installation and immediately installed. These include the Intel ipw2100 and ipw2200, Cisco Aironet cards, and NICs based on the Prism chipsets (for example, Prism 2, 2.5, and 3). If you go to the Network Manager and see your wireless card listed, then it is already supported and ready for configuration. You can just jump to the "Hacking with Wireless Tools" section.

NOTE While some manufacturers provide wireless network drivers for Ubuntu (for example, Intel), other drivers have been reverse-engineered. For example, the Broadcom drivers were built by people in the open source community and not by Broadcom.

If the wireless NIC is not supported by the base installation, consider using `apt-cache` to search for an appropriate Ubuntu driver. (See Chapter 5 for using `apt-cache`.) You may need to search based on the wireless card's chipset and not the NIC's model number or manufacturer. For example, the Madwifi driver in the `linux-restricted-modules` package (`apt-cache search linux-restricted-modules`) provides support for Atheros-based adapters. Atheros-based wireless adapters are found in many laptops as well as NICs by 3Com, D-Link, Netgear, and many other manufacturers.

WARNING Be sure to install the correct `linux-restricted-modules` package for your kernel. Use `sudo apt-get install linux-restricted-modules-$(uname -r)`. Since this comes from the restricted repository, the drivers are not necessarily free or open source.

If all else fails and you cannot find a native Linux driver for your wireless card (and purchasing a natively supported wireless NIC is not a viable option), then you can try using `ndiswrapper` to use the Microsoft Windows driver under Ubuntu.

Using ndiswrapper

Chapter 7 discusses some different emulators that work under Ubuntu. Using these emulators, you can install an entire operating system in a virtual environment. However, everything in the virtual environment stays in the virtual environment. In contrast, the Network Driver Interface Specification wrapper (`ndiswrapper`) program enables you to install some network drivers for Microsoft Windows in your actual Linux environment. The wrapper provides enough emulation to support Windows device drivers.

> **WARNING** Using `ndiswrapper` may cause your computer to hang! Save all critical files and close all unnecessary processes before attempting to install any drivers using this tool.

Installing a Driver

Before installing a Windows driver under Linux, you need a few things:

- **Get the Windows driver**—The `ndiswrapper` tool works only with Microsoft Windows XP drivers. If you have drivers for Windows 95, 98, ME, Vista, Windows 7, or some other Windows version, then it won't work unless it says that the driver also works with Windows XP. If you don't have the Windows XP driver, then you can stop here because it won't work.

- **Unpacked INF files**—Most Windows drivers come bundled in a self-extracting archive. You'll need to extract the files before you can use them. Try using `unzip` to expand a self-extracting zip file, `cabextract` for Windows Cabinet files, or `unshield` for unpacking Install Shield files. You can install these tools using:

  ```
  sudo apt-get install unzip cabextract unshield
  ```

- You will know that you have extracted the right files if you see an INF file and some device drivers (likely SYS files). You can check for them using:

  ```
  find . -type f -name '*.inf' -o -name '*.INF'
  ```

After you have gathered the necessary programs and files, you can install the drivers.

1. Install `ndiswrapper`—This can be installed using `sudo apt-get install ndiswrapper-utils`. This will give you the `ndiswrapper` program as well as a loadable kernel module.

2. If the device is an external USB device, then disconnect it before installing the drivers. Some drivers may hang the operating system if the device is installed before the drivers.

3. Find the INF files needed to install the program. In my case, there are two files needed, although other network devices may only need one INF file.

   ```
   $ find . -name '*.inf' -o -name '*.INF'
   ./athfmwdl.inf
   ./net5523.inf
   ```

4. Use `ndiswrapper` to install the files. For my USB network adapter, there were two drivers that needed to be installed, and they needed to be installed in a specific order (see "Debugging Driver Problems").

```
sudo ndiswrapper -i ./net5523.inf
sudo ndiswrapper -i ./athfmwdl.inf
```

5. Load the kernel module:

```
sudo modprobe ndiswrapper
```

6. If the device needs to be plugged in (for example, a USB network adaptor), then plug it in now.

WARNING If the system is going to lock up and hang, it will do so here. If it hangs, then go to the next section, "Debugging Driver Problems."

7. If you made it this far, then it didn't hang (that's great!). Use `ifconfig -a` to list all network devices. You should see a device called `wlan0`—this is the default name given to `ndiswrapper` devices. You can then configure it using the graphical Network Manager or command-line using the settings (see "Using the Network Manager and Configuring Networks from the Command-Line").

8. To automatically start `ndiswrapper` on boot, add the kernel module to `/etc/modules`.

```
sudo bash -c 'echo "ndiswrapper" >> /etc/modules'
```

A graphical alternative to using the command line `ndiswrapper` is `ndisgtk`:

```
sudo apt-get install ndisgtk
sudo ndisgtk
```

This tool provides a front end to `ndiswrapper` and makes it a little easier to install devices (see Figure 12-4). You can also click the Configure Network button to quickly open the Network Settings applet.

Debugging Driver Problems

Installing a driver with `ndiswrapper` is fairly straightforward, although there are a few places where things can go very bad. If the drivers are going to hang the computer, then it will likely happen when the kernel module is loaded or when the device is plugged in. However, drivers may also cause your system to hang when the devices are unloaded or detached, or when resuming after being suspended (as might happen on a laptop).

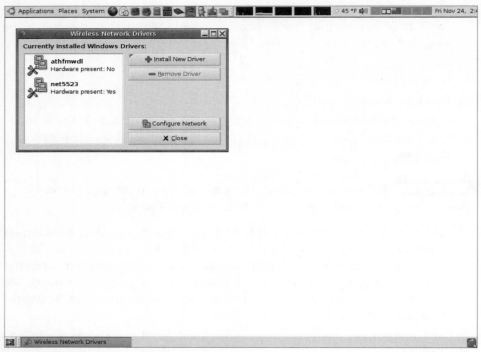

Figure 12-4: The ndisgtk interface

If the drivers are not working for you, then you can try the following:

- **Unload the drivers**—If the drivers cause your system to hang, then you should probably unload them.

  - Reboot the system (usually with the front panel's reset button, since the computer is probably hung up).

  - When Ubuntu begins to come up, press Alt+F1 so that you can see all of the init steps as they happen.

  - When you see the text "Configuring network interfaces," press Ctrl+C. This will skip the network configuration. As long as the network is not configured, the NDIS drivers will not load and the system will not hang. If you don't stop it here, then the system will hang again.

  - Allow the rest of the initialization stages to come up.

  - Log into the system.

  - Use ndiswrapper -l to list each of the loaded drivers.

  - Use ndiswrapper -e to erase (remove) the offending driver. For example, you can use:

    ```
    $ ndiswrapper -l
    ```

```
Installed ndis drivers:
athfmwdl                    driver present
net5523            driver present, hardware present
$ sudo ndiswrapper -e net5523
```

- Reboot the system (`sudo reboot`) and allow it to come up completely.

TIP For some USB network devices, simply unplugging the device and rebooting the system enables you to boot without hanging. In this case, you only need to remove the devices (`ndiswrapper -e`) and do not need to reboot the system a second time.

- **Check the drivers**—In some cases, there may be newer or more stable Windows XP drivers available. Also, drivers from compatible network devices may work better than official ones from the manufacturer.

- **Check official forums**—The `ndiswrapper` tool is very well supported and there are hundreds of network interfaces that are documented as being compatible, incompatible, or requiring additional steps. Visit `http://sourceforge.net/apps/mediawiki/ndiswrapper/`for tips and hints for specific cards. In many cases, this forum also provides links to the actual Windows drivers, ensuring that you are installing the right one.

- **Check for compatible devices**—Many manufacturers may use the same chipsets in different cards. Using `lsusb` or `lspci -n`, identify your 4-byte unique identifier for your network adapter. It should look something like "0123:89ab" (although the exact hex numbers will be different). Check the official forums for the identifier and see if any other devices use the same drivers. For example, the EnGenius EUB-862 uses the same chipset as the Airlink101 (both use the USB identifier "0cf3:0001"). Although the Windows XP drivers that came with the EUB-862 consistently hung my Linux system, the drivers for the Airlink101 worked well.

Hacking with Wireless Tools

Ubuntu includes many different tools for configuring the network. The most important ones are `iwconfig` and `iwlist`. Using these, you can configure and reconfigure most wireless options.

The `iwconfig` command is used to configure wireless devices. When used by itself, it lists every network device and, if it is a wireless device, the current configuration. For example:

```
$ iwconfig
lo        no wireless extensions.
eth0      no wireless extensions.
```

```
sit0      no wireless extensions.
wlan0     IEEE 802.11b  ESSID:"My SSID"
          Mode:Managed  Frequency:2.437 GHz
          Access Point: Not-Associated
          Bit Rate:108 Mb/s
          Power Management min timeout:0us  mode:All
packets received
          Link Quality:0  Signal level:0  Noise
level:0
          Rx invalid nwid:0  Rx invalid crypt:0  Rx
invalid frag:0
          Tx excessive retries:0  Invalid misc:0
Missed beacon:0
```

Using the `iwlist` command, you can scan for available access points (APs), as demonstrated in Listing 12-2.

Listing 12-2: Example iwlist Scan

```
$ sudo iwlist wlan0 scan
wlan0     Scan completed:
          Cell 01—Address: 00:18:39:CC:F8:C7
               ESSID:"logo1"
               Protocol:IEEE 802.11g
               Mode:Managed
               Frequency:2.412 GHz (Channel 1)
               Quality:0/100  Signal level:-87 dBm  Noise level:-256 dBm
               Encryption key:on
               Bit Rates:1 Mb/s; 2 Mb/s; 5.5 Mb/s; 11 Mb/s; 18 Mb/s
                         24 Mb/s; 36 Mb/s; 54 Mb/s; 6 Mb/s; 9 Mb/s
                         12 Mb/s; 48 Mb/s
               Extra:bcn_int=100
               Extra:atim=0
               Extra:wpa_ie=
                  3d180050f21101020050f21201002050f20211002050f20
          Cell 02—Address: 00:14:BF:9B:CA:D3
               ESSID:"My SSID"
               Protocol:IEEE 802.11g
               Mode:Managed
               Frequency:2.437 GHz (Channel 6)
               Quality:0/100  Signal level:-36 dBm  Noise level:-256 dBm
               Encryption key:on
               Bit Rates:1 Mb/s; 2 Mb/s; 5.5 Mb/s; 11 Mb/s; 18 Mb/s
                         24 Mb/s; 36 Mb/s; 54 Mb/s; 6 Mb/s; 9 Mb/s
                         12 Mb/s; 48 Mb/s
               Extra:bcn_int=1000
               Extra:atim=0
          Cell 03—Address: 00:18:39:2C:2B:51
               ESSID:"linksys"
               Protocol:IEEE 802.11g
               Mode:Managed
               Frequency:2.437 GHz (Channel 6)
               Quality:0/100  Signal level:-85 dBm  Noise level:-256 dBm
```

```
Encryption key:off
Bit Rates:1 Mb/s; 2 Mb/s; 5.5 Mb/s; 11 Mb/s; 18 Mb/s
           24 Mb/s; 36 Mb/s; 54 Mb/s; 6 Mb/s; 9 Mb/s
           12 Mb/s; 48 Mb/s
Extra:bcn_int=100
Extra:atim=0
```

TIP When used as a regular user, `iwscan wlan0 scan` will only display previous results. These may expire after a few minutes. However, if you run the command as root, it will initiate a new scan.

The example in Listing 12-2 shows a scan from `iwlist`. In the example, there are three APs that are within range of the Ubuntu system. You can combine the results from `iwlist` with `iwconfig` and connect to a specific access point (AP). For example:

```
# connect to an AP using the SSID
sudo iwconfig essid "My SSID"
# connect to SSID on a specific channel
sudo iwconfig essid "My SSID" channel 6
```

Enabling Wireless Security with WEP

The Wired Equivalent Privacy (WEP) protocol is a common method for encrypting wireless connections. The `iwconfig` program allows you to specify the physical connection. It also allows you to provide a WEP key for connecting to an AP. This can be specified on the command line as a string of ASCII text or hex values. Table 12-2 shows some of the common key formats.

Table 12-2: Examples of iwconfig Key Formats

EXAMPLE	DESCRIPTION
`iwconfig wlan0 key` `0123456789`	Specify a 10-digit (hexadecimal) key for 64-bit WEP.
`iwconfig wlan0 key` `0123-4567-89ab-cdef-0123-4567-89`	Specify a 26-digit (hexadecimal) key for 104-bit WEP. Hyphens are optional.
`iwconfig wlan0 key 's:Secret Key'`	An ASCII string can be used as the key if it is prefaced by an "s:". Be sure to put quotation marks around the string if it has spaces.

NOTE Although it has some security weaknesses, WEP is universally available and certainly better than using no security.

The key value for `iwconfig` can also be placed in the /etc/network/ interfaces file. In addition, you can specify multiple keys—if one key does not work, then it will try the next one. Multiple keys can be really useful if your home and office use the same SSID but different keys. (Or if your office has meeting rooms, each with the same SSID but different keys.) For example, to specify three keys and set the default to be #2, you could have lines similar to these in your `/etc/network/interfaces` file:

```
auto wlan0
iface wlan0 inet dhcp
wireless-essid My SSID
wireless-key1 0123456789abcdef0123456789
wireless-key2 abcdef0123
wireless-key3 s:Top Secret
wireless-defaultkey 2
```

Enabling Wireless Security with WPA

Although WEP is certainly better than no security, there are other ways to secure wireless networks. Wi-Fi Protected Access (WPA) is steadily growing in popularity and offers stronger options for privacy and authentication.

1. To configure WPA, you will need to generate a WPA configuration file. This is done by using `wpa_passphrase`. You will need to provide your SSID and a passphrase, and the program will generate a configuration file.

TIP Specifying the passphrase on the command line (as done in this example) is usually not very secure—particularly if multiple people have access to the computer. If you don't specify the passphrase, you will be prompted for it. (Prompting is much better, since the passphrase won't be stored in your shell's history.)

```
wpa_passphrase "My SSID" "Secret Password" > tempfile
sudo cp tempfile /etc/wpa_supplicant.conf
```

The contents of `/etc/wpa_supplicant.conf` lists your network's name and the associated WPA key. Although they should be autodetected, some drivers may need to you to add `proto` and `key_mgmt` fields. Listing 12-3 shows a sample `/etc/wpa_supplicant.conf` file (bold indicates optional fields).

Listing 12-3: CR Sample /etc/wpa_supplicant.conf File

```
network={
        ssid="My SSID"
        #psk="Secret Password"
psk=aa380927bc23c6a736a69fa2b395b442bade145973b3a39c25cee0c9d55b0711
        proto=WPA
        key_mgmt=WPA-PSK
}
```

TIP For security on multi-user systems, you should consider removing the `#psk` line that contains the decoded key and changing the file permissions so it is only accessible by root: `sudo chmod 600/etc/wpa_supplicant.conf; sudo chown root:root/etc/wpa_supplicant.conf`.

2. Beginning with Karmic Koala (9.10), support for `/etc/wpa_supplic-ant.conf` was removed. (Karmic's wireless network is easy to configure from the GUI, but what if you installed the Server edition and don't have a GUI?) To re-enable it, you need to edit `/etc/network/interfaces` and specify the configuration file. For example:

```
auto wlan0
iface wlan0 inet dhcp
wpa-conf /etc/wpa_supplicant.conf
```

3. After creating the `/etc/wpa_supplicant.conf` file, you should test it to make sure it works. In this example, the wireless interface is `wlan0` and it uses the generic wireless LAN extensions (`-D wext`). Other possible control extensions are listed in `man wpa_supplicant` and include `ndiswrapper`, `ndis`, `madwifi` (for Atheros adapters), and `wired` for wired Ethernet cards with WPA support.

```
sudo wpa_supplicant -D wext -i wlan0 -c/etc/wpa_supplicant.conf
```

4. To make the changes take effect every time the network interface is used, `pre-up` and `post-down` scripts can be added to `/etc/networking/inter-faces`. These scripts will start and stop WPA support. For example:

```
auto wlan0
iface wlan0 inet dhcp
pre-up wpa_supplicant -B -w -D wext -i wlan0 \
                -c/etc/wpa_supplicant.conf
post-down killall -q wpa_supplicant
```

NOTE The `-B` option to `wpa_supplicant` means to run the command in the background. The `-w` option means to wait for the interface to be added in case the wlan0 interface is not immediately available (or created) when the script starts.

Securing the Network

When you enable a network interface, you create a bidirectional path. Just as you can go out over the network, there is a path for attackers to come into your system. Firewall software, such as Tcpwrappers and IP Tables, enable you to restrict, modify, and manage network packet handling.

Using the network usually has one other limitation: there is no security. Although a user may connect remotely using SSH or some other secure protocol, the ability to connect in the first place can lead to security risks in highly sensitive environments. Fortunately, Ubuntu includes IPsec and IPv6. These network layer protocols can authenticate, validate, and encrypt network traffic. It's one thing to require a user login using SSH; it's another thing to block SSH connections in the first place if they are not authenticated.

Configuring Firewalls with Tcpwrappers

The basic Ubuntu installation includes two types of firewalls: Tcpwrappers and IP Tables. Tcpwrappers is usually used with automated services such as inetd and xinetd. This system consults two files (`/etc/hosts.allow` and `/etc/hosts.deny`) and grants access based on these settings. Both files are in the same format: *daemon*: *clients*. For example, to restrict access for incoming FTP requests to only machines in the `mydomain.lan` domain, you can use:

```
in.ftpd: .mydomain.lan
```

> **NOTE** There are many different FTP servers available. In this example, the server's executable is called `in.ftpd`. For the full list, use `apt-cache search ftpd`. You will need a server that supports libwrap or starts from `inetd`. See the section "Enabling Tcpwrappers" later in this chapter.

When a new network request for the daemon is received, Tcpwrappers first checks `/etc/hosts.allow` and then `/etc/hosts.deny`. If the restriction is found in `/etc/hosts.allow`, then the connection is permitted to contact the daemon. The `/etc/hosts.deny` restriction blocks the request from ever reaching the daemon. And if there is no restriction, then the connection is permitted.

If you don't want to list specific daemons and hosts, then you can use the keyword ALL. Very secure systems usually have an `/etc/hosts.deny` that says:

```
ALL: ALL
```

This creates a default-deny configuration and blocks access to every service from every client except when they are explicitly permitted by `/etc/hosts.allow`.

> **WARNING** If you set `/etc/hosts.deny` to ALL: ALL and forget to grant access in `/etc/hosts.allow`, then new remote access connections will fail! You may not notice this immediately if you are already remotely connected; Tcpwrappers only restricts new connections, not established ones.

Testing the Tcpwrappers Configuration

You can check your Tcpwrappers configuration using the `tcpdmatch` command. For example, to check if the host `myhost.mydomain.lan` can access the service `in.ftpd`, you can use:

```
tcpdmatch in.ftpd myhost.mydomain.lan
```

This displays any hostname warnings, service issues, and whether access is granted or denied. In addition, if any rule is matched then it will tell you which file (`/etc/hosts.allow` or `/etc/hosts.deny`) and which line.

Enabling Tcpwrappers

The active program for running Tcpwrappers is called `tcpd` (`/usr/sbin/tcpd`). This is usually found in `/etc/inetd.conf` for starting services. For example:

```
netbios-ssn    stream  tcp    nowait  root   /usr/sbin/tcpd  /usr/sbin/smbd
```

This line says to run the SMB daemon when there is a connection on port 139/tcp (the `netbios-ssn` TCP port). Before running the `smbd` daemon, Tcpwrappers is used to check if the connection is permitted.

Not every program that uses Tcpwrappers runs the `tcpd` program; Tcpwrappers is commonly compiled into some network daemons. For example, the SSH daemon (`sudo apt-get install openssh-server`) has Tcpwrappers built in. You can check for this by using the `ldd` command to list all linked libraries and search the `libwrap` shared library.

```
$ ldd /usr/sbin/sshd | grep libwrap
        libwrap.so.0 => /lib/libwrap.so.0 (0xb7eee000)
```

This means that the SSH server will consult `/etc/hosts.allow` and `/etc/hosts.deny` before allowing connections. You can generate a list of `libwrap`-enabled applications using a small script:

```
# find all executables and test for libwrap
find /bin /usr/bin /sbin /usr/sbin -type f -perm -1 | \
while read filename; do
  haslib=$(ldd "$filename" | grep libwrap.so);
  if [ "$haslib" != "" ]; then echo "$filename"; fi;
done
```

Configuring Firewalls with IP Tables

Tcpwrappers operates on the network's transport layer. It can filter TCP or UDP ports, but it cannot filter network layer (IP, IPv6, and so on) traffic. For this type of filtering, you can use IP Tables. Unlike Tcpwrappers, which runs as an application, IP Tables are provided as a kernel module. As a result, IP Tables impact all applications, not just those designed or configured to use it.

By default, IP Tables stores three types of filters:

▪ INPUT—This table identifies what type of incoming packets to accept. For example, to block SSH packets that use TCP on port 22 from the subnet 172.16.23.0/24, then you can use:

```
sudo iptables -A INPUT -p tcp --dport 22 \
   --source 172.16.23.0/24 -j REJECT
```

▪ OUTPUT—This table is used to filter outbound network traffic (from your system to a remote system). For example, to block all connections to Microsoft, you can use:

```
sudo iptables -A OUTPUT --destination 207.46.0.0/16 -j REJECT
```

▪ FORWARD—This table is used to forward traffic, in case you want to use your Ubuntu system as a network firewall. For example, to allow all traffic from my local LAN (10.0.0.0/8) to relay through my Ubuntu system, I can use:

```
sudo iptables --table nat -A POSTROUTING \
   --out-interface eth0 -j MASQUERADE
sudo iptables -A FORWARD --in-interface eth0 \
   --source 10.0.0.0/8 -j ACCEPT
```

However, if I only want to forward web traffic, then I can specify a destination port:

```
sudo iptables -A FORWARD --in-interface eth0 \
   --source 10.0.0.0/8 -p tcp --dport 80 -j ACCEPT
```

After configuring your system to forward traffic, you can use it as the network gateway for other systems on your network.

The iptables command manages a set of tables and rules, called *chains*. A single table may have many different chains. The default table is called filter and has the INPUT, OUTPUT, and FORWARD chains. Other tables include nat (for network address translations), mangle (for packet modification), and raw for low-level packet management.

The iptables command takes a variety of options. Table 12-3 lists some of the more common parameters. The full list can be found in the man page for iptables.

When you are finished, you can view your tables using sudo iptables -L. For example:

```
$ sudo iptables -L
Chain INPUT (policy ACCEPT)
target    prot opt source              destination
REJECT    tcp -- 172.16.23.0/24        anywhere
```

```
tcp dpt:ssh reject-with icmp-port-unreachable
REJECT    tcp -- 172.16.23.0/24        anywhere
tcp dpt:ssh reject-with icmp-port-unreachable
Chain FORWARD (policy ACCEPT)
target    prot opt source              destination
ACCEPT    tcp -- 10.0.0.0/8            anywhere
tcp dpt:www
Chain OUTPUT (policy ACCEPT)
target    prot opt source              destination
REJECT    all -- anywhere              207.46.0.0/16
reject-with icmp-port-unreachable
```

Table 12-3: Common Parameters for `iptables`

PARAMETER	EXAMPLE	PURPOSE
-t, --table	-t nat	Specify the table to act on, such as `filter`, `nat`, `mangle`, or `raw`. The default table is `filter`.
-A, --append	-A INPUT	Append rules to a particular chain, such as INPUT, FORWARD, or OUTPUT.
-s, --source, -d, --destination	-s 10.0.0.0/8	Specify the source (`-s` or `source`) and destination (`-d` or `destination`) network address. You may include an optional subnet mask.
-p, --proto	-p tcp	Specify the transport layer protocol, such as tcp, udp, icmp, or all. Without this option, all protocols match the rule.
--port, --sport, --dport	--port 22	If you specify a protocol with `-p`, then you can also specify the port number. This can be a source port (`sport`), destination port (`dport`), or either (`port`).
--in-interface, --out-interface	--in-interface eth0	Specify the port used for receiving (`in`) or sending (`out`) packets.
-j, --jump	-j ACCEPT	Identify how to handle the rule. Common rules usually use ACCEPT, REJECT, or DROP. There are a variety of other rules including ones for rewriting packets, triggering logs, or generating specific packet responses.

TIP If you need to support IPv6 network addresses, use the `ip6tables` command instead of `iptables`.

Saving IP Tables Settings

Changes made using IP Tables are not permanent. To make them happen every time you reboot, you will need to save the settings and reload them during boot.

1. Configure IP Tables and test them to make sure they do what you want.

CUSTOM FILTERING

Usually when administrators configure IP Tables, it is done to block external attack paths or enable routing through an existing computer. However, there is another use.

Many different types of viruses, spyware, and worms call out to remote control systems. Using the OUTPUT chain from the `filter` table, you can block known communication protocols. For example, if nobody within your network should be accessing IRC servers, then you can block TCP ports 6666 and 6667 since these are commonly used for IRC:

```
sudo iptables -A OUTPUT -p tcp --dport 6666 -j REJECT
sudo iptables -A OUTPUT -p tcp --dport 6667 -j REJECT
```

On mail servers, you can use this to block access from known spam subnets, and on proxy servers you can block access to sites that are infected with malware.

Personally, I have a different use. I perform computer network audits and some systems may be off limits or outside the scope of the audit. To prevent accidental access, I block outbound traffic to the restricted hosts. In some cases, hosts may only be accessed during certain hours (to prevent interference with regular customers). In this case, I use a `cron` job to add and remove access as needed. (See Chapter 8 for scheduling tasks with `cron`.)

---

2. Save your changes to a configuration file.

```
sudo iptables-save > iptables.conf

sudo mv iptables.conf /etc/iptables.conf
```

3. Make an init script for IP Tables. I created `/etc/init.d/iptables` and the contents are in Listing 12-4. Be sure to make the script executable: `chmod 755 /etc/init.d/iptables`.

Listing 12-4: The /etc/init.d/iptables Startup Script

```
#!/bin/sh
PATH=/usr/local/sbin:/usr/local/bin:/sbin:/bin:/usr/sbin:/usr/bin
NAME=iptables
DESC="IP Tables"

[ -f /etc/iptables.conf ] || exit 1
```

```
case "$1" in
  start)
        echo "Starting $DESC: $NAME"
        /sbin/iptables—flush -t filter
        /sbin/iptables—flush -t nat
        /sbin/iptables-restore /etc/iptables.conf
      ;;
  stop)
        /sbin/iptables—flush -t filter
        /sbin/iptables—flush -t nat
      ;;
  restart|reload|force-reload)
        echo "Restarting $DESC: $NAME"
        /sbin/iptables—flush -t filter
        /sbin/iptables—flush -t nat
        /sbin/iptables-restore /etc/iptables.conf
      ;;
  *)
        echo "Usage: $0 {start|stop|restart|force-reload}" >&2
        exit 1
      ;;
esac
exit 0
```

4. Add the script to the startup configuration. It is configured to be one of the first scripts to run.

```
cd /etc/rcS.d
sudo ln -s ../init.d/iptables S37iptables
```

Now, any configuration saved in `/etc/iptables.conf` will be included during startup. If you make new changes using `iptables`, you can save them using `sudo iptables-save`.

Using the Uncomplicated Firewall

The `iptables` system provides powerful firewall options. However, it can be fairly complicated. The Uncomplicated Firewall (`ufw`) is a front end to `iptables`. It allows you to quickly configure the network. For example, if you only want to permit SSH and HTTP connections to come into your system, you can use:

```
$ sudo ufw allow ssh/tcp      # permit ssh which is 22/tcp
Rules updated
$ sudo ufw allow 80/tcp       # HTTP is also known as 80/tcp
Rules updated
$ sudo ufw enable
Firewall started and enabled on system startup
```

```
$ sudo ufw status
Firewall loaded

To                        Action  From
–                         –––––
22:tcp                    ALLOW   Anywhere
80:tcp                    ALLOW   Anywhere
```

TIP **You can reference ports by numbers or names. The `/etc/services` files contains the list of common ports and their names. Port 22 is ssh, so `22/tcp` is the same as `ssh/tcp`.**

The `ufw` command allows you to very quickly permit (allow) or reject (deny) connection. You can even make very specific commands. For example:

```
# allow 10.1.2.0 to 10.1.2.255 to access my mail server (25/tcp)
sudo ufw allow proto tcp from 10.1.2.0/24 port 25
# Forbid FTP connections from my computer to the 192.168 subnet.
sudo ufw deny to 192.168.0.0/16 port ftp
```

When you are all done configuring the firewall, use `ufw enable` to make the rules active. This will also save the rules and enable them the next time the computer boots.

Table 12-4 lists some of the more common parameters. The full list can be found in the man page for `ufw`.

Different versions of Ubuntu offer different levels of `ufw` functionality. For example, Hardy Heron (8.04 LTS) supports the basic allow and deny rules, as well as IPv4 and IPv6 network addresses. However, Hardy's `ufw` does not have any option to limit the number of incoming connections (rate limiting). Jaunty Jackalope (9.04) includes options for rate limiting, but not filtering by interface (e.g., eth0 or wlan0). For interface-specific rules, you will need to use Karmic Koala (9.10) or fall back to `iptables`. Unfortunately, `ufw` is not available for Dapper Drake (6.06 LTS) and updates to `ufw` are not back-ported to older Ubuntu versions.

Between Hardy Heron and Jaunty Jackalope, the Uncomplicated Firewall only filters connections to incoming network services. If you want to filter outbound connections, then you will need to either use `iptables` or use the `ufw` that comes with Karmic Koala. Under Karmic, you can use `ufw` to block outbound network connections.

```
sudo ufw deny 22/tcp     # block inbound connections to
SSH (any Ubuntu)
sudo ufw deny in 22/tcp  # block inbound connections
(Karmic or later)
sudo ufw deny out 22/tcp # block outbound connections
(Karmic or later)
```

```
# block all outbout connection to a specific subnet:
sudo ufw deny out proto tcp to 192.168.0.0/16 port 22
# block all outbound connections:
sudo ufw deny out proto tcp to any port 22
```

Table 12-4: Common Parameters for ufw

PARAMETER	EXAMPLE	PURPOSE
allow *port*	allow 25/tcp	Add a rule to permit a specific port. The port can be listed by name or number. If the protocol is omitted, then it will create a rule for both TCP and UDP.
deny *port*	deny 25/tcp	Explicitly forbid access to the port.
status	status	List the current set of rules.
delete *rule*	delete allow 25/tcp	Remove a rule from the table.
default *policy*	default deny	Specify the default action in case there is no specific rule. Generally you should leave this as default deny.
enable	enable	Save the current rule list, activate the rules, and ensure that they will be enabled the next time the computer starts up.
disable	disable	Deactivate the current rule list and prevent the rules from starting up during the next boot.

Disabling Pings

Between iptables, ufw, and kernel parameters, there are plenty of ways to tweak the network and enable packet filtering. For example, the following commands are equivalent for blocking network connections to a local Internet Relay Chat (IRC) servers (port 6667/tcp).

```
sudo ufw deny 6667/tcp
sudo iptables -A INPUT -p tcp --dport 6667 -j REJECT
```

One common protocol that is frequently filtered is the ICMP Echo-request packet, also known as an echo or *ping*. Echo is part of the Internet Control Message Protocol (ICMP) and used to determine whether a remote host is reachable. Unfortunately, ping packets can also be abused. Attackers may send a ping packet as a form of network reconnaissance—if the host answers, then it is available for further scanning and attacks. Similarly, a flood of ping packets can be enough traffic to cripple a networked server.

> **NOTE** A flood of ICMP Echo-request packets is called a *Smurf attack* — named after the little blue cartoon characters from the 1980s. The cartoon emphasized the power of teamwork. A single ping packet is not a threat, but a million of them at the same time can crash a network.

Servers that are connected directly to the Internet (externally accessible) commonly disable ICMP Echo-request packets in order to deter network reconnaissance and mitigate potential Smurf attacks. Many firewall routers also drop ping packets in order to reduce unnecessary network traffic and protect servers. With Ubuntu, there are many options for disabling support for ICMP Echo-request packets:

▪ Disable with `sysctl`. Using `sysctl`, you can disable ICMP Echo-request support from the kernel. This is the most efficient way to disable support since the packet is not passed to any other kernel or application subsystems. (See "Tuning Kernel Parameters" in Chapter 8 for more information about `sysctl`.)

```
sudo sysctl -w net.ipv4.icmp_echo_ignore_all=1
```

▪ Disable with `/proc`. You can directly modify the running system configuration by editing support in `/proc`.

```
echo 1 | sudo tee /proc/sys/net/ipv4/icmp_echo_ignore_all
```

▪ Disable with `iptables`. The ICMP Echo-request is an ICMP packet type 8. Use `iptables` to block these requests.

```
sudo iptables -A INPUT -p icmp --icmp-type 8 -j DROP
```

▪ Disable with `ufw`. The `ufw` command line cannot be used to disable ICMP packets. However, you can edit the file containing the initialization rules. Normally `ufw` drops all ICMP packets. However, the default `/etc/ufw/before.rules` file enables ICMP. Edit the file and comment-out the echo-request line (and any other ICMP line) by prefacing it with a `#`.

```
# ok icmp codes
-A ufw-before-input -p icmp --icmp-type destination-unreachable \
   -j ACCEPT
-A ufw-before-input -p icmp --icmp-type source-quench -j ACCEPT
-A ufw-before-input -p icmp --icmp-type time-exceeded -j DROP
-A ufw-before-input -p icmp --icmp-type parameter-problem -j ACCEPT
# -A ufw-before-input -p icmp --icmp-type echo-request -j ACCEPT
```

> **WARNING** UFW is a little finicky about reloading the `/etc/ufw/before-.rules` configuration file. If the `ufw enable` or `ufw reload` commands do not disable ping packets, you might need to enable `ufw` and then reboot the system for the change to take effect. During the reboot process, the system will briefly

respond to ICMP Echo-request packets. This happens because the kernel loads ICMP support before `ufw` disables them.

Enabling IPsec

Although firewalls prevent some connections, they do nothing to actually authenticate the connection and offer no privacy options. If you really need to make sure the connection is permitted and don't want someone to see what you are doing, then consider using IPsec, the security extension to IP. IPsec offers digital signatures for authentication and encryption for privacy.

> **NOTE** There are two common versions of the Internet Protocol: the older IP (also called IPv4) and the newer IPv6. IPv6 uses the same security options found in IPsec. The only difference: the availability of these security functions is optional for IPv4 but mandatory for IPv6. However, *available* is not the same as *enabled*. The security in IPv6 is normally turned off unless you explicitly enable it. Turning on the security for IPv6 is exactly the same as configuring the security for IPsec.

IPsec provides point-to-point security that can be used as a secure path or as a virtual private network (VPN). The configuration happens in two stages. First you define the keys to use, and then you define the security policies.

The main program for configuring IPsec is called `setkey` and it comes from the `ipsec-tools` package.

```
sudo apt-get install ipsec-tools
```

UNMASKING RACOON

There is an alternate package to `ipsec-tools` called `racoon`. (Yes, it is spelled with one c, not like the animal with the same name.) Although `racoon` is popular with some Linux and BSD distributions, `ipsec-tools` was the first package included in the main repository for older versions of Ubuntu. This historical precedence gives it slightly more popularity with Ubuntu users. Both packages include the `setkey` program and both have nearly identical usage. Ironically, the man page for `setkey` from the `ipsec-tools` package explicitly references `racoon`, even if you don't install `racoon`.

So, what is the difference between `racoon` and `ipsec-tools`? Not much from my viewpoint. `ipsec-tools` accepts configuration commands from a file or stdin, while `racoon` also supports configurations on the command-line. The `racoon` package also uses a different configuration file: `/etc/racoon/racoon-tool.conf` instead of `/etc/ipsec-tools.conf`.

Creating IPsec Keys

WARNING   I strongly recommend against *remotely* using `setkey` to configure IPsec. As soon as you run the command, it is implemented. If you configure a rule to require a key, then your network connection may be immediately terminated. Unless you have an alternate route into the system, you can easily become locked out.

To create a key, you need to know the IP addresses for the source and destination hosts, the algorithm, and the key. For example, to define a key for 3DES encryption using cipher block chaining (CBC), I can use:

```
echo 'add 10.1.1.5 10.1.2.10 esp 0x201 -m tunnel
  -E 3des-cbc "Twenty-four characters!!"
  -A hmac-md5 0xdeadbeefcafe1234deadbeefcafe1234;' |
  sudo setkey -c
```

In this case, the 3DES key for encryption is the string `Twenty-four characters!!`, and the secret password used for authenticating the packet is the hexadecimal value `0xdeadbeefcafe1234deadbeefcafe1234`.

The `setkey` program either reads in commands from a file or from stdin. If you just want to run one setting, then place the command in an `echo` statement and pipe the data into `setkey -c`. The `-c` option to `setkey` says to read from stdin, whereas `-f` says to read from a file. The lines that it reads are commands such as `add` or `delete` and include configuration options. Each command needs to end with a semicolon.

The `add` option within the `setkey` command is used to specify a Security Association Database (SAD) entry. These are basically combinations of encryption, authentication, and compression definitions along with network addresses.

- **Addresses**—The first two options to the `add` command are the source and destination IP addresses. These can be IP or IPv6 address (although they must both be IP or both be IPv6).

- **Protocol**—The next parameter specifies the type of protocol. The available values are usually either `esp` for encapsulating security payload or `ah` for authenticated header. The former defines a protected payload, while the latter is only used for authenticating the sender. Other protocols include `esp-old` and `ah-old` (from obsolete standards), `ipcomp`, and `tcp` for using TCP with MD5 for validation.

- **SPI**—The protocol is followed by a Security Parameter Index used to identify the SAD entry.

- **Mode**—The `-m` option identifies the type of protocol. It can be `tunnel`, `transport`, or `any`. A `tunnel` is used for a VPN, while `transport` is only used for protecting the transport layer (TCP or UDP traffic). Other protocols, such as ICMP, will not pass through the secure connection when using `transport`. Specifying `-m any` allows the SAD to be used for either `tunnel` or `transport` security.

- **Encryption**—The `-E` option specifies an encryption algorithm and a secret key used for the encryption. The length of the key depends on the selected encryption algorithm. For example, `-E 3des-cbc` requires a 24-byte key. Table 12-5 lists the available encryption algorithms and the required key lengths. Keys can be provided as hexadecimal values (beginning with 0x) or as quoted strings. If you do not specify an encryption algorithm, then the entire packet will be sent unencrypted—just as when using the `null` cipher with no key.

WARNING The `setkey` program will not load the command if the key length is wrong. It will only say that the key length is wrong; it won't tell you what the key length should be. Also, the man page for `setkey` only gives you the key length in bits, not bytes or characters.

Table 12-5: Available Encryption Algorithms and Required Key Sizes for setkey

ALGORITHM	KEY SIZE IN BITS	KEY SIZE IN BYTES
des-cbc	64	8
3des-cbc	192	24
null	0–2048	0–256
blowfish-cbc	40–448	5–56
cast128-cbc	40–128	5–16
des-deriv	64	8
3des-deriv	192	24
rijndael-cbc	128, 192, or 256	16, 24, or 32
twofish-cbc	0–256	0–32
aes-ctr	160, 224, or 288	20, 28, or 36

- **Authentication**—The `-A` option specifies the algorithm for digitally signing the packet. This authentication header allows the recipient to know that the packet is actually from the sender. As with encryption, the key can either be a hexadecimal value (beginning with 0x) or a quoted string, and the key size depends on the algorithm (see Table 12-6). If this option is not specified, then the header is not authenticated.

▪ **Compression**—The -c option can be used to specify packet compression. The only available algorithm is deflate, based on the same algorithm used to compress gzip files (see RFC2394). However, unlike gzip, you cannot specify the compression level. Although compression is useful in some situations, such as transmitting large text files, it isn't ideal for all situations. For example, most encryption algorithms generate random-looking data that may not compress well. Also if the data being transmitted is already compressed, then it won't compress any further. Trying to compress data again may only consume more CPU resources. If you're transmitting small packets or not using encryption, then it might be worthwhile to enable compression since the TCP header (a significant transmission overhead) will be compressed. However, for large blocks of streaming data through an encrypted tunnel, you might see better performance without using encryption. This is because the TCP header no longer accounts for a significant amount of data, and encrypted data does not compress well. For these reasons, this option is usually not enabled.

Table 12-6: Available Authentication Algorithms and Required Key Sizes for setkey

ALGORITHM	KEY SIZE IN BITS	KEY SIZE IN BYTES
hmac-md5	128	16
hmac-sha1	160	20
keyed-md5	128	16
keyed-sha1	160	20
null	0–2048	0–256
hmac-sha256	256	32
hmac-sha384	384	48
hmac-sha512	512	64
hmac-ripemd160	160	20
aes-xcbc-mac	128	16
tcp-md5	8–640	1–80

Both ends of an encrypted tunnel need to have the same configuration. Otherwise, they will be unable to communicate. However, both directions of an encrypted tunnel do not need to use the same configuration. For example, transmitting IPsec packets may use an authenticated header with one key, and responses may use authentication and encryption with different keys.

Configuring the Security Policy Database

Whereas the Security Association Database (SAD) is used to match algorithms to a particular configuration, the Security Policy Database (SPD) says when to use the SAD entries. The `setkey` option `spdadd` defines the requirements. For example:

```
spdadd 10.1.2.10 10.1.1.5 any -P in
  ipsec esp/tunnel/10.1.2.10-10.1.1.5/require;
```

Like the `add` command, `spdadd` takes a series of parameters.

- **Addresses**—The first two parameters specify the source and destination addresses. These can be provided as IP or IPv6. They can also contain an optional subnet mask and port number. For example, `10.1.2.10` is the same as `10.1.2.10/32` and `10.1.2.10/32[any]`. If you want to allow an entire subnet, then you can use something like `10.1.2.0/24`. You can specify port (for example, port 80) as `10.1.2.10[80]` or `10.1.2.0/24[80]`. Specific ports are very useful if you are configuring a static VPN.

- **Policy**—The `-P` option specifies policy requirements. This starts with the direction of packet traversal; `-P in`, `-P out`, or `-P any`. While both sides of an IPsec connection need to have the same SAD values, the `-P` option in the SDP needs to be reversed. If one system says `-P in` then the other needs to say `-P out`. The policy also defines what should happen. The options are `ipsec` for enabling IPsec, `discard` to deny access, or `none` to allow unsecured connections.

- **IPsec**—If the policy specifies using `ipsec`, then you also need to specify which SAD to associate with the SPD and when to associate it. The specification has four parameters, separated by slashes.

  - *Protocol*—This can be either esp or ah.

  - *Mode*—This can be either tunnel or transport.

  - *Addresses*—This is only required for tunnels; it lists the source and destination addresses with optional ports. For transport mode, this field can be blank (denoted by `//`).

  - *Level*—This says when to enable IPsec. The value must be either `default`, `use`, or `require`. The `default` setting will consult the `esp_trans_deflev` kernel variable (see Chapter 7 for `sysctl`). If you have not changed anything, then this means no IPsec. The use value will try to use IPsec but fall back to regular IP if a connection cannot be established. Finally, the `require` value demands IPsec and will not establish a connection without it—this is the most secure option.

Configuring IPsec

There is a startup script called `/etc/init.d/setkey` that configures IPsec at boot. It does this by consulting the configuration file `/etc/ipsec-tools.conf`. If you want to configure IPsec, place your settings in this file. Listing 12-4 shows a sample configuration file that uses encryption and authenticated headers between two hosts.

Listing 12-5: Sample /etc/ipsec-tools.conf

```
#!/usr/sbin/setkey -f
# Flush the SAD and SPD
flush;
spdflush;

#########
# My host is 10.1.1.5
# The remote host is 10.1.2.10

#########
# Set a tunnel between 10.1.1.5 and 10.1.2.10
add 10.1.1.5 10.1.2.10 esp 0x201 -m tunnel \
  -E 3des-cbc "Twenty-four characters!!" \
  -A hmac-md5 "0123456789abcdef";

add 10.1.2.10 10.1.1.5 esp 0x301 -m tunnel \
  -E 3des-cbc "Twenty-two plus two more" \
  -A hmac-md5 0xdeadbeefcafe1234deadbeefcafe1234;

########
# Security policies
# NOTE: If this file is placed on the remote host, then
# swap the "-P out" and "-P in" values.
# All outbound traffic must go through the tunnel
spdadd 10.1.1.5 10.1.2.10 any -P out \
  ipsec esp/tunnel/10.1.1.5-10.1.2.10/require;

# All inbound traffic must come from the tunnel
spdadd 10.1.2.10 10.1.1.5 any -P in \
  ipsec esp/tunnel/10.1.2.10-10.1.1.5/require;
```

After creating the configuration file, you can test it using:

```
sudo setkey -f /etc/ipsec-tools.conf
```

If there are any errors when it loads, they will be cryptic but at least you will know that there is a problem. Errors are likely due to typographical mistakes or oversights. After it loads, you can use `setkey -D` and `setkey -DP` to view the current settings.

```
$ sudo setkey -D
10.1.1.5 10.1.2.10
        esp mode=tunnel spi=513(0x00000201) reqid=0(0x00000000)
        E: 3des-cbc   5477656e 74792d66 6f757220 63686172 61637465
                                                            72732121
        A: hmac-md5   30313233 34353637 38396162 63646566
        seq=0x00000000 replay=0 flags=0x00000000 state=mature
        created: Nov 25 16:53:50 2006   current: Nov 25 16:53:55 2006
        diff: 5(s)        hard: 0(s)       soft: 0(s)
        last:                          hard: 0(s)       soft: 0(s)
        current: 0(bytes)          hard: 0(bytes)  soft: 0(bytes)
        allocated: 0     hard: 0 soft: 0
        sadb_seq=1 pid=9861 refcnt=0
10.1.2.10 10.1.1.5
        esp mode=tunnel spi=769(0x00000301) reqid=0(0x00000000)
        E: 3des-cbc   5477656e 74792d74 776f2070 6c757320 74776f20
                                                            6d6f7265
        A: hmac-md5   deadbeef cafe1234 deadbeef cafe1234
        seq=0x00000000 replay=0 flags=0x00000000 state=mature
        created: Nov 25 16:53:50 2006   current: Nov 25 16:53:55 2006
        diff: 5(s)        hard: 0(s)       soft: 0(s)
        last:                          hard: 0(s)       soft: 0(s)
        current: 0(bytes)          hard: 0(bytes)  soft: 0(bytes)
        allocated: 0     hard: 0 soft: 0
        sadb_seq=0 pid=9861 refcnt=0
$ sudo setkey -DP
10.1.2.10[any] 10.1.1.5[any] any
        in prio def ipsec
        esp/tunnel/10.1.2.10-10.1.1.5/require
        created: Nov 25 16:53:50 2006   lastused:
        lifetime: 0(s) validtime: 0(s)
        spid=32 seq=2 pid=9864
        refcnt=1
10.1.1.5[any] 10.1.2.10[any] any
        out prio def ipsec
        esp/tunnel/10.1.1.5-10.1.2.10/require
        created: Nov 25 16:53:50 2006   lastused:
        lifetime: 0(s) validtime: 0(s)
        spid=25 seq=1 pid=9864
        refcnt=1
10.1.2.10[any] 10.1.1.5[any] any
        fwd prio def ipsec
        esp/tunnel/10.1.2.10-10.1.1.5/require
        created: Nov 25 16:53:50 2006   lastused:
        lifetime: 0(s) validtime: 0(s)
        spid=42 seq=0 pid=9864
        refcnt=1
```

Finally, you can test the connection. If you can ping the host or connect using a known service such as SSH or HTTP, then you know it is working.

Enabling Proxies

Another way to add security to the network is to relay traffic through a proxy. Chapter 6 covers how to install a SOCKS server for assisting privacy. The example relays web traffic through a SSH tunnel. However, this example works because the web browser was configured to use a proxy. Under Ubuntu, there are many different ways to configure proxies. For example, there is a general system proxy setting that few applications use. There are also some generic proxy settings that are supported by a variety of applications.

Proxies can add more than one level of indirection. Some proxy systems, such as Tor, can provide network anonymity.

Using the General System Proxy

Individual applications can be independently configured to each use a proxy. In contrast, Ubuntu's Gnome desktop supports a global proxy configuration. The theory is that all applications will immediately use the proxy rather than directly access the Internet. In reality, only specific applications use these settings and you may need to log out and log back in for all applications to use the configuration. General system proxy configurations are commonly required for corporate networks that have specific outbound relays for accessing the Internet.

To set the general proxy, use System ⇨ Preferences ⇨ Network Proxy. This opens the Network Proxy Preferences applet (see Figure 12-5). In this applet, you can declare your SOCKS, HTTP, HTTPS, and FTP proxy servers. You will need to know the hostnames (or network address) as well as the proxy port number. Under the Advanced Configuration tab, you can specify local hosts and networks that do not require proxy access.

> **TIP**   With Jaunty Jackalope and Karmic Koala, the Network Proxy Preferences allows you to store multiple proxy configurations. This way you can use one proxy setting when your laptop is at home, a different setting at the office, and a third setting for your favorite coffee shop.

Enabling Application-Specific Proxy Configurations

Although the global proxy settings are a nice idea, they are currently not supported by many applications. For example, the settings may be ignored by `firefox`, `ssh`, `wget`, and `apt-get`. If you want more general proxy support, you can use environment variables. Many applications look for HTTP, HTTPS, and FTP proxy definitions in variable names that have become de facto standards. Table 12-7 lists the more common definitions. In general, if the variable is in all capitals, only the server name and port number are specified. Lowercase variables need entire URLs.

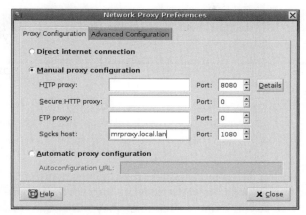

Figure 12-5: The Network Proxy Preferences applet from Hardy Heron (8.04 LTS)

Table 12-7: Common Proxy Environment Variables

VARIABLE	EXAMPLE	PURPOSE
HTTP_PROXY	export HTTP_PROXY= 10.1.2.45:8080	Define an HTTP proxy.
FTP_PROXY	export FTP_PROXY= 10.1.2.45:8081	Define an FTP proxy.
ftp_proxy	export ftp_proxy=http: //10.1.2.45:8081/	Specify a proxy for relaying FTP traffic.
http_proxy	export http_proxy=http: //10.1.2.45:8080/	Specify an HTTP proxy.
https_proxy	export https_proxy=http: //10.1.2.45:8082/	Specify an HTTPS proxy.

TIP In many corporate environments, the same server and port are used for all proxy services. They do not need to all be different.

GOPHER AND WAIS

Other network protocols, such as Gopher and WAIS, also have standard proxy support through the environment variables `wais_proxy` **and** `gopher_proxy`. For example:

```
export gopher_proxy=http://10.1.2.45:8083/
export wais_proxy=http://10.1.2.45:8084/
```

Gopher and WAIS predate the Web for providing online content. Although today you are unlikely to find them used on the general Internet, they are still used in some Universities.

These proxy definitions can be added to your `$HOME/.profile` (or `$HOME/.bashrc`) for individual user declarations. For systemwide support, they should be added to `/etc/bash.bashrc` or `/etc/profile`.

WARNING Setting the general system proxy defines many of these variables for new shells and applications. However, they are only set for Gnome applications. For example, if you start the Gnome Terminal, they will be set. However, if you start an `xterm`, they will not be set. The proxy settings will also not necessarily be available if you remotely log in. Finally, you may also need to log out and log back in for the changes to take effect. If you need these proxy settings, you should consider manually adding the to `$HOME/.bashrc` or `/etc/profile`.

Defining these proxy variables will give you proxy support for some applications, but other applications need their own configurations. For example:

- **Firefox**—Proxy settings for the web browser must be specified through the Firefox preferences. If you have multiple profiles, then you will need to set the preferences in each one of them.

- **APT**—The `apt-get` command looks for proxies in `/etc/apt/apt.conf`. The default install says:

```
Acquire::http::Proxy "false";
```

This setting disables all proxies. If you need to use a proxy, then you can change the line to something like:

```
Acquire::http::Proxy "http://proxyserver:port/";
```

This tells `apt-get` to use this specific proxy for HTTP access. If you have multiple proxies available, then you can specify multiple proxy definitions.

Enabling SOCKS Clients

While HTTP and FTP proxies forward specific protocols, SOCKS servers can forward almost any protocol. This can be specified using the SOCKS_SERVER environment variable. For example:

```
export SOCKS_SERVER=10.1.2.251:1080
```

Unfortunately, most applications do not support SOCKS, even if the environment variable is defined. For SOCKS support, you will need to socksify applications.

1. If you have not already installed it, then install the `dante-client` package. This will give you a SOCKS client:

   ```
   sudo apt-get install dante-client
   ```

2. Edit the `/etc/dante.conf` configuration and declare your SOCKS server. You will need to know the server's network address, port, and version (SOCKSv4 or SOCKSv5). My configuration specifies a SOCKS server at 10.1.2.251 and uses the standard port 1080. The configuration looks like this:

   ```
   route {
    from: 0.0.0.0/0 to: 0.0.0.0/0 via: 10.1.2.251 port = 1080
    protocol: tcp udp                  # server supports tcp and udp
    proxyprotocol: socks_v4 socks_v5 # server supports both versions.
    method: none #username            # no authentication needed
   }
   ```

3. To enable SOCKS support for non-SOCKS applications, run the application through the `socksify` wrapper. For example to use `ssh` to connect to the host `outside.local.lan` via the SOCKS server, I can use:

   ```
   socksify ssh outside.local.lan
   ```

   Similarly, I can force Firefox to use the SOCKS server without changing the Firefox proxy settings:

   ```
   socksify firefox
   ```

   > **NOTE** Socksifying Firefox will only work if there are no other open Firefox windows. This is because Firefox uses interprocess communications. When there are multiple instances running, it will use the existing instance instead of creating a new one. You can overcome this limitation by using `socksify firefox --no-xshm`.

Anonymizing with Tor

A simple proxy is good for relaying traffic, but a group of proxies can provide network anonymity. A system called The Onion Router (Tor) uses groups of linked proxies to relay traffic. The connection between each proxy is encrypted, so anyone observing the network traffic will be unable to see what is going on. From the client's end, Tor looks like just another SOCKS proxy server (although it may have significantly higher network delays).

Installing Tor requires downloading and compiling the source code. (See Chapter 5's section "Programming with C" for information on installing the full compiler.) The source code is available from `https://www.torproject.org/`. You will want to download the source tarball. This will have a name like `tor-version.tar.gz` (e.g., `tor-0.2.1.19.tar.gz` for version 0.2.1.19).

The Tor project updates versions often. Be sure to use the latest version number, and periodically check for updates. If you find that Tor is unable to connect, then you probably need to update your software.

NOTE Security conscious users should check for Tor updates at least monthly. For everyone else, just check every time it seems to be slow or unable to establish a connection.

WARNING Some Ubuntu releases have a Tor package in the repository. *Do not use it!* The Ubuntu `tor` package is not maintained. It is missing many security fixes and is not compatible with the current server lists. (As of this writing, the current version of Tor is 0.2.1.20. The version found in the Dapper Drake repository is 0.1.0.16 and the Hardy Heron repository contains 0.1.2.19. Both are more than a year out of date.)

1. Install the `libevent` and `libssl` packages (`sudo apt-get install libevent-dev libssl-dev`).

2. Download and unpack the tar file. For Tor 0.2.1.20, use `tar -xvf tor-0.2.1.20.tar.gz`. This will create a directory `tor-0.2.1.20`.

3. Enter the source code directory:

   ```
   cd tor-0.2.1.20
   ```

4. Compile and install the code:

   ```
   ./configure
   make
   sudo make install
   ```

5. If you are upgrading your installed Tor version, then you should remove your list of cached Tor servers: `rm -rf $HOME/.tor`. Otherwise your cache

may contain lists of obsolete servers and that can seriously hamper Tor's ability to establish new connections.

6. By default, Tor only listens for connections from the local system. If you plan to have other computers use your Tor connection, then you will need to alter the Tor configuration file:

```
cd /usr/local/etc/tor/

sudo cp torrc.sample torrc
```

Edit the `/usr/local/etc/tor/torrc` file. There is a line that says `Socks ListenAddress 127.0.0.1`. Add another line for each IP address on this host. For example, my computer has the external IP address 10.1.2.50, so my `torrc` contains:

```
SocksPort 9050

SocksBindAddress 127.0.0.1          # accept from localhost

SocksBindAddress 10.1.2.50:9050     # accept from the external address
```

7. Run Tor. This will start it up and retrieve the list of Tor proxies. The first time you run it, it may take a minute to fully configure itself.

```
tor
```

To run an application over the Tor network, either set the proxy to be `localhost:9050` or use the program `torify` the same way you would use `socksify`. For example, to run Firefox through the Tor network, you can use: `torify firefox --no-xshm`. When Firefox uses Tor, your external IP address may be anywhere in the world. Connecting to sites like Google (`www.google.com`) may display text in English, German, Italian, or some other language depending on where Google thinks you are coming from.

Using the Torbutton

If you find yourself using Tor often, then consider installing the torbutton plug-in for Firefox. This gives you a button in the lower-right corner of the browser's status bar, which you can click on to enable to disable connecting through the Tor proxy system.

1. Start the Firefox web browser.

2. On the Firefox menu, select Tools ➪ Add-ons.

3. Search for "torbutton."

4. Install the plug-in.

5. Restart Firefox.

6. In the bottom corner of the browser will be red text that says "Tor Disabled." This is the torbutton. Right-click on the red text to configure it.

7. Enable the custom proxy settings. The only proxy you will need is a SOCKS server on port 9050. Port 9050/tcp is the Tor port. Set the SOCKS host to be whatever server you have running Tor. If Tor is running on the same system, use 127.0.0.1.

WARNING Do *not* click the Test Settings button. This feature frequently fails, even when the connection is good. After it fails, every time you enable the torbutton, you will get a warning about it previously failing. To disable this warning, direct your browser to about:config. Change the preference extensions.torbutton.test_failed to false.

8. Close the configuration window, and toggle the orbutton by clicking on the torbutton text twice.

9. Enable the torbutton by clicking on it. The text should change to green and say "Tor Enabled."

10. Go to a web site that you know works, such as http://www.google.com/. The connection may time out while Tor tries to establish the initial connection. If it times out, then wait a moment and retry the URL.

When you finish using Tor, click on the torbutton again. This will disable the proxy connection.

Understanding Tor's Limitations

Although Tor does make all of the SOCKS connections effectively anonymous, there are still some ways to breach the anonymity.

For example, before connecting to a host, your system performs a domain name lookup using DNS to identify the host's network address. The DNS query usually does not pass through the proxy. Thus, a clever administrator could check their DNS server connections against any anonymous Tor connections in order to identify the otherwise-anonymous source.

Tor is a SOCKS server and supports socks4, socks4a, and socks5 protocols. The socks4 protocol does not support hostname lookups (DNS), but socks4a and socks5 do. With the Firefox browser, you have the option of using socks4 or socks5, and socks4 will route traffic outside of the Tor tunnel.

To overcome this limitation, you can either specify using socks5, or you can install the privoxy package. Privoxy is a non-caching web proxy. Although designed to stop undesirable web ads, it has the added bonus of using socks4a or socks5, so you won't leak information to DNS servers.

1. Install privoxy:

   ```
   sudo apt-get install privoxy
   ```

2. Configure privoxy to use your Tor server. Add the following line to the `/etc/privoxy/config` configuration file:

   ```
   # My tor server is on 127.0.0.1 (the local system).
   # Be sure to set the IP address to match your Tor configuration.
   forward-socks4a / 127.0.0.1:9050 .
   ```

3. Restart privoxy:

   ```
   sudo /etc/init.d/privoxy restart
   ```

The `privoxy` system provides an HTTP proxy interface to Tor's SOCKS interface. Since HTTP proxies do not need the client to perform hostname lookups, UDP traffic is never generated by the client. You can then use the HTTP_PROXY and `http_proxy` environment variables (or the Firefox HTTP proxy connection preference) to specify the use of the `privoxy` server on `localhost:8118`.

> **TIP** With the Firefox torbutton installed, you can configure the proxy settings to use privoxy.

While privoxy provides anonymity for web requests, it offers no security for other protocols. For example, SSH through a Tor connection will generate a hostname lookup that is traceable.

Another limitation to Tor comes from unproxied requests. For example, if your web browser spawns a RealPlayer or Totem player for streaming video, then these players may not use the proxy server.

Applying Parental Controls

Tor is an example of a network proxy that does more than just proxy traffic; Tor anonymizes network connections. Intelligent proxies can also be used to filter undesirable traffic. For example, many parents want parental controls that will filter out inappropriate sites that their children may (accidentally or otherwise) attempt to access. Parental controls can be added with few intelligent proxy servers.

To add parental controls for web filtering, you will need to install Squid, DansGuardian, ClamAV, and FireHOL. Squid is a caching web proxy server. DansGuardian is a web-based content-filtering system that includes blacklists. ClamAV is a free antivirus scanner, used by DansGuardian. Finally, FireHOL uses `iptables` to redirect network traffic.

> **TIP** Even if you don't need parental control, this is a great example of combining network and application proxy servers to filter access.

1. Install Squid, DansGuardian, ClamAV, and FireHOL:

   ```
   sudo apt-get install squid dansguardian clamav firehol
   ```

   Squid enables a proxy on port 3128/tcp. DansGuardian adds a proxy on port 8080/tcp. But when we finish, this will all be transparent.

2. Configure FireHOL by editing `/etc/firehol/firehol.conf`. Replace the default contents. The new contents forbid direct access to the Squid proxy server. Instead, all traffic will be transparently forwarded from DansGuardian to Squid.

   ```
   version 5

   # Use iptables to stop users from using the proxy without
   DansGuardian
   # NOTE: This is one really long line...
   iptables -t filter -I OUTPUT -d 127.0.0.1 -p tcp --dport
   3128 -m owner
     !—uid-owner dansguardian -j DROP

   # Setup the redirection to DansGuardian
   transparent_squid 8080 "proxy root"
   interface any world
     policy drop
     protection strong
     client all accept

   # Permit SSH into this computer.
     server ssh accept

   # If you have a mail server, uncomment this line:
   # server "smtp pop3 imap" accept

   # This line permits any computer on the network to use
   this parental
   # control system.  However, they must each be configured
   to use the
   # HTTP proxy on this computer's port 8080.
     server webcache accept
   ```

3. Edit `/etc/default/firehol` and change `START_FIREHOL=NO` to `START_FIREHOL=YES` to enable the firewall.

4. FireHOL maintains a list of reserved IP addresses. If this file is outdated, it will complain. All you need to do is update the timestamp on the reserved IP list:

```
sudo touch /etc/firehol/RESERVED_IPS
```

5. Now to configure DansGuardian. Edit /etc/dansguardian/dansguardian .conf. One of the first lines says "UNCONFIGURED." Comment out this line by inserting a # at the beginning of the line.

```
# UNCONFIGURED - Please remove this line after
configuration
```

6. A little further down in dansguardian.conf is the URL for a denied web page. Change the server name to localhost.

```
# accessdeniedaddress =

      'http://YOURSERVER.YOURDOMAIN/cgi-bin/dansguardian.pl'

accessdeniedaddress =

      'http://localhost/cgi-bin/dansguardian.pl'
```

7. DansGuardian maintains a list of undesirable sites, weighted phrases, and more in /etc/dansguardian/lists/. Even if you don't make any changes, it is worthwhile to look over the lists so you can see what is filtered by default. (The thoroughness of the default filters is impressive.)

8. Start the servers. Whereas Squid is started during the installation, the others must be started after configuration:

```
sudo /etc/init.d/dansguardian start

sudo /etc/init.d/firehol start
```

It doesn't take long to configure this parental control system, and you do not need to change your browser's configuration. If you attempt to access a filtered site, you will immediately see a banned message (see Figure 12-6).

WARNING There are plenty of ways around this parental control system. While it does a great job filtering web (HTTP) traffic, it does not filter HTTPS or other protocols. Moreover, it does not stop Tor, and any user can install Tor without requiring root access. This parental control system may prevent access by a nontechnical computer user, but it won't stop a curious, technically savvy child.

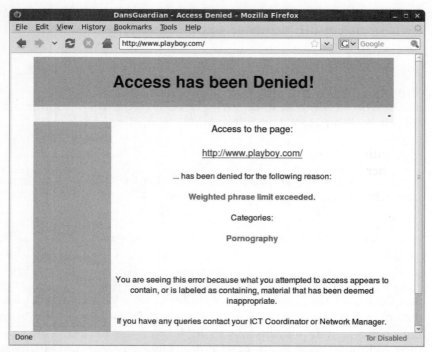

Figure 12-6: A website blocked by the default parental controls

Debugging the Network

In my own experience, configuring networks to use proxies or encryption doesn't always work right the first time. Between typographical errors and missed steps, it might take a few tries to get it right. You are probably going to need a network sniffer to diagnose bad connections and make sure the good connections are working right. (There's no point in setting up an IPsec tunnel only to discover later that all traffic is transmitted in plain text, or to configure a proxy and find that your critical applications are not using it.)

You can use a couple of different tools to diagnose network issues. They range in complexity from ''pretty pictures'' to hard-core packet analysis. The main tools that I use are EtherApe, Snort, and Wireshark.

Packet sniffers are only as good as the network that they are connected to. If your network adaptor is located on an isolated network (or behind a network switch), then you are not going to see many packets. In contrast, if you are connected to a busy network, you will see lots of packets.

NOTE Sniffers can only capture packets that reach the network adaptor. The range is limited by physical connectivity. There is no way for a remote packet sniffer to capture packets on your local network.

Using EtherApe

EtherApe is a simple packet sniffer that graphically displays all network connections. This is a great tool if you just want to know where the connections are going, without the details found in every packet.

To use EtherApe, you just need to install it and run it.

```
sudo apt-get install etherape
sudo etherape
```

The graphical display shows a large black field with every node heard on the network represented by dots (see Figure 12-7). Lines between nodes show connections, and line thickness represents the amount of traffic. Lines are color-coded based on protocols and listed in the protocol key on the left side. You can also hover your mouse over any of the lines and see the protocol's name at the bottom of the window.

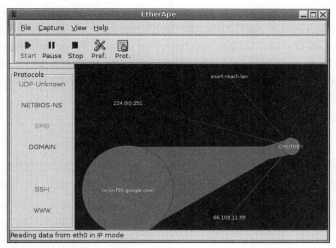

Figure 12-7: EtherApe capturing packets

EtherApe can be a quick way to identify that a proxy or secure tunnel is being used. For example, if all of your network connections should pass through a proxy or VPN, then the only connections should go to one host.

Similarly, ports map to protocols. If connections are supposed to use a specific port, then you can validate that the specific port is being used. Also, if you are using IPsec and the packet should be encrypted, then you should see an unknown protocol being displayed.

Using Wireshark

Although EtherApe can give you a very quick view of what is happening, it does not allow you to tell what traffic is being transmitted. For example, if everything should use a proxy and EtherApe shows some traffic outside of the proxy's connection, then you need some way to debug it. Wireshark is absolutely the most powerful packet analyzer I've ever come across. Not only can it collect and display packets, but it can also disassemble the packet fields and decode most protocols. If something should be encrypted, then you can confirm that the packet contents are encrypted. If some packets are unexpected, then you can capture the packets and analyze them and investigate what is really going on.

Running Wireshark is almost as easy as running EtherApe:

1. Install the Wireshark package:

   ```
   sudo apt-get install wireshark
   ```

NOTE The Wireshark packet analyzer was originally called Ethereal. In May 2006, it was renamed due to a trademark issue. The Dapper Drake repository contains the older `ethereal` package. Hardy Heron contains both `ethereal` and `wireshark` packages (`ethereal` points to `wireshark`). Later Ubuntu versions only contain the `wireshark` package.

2. Run Wireshark:

   ```
   sudo wireshark
   ```

   The user interface allows you to capture packets or analyze packets, but capturing and analyzing are usually done in two separate steps.

3. Capture some packets by selecting Capture ➪ Interfaces from the menu. This will display a list of available interfaces. From this popup window, you can click the Capture button for the appropriate interface.

4. As packets are being captured, a capture status window is available. It shows the number of each packet type collected. When you are done capturing packets, you can click Stop (or on the icon with a stop sign). This moves you from the collection phase to the analysis phase.

5. The analysis window is divided into three segments (see Figure 12-8). The top shows each packet that was collected in the order that it was collected. You can click any packet to reveal the contents in the lower two

window sections. The middle section shows the decoded components and the lower section shows the raw packet. You can click any part of the decoded section and the raw bytes in the lower section will be highlighted. Similarly, you can click any of the raw bytes to see what the decoded bytes mean.

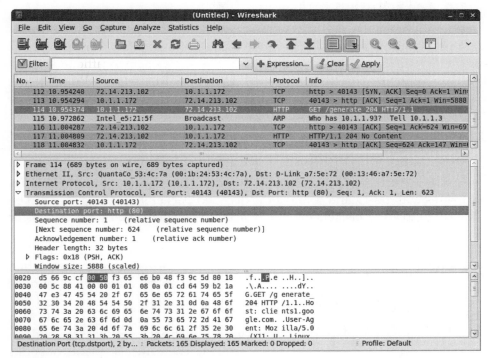

Figure 12-8: The Wireshark packet analyzer

Although Wireshark is relatively easy to use, it has some very complex packet-filtering options. Some functions have a very steep learning curve. If you have a need to use Wireshark for anything other than basic capture and analysis, then you probably should get a book dedicated to Wireshark; there are plenty of available resources. Another source for more information is the Wireshark web site: www.wireshark.org.

Using Snort and Tcpdump

Wireshark and EtherApe are very useful if you have a graphical workstation. However, if you are using a command-line terminal, remote login, or the Ubuntu Server installation, then you really need a command-line tool. The two most common are Tcpdump and Snort.

Tcpdump comes standard on Ubuntu systems. It allows you to capture packets and apply simple packet filters. For example, to capture all UDP packets, you can use: `sudo tcpdump udp`. If you want to capture all packets, use `sudo tcpdump`.

Each packet that is captured displays a line on the console. For example:

```
14:32:28.958743 IP ubuntu.roach.lan.32966 >
  dns.roach.lan.domain:  31917+ A? cow.rats. (26)
14:32:28.959476 IP ubuntu.roach.lan.32967 >
  dns.roach.lan.domain:  35645+ PTR? 251.1.1.10.in-addr.arpa. (41)
14:32:28.960760 IP dns.roach.lan.domain >
  ubuntu.roach.lan.32967:  35645* 1/1/0 PTR[|domain]
14:32:28.960929 IP ubuntu.roach.lan.32967 >
  dns.roach.lan.domain:  33818+ PTR? 5.1.1.10.in-addr.arpa. (39)
14:32:28.961467 IP dns.roach.lan.domain >
  ubuntu.roach.lan.32967:  33818* 1/1/0 PTR[|domain]
14:32:28.997905 IP dns.roach.lan.domain >
  ubuntu.roach.lan.32966:  31917 NXDomain 0/1/0 (101)
```

Each line includes a timestamp, the protocol, source, and destination addresses with ports, and some of the decoded packet flags. Tcpdump can be configured to write packets to a file which can be later used by Wireshark for analysis.

Snort (`sudo apt-get install snort`) is an alternative to Tcpdump. Just as Wireshark is more complex than EtherApe, Snort is more complex than Tcpdump. Using Snort, you can capture packets, display contents, trigger rules and alerts, and even create your own plug-in filters. As with Wireshark, if you need to use Snort for anything more complicated than displaying packets with basic filters (for example, `sudo snort -v udp`), then I strongly recommend the Snort homepage (`www.snort.org`) as a resource. There are also plenty of books on basic and advanced Snort configurations.

TIP When Snort is installed, it enables the Snort Intrusion Detection System (IDS). This IDS (covered in Chapter 13) generates one e-mail per day, summarizing the possible network attacks that were detected. If you want to disable the IDS, you can remove the `S20snort` and `K20snort` initialization scripts from the `/etc/rc*.d/` directories.

Summary

Networking with Ubuntu does not need to be static. At any time, you can enable new network adaptors and reconfigure existing ones. Network connections may be direct, routed through proxies, or protected through encrypted network connections. With tools like `ndiswrapper`, you are not limited to hardware with Linux drivers, and IPsec and Tor add security to your connections.

Configuring new network routes is not always simple. Ubuntu offers a variety of powerful packet analysis tools that you can use to diagnose network problems.

## CHAPTER 13

Enabling Services

What's In This Chapter?

Enabling common network services
How to defend against network-based attacks
Installing SSH, FTP, and web servers

I find it somewhat ironic that the final chapter in this book covers turning on essential network servers such as FTP, e-mail, and the web. Part I of this book covers installation and system tweaking, mainly focusing on the local system, not network services. Part II discusses collaboration systems, where your Ubuntu system primarily operates as a client and details some services such as Samba (SMB), Secure Shell (SSH), Socket Servers (SOCKS), and Line Print Daemon (LPD). Part III aims at improving performance, but not network services. That leaves Part IV. In Chapters 11 and 12, I show you how to lock down your system and network. In this chapter, I will show you how to open it up.

Any time you make a network service externally accessible, you open yourself up to a possible network attack. For this reason, it is very important to know exactly what services you are offering and to limit access to only the services you explicitly want to offer. You will also want to monitor your system for possible threats. Basic network services, like web and e-mail systems, should expect to receive literally hundreds of probes and attack attempts per day. As luck usually has it, the day you stop monitoring for these events will be the day one of them becomes successful in compromising your system.

Finally, when you understand the risks and how to handle them, you should feel confident enough to open a network service to other people, including everyone on the Internet. Common services that you will probably want to run include SSH, FTP, e-mail, and web servers.

> **WARNING** While booting from a USB drive is arguably the most difficult hack in this book (see Chapter 1), opening a network service (especially to the Internet) is the most dangerous. The question is not "will you be attacked?"—you will. You will probably be probed and attacked within a few hours, and the attempts will *never* end. Eventually some attack method may succeed. The only real question is, "when will you notice?"

Understanding Ubuntu's Default Services

Ubuntu has a simple default setting: no default network services. Although software firewalls are not configured (see Chapter 12), they are also not needed until you begin turning on services.

While externally accessible services are disabled, some programs do use network connections to communicate between processes on the same system. For example, X-Windows uses some local network connections to communicate between applications. There are two common ways to identify what services are running: netstat and nmap.

Using netstat

As mentioned in Chapter 8, the netstat command provides useful statistics about the network interfaces on your system. Besides summarizing traffic flows, netstat shows established network connections and open network services. Running the command all by itself generates a long list of current TCP, UDP (datagram), and Unix sockets.

> **TIP** The netstat command usually generates a large amount of data. You should pipe the output into a pager such as more or less. (The less command is similar to more, but enables you to scroll backward.)

```
$ netstat | more
Active Internet connections (w/o servers)
Proto Recv-Q Send-Q Local Address          Foreign Address        State
tcp     0      0 marvin.local.lan:55419 bugs.local.lan:ssh ESTABLISHED
tcp     0      0 localhost:44235          localhost:46274 ESTABLISHED
tcp     0      0 marvin.local.lan:38446 foghorn.local.lan:ssh ESTABLISHED
```

```
tcp    0    0 localhost:46274        localhost:44235 ESTABLISHED
tcp6   0    0 chutney.local.lan:ssh  foghorn.local.lan:1074 ESTABLISHED

Active UNIX domain sockets (w/o servers)
Proto RefCnt Flags        Type      State       I-Node Path
unix  4      [ ]          DGRAM                 13124361 /dev/log
unix  2      [ ]          DGRAM                 5610
unix  2      [ ]          DGRAM                 12548
unix  2      [ ]          DGRAM                 13232791
unix  2      [ ]          DGRAM                 13198909
unix  2      [ ]          DGRAM                 13124142
unix  3      [ ]          STREAM    CONNECTED
unix  3      [ ]          STREAM    CONNECTED   13123938
unix  2      [ ]          DGRAM                 13123531
--More--
```

The first part of the `netstat` output shows TCP connections. This can also be shown using `netstat -t`. Connections show the local address (in this case, my localhost is named *marvin*), the connected remote systems (*bugs* and *foghorn*), and the connection state. The states represent the TCP connection's status. There are two states that you will often see:

- **ESTABLISHED**—A network connection exists between the two systems.

- **TIME_WAIT**—A connection has terminated and the system is just waiting for any final packets before tearing down the connection.

Along with these common states, there are many other states that exist for very short durations. For example, SYN_SENT and SYN_RECV indicate that a connection is starting. These will quickly switch over to the ESTABLISHED state. There are also plenty of states that indicate a connection is closing. For example, FIN_WAIT1, FIN_WAIT2, CLOSE, and CLOSE_WAIT. These states rarely exist for more than the blink of an eye before switching over to the TIME_WAIT state.

The second part of the `netstat` output shows Unix services. These include connectionless UDP packets (DGRAM) and connection-oriented sockets (STREAM). You can limit the display to just these services by using `netstat -x`.

Identifying Servers with netstat

Besides showing established connections, `netstat` can display waiting network services. The command `netstat -l` shows all the listening servers.

```
$ netstat -l | more
Active Internet connections (only servers)
```

```
Proto Recv-Q Send-Q Local Address          Foreign Address     State
tcp      0      0 *:nfs                     *:*                 LISTEN
tcp      0      0 *:printer                 *:*                 LISTEN
tcp      0      0 *:40867                   *:*                 LISTEN
tcp      0      0 localhost:42309           *:*                 LISTEN
tcp      0      0 *:935                     *:*                 LISTEN
tcp      0      0 *:netbios-ssn             *:*                 LISTEN
tcp      0      0 localhost:44235           *:*                 LISTEN
tcp      0      0 *:sunrpc                  *:*                 LISTEN
tcp      0      0 localhost:8118            *:*                 LISTEN
tcp      0      0 localhost:socks           *:*                 LISTEN
tcp      0      0 *:smtp                    *:*                 LISTEN
tcp      0      0 localhost:9050            *:*                 LISTEN
tcp      0      0 localhost:6010            *:*                 LISTEN
tcp      0      0 *:668                     *:*                 LISTEN
tcp      0      0 *:microsoft-ds            *:*                 LISTEN
tcp6     0      0 *:ssh                     *:*                 LISTEN
tcp6     0      0 ip6-localhost:6010        *:*                 LISTEN
udp      0      0 *:32768                   *:*
udp      0      0 *:nfs                     *:*
udp      0      0 *:netbios-ns              *:*
--More--
```

This example shows a large number of available network services including Tor (TCP port 9050), NFS and LPD (printer), and even Samba (netbios). If you only want to list TCP or UDP services, you can use `netstat -lt` or `netstat -lu`, respectively. `netstat -lx` shows the local Unix services and sockets.

Running nmap

Although `netstat` usually shows many services, not all are accessible from across the network. For example, the Unix services are usually restricted to the local system and are not externally accessible. In addition, many TCP and UDP services may be bound to the loopback interface rather than the external network interface. These are denoted by the *localhost* interface name.

A better way to identify running services is with the `nmap` command (`sudo apt-get install nmap`). This network-mapping tool can identify every network-accessible service on a host and can even scan an entire subnet in minutes.

WARNING In some sensitive network environments, `nmap` will trigger intrusion detection systems. Before you scan any hosts, make sure that you won't get in trouble with the local network administrators.

Table 13-1 lists some of the common command-line parameters that I use with `nmap`. Other parameters are described in the man page for `nmap`.

Table 13-1: Common nmap Command-Line Parameters

PARAMETER	PURPOSE
-p portlist	By default, nmap only scans a set of well-known and common ports. This option can be used to specify one or more ports (for example, -p 80 or -p 80,443) or a range of ports (for example, -p 0-65535 or -p 1-1023).
-P0	Normally nmap pings the host before scanning it. However, if you enabled iptables or a firewall to drop ICMP packets, then the host cannot be pinged. This option disables pinging hosts before scanning them.
-sS	This option performs a SYN-scan. Rather that performing a full TCP connection, only the initial connection is performed. This type of scan is not detected by some logging systems. I use it because it is faster than performing a full TCP scan.
-sU	Rather than scanning for TCP services, this will scan for UDP services.
-sV	When a network service is identified, only the port number is known. This option tells nmap to profile what is running on the port. In many cases, it will identify the name and version of the server.
-O	While -sV profiles individual services, -O profiles the actual operating system. Using the option, nmap can try to determine the running operating system and version.

The results from an nmap scan show all of the accessible network services. For example:

```
$ sudo nmap -sS -sV -p 0-65535 -O 127.0.0.1
Starting Nmap 4.53 ( http://insecure.org ) at 2009-10-27 13:31 MDT
Interesting ports on localhost (127.0.0.1):
Not shown: 65519 closed ports
PORT       STATE SERVICE       VERSION
21/tcp     open  ftp           vsftpd 2.0.6
22/tcp     open  ssh           OpenSSH 4.7p1 Debian 8ubuntu1.2
(protocol 2.0)
25/tcp     open  smtp          Postfix smtpd
80/tcp     open  http          Apache httpd 2.2.8 ((Ubuntu)
PHP/5.2.4-2ubuntu5.7 with Suhosin-Patch)
111/tcp    open  rpcbind       2 (rpc #100000)
631/tcp    open  ipp           CUPS 1.2
2049/tcp   open  nfs           2-4 (rpc #100003)
3690/tcp   open  unknown
```

```
5432/tcp  open  postgresql   PostgreSQL DB
6000/tcp  open  X11          (access denied)
8000/tcp  open  networkaudio Network Audio System
8118/tcp  open  privoxy?
35002/tcp open  status       1 (rpc #100024)
35245/tcp open  mountd       1-3 (rpc #100005)
50962/tcp open  nlockmgr     1-4 (rpc #100021)

No exact OS matches for host (If you know what OS is running on it,
see http://insecure.org/nmap/submit/ ).
TCP/IP fingerprint:
OS:SCAN(V=4.53%D=10/27%OT=21%CT=1%CU=42723%PV=N%DS=0%G=Y%TM=4AE74AF0%P=i686
OS:-pc-linux-gnu)SEQ(SP=CE%GCD=1%ISR=CC%TI=Z%II=I%TS=7)OPS(O1=M400CST11NW7%
OS:O2=M400CST11NW7%O3=M400CNNT11NW7%O4=M400CST11NW7%O5=M400CST11NW7%O6=M400
OS:CST11)WIN(W1=8000%W2=8000%W3=8000%W4=8000%W5=8000%W6=8000)ECN(R=Y%DF=Y%T
OS:=40%W=8018%O=M400CNNSNW7%CC=N%Q=)T1(R=Y%DF=Y%T=40%S=O%A=S+%F=AS%RD=0%Q=)
OS:T2(R=N)T3(R=Y%DF=Y%T=40%W=8000%S=O%A=S+%F=AS%O=M400CST11NW7%RD=0%Q=)T4(R
OS:=Y%DF=Y%T=40%W=0%S=A%A=Z%F=R%O=%RD=0%Q=)T5(R=Y%DF=Y%T=40%W=0%S=Z%A=S+%F=
OS:AR%O=%RD=0%Q=)T6(R=Y%DF=Y%T=40%W=0%S=A%A=Z%F=R%O=%RD=0%Q=)T7(R=Y%DF=Y%T=
OS:40%W=0%S=Z%A=S+%F=AR%O=%RD=0%Q=)U1(R=Y%DF=N%T=40%TOS=C0%IPL=164%UN=0%RIP
OS:L=G%RID=G%RIPCK=G%RUCK=G%RUL=G%RUD=G)IE(R=Y%DFI=N%T=40%TOSI=S%CD=S%SI=S%
OS:DLI=S)

Uptime: 33.765 days (since Wed Sep 23 19:11:15 2009)
Network Distance: 0 hops
Service Info: Host:  marvin.private.lan; OSs: Unix, Linux

OS and Service detection performed. Please report any incorrect
results at http://insecure.org/nmap/submit/ .
Nmap done: 1 IP address (1 host up) scanned in 84.451 seconds
```

Using nmap to scan your local system won't generate the same results as scanning from a remote host. This is because some network services are restricted to the local host or remote network interface. Also, some network services do their own filtering (for example, the Tcpwrappers described in Chapter 12) and only permit local connections. Ideally, you will want to scan your system from a different host on the same local network. Scanning my host from a remote system shows:

```
$ sudo nmap -sS -sV -O -p 0-65535 marvin
Starting Nmap 5.00 ( http://nmap.org ) at 2009-10-27 13:30 MDT
Interesting ports on marvin.private.lan (10.1.100.6):
Not shown: 65522 closed ports
PORT      STATE SERVICE      VERSION
21/tcp    open  ftp          vsftpd 2.0.6
22/tcp    open  ssh          OpenSSH 4.7p1 Debian 8ubuntu1.2
(protocol 2.0)
25/tcp    open  smtp         Postfix smtpd
80/tcp    open  http         Apache httpd 2.2.8
((Ubuntu) PHP/5.2.4-2ubuntu5.7 with Suhosin-Patch)
111/tcp   open  rpcbind
```

```
2049/tcp  open  rpcbind
3690/tcp  open  svnserve      Subversion
6000/tcp  open  X11           (access denied)
8000/tcp  open  networkaudio Network Audio System
MAC Address: 00:22:15:5F:35:20 (Asustek Computer)
Device type: general purpose
Running: Linux 2.6.X
OS details: Linux 2.6.9—2.6.28
Network Distance: 1 hop
Service Info: Host:  marvin.roach.lan; OSs: Unix, Linux

OS and Service detection performed. Please report any incorrect
results at http://nmap.org/submit/ .
Nmap done: 1 IP address (1 host up) scanned in 16.96 seconds
```

Note that the remote scan shows fewer ports and a slightly different operating system profile. (You can also see my Subversion source code server on 3690/tcp, which is only accessible from the external network interface.)

WARNING The `nmap` network profile may not identify the scanned system. Sometimes it will profile an intermediate router or firewall located between the scanning system and scan target, or it may return an encoded fingerprint if the system is unknown.

Recognizing Network Threats

Every network service that is remotely accessible offers a path onto your system. If there is an exploit (available today *or* sometime in the future), then you will have a risk that needs to be addressed. In addition, many network services run with root privileges; an exploit can potentially allow an attacker to access your entire file system as root. Even if the exploit only gives user-level access, there are plenty of options for escalating privileges from a "regular" local user to root.

TIP As far as bug discovery goes, local exploits are much more common than remote exploits. However, if you periodically update your system with `apt-get update` and `apt-get upgrade`, then you should have most of the local exploits under control. Periodically updating your system will also take care of any known remote exploits.

Having open ports accessible within your home or office network is usually not as serious as having ports accessible to anyone on the Internet. For example, I'm not too worried about my RedHat system having access to my Ubuntu box. On the other hand, I certainly don't want everyone in the world to access my Ubuntu NFS service.

WHAT'S MY MOTIVATION?

Security is a measurement of risk. A good system is "secure enough" for your needs. With security comes tradeoffs for performance, accessibility, and functionality. In order to understand your risks, you need to understand your potential attacker. For example, in your home environment, your main risks are probably restricted to physical access from kids, cats, and the occasional guest (anyone who might download a virus or accidentally delete something critical). However, other risks may include burglary, disk crashes, and viruses that you accidentally download.

Threats at home are different from threats at work. In your office are dozens or hundreds of people with network access, including a few disgruntled employees, and sensitive or company confidential information. However, local access is still limited to people who are usually trusted. This is different from Internet-accessible services, where anyone in the world has access and you *know* that you cannot trust everyone.

The big question becomes: Who is your likely attacker, and what does the attacker probably want? In directed attacks, someone wants something on your system—files, passwords, credit card numbers, secret files, or anything else of value. However, more common are broadcast attacks, where the attacker wants *a* computer and not specifically *your* computer. Even if you have a slow CPU and very little disk space, the fact that you have Internet access means that you can relay spam, act as a proxy for anonymous attacks, or become part of a botnet. If you happen to have a fast computer or a few gigabytes of disk space, then that's just icing on the cake for the attacker. They can use your computer to store porn or warez (stolen software), crack passwords, host chat rooms for other undesirable associates, or worse. That one network service that you temporarily opened to the Internet could be the reason you are at the epicenter of a massive network attack and child pornography ring.

Attackers are constantly scanning the Internet for computers with vulnerable network services. If you open up a web, FTP, or e-mail server, then potential attackers will probably discover it within a few hours. If you open some other service, then it might take longer to be discovered, but eventually someone will find it.

Mitigating Risks before Going Public

There are a couple of things you can do to mitigate risks before opening a network service to the Internet.

- **Remove defaults**—Any sample scripts and default documentation should be removed. In many cases, sample code can be used to exploit a system, and documentation usually tells an attacker what they are up against. If there is a default login or account name, then change it.

- **Limit service access**—Restrict Internet access to only the necessary services. For example, if you only want to give access to your SSH server, then you don't need to offer your HTTP server to the world. You can restrict access with Tcpwrappers, IP Tables, or ufw (see Chapter 12). Some services can be bound to the loopback interface rather than the network card. A better alternative to local access restrictions is to use a standalone firewall. This way, hostile network traffic never reaches your computer in the first place.

- **Limit services per system**—Ideally, each open network service should be on a different computer system. This way, an attacker who compromises your web server won't also have access to your e-mail, SSH, and other services. In reality, you may not have many computers sitting around, acting as dedicated service providers. Maintenance may also be a hassle. However, if you have a particularly critical service, definitely consider placing it on a standalone system.

- **Limit host access**—If only a few hosts will be accessing the service, consider restricting connections to just those hosts. The restrictions may be based on IP addresses (if they are static) or on VPN technology, such as IPsec (see Chapter 12) or SSH (see Chapter 6).

- **Use a firewall**—Anyone using a computer connected to the Internet (or an ISP) without a firewall is just asking for trouble. A simple NAT-based home firewall usually costs under $30 and is well worth the investment.

NOTE A NAT router performs a *network address translation*. NAT is used to share one external IP address with a bunch of internal computers. The router maps every outgoing connection to a network port, so replies can be returned to the correct system. However, externally initiated inbound connections (such as a network attack) do not map to any established routes, so the packet never reaches a computer and the attack fails. Because NAT routers drop incoming connections, they are commonly called *firewalls*.

- **Use a DMZ**—A DMZ (demilitarized zone) is a network buffer region that is surrounded by firewalls. The concept is pretty simple: all inbound traffic must stop at the computer in the DMZ before continuing into the internal network. The DMZ provides a choke point for monitoring suspicious network traffic and authenticating desirable traffic. Configuring a DMZ requires two firewalls and one computer (the computer can even be that old 75-MHz Pentium that you have collecting dust in your closet).

- **Configure an IDS**—An IDS (intrusion detection system) watches network traffic for potential threats and alerts you when something questionable is identified.

- **Monitor logs**—Local network services usually generate log files. So do firewalls and IDSs. If you don't periodically look at the logs, then you will never see attacks when they happen.

- **Keep backups**—Being able to recover from a compromise is just as important as knowing how and when the compromise happens. Chapter 3 offers a very simple backup system, but your backups should really match your needs.

- **Patch! Patch! Patch!**—While a home computer with no services may only need to be updated monthly, systems with Internet-accessible services should be patched much more often. Attackers won't wait for you to catch up with the latest exploits.

Monitoring Attacks

Regardless of the type of network service you want to enable, you should have lots of log files that identify what happened and when. You're going to need a way to sort through all the noise and clutter for those few items that might indicate a possible attack—or a successful attack.

What Should You Look For?

There are a couple of different types of attacks, each of which should show up in various log files.

- **Brute force**—Brute force attacks are usually tried against login systems. You should see logs that have a high number of failed connection attempts.

- **Reconnaissance scans**—Before attacking, many systems initially perform some type of reconnaissance. This should appear in the logs as a scan. Scans usually look like a bunch of connections or simple queries. There may be one per host, or a suite of connections per host. If the scan finds anything useful, then the attack will come later.

- **One-time tries**—Many automated attack systems blindly try exploits. If the attack works, then you are compromised. If it fails, then you're safe. These should appear in log files as one-time oddities. Or in the case of a massive worm, lots of the same oddity as each infected system tries to spread.

A quick hack for analyzing log files simply looks at file size. If you rotate logs hourly or daily, then look for a sharp increase in log size—this will indicate some new worm or network scan. As far as one-time attacks go, look over some logs to get an idea of "normal" and then look for things that stand out as odd.

Periodic scans of your own systems with tools like `nmap` should be used to look for new, unexpected services. If there is a new, unexpected service running on your system, then take the time to find out why. If there are lots of new ports, then it is a strong indication that the system is compromised. Similarly, look for unexpected network traffic. If you never use IRC and start seeing IRC traffic, then find out where it is coming from!

What Now? After a Compromise. . .

Okay, so you started a new network service, you put it on the Internet, and you've been compromised. Do you know what you will do? Turning off the system is a good start, but how and when will you turn it back on? Do you reset or restore the system? This could simply reintroduce the same environment that led to the initial compromise!

Regardless what you plan to do, have a plan in place *before* making a service public. For example, what will you do if you are on vacation and you suddenly hear that your hobby FTP server is sending millions of spam e-mail messages? It is better if you take care of it than having your ISP disconnect you.

I have a very simple plan: there is always someone available to pull out the power cord if a system is acting fishy. Later, I can remove the hard drive and mount it under a different Linux system to see what went wrong and recover log files. Subsequently, I can restore from a backup and apply the most recent patches as needed.

Logging Logins

Many types of services provide login access. Failed logins should be placed in log files. Under the default Ubuntu installation, successful logins are stored in /var/log/wtmp. This is a binary file that stores the login account name, date of access (login and logout), and if it is a remote connection, the name of the remote host. You can access this log file with the last command.

```
$ last
nealk    pts/0      10.1.100.7        Tue Oct 27 13:22    still logged in
nealk    pts/2      :0.0              Tue Oct 27 13:20    still logged in
nealk    pts/1      :0.0              Tue Oct 27 13:20    still logged in
nealk    tty7       :0                Tue Oct 27 13:19    still logged in
nealk    pts/0      10.1.100.7        Tue Oct 27 13:14 − 13:22   (00:07)
reboot   system boot 2.6.31-11-generi Tue Oct 27 13:14 − 15:08   (01:54)
```

Recording Failed Logins

Ubuntu stores failed login attempts in /var/log/btmp file. If the file exists, then it will store failed logins. If it does not exist, then no failures will be recorded.

```
sudo touch /var/log/btmp
sudo chown root:utmp /var/log/btmp
sudo chmod 660 /var/log/btmp
```

TIP The `/var/log/btmp` file is usually used by text-based logins. Graphical login screens, such as Gnome's `gdm`, do not record login failures to `btmp`. Similarly, SSH logs to `/var/log/auth.log` and not `btmp`. To test `btmp`, press Ctrl+Alt+F2 and try a few failed logins, then log in and use `lastb` to see the results.

You can access the `btmp` logs using the `lastb` command:

```
$ sudo lastb
nealk     tty2                        Tue Oct 27 15:32—15:32  (00:00)
UNKNOWN   tty2                        Tue Oct 27 15:32—15:32  (00:00)
UNKNOWN   tty2                        Tue Oct 27 15:32—15:32  (00:00)
root      tty2                        Tue Oct 27 15:15—15:15  (00:00)
UNKNOWN   tty2                        Tue Oct 27 15:15—15:15  (00:00)
(unknown  tty7          :0            Sat Oct 17 21:57—21:57  (00:00)
nealk     tty7          :0            Thu Oct  8 09:45—09:45  (00:00)

btmp begins Thu Oct  8 09:45:49 2009
```

TIP The `wtmp` and `btmp` log files rotate. You may need to use `lastb -f` to specify a log file. For example, `sudo lastb -f /var/log/btmp.1`.

Enhancing Failed Login Records

Normally `btmp` only logs valid usernames and the time of the failed login attempts. Unknown usernames are logged as UNKNOWN. You can change `btmp` to log all unknown usernames, enabling you to see what usernames are used by a brute force attack:

1. As root, edit `/etc/login.defs`.
2. Change `LOG_UNKFAIL_ENAB` from `no` to `yes`. There is no need to restart the system—this change takes effect immediately.

WARNING Users sometimes accidentally enter their password instead of a username. This means that their passwords will be logged to `/var/log/btmp`. If you accidentally enter your password at the login prompt of a multi-user system, then log in and immediately change your password.

TIP To prevent other users from potentially seeing login-password mistakes, make sure that `btmp` is not world-readable (`sudo chmod o-r /var/log/wtmp`). Also edit `/etc/logrotate.conf` and change the `btmp` rotation. The new file mode should be `660`, not `664`. With these changes, only users with root access can check failed logins.

Although `last` and `lastb` record login events, not every remote-access system uses them. For example, the SSH daemon logs to `/var/log/auth.log`. To see the list of failed logins, you will need to search the log files:

```
$ zgrep "Invalid user" /var/log/auth.log* | sed -e 's/^.*: //' |
sort| uniq -c
```

```
2 Invalid user bill from 127.0.0.1
1 Invalid user cow from 10.1.30.25
3 Invalid user dog from 127.0.0.1
```

This command searches all of the `auth.log` files for the lines containing `Invalid user`. It then displays each invalid username, where the attempt came from, and how many times it was tried (sorted by username).

TIP The `zgrep` command searches regular logs and compressed (`.gz`) files.

Enabling Intrusion Detection Systems

Snort is a very powerful tool. As mentioned in Chapter 12, it can be used to sniff packets. However, Snort can do much more than just collect packets. The default installation (`sudo apt-get install snort`) enables an intrusion detection system (`/etc/init.d/snort`). This constantly watches for suspicious traffic and generates an activity report. To generate a report, you can use the `snort-stat` command:

```
# make sure the next sudo command does not prompt for a password
$ sudo id
$ sudo cat /var/log/snort/alert | snort-stat -a | less
Events between  11 28 05:29:52  and  12 02 10:26:15
Total events: 1289
Signatures recorded: 21
Source IP recorded: 8
Destination IP recorded: 21
Events from same host to same destination using same method
=======================================================================
 # of  from             to                method
=======================================================================
 1088  10.1.30.10       10.255.255.255    NETBIOS name query
overflow attempt UDP
   73  10.1.30.5        65.19.187.154     WEB-IIS %2E-asp access
   24  204.11.52.67     10.1.30.5         ATTACK-RESPONSES 403 Forbidden
   21  64.127.105.40    10.1.30.5         ICMP Destination Unreachable
Communication with Destination Host is Administratively Prohibited
    9  64.127.105.44    10.1.30.5         ICMP Destination Unreachable
Communication with Destinat0ion Host is Administratively Prohibited
    6  10.1.3.5         209.97.46.5       (http_inspect) DOUBLE DECODING
ATTACK
    4  10.1.30.25       10.1.30.5         SNMP trap tcp
    4  10.1.30.25       10.1.30.5         SNMP AgentX/tcp request
    3  10.1.30.5        72.21.210.11      WEB-CGI redirect access
    3  10.1.30.25       10.1.30.5         (spp_rpc_decode) Multiple RPC
Records
    3  10.1.30.5        203.0.178.91      WEB-CGI count.cgi access
    2  10.1.30.30       10.1.30.5         (portscan) TCP Portscan
    2  10.1.30.25       10.1.30.5         (portscan) TCP Portscan
    2  10.1.30.25       10.1.30.5         (portscan) TCP Portsweep
--More--
```

The log report shows the number of suspicious packets, as well as the type of attack. For example, there were a couple of port scans and port sweeps identified, as well as some suspicious web traffic, but the main concern is a NETBIOS name query overflow attempt. (In this case, it was due to a misconfigured OS/2 system running an old SMB configuration.) Although there are likely to be many false-positive findings, items such as port scans and known attacks should be closely examined. All of the suspicious packets are saved in `/var/log/snort/tcpdump.log.*` files. These can be viewed using Wireshark (see Chapter 12).

The actual set of IDS rules used by Snort is found in `/etc/snort/rules/`. There are dozens of attack signatures that trigger alerts. If you have some known false-positives, you can remove the IDS rule by commenting out the rule in the `/etc/snort/snort.conf` configuration file. Similarly, if you learn of a new rule, then you can easily add it to the rules directory and tell `snort.conf` to include the new rule. After changing any of the rules, be sure to restart the IDS: `sudo /etc/init.d/snort restart`.

The Snort IDS configuration files (`/etc/snort/snort.conf` and `snort.debian.conf`) have a large number of configuration items, and most have excellent default values. The main items you may want to change are your home network (the HOME_NET variable) and the interface. For example, one of my systems has two network adapters: `eth0` and `eth1`. One adapter (`eth0`) is used for regular network traffic, while the other (`eth1`) is connected to a hub in the DMZ and monitors suspicious traffic. To change Snort so that it watches only the second network card, I changed the interface name in `/etc/snort/snort.debian.conf` from `DEBIAN_SNORT_INTERFACE="eth0"` to `DEBIAN_SNORT_INTERFACE="eth1"`.

Running Services

There are literally hundreds of different types of servers that you can install and use. However, when it comes to services on the Internet, there are a few main ones that you will probably want to enable. These include SSH, FTP, e-mail, and web.

Hardening SSH

The Secure Shell server (`sshd`) provides encrypted and authenticated remote connectivity for logins, file transfers, and remote command execution. The basic SSH server installation (`sudo apt-get install openssh-server`, discussed in Chapter 6) is secure enough to be immediately place on the Internet. However, there are some parameters in the `/etc/ssh/sshd_config` file that you might want to modify for added security (see Table 13-2).

Table 13-2: Commonly Modified SSH Server Parameters

OPTION	DEFAULT VALUE	PURPOSE
AllowUsers	AllowUsers *	Restricts login access to a list of usernames (separated by white space). You can also specify *user@host* to restrict access to a specific user logging in from a specific host. If only some users should have remote access, then you can use this to explicitly block all other users.
AllowGroups	AllowGroups *	Similar to AllowUsers, you can specify group names found in /etc/group. Only users who are members of the specified groups are allowed to login. To find the groups you are in, use the groups command.
LoginGraceTime	LoginGrace Time 120	Specifies the number of seconds a user can sit at the password prompt before being disconnected. The sshd has a limit on the number of concurrent connections. If someone is trying to block your connection by tying up all available connections, then consider lowering this value from 120 seconds to 5. You may also want to lower this value if you have users who connect but take too long trying to remember their passwords.
MaxStartups	MaxStartups 10	Specifies how many concurrent login attempts are permitted (before successfully entering your password). The default is 10 concurrent, unauthenticated connections. You should consider changing this to 10:30:60. This specifies allowing 10 concurrent. If the 10 are connected, then drop them at a rate of 30/100—there is a 30 percent chance that some connection will be dropped before LoginGraceTime. This will continue until the maximum of 60 connections is reached; then all new connections are dropped.
Port	Port 22	For servers on the Internet, consider moving them to a port other than 22/tcp. Although this is technically security by obscurity, it will deter most simple reconnaissance attacks from finding your server and attempting brute force logins.

TIP There are two parameters in `/etc/ssh/sshd_config` that are serious risks any to system on the Internet: `PermitRootLogin` and `PermitEmptyPasswords`. By default, users with empty passwords cannot log in. Although the default setting does permit root logins, Ubuntu does not give root a password. Still, setting either of these to `yes` is a serious risk for system on the Internet. You should consider changing both of them to `no`.

After you change the `/etc/ssh/sshd_config` file, you will need to restart the server:

```
sudo /etc/init.d/ssh restart
```

Restarting the server applies all the changes to new connections, but existing connections will be unaffected. You can even restart the server while remotely connected over SSH.

Using SSH Keys

SSH supports different types of authentication. Basic password authentication is the most common approach. However, password authentication isn't very good for automated tasks like `cron` jobs (see Chapter 8) that use SSH for network administration.

Another form of authentication uses keys in place of passwords. The SSH keys are similar to Pretty Good Privacy (PGP, see Chapter 11) in that they are asymmetrical; there is a public and a private key. Creating SSH keys requires generating keys on the client and transferring the public key to the server.

1. The `ssh-keygen` program is used to generate SSH keys on the client. You will need to specify the algorithm (DSA or RSA) and the bit size. For stronger security, use RSA with a key size of at least 2048 bits.

```
% ssh-keygen -t rsa -b 2048
Generating public/private rsa key pair.
Enter file in which to save the key (/home/user/.ssh/id_rsa):
Enter passphrase (empty for no passphrase): [password]
Enter same passphrase again: [password]
Your identification has been saved in /home/user/.ssh/id_rsa.
Your public key has been saved in /home/user/.ssh/id_rsa.pub.
The key fingerprint is:
5b:6b:3d:58:32:0f:56:40:54:6d:8a:96:f1:96:60:d2 user@karmic-laptop
```

Generating keys longer than 2048 bits may take awhile. Be patient and the program will eventually ask you where to save the keys.

WARNING In general, RSA keys are preferred since DSA is cryptographically weaker. Also, while OpenSSH version 4.2 (found in Dapper Drake) permits large key sizes with DSA (such as **-t dsa -b 2048**), later versions of OpenSSH found in Hardy Heron and other Ubuntu versions only permit a DSA key size of 1024. For larger key sizes, use RSA.

TIP The passphrase is used to protect the key from theft. If you are not worried about other users on the system stealing your SSH key file, then you can leave this blank. For an automated system that cannot enter passwords, you should probably leave it blank.

2. Generating keys creates two files. `$HOME/.ssh/id_rsa` (or `id_dsa`) holds the private key, whereas `$HOME/.ssh/id_rsa.pub` (or `id_dsa.pub`) is the public key. Transfer the public key from the client to the remote server.

   ```
   scp $HOME/.ssh/id_rsa.pub remote:id_rsa.pub
   ```

   This will use SSH to copy the public key from your local system to the server named *remote*. The file will be copied to `$HOME/id_rsa.pub` (not `$HOME/.ssh/id_rsa.pub` on the remote host).

3. You will need to tell the server which keys are permitted for logins. Copy the contents of `id_rsa` to `$HOME/.ssh/authorized_keys`. If the file exists, then you can just append to it.

   ```
   mkdir $HOME/.ssh   # in case it does not exist
   cat $HOME/id_rsa.pub >> $HOME/.ssh/authorized_keys
   ```

4. On some SSH servers, you may need to make sure that the server accepts keys. Edit (or have the administrator edit) the `/etc/ssh/sshd_config` file and make sure that `RSAAuthentication` and `PubkeyAuthentication` are both set to `yes`. (Under the default installation for Ubuntu, they are already set to `yes`.) If you made changes, then you will also need to restart the SSH server.

5. Test the connection. You should be able to use `ssh` and connect to the host using only your key. If you entered a passphrase for the key, then you will be prompted for it but it will not be transferred across the network. Without a passphrase, you should immediately get a command-line prompt.

TIP If the server does not accept the key, then it will regress to using the user's login password. If you want to disable password-based logins, then set **PasswordAuthentication** to no in **/etc/ssh/sshd_config**.

Debugging SSH Connections

The most common problem with SSH is an unknown server key. During the server installation, a server key is generated. The OpenSSH client caches this key the first time you connect to the server, and then compares new keys during subsequent connections.

There are only a few real reasons why the server key may not match. First and most common, the SSH server was reinstalled for some reason and generated a new key, or was replaced by a different server with a different key. The alternative is that someone is trying to hijack your connection. Both will appear as a message that looks something like this:

```
@@@@@@@@@@@@@@@@@@@@@@@@@@@@@@@@@@@@@@@@@@@@@@@@@@@@@@@@@@@@@
@    WARNING: REMOTE HOST IDENTIFICATION HAS CHANGED!    @
@@@@@@@@@@@@@@@@@@@@@@@@@@@@@@@@@@@@@@@@@@@@@@@@@@@@@@@@@@@@@
IT IS POSSIBLE THAT SOMEONE IS DOING SOMETHING NASTY!
Someone could be eavesdropping on you right now (man-in-the-middle
attack)!
It is also possible that the RSA host key has just been changed.
The fingerprint for the RSA key sent by the remote host is
7f:23:ac:9d:4f:6d:88:eb:db:61:85:af:8b:c6:f3:21.
Please contact your system administrator.
Add correct host key in /home/user/.ssh/known_hosts to get rid of this
message.
Offending key in /home/user/.ssh/known_hosts:7
RSA host key for localhost has changed and you have requested strict
checking.
Host key verification failed.
```

To resolve this problem, you'll need to remove the offending server's key from the SSH cache file: $HOME/.ssh/known_hosts. In this case, delete line 7 as specified in the warning: /home/user/.ssh/known_hosts:7.

WARNING Although hijacking is extremely rare, it is definitely possible! Do not just fix the cache file without making sure that it isn't a real attack. If you are at a coffeehouse (or hacker conference) and you own this server and nothing should have changed, then don't try to fix the connection to the server! If nothing should have changed then this probably *is* an attack. If you remove the cached entry then the attacker will receive your login credentials and could gain access to the real system.

Enabling FTP

I use a variety of operating systems—some new and some very old. Using SSH to log in and transfer files between Unix and Linux systems is convenient. However, other operating systems may not be as convenient for using SSH. For example, Windows has free SSH clients like PuTTY, but many SSH servers for Windows are commercial and costly (although some free servers do exist). In some cases (for example, my old OS/2 system) an SSH server is unavailable.

Since I need to transfer files between systems on my local network, I have found that FTP is ubiquitous, and usually a little faster than SSH even if it is not as secure. For a local network, FTP is a great file transfer option. For direct

Internet access, FTP can be secure enough as long as you lock down the system and recognize that anyone may gain access to the server since your user name and password are passed as plain text across the network. Consider using FTP for non-critical accounts and transferring data that is not sensitive.

> **WARNING** While FTP is usually safe enough within your home or corporate network, it is usually not safe enough for accessing sensitive files or accounts across the Internet.

Besides being universally available to all clients, FTP also overcomes one serious limitation found in SSH: SSH does not permit anonymous logins. With FTP, anyone can connect to a shared directory for collaboration.

Installing VSFTPD

Ubuntu offers a variety of FTP servers (`apt-cache search ftpd`). My personal preference is the Very Secure FTP Daemon (VSFTPD). I like all of the customizable features and the fact that the default installation activates one anonymous account and no user accounts. However, you'll probably want to customize the system since the basic installation gives no access.

Installing the server is straightforward:

```
sudo apt-get install vsftpd
```

The installation will start the server as a stand-alone process (not requiring `inetd`), configure the `/etc/init.d/vsftpd` startup script, and create the user *ftp* for anonymous access. The server immediately permits anonymous read-only access to the directory `/home/ftp`. You can log in using the username *anonymous* or *ftp* with any password.

```
$ ftp localhost
Connected to localhost.
220 (vsFTPd 2.0.4)
Name (localhost:ubuntu): anonymous
331 Please specify the password.
Password: ********
230 Login successful.
Remote system type is UNIX.
Using binary mode to transfer files.
ftp> ls -la
200 PORT command successful. Consider using PASV.
150 Here comes the directory listing.
drwxr-xr-x    2 0        65534        4096 Dec 09 16:30 .
drwxr-xr-x    2 0        65534        4096 Dec 09 16:30 .
226 Directory send OK.
```

Any files or directories placed in the `/home/ftp/` directory will be accessible by the anonymous FTP user. However, regular users do not have access until you explicitly enable it (see the section "Adjusting Regular FTP Access" later in this chapter).

Adjusting Anonymous FTP Access

If you don't want anonymous FTP access, then you can disable it.

1. As root, edit `/etc/vsftpd.conf`.

2. Change the configuration value `anonymous_enable=YES` to `anonymous_enable=NO`.

3. Restart the FTP server:

   ```
   sudo /etc/init.d/vsftpd restart
   ```

TIP You will need to restart the server any time you make a change to `/etc/vsftpd.conf`.

However, if you want to use anonymous FTP access, then there are many configuration options you might want to change. Table 13-3 shows some of the anonymous FTP configuration options. Other options can be found in the online manual (`man vsftpd.conf`).

TIP If you allow anonymous users to upload files, consider enabling disk quotas for the FTP user (see Chapter 9). This way, anonymous FTP users won't consume all of your disk space.

Adjusting Regular FTP Access

By default, VSFTPD disables FTP access for regular users. To enable FTP access for local (non-anonymous) users:

1. Edit `/etc/vsftpd.conf`.

2. Uncomment the `local_enable=YES` line.

3. Restart the server:

   ```
   sudo /etc/init.d/vsftpd restart
   ```

After these changes, any user may FTP to his or her account by specifying a valid username and password. There are other local user options for `/etc/vsftpd.conf` that you may want to modify (see Table 13-4).

TIP VSFTPD logs every connection, file transfer, and anonymous login password to the file `/var/log/vsftpd.log`. If your system is connected to the Internet, then you should monitor this log file for possible attacks or abuse. The log file is rotated weekly by the `logrotate` configuration file `/etc/logrotate.d/vsftpd` (see Chapter 11 for rotating log files).

Table 13-3: Anonymous FTP Options for /etc/vsftpd.conf

OPTION	EXAMPLE	PURPOSE
anon_upload _enable	anon_upload _enable=YES	Allow anonymous users to upload files to the `/home/ftp/ directory`.
anon_mkdir_write _enable	anon_mkdir_write _enable=YES	Allow anonymous users to create directories under `/home/ ftp/` with the `mkdir` FTP command.
anon_other_write _enable	anon_other_write _enable=YES	Allow anonymous users to rename or delete files under `/home/ftp/`.
anon_max_rate	anon_max_rate =131072	Throttle file transfer rates for anonymous users. This specifies 131,072 bytes per second (or 1 megabit per second).
anon_world _readable_only	anon_world_readable _only=YES	Restrict anonymous users to downloading only files that are world-readable. This way, the user *ftp* may have private files that cannot be downloaded.
hide_ids	hide_ids=YES	Changes all user and group IDs so they look like FTP. By default, all IDs are shown by their numeric values.
secure_email_list _enable	secure_email_list _enable=YES	Force anonymous users to provide a valid password. You will need to create the file `/etc/ vsftpd.email_passwords` and give it a list of passwords, one per line. Any of these passwords are acceptable for anonymous access.

Securing Internet FTP

FTP is not a secure protocol. Every username and password is transmitted in plain text across the network. If your server is accessible from the Internet, then anyone capable of capturing your packets will see your valid username and password. If you need to give users FTP access, consider creating a second account strictly for FTP access. By default, new accounts are given a unique group name. You can create an FTP-only account for each user, and assign the accounts to the user's group name. For example, user *bill* can be given the account *bill-ftp* in the group *bill*:

```
sudo useradd -m -g bill -c "FTP for Bill" bill-ftp
```

Be sure to give Bill write-access to the `bill-ftp` directory:

```
sudo chmod -R g+w /home/bill-ftp
```

Table 13-4: Local User FTP Options for /etc/vsftpd.conf

OPTION	EXAMPLE	PURPOSE
max_clients	max_clients=20	Limit the number of client connections. In this case, up to 20 clients can be connected at once. The default value is 0 meaning *no limit*.
max_per_ip	max_per_ip=2	Specify how many FTP connections may come from the same IP address. The default is 0 meaning *no limit*.
local_max_rate	local_max_rate= 1048576	Specify the number of bytes per second for throttling FTP connections. This example sets a limit of 1 megabyte (8 megabits) per second. If you have an 8-Mbps connection, then consider setting the limit to 6 Mbps or less so that the FTP server will not consume all available network bandwidth. The default value has no limit.
chroot_local _user	chroot_local _user=YES	Restrict local users to their home directories rather than letting them access anything on the system.
chroot_list _enable	chroot_list _enable=YES	Specify a list of users that should or should not be limited to their home directories. If `chroot_local_user` is NO, then this is a list of users who should be restricted. If `chroot_local_user` is YES, then this is a list of users who should not be restricted. The list of users (one username per line) is stored in `/etc/vsftpd.chroot_list` (you'll need to create this file).

Then you can give this account a different password than Bill's regular account.

```
sudo passwd bill-ftp
```

Finally, you can block SSH and remote login access for any account containing `-ftp` in the account name.

1. Edit `/etc/ssh/sshd_config`.
2. Add the following option:

   ```
   DenyUsers *-ftp
   ```
3. Restart the SSH server:

   ```
   sudo /etc/init.d/ssh restart
   ```

This way, user *bill* can access the directory `bill-ftp`. But if his login credentials are ever compromised, then the attacker will be unable to access the account through SSH.

Enabling Postfix

E-mail is pretty much a mandatory network service. If you don't want to host your own e-mail, then you just need an e-mail client (see Chapter 6). However, if you plan to actually receive e-mail on your own system, then you will need an e-mail server. In addition, many applications generate status reports using e-mail. You will need a server if you want to send the e-mails directly to yourself.

TIP I have a home firewall that can e-mail its system logs. Rather than sending the logs out to my ISP, I have them sent directly to my own, internal mail server running on an Ubuntu system.

Ubuntu offers many different e-mail servers. However, Sendmail, Qmail, and Postfix are the most common under Linux. Of these servers, Sendmail is the oldest and most widely used, but it is also historically the most insecure. My personal preference is Postfix because of its security, speed, and reliability. Each of these mail servers supports configurations that vary from plug-and-play simple to extremely complex. Unfortunately, none of these mail servers is trivial to configure. (Sendmail is one of the most complicated ones to configure—another reason that I like Postfix.)

To get started with your mail server, you will need to install the server package, configure it, and test it. If it tests well and seems to work, then you can be really daring and open it to the world.

1. Install the Postfix server. This will create the appropriate startup scripts, place default files, and start the server:

   ```
   sudo apt-get install postfix
   ```

> **TIP** If Postfix is already installed, then you can reconfigure it using `sudo dpkg-reconfigure postfix`.

2. During the installation, you will be prompted for the type of installation. Your options are:

   - **No configuration**—Install the server but leave it unconfigured. (Probably not what you want unless you are trying to repair a broken installation.)

   - **Internet Site**—Assume that the server will be directly connected to the Internet. Use this if you actually intend to send and receive e-mail directly. This is the default option but it is probably not what you want if you are installing on a home system, private network, or for a small business.

   - **Internet with smarthost**—This configuration is useful for most home users who need to relay outbound e-mail through an ISP's mail server. This can be used to provide mail to a local never even if the host is not accessible from the Internet.

> **NOTE** A *smarthost* is a mail relay that knows how to route e-mail across the Internet. Many ISPs provide a smarthost for sending e-mail. You'll need to ask your ISP if they have an SMTP server for outbound delivery.

   - **Satellite system**—This option configures Postfix as a system for sending e-mail through a smart mail relay but not for receiving e-mail. This is a great option if your actual e-mail is stored on some other server.

   - **Local only**—Choose this configuration if you have no other systems that will be relaying e-mail through this host.

   I usually choose the Internet Site or Internet with smarthost option for primary servers. However, for secondary servers and workstations, I use the Satellite system. Depending on the option you choose, you will be prompted to supply your own mailing domain, smarthost name, and other configuration values. Then the installation will complete and the server will start up.

Post-Installation Configuration

There are a couple of options in `/etc/postfix/main.cf` that you might want to modify or add after the installation.

■ `relayhost`—This option is the IP address or host name of the smarthost. If it is blank, then no smarthost is used.

■ `mydestination`—This is a comma-separated list of host names and domains that are used for local delivery. You probably should add your system's host name to this list. Also, if this server is expected to receive e-mail for multiple domains, then you'll want to add every domain here.

■ `myhostname`—This option specifies your host's Internet host name that is revealed when sending e-mail. I usually make this my Internet domain name rather than my private LAN's domain since seeing e-mail from `neuhaus.roach.lan` won't make sense to anyone but me.

■ `mydomain`—Similar to `myhostname`, this specifies your Internet domain name. If you have a vanity (personal) domain, you can put it here rather than using your ISP or other private domain name.

■ `inet_interfaces`—You can specify one or more network interfaces for receiving e-mail. If your system has multiple network interfaces but only one that should receive e-mail, then you definitely need to modify this line. If you're just testing, you can always say `inet_interfaces = loopback-only` and only receive e-mail from yourself.

■ `mynetworks`—If other systems will be relaying e-mail through your server, then you will need to specify the networks that can relay e-mail. For example, I use:

```
mynetworks = 127.0.0.0/8, 10.0.0.0/8
```

This setting enables me to send e-mail from localhost (the 127.0.0.1 subnet) and from my private, local network: 10.*x.x.x*. All other machines (not on these networks) that connect to my mail server can only deliver e-mail directly to this host; they cannot relay. This way, my host will not be used to relay spam to other networks.

■ `smtpd_banner`—This is the welcome banner that is displayed any time a mail client connects to the mail server. For security, it should display as little information as possible about the system—don't display the server's version since that can be used by an attacker to gain knowledge about the server. The default setting does not give a version, but it does state Ubuntu (I recommend removing that). I usually make a simple banner:

```
smtpd_banner = Private System - All connections are logged.
```

There are many more configuration options. The file `/usr/share/postfix/main.cf.dist` is a template that describes every default option and configuration. Alternately, you can consult the man page: `man 5 postconf`. When you finish tweaking your configuration file, you need to tell Postfix to reload it:

```
sudo /etc/init.d/postfix reload
```

Testing Postfix

When you have it all configured, try sending an e-mail to yourself—both locally and to a remote system so that you can verify network access. Also, if any systems on your network will be relaying through your server, then try relaying e-mail. If there are any problems or errors, you should see them logged in `/var/log/mail.log`.

Opening Postfix

If you are going to be making your mail server publicly accessible from the Internet, then you will need to open port 25/tcp in your firewall. This traffic should go to your mail server. After opening the firewall, you can try e-mailing yourself from outside your network and see if you receive it.

> **WARNING** Opening your mail server to the Internet is not as easy as opening a port in a firewall. You're also going to need to configure your DNS entry for your domain so that the server is listed as a mail exchanger (DNS MX record). How you do this depends on your domain registrar or DNS hosting provider. Contact them if you have questions.

Enabling Apache

Web servers play an important role on most networks. You can use them to create official web sites, or to test web pages before making them public. On internal networks, placing a file on a web site for download can be more convenient than using an FTP server. In addition, server-side scripts such as CGI scripts and PHP can create dynamic content. As a software developer, I frequently use HTML and CGI scripts to mock up graphic interfaces and user flows before devoting time to creating the final "real" interface.

The Ubuntu repositories contain a wide variety of web servers. For example, `thttpd` is a tiny server that is ideal for minimal-resource systems. Other server packages include `dhttpd`, `fnord`, and the Roxen WebServer (`roxen4`). However, Apache is by and far the most common server. Although it isn't tiny, it is fast, stable, secure, and extremely flexible.

The basic Apache package installs the core web server: `sudo apt-get install apache2`. This provides the server (`apache2`), startup script (`/etc/init.d/apache2`), and log management file (`/etc/logrotate.d/apache2`). You should be able to connect to it using `http://localhost/` and see a generic web page (see Figure 13-1).

> **ARE YOU BEING SERVED?**
>
> There are actually two different branches of Apache web servers: 1.x and 2.x. The Apache Software Foundation (www.apache.org) supports both versions. Basically, the 2.x branch is a complete rewrite and offers features such as IPv6 support and a new software API. However, unless you plan to create plug-ins for Apache (not CGI), you'll probably never notice a difference.
>
> For Ubuntu's Dapper Drake (6.06 LTS), the apache package installs Apache 1.x, while apache2 installs the 2.x version. Later versions of Ubuntu only include apache2 in the repositories.

Figure 13-1: The default Apache2 server web page from Karmic Koala (9.10)

Post-Installation Configuration

After installing Apache, there are a few configuration items that you will want to tweak. The Apache server manages content for multiple domains. Each domain's configuration is stored in /etc/apache2/sites-available/ and linked by /etc/apache2/sites-enables/. Only domains linked into the sites-enabled directory are accessible. By default, there are two available domains (default for HTTP and default-ssl for HTTPS), but only default is enabled.

For customizing your server, you will want to edit these default files, or create your own. Some common parameters that you will probably want to modify:

■ ServerAdmin—This is the person to contact in case of problems. It defaults to webmaster@localhost. I recommend creating a webmaster account for your domain and setting that as the contact. I try not to use specific users since people in companies have a tendency to move around—it's easier to change the mail alias than contact everyone who has the webmaster e-mail address.

■ DocumentRoot—The default root is /var/www/. I usually change this to /home/www-data/ after creating a directory for the www-data user (if it does not already exist).

```
sudo useradd -c "Web Server" -m www-data
```

I do this because on my systems /home/ usually has more disk space than /var/ and if I'm enabling disk quotas, then /home/ usually has quotas enabled.

Beyond the basic contact and host name configurations, I also modify some of the default directories. Most of this is done for additional security.

■ **Remove unneeded aliases**—Anything that is not needed on the server can be used to profile and potentially attack the server. I usually remove the web server's /doc/ entry, /images/, and /perl/. For example, /doc/ is defined as:

```
Alias /doc/ "/usr/share/doc/"
<Directory "/usr/share/doc/">
  Options Indexes MultiViews FollowSymLinks
  AllowOverride None
  Order deny,allow
  Deny from all
  Allow from 127.0.0.0/255.0.0.0::1/128
</Directory>
```

I remove all of this. Even though /doc/ is only accessible from the local system, I have never needed to use any of these files from the web browsers. Providing these files over the web could tell an attacker exactly what software (and vulnerabilities) are on my system.

■ **Disable indexes**—Throughout the configuration file are Options lines that reference Indexes. For example:

```
<Directory /var/www/>
Options Indexes Includes FollowSymLinks MultiViews
...
```

Just remove the Indexes keyword. With this option, a directory without an index.html file will actually show the directory contents. This enables anyone to browse any file that may be accessible from the web server—including backup versions, temporary files, and hidden or personal directories. Removing the Indexes option blocks open directories and returns an error. If a specific directory should be open, then I can open it on an as-needed basis.

- **Enable home directories**—The default Apache2 installation does not enable home directories. However, they can be added by linking in the `userdir` modules. The quick way to link them is with the `a2enmod` (Apache2 Enable Module) command:

```
sudo a2enmod userdir
sudo /etc/init.d/apache2 restart
```

The `userdir` module enables every user to have a `$HOME/public_html` directory for storing web content. This way, the user *tim* can access his files web using `http://localhost/~tim/`. Any users who do not want a web presence can just remove the `public_html` directory.

TIP Consider adding the public directory to `/etc/skel` (sudo `mkdir` `/etc/skel/public_html`) so that new accounts will have it created by default. For existing accounts, you can run the following commands as root to create the directories:

```
cd /home
for i in *; do
  if [ ! -d "$i"/public_html ]; then
    mkdir -m 766 "$i"/public_html
    chown "$i":www-data "$i"/public_html
  fi
done
```

WARNING If the web server returns a "Forbidden" message, then check the directory permissions. The Apache2 web server does not run as root, so it will need access to the `public_html` directory as a regular user. At minimum, the permissions should be accessible to the home directory (chmod `o+x` /home/*user*) and readable to the `public_html` directory (chmod `o+rx` /home/*user*/public_html). In addition, all files under the `public_html` should be world-readable (a+r).

- **Enable CGI scripts**—I do a lot of programming, so I like to have CGI scripts enabled. I usually edit `/etc/apache2/mods-available/userdir` `.conf` and add `ExecCGI` to the list of options. This way, any executable in any user's `public_html` directory will act as a CGI script. The entire `userdir.conf` file ends up looking like this:

```
<IfModule mod_userdir.c>
        UserDir public_html
        UserDir disabled root
        <Directory /home/*/public_html>
                AllowOverride FileInfo AuthConfig Limit Indexes
                Options MultiViews SymLinksIfOwnerMatch ExecCGI
                <Limit GET POST OPTIONS>
                        Order allow,deny
```

```
                              Allow from all
                    </Limit>
                    <LimitExcept GET POST OPTIONS>
                            Order deny,allow
                            Deny from all
                    </LimitExcept>
            </Directory>
    </IfModule>
```

You will also need to edit `mods-enabled/mime.conf` and add a line so files ending with .cgi, .sh, and .pl will run as CGI scripts:

```
AddHandler cgi-script .cgi .sh .pl
```

This handler allows any file that ends with `.cgi`, `.sh`, or `.pl` to be used as a CGI script.

WARNING Enabling CGI scripts is definitely *not* for everyone. There are huge security implications here. If you enable CGI scripts for everyone, then there is a very serious threat of an attacker exploiting a weak script and compromising your system. For public servers that host many different users, I strongly recommend *not* enabling `ExecCGI` for everyone. But if it is just you on a private server, then this is a very convenient option.

After changing the Apache configuration files, you will need to reload the server.

```
sudo /etc/init.d/apache2 reload
```

Enabling HTTPS

The Hypertext Transfer Protocol (HTTP) can be combined with the Secure Socket Layer protocol (SSL) to form HTTPS. With HTTP, all information transferred across the network is unencrypted. Any attacker with network access between the web server and browser can intercept the data. HTTPS provides a framework for encrypting web traffic. Simply enabling HTTPS for Apache2 is straightforward. However, the basic system will not be secure.

```
sudo a2enmod ssl             # enable mod_ssl
sudo a2ensite default-ssl    # enable the default SSL site
configuration
sudo /etc/init.d/apache2 reload  # load the new configuration
```

You can test the SSL configuration by connecting to the server with `https://localhost/`. If there are problems, they will be denoted in `/var/log/apache2/error.log` and `ssl_access.log`.

VIRTUAL SSL SERVERS

While Apache2 can host many different virtual web servers on the same system, it can only have one SSL certificate installed at a time. This is because SSL is a lower network protocol than HTTPS and is accessed before the web server's name is transmitted. Thus, every HTTPS server on the same port (port 443/tcp is HTTPS) must have the same SSL certificate.

If you want your server to host different web sites with different SSL certificates, then there are two options, and both have limitations.

First, you can run each site on a different and nonstandard port. This way, the configuration permits one domain on the standard port (`https://domain1/`) and another domain on a nonstandard port like 10443/tcp (`https://domain2:10443/`).

The other option is Server Name Indication (SNI). SNI is an extension to SSL and permits the web browser to specify the domain name prior to requesting the SSL certificate. The problem is, SNI is relatively new. It requires Apache 2.2.12 or later (the Hardy Heron 8.04 LTS repository includes Apache 2.2.8—you will need Karmic Koala 9.10 or later) and is only supported by newer web browsers; you need Firefox 2.0 or later or Internet Explorer 7 for Windows Vista (not XP). Until SNI becomes more widely accepted, this is not a great option.

Unfortunately, just enabling HTTPS is not enough. SSL uses server certificates to perform the encryption. The web browser is supposed to compare the certificate with a trusted third-party certificate authority (CA), such as Verisign, Thawt, or DigiCert for validation. The default certificate was created without a trusted CA; web browsers will be unable to validate the certificate. Ideally, you will want to contact a trusted third-party provider and acquire (or purchase) an SSL certificate.

The acquisition process varies by provider, but eventually you will receive a privacy enhanced mail (.pem) and private key (.key) file. The PEM will look something like:

```
-----BEGIN CERTIFICATE-----
MIIBmTCCAQICCQDC+F19KWjYKTANBgkqhkiG9w0BAQUFADARMQ8wDQYDVQQDEwZ1
YnVudHUwHhcNMDkxMDA1MjEzODE5WhcNMTkxMDAzMjEzODE5WjARMQ8wDQYDVQQD
EwZ1YnVudHUwgZ8wDQYJKoZIhvcNAQEBBQADgY0AMIGJAoGBAOtMuVKMp/QPeZW2
0vx5UijAqJJjH0pOYhR7GOyFmLJYh2l/EVHzns1IW0zxQvC0wQmk4Q0hHlkt4j2x
YonPvqZ2dAD+a7c7PVNxewds0AsPYIp8/CWZztA1ZK9ZbOIa+kG2wlAqcV+SSzeW
Z2ASdQNLvgSWixlNqKEENp0FWt3XAgMBAAEwDQYJKoZIhvcNAQEFBQADgYEA4LLT
Q5bqX96yN/STqSRpM/GkuY2oMGRnwYOaUX/tcyQBpqOYvfZ/9vnohMGJFKvaaUVB
wWO7eGTHmXMY1smZuUCfqqcynFPx6reR9yaXYiuEHDITJYj/Zl9PNGH+Bym8XCDJ
QcPxlOjHfp3ca5Dxby+KfsR3fvfHdc3QPJjQX6A=
-----END CERTIFICATE-----
```

WARNING The key file can be, and usually is, encrypted with a password when it is created. For most Apache server installations, you do not want to set a password. The reason is simple: Apache is a program that cannot automatically enter a password. So unless you are sitting at the console, the server will just wait until a password is entered. With no password on the key file, the web server will start up automatically.

The key file will look similar to the PEM file, but it will contain a private key heading. Both files will need to be installed on your web server.

1. Save the PEM file in `/etc/ssl/certs/myhost.pem`. Be sure to make the file world-readable, but not world-writable: `chmod 644 myhost.pem`.

2. Save the key file in `/etc/ssl/private/myhost.key`. This file should only be accessible by the root user and group `ssl-cert`: `sudo chown root:ssl-cert myhost.key; sudo chmod 640 myhost.key`.

3. Edit `/etc/apache2/sites-available/default-ssl`. Search for the `SSLCertificateFile` and `SSLCertificateKeyFile` lines and change them to point to your PEM and key files, respectively.

   ```
   SSLCertificateFile    /etc/ssl/certs/myhost.pem
   SSLCertificateKeyFile /etc/ssl/private/myhost.key
   ```

4. You may need to configure the `SSLCertificateChainFile` and `SSLCACertificateFile` variables to identify your CA server. Your certificate authority should provide you with the configuration information.

5. Restart your web server. It should start up and use the new certificates.

WARNING While an established HTTPS connection is difficult for an attacker to hijack, there are vulnerabilities related to establishing and authenticating the connection. In addition, SSL provides no protection against web-based attacks or vulnerabilities in your CGI scripts. Even though you use the Secure Socket Layer protocol, it does not mean that you are secure.

Extending Apache

The basic Apache installation is good for serving web pages and handling basic CGI scripts. However, there are many additional packages that can be added to extend the server's functionality. These additional modules provide functionality that integrates into the web server. The full list of available modules can be found with `apt-cache search libapache2-mod`. Table 13-5 lists some of the available packages and the functionality that they provide. You can install any of them using `apt-get install` *package*. In some cases, there will be additional configuration steps needed before the modules can be used.

Table 13-5: Additional Apache Packages

PACKAGE	FUNCTIONALITY
`libapache2-mod-perl`	Adds `<Perl>...</Perl>` sections in your HTML to execute server-side scripting with Perl.
`libapache2-mod-gnutls`	Adds SSL support to the Apache server. This enables you to use HTTPS. However, you will need to configure your SSL certificates before enabling SSL.
`libapache2-mod-php5`	Provides PHP version 5 server-side scripting support for Apache2. Unfortunately, at the time of this writing, `libapache-mod-php5` was not available as a package for the Apache 1.*x* server. However, the `php5-cgi` package provides similar functionality.

Not every Apache module is simple to install. For example, Ruby on Rails is a popular programming language (Ruby) and web application framework (Rails). The installation requires installing many dependencies and then manually enabling them.

```
# The following apt-get will install dozens of required packages.
sudo apt-get install ruby rails
sudo apt-get install libapache2-mod-ruby libapache2-mod-fcgid
sudo a2enmod ruby
sudo a2enmod fcgid
sudo /etc/init.d/apache2 restart
```

Creating Web Pages

After configuring the web server, you will want to create some HTML web pages. At minimum, you will want to replace the default placeholder (as previously shown in Figure 13-1) with your own page—or a blank page. Unless you change it (like I usually do), the default server web pages are located in `/var/www/` and the placeholder is `/var/www/index.html`.

As previously mentioned, individual users can create a `public_html` directory (`mkdir $HOME/public_html`) and place their personal files in this directory. For example, Tim (my technical reviewer) can use:

```
mkdir /home/tim/public_html
echo "Test page" > /home/tim/public_html/index.html
```

He can then access his test page using `http://localhost/~tim/`.

Summary

It does not take much skill to install a basic Ubuntu system and use the out-of-the-box configuration. However, configuring, tuning, optimizing, and securing the system to fit your needs takes serious skills. If you want to safely enable network services, then you'll need to start with a basic system and customize it to your needs. Although these services enable you to provide support for other systems on the network, they also open up your system and provide vectors for attackers. However, these hacks for network services should enable you to run the servers you want and need, without opening you up to too much risk.

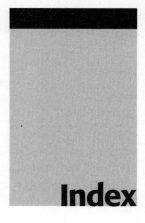

Index